Queers in American Popular Culture

Queers in American Popular Culture

Volume 3
Sports, Leisure, and Lifestyle

Jim Elledge, Editor

Praeger Perspectives

PRAEGER

AN IMPRINT OF ABC-CLIO, LLC
Santa Barbara, California • Denver, Colorado • Oxford, England

Library of Congress Cataloging-in-Publication Data

Queers in American popular culture / Jim Elledge, editor.
p. cm.
Includes bibliographical references and index.
ISBN 978–0–313–35457–1 (set. : alk. paper) — ISBN 978–0–313–35458–8 (set : ebook)
1. Gays in popular culture—United States. I. Elledge, Jim, 1950–
HQ76.3.U5Q447 2010
306.76′60973—dc22 2010023183

ISBN: 978–0–313–35457–1
EISBN: 978–0–313–35458–8

14 13 12 11 10 1 2 3 4 5

This book is also available on the World Wide Web as an eBook.
Visit www.abc-clio.com for details.

Praeger
An Imprint of ABC-CLIO, LLC

ABC-CLIO, LLC
130 Cremona Drive, P.O. Box 1911
Santa Barbara, California 93116-1911

This book is printed on acid-free paper. ∞

Manufactured in the United States of America

For David

Contents

Set Introduction

Jim Elledge

Queers in American Popular Culture attempts to cover, in a comprehensive way, the presence of gay, lesbian, bisexual, and the transgendered persons in popular culture venues of the United States. Although largely post-Stonewall in scope, this three-volume set also, at times, investigates queers and their representation in periods as early as the late 1880s. The topics covered may be new to a non-queer readership (and even to some queer readers), perhaps even strange to them, but they are always eye opening and thought provoking.

While most readers will have seen episodes of *Will & Grace* or may even be diehard fans of the popular television sitcom, for example, only a handful will have heard of—much less seen—the post-op, female-to-male-with-a-vagina porn star, Buck Angel. Fewer yet will have been enthralled by his body, his rugged sexuality, and his sexual appetite(s). Transforming from man to woman to pop icon, RuPaul has "sashayed shante" very visibly across *Billboard*'s charts, becoming the best-known drag queen entertainer in the United States and across the globe since Boy George. Yet while RuPaul is taking her turn on the catwalk, "boi"—a personality as important to contemporary queer culture as the fairy was to our grandfathers and grandmothers a century ago—scoots along the streets, hangs out, and clubs hard virtually unknown and unnoticed by all but those in the know. *Queers in American Popular Culture* gives notice to, and provides a forum for discussion about, both "boi" and Buck Angel, along with the much more visible RuPaul and Will.

Queers in American Popular Culture attempts to be comprehensive and strives diligently to obtain that goal. The number of possible topics to cover is so immense that it would be impossible to produce a work that truly covered, even only minimally, every queer topic and every queer personality in American popular culture. Queers have been associated with U.S. popular culture for so long now that many of those involved with it, their representations in it, and what they produced have simply faded away—"like sand through the hour glass"—from current, cultural awareness. Those of us of a certain age will remember when the country's attention was focused on Glenn Burke and Colonel Martgarethe Cammermeyer or when *Torch Song Trilogy* and *Go Fish* caused a stir, although not one of them is mentioned in these pages.

The truth is that what was once so important to gay men, for example, has now all but vanished from the scene. Beginning with the riots at the Stonewall Inn in New York's Greenwich Village during the last weekend of July 1969 and for the next two or three decades thereafter, personalities like Paul Lynde, who was a regular "center square"—an oxymoronic handle if there ever was one—on the TV game show *Hollywood Squares*, was perhaps the most recognizable queer funny man to most Americans. During the approximate same period of time in which Lynde was delivering belly laughs, many of the diehard fans who watched the wigged-out, dark comedy *Soap* became fascinated by the quirky boy-next-door Jodie Dallas, played by Billy Crystal, a less bitchy and bitter, and a more bittersweet, character than Lynde's persona. Jodie, who did not elicit the guffaws that Lynde did, tempered the image most Americans had when they thought of queer men.

A third personality appeared during the same period, one that would further complicate the image. Hunky, handsome, blonde Steven Carrington of the nighttime soap opera *Dynasty*, a number-one hit within a few seasons, got no laughs, only *ooohs* and *ahhhs*. He quickly won the hearts of gay men and imaginative straight women alike. Played first by Al Corey, then by Jack Coleman, Steven seemed, at the time and to many gay men, to be the first "realistic" depiction of a gay character, one who struggled with his sexual identity and took missteps, but eventually "got it together." He was vastly different from both Lynde and Jodie. As important as these three television personalities were in queer male popular culture in the 1970s and 1980s, few remember them now and, perhaps, even fewer care.

There were many others, including lesbians and bisexuals, who like Paul Lynde, Jodie Dallas, and Steven Carrington would become well-known, even liked, admired, and emulated, gathering a large fan base and accruing large revenues—and a great deal of right-wing, fundamentalist hatred—but each has now been edged out by the *new*. Typically, what any book like *Queers in American Popular Culture* covers depends, to a large extent, on what is currently hot, what is currently the buzz, what is currently aflutter in our—queers' *and* non-queers'—collective consciousnesses: gay marriage, Ennis and Jack (or is it Heath and Jake?), Ellen, and so on. In short, currency is all too often the capital for critical or scholarly interest in popular culture whether we want it to be or not.

Nevertheless, *Queers in American Popular Culture* purposefully includes a number of chapters that cover topics that are not *currently* hot, not the buzz, nor even vaguely on our minds as we drive or walk or take the subway to and from work, but which have a timeless value. Certainly, we do not typically mull over the place of lesbian and gay pulp fiction in the larger, non-queer culture during coffee breaks, nor do most of us ponder lesbian cookbooks (of which there are a surprising number) while eating a Big Mac at lunch. Yet in these volumes, some little-thought-of subjects as well as some forgotten personalities point out the fact to us over and over again that popular culture, and the queer's place in it, is remarkably vast and varied, flexible, and timeless.

Even some topics covered in *Queers in American Popular Culture* that are current have had lives in previous eras. Some were extant and even recorded decades before the dawn of the twentieth century, helping in their own way to give birth to the Pansy Craze, approximately a decade and a half or so (from the 1920s through the mid-1930s) in which gay men were quite visible, particularly on stage and screen but also in restaurants, department stores, on the streets, and elsewhere. By 1935 or so, the pansy began to fade from popular culture. Through the 1940s and 1950s, and almost to the close of the 1960s—decades that are often dubbed the Lavender Scare—queers, so visible during the Pansy Craze, were forced into invisibility, finding refuge in the closet. Police raided their meeting places time after time and closed them. They were arrested, tried, jailed—then fired from their jobs, expelled from their families, and rejected by their friends. During the Lavender Scare, if popular culture represented queers at all, they were targets of ridicule, paranoia, even outright hatred.

As one might expect, the majority of the chapters in a set of books like *Queers in American Popular Culture* will focus on television and film, not because those two media are more important in queer popular culture than others are, but because they are the most accessible of all popular culture venues and so are the most "popular" of all, what most people think of when they think about *popular* culture. Whether developed by heterosexuals or queers, the popular culture scene in which queers find their most immediate and overt representation these days is in TV Land. The vast majority of U.S. citizens have television sets, often very large ones and often more than one per household, and the producers of television programs have found that some series with substantial queer representation have been a lucrative business proposition. (Advertisers, too, have come to realize that such programs bring in the loot.) *Queers in American Popular Culture* does not ignore television and film. It acknowledges both, and it puts them on equal par with other popular culture venues.

Said in a different way, "popular culture" is far larger than sitcoms on the boob tube or flicks on the silver screen. In fact, television and the cinema, as popular as each is in our culture, are only two facets of a multifaceted phenomenon that includes sports, fashion, literature, art, music, performances of various sorts, advertising (in popular magazines and even on television: between individual programs and within the programs themselves), and the Internet that, as many believe, is giving both television and the film industry a run for their money.

The chapters in *Queers in American Popular Culture* are divided into large categories that highlight the range of popular culture venues. Volume 1 is devoted to television and film; Volume 2 contains chapters on many different topics, among them, popular art, the Internet, popular literature, performance, and youth-related subjects; and Volume 3 covers advertising, fashion, leisure, lifestyle, and sports. These categories are decidedly subjective, and a different editor might have arranged the volumes quite differently. All but four of the chapters have never appeared elsewhere in print before, giving this three-volume set a fresh approach that is rare in other popular culture anthologies. As readers of these pages will quickly discover, each of the authors is an acute observer of U.S. popular culture and the queer's place in it. In fact, contributors to *Queers in American Popular Culture* include a number of scholars from countries other than the United States.

Also unlike other anthologies on similar topics, "popular culture" is broadly defined by the authors whose chapters fill the three volumes' pages to cover what many might not think of as "popular culture" in its narrowest definition. In short, while the expected is certainly represented in *Queers in American Popular Culture,* the unexpected has also found its way into the collections. Readers will expect chapters on *Brokeback Mountain*, *The L Word*, and *Queer as Folk* in Volume 1, for example, but they will also be delighted to discover chapters on *Noah's Arc*, a series on Logo about a group of African-American gay men in Los Angeles, and on queers in 1970s blaxploitation films, and on gay themes/representations in animation. Students who open Volume 2 will probably anticipate finding a chapter on gay pulps and *Dykes to Watch Out For*, but they will be surprised by chapters on lesbianism in Latina popular literature, on queer vampires, on the blogs of transwomen, or on pornography. Also, readers of Volume 3 might be amazed to read that the concept of gay marriage has been discussed since the 1950s, that there are cookbooks aimed at lesbians, that the father of modern bodybuilding was queer, and that not all queers worship within any mainstream faith system.

While the authors of the chapters in all three volumes are to be thanked for their devotion, intelligence, and savvy, *Queers in American Popular Culture* could not have been produced without the help and diligence of my graduate research assistant, Sara Meyer, or Lindsay Claire, my second set of eyes at Praeger. I owe both more gratitude for their help than I could ever express.

Chapter 1

Marry, Mary! (Quite Contrary): Homosexual Marriage in *ONE* Magazine, 1953–1959

C. Todd White

SEX BEFORE MARRIAGE?

When the first issue of *ONE* magazine was launched in January of 1953 and distributed hand-to-hand through the dark streets and shady bars of downtown Los Angeles, there was no mention of homosexual marriage in this premier issue. But there was much talk of love.

A poem attributed to "Helen Ito" proclaimed the purpose of this new magazine: " . . . To bring our love out into the sunshine/And proclaim to the world, "We love! We love." With a nod to the German magazine *Die Insel*, the editors of *ONE* promised that this new magazine would engage in thoughtful and lively discussion regarding the rights of the "homophile," a word they used to signify men who love men and women who love women. It was thus inevitable that an issue of *ONE* produced eight months later, in August of 1953, should pose the question, "Homosexual Marriage?"

When the contemporary gay or lesbian person reads this plug, they are probably as intrigued by the first word as the second. Homosexual? Why not gay? The short answer to that is that the West Coast homophile movement did not start to use the word gay in modern parlance until the late 1960s. So why not homophile? Probably because, though attributed to "E. B. Saunders," I suspect the article was written by

ONE's editor-in-chief, Dale Jennings, who did not like that term—simple as that (see White 2002). To many in Los Angeles at this time, the term "gay" signified an effeminate male homosexual, one to be shunned and avoided. The second word, though, "marriage," might also cause us to anticipate several things: a demand for civil recognition on par with legally recognized heterosexual partnerships. We might expect to find within a discussion of whether "homosexual marriage" should be a civil or a religious issue or perhaps find a diatribe on the unfair tax burden levied on single, often childless adults. But what we find in this eighth issue of *ONE* magazine is contrary to what most of us would expect.

The article is titled "Reformer's Choice: Marriage License or Just License?" Its teaser forewarns the reader of the magnitude of the topic: "The following paper is, in the opinion of the editorial board, one of the most important which *ONE* has published. Its implications are staggering. The author(ess?) was little short of staggering, too, in the mild letter which accompanied this historic essay: 'I hope the enclosed will not seem an impertinence.' But on second thought, Writer Saunders, It is impertinent and exactly the type of impertinence all thinking persons and this magazine vitally need!"

So the reader is thus enticed to engage the topic in a most serious light. The prose of the essay is sober and pedantic. The article posits that the editors of *ONE*, like their progenitors in the Mattachine Society, aspire to fight for the social acceptance of the sexual deviate. But what then? Could there be unanticipated repercussions? Saunders transports us to the year 2053, "when homosexuality has been accepted to the point of being of no importance." Saunders asks, "Now, is the deviate allowed to continue his pursuit of physical happiness without restraint as he attempts to do today? Or is he, in this Utopia, subject to marriage laws?" At this point, the alert reader might begin to suspect that this is a Swiftian satire, for things are already the opposite of what we would expect. Few after all, in this era of the Ricardos and Kramdens, would equate marriage with utopia.

In Saunders's brave new world, promiscuity must be guarded against at all costs lest it "loosen heterosexual marriage ties, too, and make even shallower the meaning of marriage as we know it." Wanton homosexuality would thus be an attack on heterosexual marriage—an assault that would not be tolerated by the heterosexual majority. "For why should [the homophile] be permitted promiscuity when the heterosexuals who people the earth must be married to enjoy sexual intercourse?"

Would homosexual men desire such a burden? No way. "Available statistics do not indicate that most or even a large percentage of deviates want a binding and legal marriage," states Saunders, though "undoubtedly if it were possible there would be more who attempted it and many who might make it work." And anyway, who would wear the pants in the marriage? Would the "Mr." and "Mrs." idea be retained? If so, "what legal developments would come of the objection by the 'Mr.' that the 'Mrs.' doesn't contribute equally?" What of adoptions? Would a Lesbian retain her rights as a mother after divorcing her husband? How will this affect the "masses of children" who lived in such a futuristic household? What of adultery? Surely this would not be tolerated, for "equal rights mean equal responsibilities: equal freedoms mean equal limitations." Saunders's article indeed makes many astute and prescient observations by asking several of the questions that haunt us today.

Here we have the true heart of the matter. *ONE* was dedicated to the cause of equality, of living up to the ideals set forth in the Declaration of Independence and the Bill of Rights. But if these rights were to truly be secured, perhaps homosexuals and homophiles (men in particular, reflecting the biases of *ONE*'s editorship) would lose out in some surprising and undesirable ways.

Compulsory marriage for homosexuals? What kind of freedom would that be? Could it be that homosexuals *sub rosa* have more freedoms than they would should they be accepted? "Are we willing to make that trade?" Saunders asks. And here is the crux of the irony: in their quest for equality, homosexual men may get more than they bargained for. Saunders advised the activists within *ONE* and Mattachine to choose their battles—and their path—wisely. "When one digs, it must be to make a ditch, a well, a trench: something! Otherwise all this energetic work merely produces a hole. Any bomb can do that."

There is one further observation that compounds the irony of this essay: Is it not a bit crazy to talk of homosexual marriage when homosexual sex is still forbidden? The key is in understanding that this article is itself a teaser, a simple ploy to get the attention of an audience, to challenge it to think in new and different ways—and to subscribe.

THE LEGAL RAMIFICATIONS OF HOMOPHILIA

And the ploy worked—in fact, perhaps too well. We must remember that at the time of this publication, homosexual sex was illegal in every state. "*ONE* by its very nature often discusses illegal sexual practices as well as the legal rights of those who commit them," warned an editor's blurb printed at the close of the marriage article. "Yet, until the nature of a sex crime is so defined as to most benefit society, *ONE* wishes to clearly state that its aims do not include converting any man, woman, or child to ways alien to their natures nor does is [*sic*] condone any behavior which is actually 'against nature' and not to the best interests of society." Much time could be spent unpacking the innuendo and double entendre of this disclaimer. But clever as it may be, it did not at all impress the authorities. This August 1953 issue of *ONE* magazine was confiscated the day it was dropped off at the Los Angeles post office, and the postal authorities in Los Angeles and Washington, D.C. withheld it for 16 days.

There was a two-month lag in *ONE* magazine between the time an issue was published and the time the commentary on that issue would run in a subsequent issue. Therefore, the topic of homosexual marriage was dropped in the September issue of *ONE*, which turned its attention instead to Communists, effeminate men, and even, believe it or not, effeminate gay Communists. This brings me to the other "Mary" of my title, for, though I do not have the time to address it in depth here, the trouble of effeminacy was often discussed in the pages of *ONE* in its early years. This was suggested in the Saunders article: If two men get married, which of them was the woman? If two women got married, which was to be the man? Though this might seem like an absurd thing to ponder in our enlightened eyes, to the homophile of the 1950s, these were serious matters to be returned to presently.

The October 1953 issue of *ONE* magazine was seething: "ONE is not grateful," the editors proclaimed across the cover; there was absolutely no gratitude to the authorities for having ultimately declared *ONE* "suitable for mailing." To fight back, readers were encouraged to spread the word and subscribe to the magazine. To stand up against the oppressive postmaster and the federal government, "deviants": needed a voice. They needed to be reminded of their constitutional rights especially as set forth under the Fifth Amendment which provided that "No person . . . shall be compelled in any criminal case to be a witness against himself." To subscribe to *ONE* was to defend American civil liberties. *ONE*'s editors were dedicated only to truth, to "bring about a better understanding of sexual deviation by both heterosexuals and homosexuals." They were willing to risk their own reputations, careers, and lives for this sake; they were "willing to stand up and stick out their necks for all deviates because they believe **someone** has to **sometime**" (emphasis in the original). For those readers in remote locations such as "Paducah," who were loath to have their name on *ONE*'s mailing list, the editors swore that they would "rot in join before handing over one single name of a subscriber." All the reader needed to do to help was to subscribe. "*ONE* is yours. Keep it yours. Isn't it worth a buck to know you're not alone?"

The ploy was working. *ONE* was being distributed in newsstands from coast to coast. Readership had quadrupled, from 500 issues in January to over 2,000 by the fall of 1953. To grow further, *ONE*'s editors knew that they would have to establish a core group of subscribers—a fact certainly not lost on the Los Angeles postmaster, Otto K. Olesen.

As for the topic that likely triggered the postmaster's scrutiny, there was no further discussion of homosexual marriage in this October issue outside of the Letters column. And here, the question was tossed aside as absurd. A writer from Berkeley, California stated that "marriage was a heterosexual concept buttressed and blessed by the Church and State since man emerged out of the miasma of pre-history." Another wrote that marriage existed solely for the sake of children, so why should we "try to legislate lasting mutual love on the part of any tow homosexuals?" This writer believed that the Saunders article posited that "legalized marriage should be one of our primary issues as a group seeking acceptance," and to that he said: "Balderdash!" He continued: " 'Marriage' between two men is, in the eyes of society, the ultimate manifestation of what it considers the 'mental illness' in homosexuality. Indeed, when it is called 'marriage,' I agree with them."

It is striking to me the vitriolic revulsion these writers had for the idea of homosexual marriage. This hardly anticipates the current battle for same-sex marriage rights currently debated daily, in newspapers from all across the United States and the world. But this second writer got one thing profoundly correct: the thought of same-sex sex perturbed heterosexuals because it somehow fed into their notions of homosexuals as psychological maladjusted deviates. The thought of same-sex marriage, the idea that two men or two women could enter into a loving and enduring, mutually-supportive relationship on par with a heterosexual union—that idea terrified them. It was a truly subversive idea, one that must be guarded against. It was therefore the talk of love, not the talk of sex, that made *ONE* lewd, lascivious, and very, very dangerous.

To clarify this point, I draw attention to the famous October 1954 issue of *ONE* that was also withheld by the Postmaster, Otto Olesen, for being, in his words, "obscene, lewd, lascivious, and filthy." Since Postmaster Olesen was not required to specify exactly what content it was that he deemed offensive, it was left to *ONE*'s senior editor, Don Slater, and

ONE's white-knight attorney, Eric Julber, to figure it out.[1] They determined that the most likely candidate was a short story attributed to Jane Dahr titled, "Sappho Remembered," in which two women were seen to fall in love—and display their affection for one another:

> Pavia closed the door of their suite behind them, tossed her coat on the chair and gently drew the girl to her. "Forgiven?" she asked at last. She touched the delicate pulse beat beneath the light golden hair on the child-like temple. "Will their ever be a day when you don't blush when I do that," she murmured.

This passage is certainly suggestive, and it probably depicts a love relationship. But by what standard is it lewd, lascivious, and filthy? Federal law at the time specified that to be lewd, there must be a "likelihood that the work will so much arouse the salacity of the reader to whom it is sent as to outweigh any literary, scientific, or other merits it may have in [the average] reader's hands." Julber, in his Appellants' Opening Brief[2] filed in the Ninth Circuit Court of Appeals on January 16, 1956, argued that this standard did not hold to any of the contraband *ONE*'s content. And he lost that argument.

On March 2, 1956, Judge Thurmond Clark entered a judgment in favor of Postmaster Olesen. However, while totally ignoring the many good arguments Julber had made in his 55-page brief, Judge Clark added a surprising remark: "The suggestion that homosexuals should be recognized as a segment of our people and be accorded special privilege as a class is rejected." This is puzzling, as nowhere in his brief did Julber suggest that homosexuals were a distinct class of people deserving special protection. Nevertheless, Julber and Slater were defeated—for the time being, at least.

ONE's case continued up the appeals process until it reached the Supreme Court. Julber filed a petition for a rehearing on March 14, 1957, that was denied a month later, on April 12, by judges Barnes, Hamley, and Ross (see Eskridge 1997, 804). Next, Julber wrote a Petition for Writ of Certiorari to the U.S. Court of Appeals for the Ninth Circuit and filed it with the Supreme Court on June 13, 1957. In the short nine-page writ, Julber asked the Court to rule that the Court of Appeals had erred in finding the magazine obscene. It had misrepresented and incorrectly gauged "the moral tone of the community" and failed to take into consideration the bibliographic appendix.

Finally, on January 13, 1958, the Supreme Court reversed the Ninth Circuit Court's rulings in *ONE v. Olesen*. Joyce Murdoch and Deb

Price, in their comprehensive study of the history of lesbians and gays in the Supreme Court, conclude:

> The significance of *ONE*'s three-year, largely forgotten legal battle is almost impossible to overstate. The written word has been the first path that countless gay men and lesbians have found out of isolation. The 1958 *ONE* ruling flung open the door for gay publications, which began to proliferate. Gay magazines and newspapers became a cornerstone for building gay communities and by encouraging people to come out, to connect with one another and to share a sense of identity and injustice. Millions of American gay men and lesbians have learned to hold their heads up high in part because an obscure little magazine successfully stood up for itself long before many of them were born. (2001, 50)

Though the subject of same-sex sex was incendiary and controversial, it was not a discussion of sex that caused the Los Angeles postmaster to twice withhold *ONE Magazine*. It was, instead, the frank discussion of same-sex marriage—and the thought of enduring romantic same-sex partnerships—that was found to be truly "lewd, lascivious, and filthy."As I am not a psychologist, I have no idea why the thought of same-sex love should so affront the heterosexual majority, but it clearly it does. For this reason, as I have argued elsewhere, perhaps LGBT lovers are the ideal LGBT activists (White 2009, 225)? In any event, we can learn from our pre-Stonewall forbears to discern and devise strategies by which we can secure a social and legal space for LGBT people whereby they can form and foster same-sex relationships. In following in the tradition of Eric Julber and Don Slater, we just might find that we do not need identity politics order to do this. Recall that Julber never grounded his argument on the rights for homophile people to be recognized as a class. Like Slater, Julber realized that if you secured the right of the individual, the right of the group would follow. It was Judge Clark who brought up the "class" argument. To my mind, it is almost as if he was trying to bait Julber and Slater, to get them to engage him in an argument that he knew they could not win.

THE TROUBLE WITH MARY . . .

Earlier, I noted that how the article attributed to Saunders in *ONE*'s August issue of 1953 was haunted by the specter of two men living together and asking which would be expected to be the woman.

Would a law need to be enacted in this futuristic utopia that would "prohibit one person to be 'kept' by another then?" In a recent publication, I have argued that this fear and intolerance of the effeminate or "gay" man is one of the fundamental characteristics between the early homophile movement as manifest in southern California and the later post-Stonewall gay or LGBT movement (White 2009, 55–56). While I do not want to suggest that Sunder's article was driven or motivated by a fear of effeminacy, it does point toward what were perceived as the two greatest threats to social acceptance of the male homosexual deviant: promiscuity and effeminacy, as a very astute writer from Quebec observed in the October 1953 issues (17–19). Caught between a monster and a maelstrom, *ONE*'s editors were trying to navigate between the Skylla of unbridled promiscuity and the swishy effeminacy of Kharbybis.

The prescient Canadian advised *ONE's* writers that "effeminacy as such maligns no one except females" and yet "they, the genuine article, take no umbrage; homosexuals who are still farther removed from the copy might show some common sense." The writer continues: "If we can face the promiscuity and the effeminacy of our group we can face this as well: that we are a true living group; one that exist because of its inner coherence, not fortuitously through pressure from outside. . . . All repressed groups faced with the first step toward emancipation face this too: that the group must free itself also from within."

CONCLUSION

While researching some of the first public discourse on homosexual marriage, I found that many of the arguments were contrary to what I had expected them to be. In short, rather than truly propose that homosexuals be given the right to marry, the dialogue in the early issues of *ONE* served two purposes. First, the editors of *ONE* were fighting the two most prominent and enduring stereotypes of the male homosexual. Evidence of the enduring nature of these stereotypes is given in a 1970 article by Julian Stanley who finds that "core vocabulary" words signifying effeminate homosexuals, such as "queen," "camp," "drag," and "Mary!"—and terms of gay promiscuity including "trade," "trick," "basket," and "one-night stand"—had percolated into popular culture enough that these could not be considered a "sign of group solidarity as slang of some other subcultures" (Stanley 1970, 50; see also Kulick 2000, 251). Second, while the stated purpose of the magazine was to hold a frank and honest discussion of homosexuality, it was also engaging a broad audience on the rights for homophiles to establish long-term relationships that were grounded on love and had the potential to be just as enduring as heterosexual marriages. As I have shown, it is this latter purpose that seems to have most stoked the ire of heterosexual moralist such as Postmaster Oleson and Judge Clark.

In 1953, the thought of compulsory marriage for homosexuals was indeed absurd enough to index the high irony of Saunders's satiric essay. But this paper suggests that Saunders (or more likely Dale Jennings) was as right as he was wrong. Perhaps, indeed, we should be careful lest we achieve that for which we strive. But more so, history indicates that the battle for lesbian and/or gay marriage is not the same as the battle for same-sex marriage. Perhaps the reason for the initial success of the marriage battle in California was due to Gavin Newsom's approach is treating marriage as a fundamental right to all, and that to deny a person from wedding another of the same sex was a simple matter of gender discrimination. Perhaps this strategy will work in other states as well. Perhaps, in some states, the rhetoric surrounding gay marriage is holding back the legalization of same-sex marriage and domestic partnerships? In short, the lessons of the past have taught us that while it is important to stand up and be recognized as gay, perhaps it is also important to know when to put the labels aside. To paraphrase Hillary Clinton, perhaps we need to learn when to stop fighting for gay rights, and start fighting for human rights. Though the words might be different, the objectives are the same.

The lessons that we have to learn from the pre-Stonewall activists are many. But in order for us to learn, those primary source materials must continue to be available to us. For this reason, sources like the new www.outhistory.org Web site of the Center for Lesbian and Gay Studies are crucial for the ongoing success and progress of our movement. Here, historic materials, such as the entire text of Julber's opening brief in the case of ONE, Incorporated versus Otto K. Oleson, can be accessed by anyone in the world with unfettered access to the Internet. Also, while it is important for today's queer scholars to mine, interpret, and present this historic information, I hope that we will all stop to remember that history and these resources need our continued help. Our queer history will not endure on its own.

NOTES

This paper was originally presented for the Sixteenth Annual American University Conference on Lavender Languages and Linguistics, February 14, 2009. I am grateful to William L. Leap for coordinating this conference and to

Robert Hill for organizing the panel on Recovering Lavender History. I would also like to thank Brett Abrams and Michael Ryall for their comments on the presented draft of this paper.

1. According to William Eskridge, this issue was found by Postmaster Oleson to be lewd based on three items printed therein: the short story "Sappho Remembered," a poem titled "Lord Samuel and Lord Montagu" that warns of the perils of T-room cruising, and a printed advertisement for a Swiss magazine, *Der Kreis* (1997, 58, 102).

2. The complete text of this brief has been posted online at http://www.outhistory.org/wiki/JulberAppeal.

REFERENCES

Eskridge, W. N., Jr. "Privacy Jurisprudence and the Apartheid of the Closet, 1946–1961." *Florida State University Law Review* 24 (4) (1997): 703–840.

Kulick, D. "Gay and Lesbian Language." *Annual Review of Anthropology* 29 (2000): 243–85.

Murdoch, Deb, and Deb Price. *Courting Justice: Gay Men and Lesbians v. the Supreme Court*. New York: Basic Books, 2001.

Stanley, J. P. "Homosexual Slang." *American Speech* 45 (1/2) (1970): 45–59.

White, C. T. *Pre-Gay L.A.: A Social History of the Movement for Homosexual Rights*. Champaign, IL: University of Illinois Press, 2009.

———. "Dale Jennings: ONE's Outspoken Advocate." In *Before Stonewall: Activist for Gay and Lesbian Rights in Historic Contexts*, edited by Vern L. Bullough et al., 83–93. Binghamton: Harrington Park Press, 2002.

Chapter 2

Queer Appetites, Butch Cooking: Recipes for Lesbian Subjectivities

Katharina Vester

In 1998, Ffiona Morgan published *The Lesbian Erotic Cookbook: Cuisine Extraordinaire to Caress and Fondle the Palate.*[1] The cookbook features recipes such as "Raging Hormone Rice," "Get Down Crepes," "Road to Ecstasy Applesauce Bread," and "Peel My Clothes Off Fried Rice," and these are only some of the tamer recipe titles. Beyond the racy titles, however, the recipes themselves are not different from those in other cookbooks; they feature lists of commonly available ingredients and detailed instructions, and the dishes they produce are similar to the dishes that are produced by recipes in mainstream cookbooks. What makes this text explicitly queer and erotic is the narrative context in which the recipes are embedded: suggestive short stories and photos that present as erotic a diversity of female bodies in various states of dress or undress, displaying voluptuous, slender, aging, muscular, sagging, pierced, soft, or flabby bodies with firm, spotless, or wrinkled skin. The text thus defies with each page the main-streamlined version of female nakedness. Clearly in love with female muscle and body fat, the cookbook defines the lesbian body as less regulated by hegemonic beauty standards and erotic in and because of its individuality. The cookbook, fully functional as a manual, becomes a tool of resistance against the embodiment of normative gender performances and the incorporation of heteronormative narratives. Cooking and eating are identity-producing acts. *The Lesbian Erotic Cookbook*, with its title, narratives and images makes this visible.

It is central to the cookbook genre that recipes come in specific narrative contexts. These narratives recommend the recipes, and promise that they will be worth the work we are about to put into them. They also locate the recipes for us culturally and attach identity categories to them. Recipes in the late *Gourmet* magazine, in soul food cookbooks or *Martha Stewart's Living* promise that if you cook these specific dishes you will be more sophisticated, more cosmopolitan, more authentically ethnic, more motherly or more whatever flavor you want to be. As self-regulatory somatic selves—subjects that are always already embodied when they come into existence—we discipline our bodies in many ways into the subjectivities we believe to be desired by our cultural surrounding, so we often eat what we aspire to be. Culinary discourses provide us with the appropriate recipes.

Since Alice Toklas published her cookbook in 1954, a very small corpus of texts has come onto on the American market reflecting on or addressing homosexual cooks.[2] However, the even smaller corpus of cookbooks explicitly targeting a lesbian audience, such as *The Lesbian Erotic Cookbook*, goes beyond merely providing a culinary identity for self-identifying dykes. These texts make it evident that traditionally the identity-constructing narratives that accompany recipes are heteronormative.[3] For almost 200 years American cookbooks addressed women who were imagined to prepare the food men eat. In the process of increasing urbanization and the atomization of families, the emancipation of slaves and dwindling numbers of servants, the naturalization of the separation of spheres and the fear that household work may be unaccounted for with the growing numbers of women in the labor force, cooking became firmly associated with a woman's love and her performance of femininity. This connection is a cultural strategy that ensures that the cooking gets done even when women find employment and/or fulfillment outside of the domestic sphere. Since the late nineteenth century, women's journals, food advertisement, and household manuals have claimed that food preparation was a central part of what it meant to be a woman. They also constructed cooking as satisfying and fulfilling (*The Joy of Cooking*), as a means to gain recognition, and as an appropriate outlet for a woman's creativity and emotional caring.[4]

Cookbooks addressing a lesbian audience make these claims visible and dispute them. Three cookbooks analyzed here use strategies to resist hegemonic notions of femininity, but by no means are these texts only liberating. Since they explicitly address a lesbian readership, all three texts struggle to define the lesbian body and self. In the process of voicing a culinary identity, they produce new normative imperatives and complex exclusionary mechanisms that demand further scrutiny.

The Lesbian Erotic Cookbook, for instance, queers ideas of the female nude and the erotic, but it presents as erotic only able bodies and almost exclusively white ones. (The few black bodies, though, are presented prominently, such as on the cover page.) While variety and individuality are important in the depictions of queer female bodies in this text, they are not free of normative assumptions. Most of the depicted women wear their hair short and no make-up, but compromise with hegemonic beauty ideals in displaying their bodies (and faces) hairless. The text stretches and bends ideas of ideal femininity but it also uses familiar images from a culturally sanctioned reservoir of depictions of women's sexuality, such as voluptuous flowers and luscious fruits and curvy statues of fertility goddesses. The cookbook thus reiterates well-worn notions of women as soft, swollen, delicious, and sweet-smelling, showing how impossible it is to escape from cultural stereotypes entirely.

The staging of the erotic, too, utilizes conventional imagery, such as the display of fragmented naked bodies emphasizing similar body parts that would be presented in the context of the heterosexual erotic, most prominently breasts. But the text does not only offer conventional productions of the erotic; it also gives space to alternatives. Biceps, for instance, are staged as sexually attractive female body parts. Juxtaposed to breasts they mediate between hardness and softness, concepts that have traditionally been misused to distinguish between the sexes. Hidden between the depictions of breasts, bellies, and bottoms is also a photo of hands, body parts commonly neglected in heterosexual porn. Showing hands in this context sexualizes them and acknowledges their importance for the erotic experience.

Perhaps most notable are the many depictions of women eating and feeding each other. As Susan Bordo has argued, representations of eating women have almost entirely vanished from public discourse as a radical consequence of the cultural dictum of "women cook, men eat."[5] In these images of women feeding each other, the symbolic connection between feeding and loving is left intact, but re-appropriated to define the female body as a non-heterosexual body. There is a long tradition in U.S. culture that values a woman's restraint of her appetite as a positively connoted sign of control over her sexual desires and other ambitions and thereby her acceptance of male privilege. *The Lesbian*

Erotic Cookbook presents women's lustful eating as desirable and the lesbian subject as guiltlessly giving into all her cravings. This, of course, is a highly romanticized notion of queer subjectivity.

The Lesbian Erotic Cookbook queers the rules of the cookbook genre. It unmasks the underlying sexual assumptions and silently implied heteronormativity, renegotiates the representation of gender and the erotic, and presents a number of decent recipes. *Red Beans and Rice: Recipes for Lesbian Health & Wisdom* by Bode Noonan is even more radical when it comes to undermining the parameters of cookbook writing.[6] Her cookbook bears only faint resemblance to what we have learned to recognize as elemental to the genre: There are no lists of ingredients, no imperatives, no instructions, no claim to authority. Each of the mere five recipes in the book is presented as its own chapter written in essayistic prose. Only by reading the entire chapter can the dish be assembled. The instructions given are vague enough to ensure that the cook will produce her own dish rather than simply clone the author's dish. Creative experimentation is explicitly encouraged. The recipes blend into what Noonan has to say about life. Meandering between unconventional wisdoms, general advice, her own biography, and food memories, she tells us how to make egg salad, red beans and rice, bread and spinach casserole, potato salad and fruit juice—all comfort foods for the bruised and battered soul.

The text was written in the 1980s, and it is conscious of the problems that come with identity politics. It tries to emphasize diversity and individuality while simultaneously imagining an identity-based community for political and emotional support. This does not have to be a contradiction, as the author explains in her chapter on potato salad:

> Potatoes, I thought. Potatoes are a lot like Lesbians. They're all the same and they're all different. You have New potatoes, Russett potatoes. Red potatoes, brown potatoes, peeled potatoes. But all potatoes are composed of carbohydrates and water. . . . Some of us play softball. . . . Some of us wear three piece suits and do our daily work in courtrooms where we defend against what we see as unjust. Some of us don't do a damn thing at all. Some of us aren't even gay. Some of us are men. Men? What am I saying? (46–47)

While Noonan obviously tries to avoid an essentialist definition of what constitutes the lesbian subject, she still grasps for a way to define what it means to be a lesbian, what constitutes the community's water and carbohydrates. In this process, she severs lesbian identity entirely from sexual acts and rearranges it around the experience of exclusion and marginalization. However, she specifies this experience as different from the experience of racism and sexism insofar as it has at its core the pain of being rejected and disowned not only by society but even worse: also being rejected by your own family and childhood friends—an experience, she argues, that is central to lesbian identity. Hence the emphasis on comfort food in the text: it is the familiar childhood food that in a Proustian manner brings back with its flavors the memory of unconditional love and acceptance. Giving you the knowledge to prepare these dishes gives you the possibility to care for yourself and to be your own family, the author argues.

In *Red Beans and Rice* Noonan also discusses lesbian identity in terms of gender. She describes how her mother labored unenthusiastically over her much acknowledged signature potato salad, despising the process of preparing it but doing it anyway. Cooking disciplined her mother's body into gender-appropriate behavior. She contrasts this description with one of her former lovers, who made her less-than-perfect potato salad with gusto and intensively enjoyed every minute of the process. The difference, Noonan suggests, is that cooking can be a liberating and creative act for women who are aware of the gender traps that come with it and are successful in avoiding them. The mother is expected to cook and cannot escape from these expectations because her self-esteem depends on the acknowledgment she gains for her flawless performance of hegemonic femininity. The lesbian lover, in contrast, makes up her own gender performance. Lesbian identity in *Red Beans and Rice* is therefore not only centered around the experience of rejection but is also described as an alternative, more liberated and maybe more enlightened form of feminine gender performance. The lesbian subjectivities Noonan constructs in the text thus waver between victimization and empowerment, defying easy assignments.

The Butch Cook Book redefines and negotiates gender identities, too. Published in 2008 by Lee Lynch, Nel Ward, and Sue Hardesty, it is a compilation of recipes sent in by cooks who self-identify as butch.[7] Compiled cookbooks have traditionally been used to create a sense of community. Simultaneously, they defy the notion of a central, authoritative voice, as all contributors share in defining the community they belong to. *The Butch Cook Book* utilizes both of these aspects to deal with the problems that come with the term butch (a term that has been called "overtheorized," "underdetermined," and "infinitely elastic").[8] The cookbook struggles hard for a complex and inclusive description of butch identity. It also shamelessly exploits every known stereotype. It often but not always does so playfully, with great humor, and lots of self-deprecation. The illustrations in the book feature—quite out of context—trucks and motor bikes. One of the contributors advises: "Use a food processor—what's a butch without power tools?" To no surprise many illustrations present real power tools in the kitchen. Some recipes call for beer, either as an ingredient or as "emotional" support for the butch who has to face the dangers of the kitchen (102, 115). Between the recipes one can find tips for "how to buff up your abs with potato sacks." Or for how to cook for a new girlfriend:

> **Tips for First Dinner Cooked by Butch for New Girlfriend**
>
> Take a deep breath and remember this is the only meal you'll have to cook.
> Go to deli and pick up something green, something red or orange, and something pre-cooked.
> Check to make sure she doesn't buy at the same deli.
> Check to see if the microwave is working.
> Serve deli stuff in dishes borrowed from gay guys next door.
> If you're lucky, the guys will jump at the chance to cater the meal for you. Take their offer without question. They'll disappear at the last moment and give you all the credit.
> Hide all the deli cartons before she arrives. (87)

The cookbook also provides (jokingly) a test to distinguish a butch from a femme. It asks you to look at your nails. If you curl your fingers inward you are butch, while the femme looks at the back of her hand (as if in the act of checking her nail polish). The test shows that butchness is not only about attitude, it is also queer embodiment, a form of resistance against the hegemonic production of the female body. The text claims that butchness undermines the disciplinary mechanisms that render the female body as dainty, incapacitated, fragile, and decorative. The butch body needs specific nourishment and this, not surprisingly, excludes some of the items that are connoted as feminine in society. For instance, the text claims, a butch only eats vegetables if her femme makes her.

The hyper-butchness that is displayed throughout the text is, of course, constantly undermined by the fact that the text is a cookbook. The editors jokingly admit that when they started to collect recipes they expected "30 recipes for boxed mac and cheese," but learned to their surprise "that butches can cook." Because cookbooks have a long tradition of being associated with hegemonic feminine gender performance, therefore the cookbook context implicitly subverts the performance of butchness as renegade gender identity. Again the text and its authors deal with the dilemma playfully. To neutralize the cookbook's gender norm-affirming potential, the contributors and editors use three strategies. First, the butch cooks for sexual gratification. Recipes feature titles such as "Green Beans for Butches Hoping for Sex on the First Date" (55). The drink section of the cookbook is called "Love Potions," and the breakfast section "The Morning After" (163). Wowing women is a sufficiently butch endeavor to limit the damage cooking may be doing to the cook's renegade gender identity. Second, many of the contributors explain in detail why they took up cooking in the first place: a partner got sick and the butch took over the household chores; it serves as a creative outlet to balance a more menial day job; or, in a more unusual explanation, she was in a Zen cloister and was ordered to cook to further her spiritual enlightenment. All these explanations make it obvious that the butch does not cook because it came naturally to her (as is implied for women within the heterosexual economy) but because of very specific circumstances that make the act an individual choice or the result of necessity.

The third strategy is the contribution of specifically butch recipes. These are recipes that are centered on the idea of speed, simplicity, and convenience. For instance, the recipe for "Mostly Peas" asks for only three ingredients: 1 can of V8 juice, half cup of frozen peas, and Tabasco sauce to taste. No fussing around in the kitchen is required here, only a microwave and a spoon. Only a few of the recipes produce food from scratch. Recipes for pancakes, pies, and cakes usually start with boxed mixes. One recipe suggests bagged salad as a side dish and advises the reader to take the salad out of the bag before serving it (184). The butch recipe stages a lack of competence and unfamiliarity with the kitchen, rejecting the expertise and authority culture has traditionally assigned to women in the kitchen and thus disassociating itself from hegemonic ideas of what constitutes an ideal woman.

But these simple definitions and descriptions of butchness are complicated on every page of the text. Contradictions are invited and not silenced in the attempt to homogenize butch identity. The cookbook, for example, features very complex and sophisticated recipes too, as well as not-so-butch recipes for Lemon Chiffon Pie, Mushroom Risotto, and Mango Compote.

All the recipes are accompanied by short texts in which the contributors explain what the recipes and butchness mean to them. Under the title "Butch Bio" we find blacksmiths, community organizers, and writers, but also stay-at-home-butches like Barb Bayenhof, who chose to devote her life to feeding her partner for the better of 11 years. Truck driver Bevin Allison calls herself a "domestic butch" (159); Melissa Freet describes herself as a cross of Martha Stewart and Mac Gyver; and Marythegood writes, "Can handle sheetrock and split wood, but my pie crust will melt in your mouth" (99). These bios show how butches cross the gender dichotomy back and forth in their daily lives.

In the end, the cookbook seems to argue that butch is an umbrella term for a great variety of gender performances that do not—or not entirely—conform to ideas of hegemonic femininity and that are directed at an audience of women. (About half of the contributors take pride in cooking for another woman and make this known to the readers.) The definition of butchness oscillates in the text between gender and sexual identities and produces an infinite number of potentialities.

All three cookbooks struggle to define the queer self and body in non-normative and non-exclusionary ways. Of course, they eventually all have to fail. Lee Lynch acknowledges this humorously when she writes in the introduction of *The Butch Cook Book*, "Finally we can tell you: this is what lesbians do, we cook." The alleged difference between "you" and "we" implodes in the quotidian act of cooking. But the texts are successful in queering the cookbook genre, making its heteronormative strategies and identity-producing narratives visible, and utilizing them for their own political agendas and playfully delicious pleasures.

NOTES

1. Ffiona Morgan, *The Lesbian Erotic Cookbook: Cuisine Extraordinaire to Caress and Fondle the Palate* (Novato: Daughters of the Moon, 1998).
2. Alice B. Toklas, *The Alice B. Toklas Cook Book* (New York: Harper and Row, 1984 [1954]). Examples of queer cookbooks and literary culinary texts, (besides those discussed in this paper) include Lou Rand Hogan, *The Gay Cookbook* (New York: Bell Publishing Company, Inc., 1965); Amy Scholder, ed. *Cooking with Honey: What Literary Lesbians Eat* (Ithaca: Firebrand Books, 1996); and some of the short stories in Arlene Voski Avakian, *Through the Kitchen Window: Women Explore the Intimate Meanings of Food and Cooking* (Boston: Beacon Press, 1997).
3. Katharina Vester, "Tender Mutton: Recipes, Sexual Identity and Spinster Resistance in Gertrude Stein," in *Another Language: Poetic Experiment in Britain*

and North America, edited by Kornelia Freitag and Katharina Vester (Berlin: Lit Verlag, 2008), 289–300.

4. For further discussion, see: Sherrie A. Inness, *Dinner Roles: American Women and Culinary Culture* (Iowa City: University of Iowa Press, 2001).

5. Susan Bordo, *Unbearable Weight: Feminism, Western Culture and the Body* (Berkeley and Los Angeles: University of California Press, 1993), 99–138.

6. Bode Noonan, *Red Beans and Rice: Recipes for Lesbian Health and Wisdom* (Trumansburg: Crossing Press, 1986).

7. Sue Hardesty, Lee Lynch, and Nel Ward, eds. *The Butch Cookbook* (Newport: Teal Ribbon Publications, 2008).

8. Sherrie A. Inness, *The Lesbian Menace: Ideology, Identity, and the Representation of Lesbian Life* (Amherst, MA: University of Massachusetts Press, 1997), 81.

Chapter 3

Advertising: Gays Conquer Another Media Venue

Rodger Streitmatter

In some ways, the content of the 2003 advertisement was downright mundane. The image showed the top tier of a wedding cake, covered with creamy white frosting and accented with fresh flowers and a miniature couple all gussied up in their matrimonial finery. The copy for the ad, centered underneath the image, seemed conventional as well: "Help them stay on top of the world. It's an ideal way to give two people a bright—and inspired—future. Save 50 percent for a limited time when you give the *New York Times* as a gift. There's no present like the *Times*. Call 1-800-251-4853." In short, the country's preeminent journalistic voice was making a pitch for people to forego a toaster or a place setting of china and, instead, give their newly married friends and relatives a newspaper subscription.[1]

But for anyone familiar with those days in 1950 when the *New York Times* had published headlines such as "Perverts Called Government Peril," the ad was extraordinary. For neither member of the wedding couple pictured in the ad wore the lace veil or the billowing white dress that would have identified her as the blushing bride, as both plastic figures wore black tuxedos and tiny bowties—they were two grooms. And so, America's most respected news organization, the one that half a century earlier had consistently vilified homosexuals, was now using same-sex couples to try to sell newspapers to its liberal readers while, at the same time, not-so-subtly supporting one of the most hotly debated initiatives of the day: allowing gay couples to marry.

Although the advertisement was remarkable in the context of the *Times* earlier treatment of homosexuals and in the paper's bold endorsement of such a culturally and politically divisive issue, it was merely one among a legion of print ads and television commercials featuring gay men that proliferated in the American media by the early 2000s.

Indeed, gay-themed ads were appearing so frequently that newspapers all across the country reported on the phenomenon. "Advertisers are feeling much more comfortable using gay content," wrote the *San Francisco Chronicle*;[2] "People with something to sell are increasingly dropping their inhibitions about the homosexual community," agreed the *Washington Post*.[3] The *New York Times* was another journalistic voice that took notice of the development that its own wedding-cake ad contributed to, saying, "Same-sex images are showing up more and more in national advertising, in consumer categories from automobiles and beer to soft drinks and home furnishings." The *Times* supported its point by quoting the editor of an advertising publication as saying, "A trend is underway, and companies are jumping on the bandwagon."[4]

While the trend was widespread both geographically and with regard to the kinds of items being hawked, most of the companies did not cross the gender line. "Lesbians have generally not received equal treatment in the ads," the *St. Louis Post-Dispatch* reported. "They appear only rarely either in print ads or on television commercials."[5]

As for exactly why so many companies were now eager to include gay men—and an occasional lesbian—in their ads, the news organizations gave other media products some of the credit, with the *New York Times* stating, "*Will & Grace* on NBC and *Queer as Folk* on Showtime have brought a major shift in attitudes about gay subjects."[6] But the various journalistic voices reported that the primary factor fueling the trend was the growing body of market research that had identified the impressive size of gay buying power. "The average income for gay and lesbian households is estimated at more than $55,000 a year, compared with about $40,000 a year for households in the general population," according to the *Washington Post*. "The aggregate buying power of the gay-lesbian market is estimated at more than $500 billion annually."[7] The Fox News Channel cited similar statistics and then stated pointblank, "Gays are essentially an untapped consumer market that corporate America can no longer ignore."[8]

Like the various television shows, motion pictures, and news stories from the previous fifty years that contained gay content, the plethora of print and television ads sent several messages about their subjects. At the top of the list was a statement that the various other media venues had been obsessing about for half a century: Gay men are highly sexual beings. But, in contrast to many of the products of early eras, the ads generally did not suggest that gay men were so sexual that they were promiscuous but that they, in fact, place enormous value on committed relationships. Additional messages that the abundance of ads communicated—all familiar to anyone who had examined how gays had been depicted in the past—included that gay people deserve equal rights, that they are fun-loving, and that they have large expendable incomes.

GAY MEN ARE HIGHLY SEXUAL

The single gay-themed advertising campaign that attracted the most newspaper ink, with such major dailies as the *Washington Post*[9] and *New York Times*[10] writing stories about it, was for Abercrombie & Fitch clothing store. "The company has been successful in creating a buzz," the *Post* reported.[11] And, indeed, anyone seeing the highly sexual ads instantly knew what all the buzzing was about.

One eye-popping image showed several handsome young men—all of them having removed their shirts to expose their well-defined chests—in a communal shower where they are smiling and laughing as they playfully tug and pull in an effort to remove the boxer shorts from another young man who is bent over with his butt partially exposed—and who clearly does not mind the attention he's getting.[12] Another ad featured a cluster of pretty boys who apparently have just finished showering, as they are naked except for the strategically draped bath towels that just barely cover their genitals, with the very center of the image showing the bare buttocks of one of the lads.[13]

An Abercrombie & Fitch spokesman denied that the examples of male eye candy in the ads were gay men, saying, "People are reading into the images and projecting their own sexuality on them."[14] Journalists who wrote about the ads, however, did not buy that denial, with a *Washington Post* reporter saying of the ads, "They are obviously homoerotic."[15]

Abercrombie & Fitch was by no means the only company to use references to gay sex to sell its products. Two popular brands of beer produced so many ads of this ilk that news organizations reported they were engaged in a duel to see which of them could come up with the cleverest concept. The *Wall Street Journal* handed the trophy to Bud Light for the double-entendre that was central to a print ad showing a man carrying a six-pack and with two words printed across the bulge in the front of his jeans just below the waist: "Nice Package."[16] The *Miami Herald* disagreed, arguing that Miller Lite deserved to win the competition for a television commercial featuring two women beer drinkers flirting with a good-looking man across the bar—until a second guy arrives and holds his boyfriend's hand; that development prompts one of the disappointed women to say, "Well, at least he's not married."[17]

Benetton approached the subject of sex from a dramatically different perspective, using the content of its clothing ads to remind media consumers about HIV/AIDS and to promote safe sex. One memorable ad featured an image of a huge hot pink condom covering all 74 feet of the obelisk at the center of the Place de la Concorde in Paris,[18] while three others showed the words "HIV POSITIVE" tattooed on various body parts of muscular male models—one ad focused on the biceps, the second on the buttocks, the third on the groin area.[19] Still another eye-catching ad featured the buff torsos of two men, one black and one white, wearing nothing but boxer-briefs; instead of being stark white, the underwear was adorned with a bright red AIDS ribbon positioned squarely in the center of each man's crotch.[20] The most controversial of the Benetton ads was titled "Pieta" and showed an emaciated David Kirby on his deathbed, his father cradling the AIDS activist in his arms as the young man took his final breath.[21]

GAY MEN VALUE COMMITTED RELATIONSHIPS

Only a few of the milestones in the decades-long evolution of gays in the media had included committed couples—the Robin Williams and Nathan Lane characters in *The Birdcage* come to mind, as do the HIV-positive and HIV-negative partners on *Queer as Folk*. But with the explosion of gay-themed advertisements, such pairings became the rule rather than the exception.

The phenomenon began in 1992 when *Vanity Fair* became the first major American magazine to publish an unambiguously gay ad. The two-page image featured two slender young men standing on a rooftop with several tall buildings behind them. The background is noticeably tilted, while the men and the words "Banana Republic," in the lower right hand corner, and "free souls," in the upper right, are level.

The most important element of the ad, though, is not the background or the camera angle or the text—but the hand. For one member of the couple has the fingers of his right hand resting, gently and tenderly, on the other man's chest.[22]

Two years later when American television aired its first gay-themed commercial, the coupling phenomenon continued. This pioneering advertisement by Ikea, the Swedish furniture company, showed two men shopping for a new dining room table. Television viewers had no trouble identifying the men as a gay couple, as the dialogue had them finishing each other's sentences and one of them looking solemnly at the other and saying, "a leaf means commitment."[23]

After Banana Republic and Ikea broke the gay advertising ice, companies selling a broad range of products followed suit by depicting gay men in a plethora of one-on-one relationships. Bridgestone/Firestone became the first tire manufacturer to enter the gay market with a magazine ad showing two attractive guys leaning against a stack of tires; it was clear that the men were intimately acquainted, as one of them had his arm around the other.[24] Philadelphia was the first American city to create ads aimed specifically at gay travelers; one spotlighted two men, one white and one black, holding hands in front of the Liberty Bell.[25] Diesel jeans aired a television commercial showing a dark-haired Boy Scout teaching a blond boy how to give mouth-to-mouth resuscitation by having the novice practice on him; at the end of the ad, the two young men are shown galloping off together on horseback—the recently resuscitated member of the pair winking triumphantly at the camera.[26]

While all of these companies sent the message that gay men value committed relationships, some went further than others to make their point. A 2003 Avis rental car ad featured an image of two handsome young hotties smiling happily as they sit inside a car. The headline read "Share the Experience," and the copy stated: "At Avis, we know the value of great relationships. That's why domestic partners are automatically included as additional drivers. No extra fees. No questions asked."[27]

GAY PEOPLE DESERVE EQUAL RIGHTS

The *New York Times* wedding-cake ad was remarkable partly because placing two grooms on top of a sea of white icing meant that the nation's most influential news organization was unabashedly endorsing the proposal to legalize same-sex marriage. But that ad was by no means the only one through which an American business enterprise stated, during the early 2000s, that gay people deserve equal rights.

Snapple was among the advertisers that joined the *Times* in supporting same-sex marriage. The company's off-beat television commercial, inspired by a scene from the film *The Graduate*, began with one bottle of the soft drink, wearing a lacy veil, walking down the aisle of a church. But when the bride reaches the altar and her bottle/groom, who's wearing a bowtie, the ceremony is disrupted by a third bottle, this one sporting a long necktie, making a ruckus in the balcony and prompting the guests to gasp. By the final scene, the two men—the bottle/groom and the bottle/disrupter—are shown leaving the church hand in hand as "The Wedding March" is being played.[28]

Another issue that gay-themed ads spoke to was domestic partner policies, by which employers extend the same benefits offered to the spouses of straight workers, such as health insurance, to the committed partners of gay workers. In 2000, Coors beer endorsed the policy by running a print ad that showed two bottles of its beer—one light, the other original—positioned so they were touching, similar to how two members of a gay couple might stand, below the headline "Domestic Partners!" The ad's copy made it clear that the company didn't merely talk the talk but also walked the walk, stating, "We were the first brewery to offer same-sex, domestic-partner benefits." Coors's corporate relations manager for gays and lesbians, Mary Cheney—who would leave that job when her father Dick Cheney was elected the country's vice president—boasted to reporters that her company had adopted the policy in 1995.[29]

Whether or not gay people choose their sexuality was another issue that made its way into ads, as well as the news coverage of them. Subaru began targeting gays as potential buyers in 1997 by picturing cars in its ads that sported "P-TOWN" on their license plates, a reference to the nickname of the popular gay vacation destination of Provincetown, Massachusetts. Many Subaru ads also featured the tagline "Get out. And stay out," a double-entendre that could be read either as a statement encouraging outdoors-oriented people to buy Subarus or as a statement urging closeted gay people to acknowledge their sexuality—and also buy Subarus. Then, in 2000, the company released an ad showing one of its cars under the headline "It's Not a Choice. It's the Way We're Built." The *Washington Post* promptly reported that Subaru had become one of the first companies to aim its ads specifically at lesbians and that the strategy had led to so many sales that gay women were now referring to the brand of cars as "Lesbarus."[30]

Some companies that sailed into the uncharted sea of gay rights, however, encountered troubled waters. In early 2000, John Hancock Financial Services aired a commercial on network television that featured two women standing in line at an immigration office, holding an infant girl. "Hi, baby, this is your new home," one of the women whispers to the child, who has Asian facial features. The other woman then smiles and tells her partner, "You're going to make a great mom," prompting the first woman to respond, "So are you." The tagline that then appeared on the screen stated: "Insurance for the unexpected. Investments for the opportunities. John Hancock."[31] But anti-gay activists protested the commercial so vehemently, the *San Francisco Chronicle* reported, that when the company re-aired it later in the year, the dialogue about being "a great mom" had been deleted, allowing viewers to think that the two women might merely be sisters or close friends.[32]

GAY PEOPLE ARE FUN-LOVING

My Best Friend's Wedding and *Will & Grace* were among the media products that had, during the 1990s, used witty repartee to portray gay men as fun fellows to be around. Many of the advertisements that exploded onto the American cultural scene a decade later sent a similar message, although they generally did so through images rather than dialogue.

The boys of Abercrombie & Fitch did their part. Those images of bare-chested young men fooling around in the shower were definitely sexual, but they also were lighthearted and playful. The *Washington Post* described the winsome lads as "frolicking" and as "being happy and open."[33] Numerous other ads distributed by Abercrombie & Fitch communicated that anyone wearing its brand of clothing was virtually guaranteed of engaging in fun activities. One had a buff boy entertaining a crowd of inebriated onlookers by stripping down to his boxer-briefs as he danced on a bar;[34] another had a line-up of four carefree young hunks—three white, one black—as they roller skated near a beach while wearing nothing but boxers;[35] and an ad that consisted of several images showed a middle-aged man paired with a much younger one as they somehow managed to pilot their small sailboat while also hugging, kissing, and otherwise cavorting.[36]

Gay men being depicted as fun to be around jumped to a whole new level in 2003 when the Chili's restaurant chain selected Esera Tuaolo to appear in a TV commercial. The ad showed the former professional football player, who retired from the Minnesota Vikings in 1999 and came out as a gay man three years later, with a huge smile stretched across his face as he strummed a ukulele and sang about the "awesome taste" of a Chili's sizzling steak.[37] "The statement we are making is that we're a fun, casual restaurant," a spokesman for the company told *USA Today*.[38] Indeed, the six-foot-three-inch, 270-pound defensive tackle, wearing a tight black T-shirt and with a tattoo visible on his bulging right bicep, clearly was a guy who enjoyed chowing down on a hunk of beef. When the *Atlanta Journal* reported on the Samoa-born Tuaolo appearing in the ad, the paper talked about his "infectious smile" and his "hearty laugh," described him as "biggie-size joy," and brought home its point about the gay man being fun to be around by saying, "If you're not smiling when Esera Tuaolo is in the room, then you're either a running back with a grudge or you're dead."[39]

Subaru crossed another threshold by communicating that being fun-loving is not a trait exclusive to gay men but one that characterizes many gay women as well. In 2000, the car company began airing a television commercial featuring openly lesbian tennis star Martina Navratilova, who had won some 170 tournaments. "She personifies the attributes of our brand as a go-anywhere, do-anything type of individual," a Subaru spokesman told the *New York Times*. "We view her as an active lifestyle woman." The message that lesbians were fun-loving was sent by the fact that the commercial, as the *Times* pointed out, had "a humorous tone."[40] The ad consisted of images of Navratilova, a female golfer, and a female skier playing their respective sports while they made verbal comments about grip, control, and performance—meant to refer to attributes shared by the women athletes and by Subarus. At the end of the commercial, Navratilova smiles directly into the camera and delivers the tongue-in-cheek punch line: "But what do we know? We're just girls."[41]

GAY PEOPLE HAVE LARGE EXPENDABLE INCOMES

The abundance of ads sent messages both about gay men and about lesbians, but anyone looking closely at the phenomenon had to acknowledge that the primary motivation of the companies either publishing the ads in print or airing them on TV was not to advance the cause of a stigmatized minority group, but to sell their products. Likewise, there was no question that part of the appeal of gay Americans was that they were perceived to be affluent.

From the moment the first gay-themed ads began appearing in the early 1990s, news organizations started reporting on the large expendable incomes among gay men. "There's no dispute that gays control many billions of dollars of disposable income," according to a 1993 story on the front page of the *Washington Post* financial section. "Most also are considered robust and young consumers with high incomes, high education and upscale tastes." The article also pointed out that the majority of gay men do not have children and, therefore, do not have to spend their hefty incomes on braces or tuition to private school. "Because gay men have fewer dependents than the general public and therefore more disposable income, they are more likely to spend that money on clothes, eating out, furniture, cars and travel."[42]

By the early 2000s when news organizations across the country were reporting on the mushrooming number of gay-themed ads, the myriad news stories reiterated that many gay people have much more money to spend than their straight counterparts do. "Gay men especially are now seen as more wealthy with more disposable income than consumers at large," the *St. Louis Post-Dispatch* wrote.[43] "This is a market segment that is very affluent with a good disposable income, and in many cases you have dual-income households without kids," the *Cleveland Plain Dealer* wrote.[44] Television newscasts made the same point, with the Fox News Channel stating: "Marketing experts say when it comes to selling their goods, companies go where the dollars are, and base their marketing decisions on pure economics. They will create products and advertising campaigns to appeal to a certain group if that group is ready to buy."[45]

To support their assertions that gays have large disposable incomes, several of the news outlets listed some of the luxury items that companies were pitching toward them, along with descriptions of the relevant ads.

The *Wall Street Journal*, the country's leading business-oriented daily, took the lead on this particular topic by publishing several such articles. In 1999, a *Journal* story highlighted some of the clever puns that abounded in gay-themed ads, including "It's time your crystal came out of the closet as well" (Waterford crystal) and "Every twelve years, thousands of us come out" (Chivas Regal aged scotch).[46] Two years later, another *Journal* story applauded a pair of ads that focused specifically on gay couples. The first one showed two men laughing and hugging while standing in front of their grand piano; the ad was for Moet et Chandon champagne and carried the tagline "When you know in your heart that your future is with him." The second featured a close-up photo of lesbian singer Melissa Etheridge and her partner

Tammy Lynn Michaels wearing elegant white gold bracelets; the ad was for Cartier jewelers and read "Cartier's Menotte handcuff bracelets symbolize everlasting love"—the ad did not include the fact that each item of jewelry carried a $4,000 price tag.[47]

"TARGETING GAY POCKETBOOKS"

If a single gay-themed advertisement were to be spotlighted as the most significant one of the early 2000s, it would be tempting to select the one featuring the two grooms standing on top of a wedding cake. The justification for that choice would be that the ad not only illustrated how major companies such as the *New York Times* were incorporating gay content into their ad campaigns but also that the image showed that the country's most influential news organization unequivocally supported same-sex marriage.

Another candidate for that solo spotlight, however, would be an ad that showed a balding, average-looking man in front of a shiny green automobile next to the words "Rob has changed our policies, our politics, our culture, and our future." The ad, which appeared in 2000, was remarkable not because of its image or its tagline, but because of the company whose products it was promoting. For in 1997, the Ford Motor Company had been among the first advertisers to announce that it was canceling its commercials that had been appearing on the *Ellen* television show because the star was coming out of the closet.[48]

What a difference three years make!

According to the copy for the 2000 Ford ad, the man in the photo deserved a portion of the credit for the company's 180-degree turn vis-à-vis gay people because he had persuaded executives to change the policy on employee benefits, including extending health care coverage to the domestic partners of gay and lesbian employees. "Today, thanks to Rob's efforts and those of numerous other Ford employees, we're creating a truly diverse and harmonious workplace for every member of the Ford family—whatever their sexual orientation."[49]

Those laudatory words notwithstanding, an objective observer who analyzed the forces behind the explosion of gay-themed ads might suggest that the turnaround had come about primarily because of the realization by Ford and other members of the American business community, thanks to market research data, that gay consumers simply had too much disposable income to ignore. Indeed, that conclusion is supported by considering some of the headlines that the country's newspapers had crafted to run above their stories reporting the glut of gay-themed ads in the initial years of the new millennium—"Targeting Gay Pocketbooks" in the *San Francisco Examiner,*[50] "More Advertisers Pursue Gay and Lesbian Consumers" in the *St. Louis Post-Dispatch,*[51] and "A Welcome Mat for Gay Customers" in the *Chicago Tribune.*[52]

While the media venue of advertising was a new one for gay content, most of the broader messages that the print ads and TV commercials sent were generally familiar to anyone who had tracked the evolving depiction of gay men and lesbians during the previous half-century. All those buff boys in boxers who populated the Abercrombie & Fitch ads—including several of them tugging at another lad's underwear—communicated that gay men are highly sexual beings. Likewise, the dozens of loving gay couples who proliferated in ads for products ranging from tires to dining room tables also brought home the point that gay people place enormous value on committed relationships. Other themes that had been portrayed in previous media products and that were reiterated by the advertisements included gay people deserving equal rights, being fun-loving, and having hefty expendable incomes.

The parade of advertisements that marched through the nation's mainstream newspapers, magazines, and television programs also deserve praise for having reflected two realities that many of the milestones that preceded them had not. First, the men and women in the ads were not lily white but included at least a smattering of persons of color who communicated that Gay and Lesbian America is a racially diverse community. Second, the series of eye-catching ads from Benetton served to remind the media-consuming public that HIV and AIDS continued to play a major role in the lives of men who had sexual desires for other men.

Perhaps the most intriguing observation vis-à-vis the media's depictions of gay people in advertisements is one that had been hinted at when looking at other milestones from earlier eras but that came into sharp focus with the mushrooming number of gay-themed ads in the new millennium. Specifically, race and sexual orientation both had traditionally been recognized as factors that propelled individuals into minority status. Just as persons of color had historically been marginalized and underserved by the nation's political elite, so had gay men and lesbians. However, market research data that surfaced in the 1990s and early 2000s suggested that persons of color and persons with same-sex desires differed dramatically when it came to economics.

More specifically still, while a huge percentage of racial minorities such as African Americans and Latinos suffered from severe economic deprivation, many gay Americans—particularly gay men—were securely positioned in either the middle class or the upper class. This distinction between the two minority groups surfaced with regard to advertising because promoting products to would-be buyers understandably involves the purchasing power of the target audience of the ads. It would seem downright foolish for Cartier to aim its ads for a $4,000 bracelet to a segment of the population that struggles to pay the electric bill. More complicated, however, is to speculate about how the relative wealth enjoyed by many gay people, particularly compared to the poverty endured by many persons of color, might influence the other media venues, as the cultural stigma attached to being gay was fading.

Does it not make sense—from a business perspective—for a major motion picture studio to crank out films depicting positive gay characters when the executives know that a critical mass of gay men can afford to pay $9 for a movie ticket to see people like themselves portrayed on the big screen? (Not to mention $3 more for a soda and $5 on top of that for a bag of popcorn.)

Likewise, does it not make sense for a cable channel such as Showtime or Bravo to develop programming that depicts gay characters and explores gay issues when The Powers That Be who are making decisions at those business enterprises are fully aware that well-heeled gay men—and an ever-growing number of well-heeled lesbians—are willing and able to pay a monthly fee to watch shows that focus on topics the major networks have largely ignored?

More difficult is the dilemma facing the country's journalistic organizations. Like their media counterparts in the fields of advertising, film, and entertainment television, the decision-makers in the world of newspapers and television news also are eager—particularly during an era when the Internet and any number of wireless products are exploding onto the media landscape—to expand their audiences. But news organizations have commitments not only to their stockholders but also to the public that depends on them for information as well as a spectrum of views on controversial issues. A motion picture studio or cable channel has every right to increase its gay and lesbian entertainment content in hopes of attracting more theatergoers or subscribers, but a newspaper also must consider if expanding its coverage of gay topics ultimately distorts the perception of its readers with regard to the size and importance of the local community compared to, for example, the size and importance of the local

African-American community. The wedding-cake ad in the *New York Times* suggested that, at least on some occasions, the country's leading news outlets were willing to take sides on hot-button debates regarding gay and lesbian rights.

NOTES

1. For discussion of and an image of the *New York Times* ad, see http://www.commercialcloset.org/cgi-bin/iowa/portrayals.html?record=1418.
2. Carrie Kirby, "Hyundai 'Boy Toy' Ad Tops PlanetOut Poll," *San Francisco Chronicle*, June 6, 2001, B2.
3. Kara Swisher, "Targeting the Gay Market," *Washington Post*, April 25, 1993, H1.
4. William L. Hamilton, "When Intentions Fall Between the Lines," *New York Times*, July 20, 2000, F1. The editor was Rogier van Bakel of *Ad Age's Creativity*.
5. Greg Jonsson, "More Advertisers Pursue Gay and Lesbian Consumers," *St. Louis Post-Dispatch*, June 22, 2001, A1.
6. Bernard Weinraub and Jim Rutenberg, "Gay-Themed TV Gaining a Wider Audience," *New York Times*, July 29, 2003, A1.
7. Richard Harwood, "Gay Chic," *Washington Post*, November 22, 1997, A19.
8. Robin Wallace, "Does Spending Power Buy Cultural Acceptance?," Fox News Channel, September 16, 2003.
9. Robin Givhan, "The Fetching Men of Abercrombie & Fitch," *Washington Post*, August 7, 1998, D1, D5.
10. Stuart Elliott, "Advertising: Abercrombie & Fitch Extends a Print Campaign to TV," *New York Times*, August 6, 1999, C5.
11. Robin Givhan, "The Fetching Men of Abercrombie & Fitch," *Washington Post*, August 7, 1998, D1, D5.
12. For discussion of and an image of the Abercrombie & Fitch ad, see http://www.commercialcloset.org/cgi-bin/iowa/portrayals.html?record=350.
13. For discussion of and an image of the Abercrombie & Fitch ad, see http://www.commercialcloset.org/cgi-bin/iowa/portrayals.html?record=1037.
14. Robin Givhan, "The Fetching Men of Abercrombie & Fitch," *Washington Post*, August 7, 1998, D1. The Abercrombie & Fitch spokesman was Lonnie Fogel.
15. Robin Givhan, "The Fetching Men of Abercrombie & Fitch," *Washington Post*, August 7, 1998, D1.
16. Ronald Alsop, "Cracking the Gay Market Code," *Wall Street Journal*, June 29, 1999, B1.
17. Steve Rothaus, "TV Ads Kick Down Closet Door," *Miami Herald*, March 16, 2002, C1.

18. For discussion of and an image of the Benetton ad, see http://www.commercialcloset.org/cgi-bin/iowa/portrayals.html?record=239.

19. For discussion of and images of the three versions of the Benetton ad, see http://www.commercialcloset.org/cgi-bin/iowa/portrayals.html?record=560, http://www.commercialcloset.org/cgi-bin/iowa/portrayals.html?record=562, and http://www.commercialcloset.org/cgi-bin/iowa/portrayals.html?record=561.

20. For discussion of and an image of the Benetton ad, see http://www.commercialcloset.org/cgi-bin/iowa/portrayals.html?record=1116.

21. For discussion of and an image of the Benetton ad, see http://www.commercialcloset.org/cgi-bin/iowa/portrayals.html?record=559.

22. *Vanity Fair*, September 1992, 262–263. For discussion of and an image of the Banana Republic ad, see http://www.commercialcloset.org/cgi-bin/iowa/portrayals.html?record=516. On the ad being the first gay-themed ad to appear in a major American magazine, see Larry Gross, *Up from Invisibility: Lesbians, Gay Men, and the Media in America* (New York: Columbia University Press, 2001), 238.

23. For discussion of and images from the Ikea commercial, see http://www.commercialcloset.org/cgi-bin/iowa/portrayals.html?record=76. On the commercial being the first gay-themed one on American television, see Carrie Kirby, "Hyundai 'Boy Toy' Ad Tops PlanetOut Poll," *San Francisco Chronicle*, June 6, 2001, B2; Bruce Mirken, "Targeting Gay Pocketbooks," *San Francisco Examiner*, January 10, 1999, B4.

24. Steve Rothaus, "Big Business Looks to the Rainbow," *Miami Herald*, August 26, 2002, Business Monday 22, 25.

25. Deborah Sharp, "Cities Come Out About Wooing Gays—and Their Dollars," *USA Today*, December 8, 2003, A3.

26. Stuart Elliott, "Advertising: Homosexual Imagery Is Spreading from Print Campaigns to General-Interest TV Programming," *New York Times*, June 30, 1997, D12.

27. For discussion of and an image of the Avis ad, see http://www.commercialcloset.org/cgi-bin/iowa/portrayals.html?record=1325.

28. For discussion of and images from the Snapple commercial, see http://www.commercialcloset.org/cgi-bin/iowa/portrayals.html?record=1253.

29. For discussion of and an image of the Coors ad, see http://www.commercialcloset.org/cgi-bin/iowa/portrayals.html?record=929.

30. Kimberly Shearer Palmer, "Gay Consumers in the Driver's Seat," *Washington Post*, July 4, 2000, C1, C7.

31. For discussion of and images from the John Hancock commercial, see http://www.commercialcloset.org/cgi-bin/iowa/portrayals.html?record=216.

32. Carrie Kirby, "Hyundai 'Boy Toy' Ad Tops PlanetOut Poll," *San Francisco Chronicle*, June 6, 2001, B1, B2.

33. Robin Givhan, "The Fetching Men of Abercrombie & Fitch," *Washington Post*, August 7, 1998, D5.

34. For discussion of and an image of the Abercrombie & Fitch ad, see http://www.commercialcloset.org/cgi-bin/iowa/portrayals.html?record=1036.

35. For discussion of and an image of the Abercrombie & Fitch ad, see http://www.commercialcloset.org/cgi-bin/iowa/portrayals.html?record=348.

36. For discussion of and images from the Abercrombie & Fitch series of ads, see http://www.commercialcloset.org/cgi-bin/iowa/portrayals.html?record=413.

37. For discussion of and images from the Chili's commercial, see http://www.commercialcloset.org/cgi-bin/iowa/portrayals.html?record=1284.

38. Michael Hiestand, "Gay Former NFL Player Lands Role in Restaurant Ads," *USA Today*, July 10, 2003, C2. The spokesman was Louis Adams.

39. L. Z. Granderson, "Tuaolo Tackles NFL Homophobia," *Atlanta Journal*, June 26, 2003, P27.

40. Stuart Elliott, "Advertising: Martina Navratilova Enters the National Mainstream Market in a Campaign for Subaru," *New York Times*, March 13, 2000, C14.

41. For discussion of and images from the Subaru commercial, see http://www.commercialcloset.org/cgi-bin/iowa/portrayals.html?record=159.

42. Kara Swisher, "Targeting the Gay Market," *Washington Post*, April 25, 1993, H1.

43. Greg Jonsson, "More Advertisers Pursue Gay and Lesbian Consumers," *St. Louis Post-Dispatch*, June 22, 2001, A13.

44. Mya Frazier, "Ads Increasingly Target Gay Market," *Cleveland Plain Dealer*, May 15, 2001, C2.

45. Robin Wallace, "Does Spending Power Buy Cultural Acceptance?," Fox News Channel, September 16, 2003.

46. Ronald Alsop, "Cracking the Gay Market Code," *Wall Street Journal*, June 29, 1999, B1. For discussion of and an image of the Waterford ad, see http://www.commercialcloset.org/cgi-bin/iowa/portrayals.html?record=299; for discussion of and an image of the Chivas Regal ad, see http://www.commercialcloset.org/cgi-bin/iowa/portrayals.html?record=360.

47. Ronald Alsop, "As Same-Sex Households Grow More Mainstream, Businesses Take Note," *Wall Street Journal*, August 8, 2001, B4. For discussion of and an image of the Chandon ad, see http://www.commercialcloset.org/cgi-bin/iowa/portrayals.html?record=688; for discussion of and an image of the Cartier ad, see http://www.commercialcloset.org/cgi-bin/iowa/portrayals.html?record=1455.

48. For discussion of and an image of the Ford ad, see http://www.commercialcloset.org/cgi-bin/iowa/portrayals.html?record=841.

49. For discussion of and an image of the Ford ad, see http://www.commercialcloset.org/cgi-bin/iowa/portrayals.html?record=841.

50. Bruce Mirken, "Targeting Gay Pocketbooks," *San Francisco Examiner,* January 10, 1999, B1, B4.

51. Greg Jonsson, "More Advertisers Pursue Gay and Lesbian Consumers," *St. Louis Post-Dispatch,* June 22, 2001, A1, A13.

52. Cliff Rothman, "A Welcome Mat for Gay Customers," *Chicago Tribune,* September 16, 2001, L1.

Chapter 4

"We're Paying Customers Too": Gay Viewers Call for the Conspicuous Representation of Gay Characters

Lyn J. Freymiller

The social significance of gay[1] representations in American media, particularly the highly accessible portrayals on television, is much-debated in modern society (Svetsky 2000). Some speculate that media visibility helps to facilitate heterosexual acceptance of gay and lesbians in society (Weinraub and Rutenberg 2003). The effect of media portrayals of gay people on heterosexual viewers remains in question, but the potential implications are significant. As Rich posits about the media's potential impact, "entertainment has often been the vanguard of familiarizing America with gay people, much as it was in spreading homophobia before that" (2003, 7). Even the battle for gay marriage or other gay rights issues might be influenced by gay visibility from television shows such as *Will & Grace* and *Queer Eye for the Straight Guy,* if indeed such programs contribute to the sensitization of the heterosexual population to gay people (Streitmatter 2009). In the general focus on heterosexual media consumers of gay portrayals, however, another audience has seldom been asked about how they are impacted by gay representation in the media: gay audiences.

The present study seeks to bring in the most important voices related to the matter of representation of gay people in the media, voices that remains almost completely unheard: the voices of gay audience members themselves. If conceptions of identity are socially constructed through an individual's engagement with the world (Berger and Luckmann 1966), it is worth exploring how gay people respond to media portrayals of gay identity. It is also worth exploring what gay viewers perceive to be the obligations of the media in regard to depiction of gay characters. As gay men and women gain a degree of representation in the media, do gay audiences think that media programmers have some responsibility to offer gay portrayals?

Gay representation in the American media notably increased in the late 1990s and in the first decade of the new century (Capsuto 2000; Gross and Woods 1999; Keller 2002; Svetsky 2000; Streitmatter 2009; Tropiano 2002). A number of studies uncover some disturbing implications of the portrayals of gay people in the media (Battle and Hilton-Morrow 2002; Dow 2001; Fejes and Petrich 1993; Lacroix and Westerfelhaus 2005; Shugart 2003; Streitmatter 2009). As these authors suggest, more notable media portrayals does not necessarily mean that portrayals are positive or serve to challenge societal stereotypes about the gay community. Walters suggests that while media depictions present representations of gay identity to large audiences, such visibility has made it take on "the dubious distinction of public spectacle" (2001, 10). Some scholars speculate that television portrayals could be of great practical value to gay people. Significantly, Fejes states that "[m]edia images are very powerful in helping one develop a sense of identity" (2000, 115). Meanwhile, Gross (1998) also indicates that gay people may reap benefits from positive portrayals of gays on television. Notably, Kama (2002) studied the response of gay Jewish-Israeli men to media portrayals of gays and found that the men desired more inclusive representations. However, the question of what American gay audiences feel they should be able to expect from American media programmers is not yet answered.

This chapter draws from the transcripts of in-depth interviews with 22 self-identifying lesbian, gay, and bisexual people. The present study is part of a larger project that seeks to understand how notable television programs depict gay identity on the different dimensions suggested by the communication theory of identity (Hecht, 1993), and also assess the responses of gay viewers to representations of gay identity on television. Specifically, this study explores a cohesive theme that emerged when interviewees were asked if they thought that media outlets had any obligation to portray gay and lesbian characters. A significant number of interviewees responded to the question by offering some variation on the notion that media outlets would profit from cultivating gay audiences, and thus it would be in their business interests to offer programming that appeals to gay audiences. In other words, various interviewees endorsed or at least recognized a notion that will be described as "conspicuous representation," or a portrayal of diverse gay characters in the media as a conduit to financial gain for media outlets.

I first offer context by discussing the gay population as a consumer culture that is increasingly courted by advertisers. In the next section, I discuss the methods used in the interview project that generated the comments discussed here. Then, I explore the theme that emerged in the interviews related to the concept of conspicuous representation and illustrate it through various interview excerpts.

GAY CONSUMER CULTURE

A growing body of literature recognizes the existence of the consumer culture of gay America. Indeed, the gay population of the United States is gaining recognition as a consumer culture to be reckoned with. As noted by Sender (2004), "(s)ince the early 1990s, the United States has seen a rapid increase in the visibility of a new consumer niche: the gay market" (1). More specifically, Iwata (2006) states, "(t)he 16 million gay consumers age 18 and older in the USA boast $641 billion in buying power," or cash to spend after taxes. Considering the disposable income the population has, maybe it was only a matter of time before the buying power of the gay community came to the attention of advertisers. Streitmatter (2009) draws a parallel between the expansion of positive portrayals of gay characters on television and film with the increase of awareness of the buying power of the gay population.

In response to this growing awareness, Witeck and Combs (2006) provide a full-fledged manual for appealing to gay consumers. They note that the emergence of media (particularly print media) directed toward a gay readership over the last several decades gave rise to a concurrent advertising niche. The niche is still developing and maturing and offers ample opportunity for companies to establish brand loyalty in the gay community. In another volume directed at businesses for marketing to gay consumers, Lukenbill (1999) suggests that mainstream advertising has always included images that appealed to gay consumers. However, these historical images were coded in such a way that non-gay audiences would not necessarily note the gay-inclusive cues. Now that appeals to gay consumers are much more overt, companies have ample opportunity to exploit the demographic.

There is additional evidence that the gay community has shown a measure of muscle in the marketplace in recent years. Logo, a cable television channel centered on programming that appeals to gay audiences, debuted in 2005 (Hernandez 2006). Major companies like travel Web site Orbitz specifically seek to cultivate gay customers. More major corporations than ever are sponsoring gay pride parades and events (Leff 2005). Whether it represents a trend or a permanent commitment to gay customers remains to be seen, but at present numerous companies are jumping on the court-the-gay-customer bandwagon.

However, it is important to note that the increase in companies seeking gay patrons is rarely connected in any significant way to the fight to live free of discrimination and be accorded equal rights in society. The very title of Sender's (2004) volume, *Business, Not Politics*, clearly implies that advertisers may be advertising to gay consumers for purely business purposes. The political agenda of the gay community is not the focus for many advertisers, and the impetus for seeking gay consumers is strictly something that makes sense in economic terms. Chasin (2000) considers the implications of how gay political priorities are generally not recognizably advanced by advertisers seeking gay consumers. Additionally, the author questions the lack of diversity in the gay-directed advertisements that do exist. Such advertisements largely depict and/or are largely directed toward financially well-off gay white males. While this segment of the gay population indeed has formidable market clout, the images do not begin to reflect the diversity of the gay community.

At least one study has explored the nexus between gay identity and gay consumer culture. Kates (1998) conducted interviews and participant observation to assess the consumer habits of gay men. He found that the buying habits varied, and much of the time matched individual preferences more than buying in to perceived trends. The study suggests that gay male culture is very diverse, and that a sense of personal identity is exemplified through buying patterns. However, to date there have been no notable studies that investigate recognition of, and responses to, gay consumer culture for gay media audiences. This theme, an unanticipated finding within a larger investigation, is the focus of this study.

PROCEDURE

I conducted a single, sit-down interview with 22 individuals who self-identified as gay, lesbian, or bisexual. After I received the necessary approval to involve human participants in the project from a large public university in the eastern United States, I sent an informational e-mail about the study to several contacts that then sent the message out on various e-mail lists at the university. A print version of the informational e-mail was also left in the Lesbian, Gay, Bisexual, Transgender (LGBT) student center on campus. The flier and the informational e-mail noted that the study sought "members of the LGBT community" for an interview project "investigating LGBT responses to LGBT depictions on television." Three criteria were noted as qualifications for the study. The first criterion was that the individual self-identified "as having a sexual orientation other than heterosexual." I chose this phrasing in order to be sensitive to individuals who might resist "labeling" their sexual orientation in any way, or may see such labels as fluid and changeable. I determined that the most crucial idea was that a participant did *not* identify with heterosexual orientation, not that a participant *did* identify with a specific designation such as "gay" or "lesbian." The second criterion was that the individual has "seen any television programs with fictional LGBT characters." Mainly, the interview assessed responses to gay characters on television. For the question under investigation in this essay, however, the focus of the interview question broadened somewhat to allow for responses relating to any type of media outlet. The third criterion was that the individual was 18 to 65 years of age.

A volunteer sample contacted me via phone or e-mail to express interest in participating, and interviews were generally scheduled through e-mail. The interviews were conducted in private spaces. Before commencing the interview, participants were briefed on the project, their rights as participants, and the trajectory of the interview questions, and signed an informed consent form. Participants were not paid for their participation.

Prior to the interview each participant filled out a short demographic profile providing information on gender, age, and sexual orientation. Code names were assigned to all interviewees, and 22 interviews were completed. There was reasonable diversity in the age range of participants, and at least five interviewees identified with each of the three sexual orientations included in the study. All interviewees self-identified themselves as gay, lesbian, or bisexual; none preferred a different term, and none preferred not to label their orientation. The 22 interviewees include 12 women, 7 of whom identified as lesbian and 5 of whom identified as bisexual. All 10 male participants self-identified as gay. Participants ranged in age from 18 to 54. Median age was 23 years, while mean age was just under 28.4 years. All participants identified as white or Caucasian except for one African-American woman and one man who self-identified as Hawaiian-American. Interviews lasted from approximately 40 minutes to about 85 minutes.

The first set of interview questions addressed the codification of the interviewee's sense of his or her gay identity. The second phase of the interview addressed the interviewee's responses to portrayals of gay characters on television, and how the interviewee saw the characters constructed in terms of personal characteristics, relationships, and sense of community. In the third and last phase of the interview, interviewees were asked if they felt that media depictions had influenced their own identities.

Interviews were audio taped and transcribed verbatim. Only code names appeared on demographic profiles, the cassette tapes of recorded interviews, and the written transcripts. A coding process was used to analyze the interview data related to specific questions that were asked of all interviewees, and thematic analysis ensued. The results of the present study are drawn from a question that was posed in the third phase of the interviews, the question of whether or not the interviewee thought media outlets had any obligation to portray gay characters. The coding procedure and the determination of notable themes across interviews were guided by the recommendations of Strauss and Corbin (1990).

The present study was initially conceived as an investigation of the different significant themes offered in response to the question posed to interviewees about whether or not media programmers held any obligation to portray gay characters. However, during analysis one theme emerged in such a notable fashion, with multiple interviewees offering remarkably similar ideas completely independent of one another, that I determined that the theme merited in-depth exploration as a self-contained study. In the next section, I exemplify and amplify the theme of gay viewers suggesting that media portrayals of gays make good business sense for media outlets by coining the term "conspicuous representation" to represent the theme. (*Note:* Interviewees are identified by age and the sexual orientation designation they used to identify themselves in the interview questionnaire; this data is provided for informational purposes and is not intended to reduce any of these complex individuals to such a limited definition of their personhood. Also, in some instances I have elected to offer what some might consider to be "extended" snippets to allow the voices of the interviewees to be recognized in more than sound bytes.)

THE CALLS FOR CONSPICUOUS REPRESENTATION

It's—they're in it for money.

—*Julie, 19-year-old lesbian*

A significant portion of interviewees suggest that media programmers generally, and television programmers specifically, should indeed feel some sense of obligation to include representations of gay and lesbian characters. In some cases, the interviewee responses explored moral, ethical, and/or altruistic reasons why media should offer such portrayals. But many interviewees immediately framed the obligation as being in the best interests of media outlets not because of their duty to show as much of the human experience as possible, but rather to enhance their bottom lines. Like Julie, many interviewees quickly assumed that media outlets are likely to be driven by dollar signs rather than any form of deep-seated commitment to diversity in media portrayals. This theme is coined here as a recommendation for "conspicuous representation."

Conspicuous representation, quite obviously, is an adaptation of the concept of conspicuous consumption, or the notion of making status-symbol purchases to flaunt one's wealth and/or appear to be among the trend-setting portion of society ("What is conspicuous consumption?," 2009). The term was defined by Thortstein Veblen in his 1899 tome *The Theory of the Leisure Class* as a proclivity of the wealthy class to spend money on items that would enhance their notoriety and position in society (1994). Mason (1998) suggests that conspicuous consumption began with the advent of consumer cultures as early as the seventeenth century; the author also notes that in the modern era all strata of society are affected (or afflicted) by the tendencies to some degree, not just the upper class.

Conspicuous representation refers not to consumer behavior but rather the notion that media programmers would benefit, in a business/marketing sense, from diverse portrayals of gay characters due to the expectation that such portrayals would win over the loyalties—and dollars—of members of the gay community. Many interviewees express significant awareness of the consumer cachet that they hold as members of the gay community. The endorsement of diverse media depictions due to the accompanying profit incentive is exemplified by Doug (21-year-old gay man). When queried about media obligations to portray gays, he states:

> I mean when I think of programmers or anyone running a business, I took business classes in high school, it's always about the money. So I mean you have a ten percent base that of-, often has been shown to have more money when you compare them to the other percentages so I mean, in theory they should have an obligation [to portray gay characters] because they want more money and their advertisers are going to realize they're opening up to new markets so I think they have, I don't know if it's an obligation of the social or even of their conscience but more along the lines of their greed. I mean, money should obligate them to it.

Doug assesses the gay population of the United States to be somewhere in the vicinity of 10 percent. As such a figure would translate to 25 to 30 million gay consumers in the country, it obviously does not match Iwata's (2006) estimate of 16 million adult gay would-be consumers. The specifics of the estimates are beside the point, however. They buying power is unquestionably significant, and Doug also invokes the notion that gay consumers putatively have more disposable income than other social groups. While this notion is based on the assumption that gay consumers are not likely to have children and are more trend-conscious, the idea of gay Americans as a wealthier class may be based on a well-off, white segment of the population that is not of the whole non-heterosexual population. In any event, Doug suggests that media programmers need only follow business instincts to feel a sense of duty to offer gay portrayals, or what could be described as conspicuous representation. He does not particularly place faith in the social conscience of media outlets, but still sees gay media portrayals as a situation in which the media outlets would benefit.

Interviewees differ on the implications of the profit-driven motive for media programmers. Does profiting from media portrayals of gays reflect a win-win situation for the media outlets and the gay community? After all, the media outlets get the bucks and the gay audiences get media representation that may be very valuable to them, as well as valuable in acclimating heterosexual audiences to them. Conversely, is the profit motive a sad comment on the American media, which should be aspiring to a higher calling in relation to representing a wider spectrum of American experience? In the same sense that conspicuous consumption may easily be viewed as a woeful misdirection of resources to unnecessary ends, conspicuous representation may be a cynical move on the part of media programmers that deserves more scorn than praise. Debbie (42-year-old lesbian), like Doug, immediately invokes a business model in relation to greater gay visibility in the media. But while she notes that indeed media might be driven to provide such portrayals, she sees great limitations to their potential effect:

> Well, in the United States we put television in the category of business and therefore one's only responsibility basically is to make money um and then we sort of kind of layer on a little bit of other stuff, and we put a few lines, but not very many, particularly around issues like, issues of class. Um, so even asking that question puts you in the position of saying, okay, what superficial veneer are we willing to ask them to take a crack at, knowing full well that what really matters to them is what Wall Street thinks and the bottom line. And can you ever expect that process of applying a veneer to ever really help anybody? It's kind of like asking, you know, should there be token hiring of gays and lesbians? No, there shouldn't be token hiring of anybody, you know, tokenism is the problem. So I, kind of feel that isn't a very—that's kind of a battle we're never gonna win as long as the only function of television is to make money, that's why the non-commercial sector is so vitally important, and that's why I think it'd be most beneficial to all of who are excluded from the people that TV programmers want to sell to, to build up alternative non, non-private sources of media.

Debbie holds out little hope that corporate-driven media representations of gay people, and other socially disenfranchised groups, will do any more than scratch the surface of the real experience of the group. Representation of such groups is destined to be token representation, undertaken for spurious reasons and of extremely limited value to audiences. We should be suspicious of conspicuous representation and the motives of companies that indeed seem to court the gay audience, as the resulting content is likely to be compromised by the corporate machine.

Another interviewee, Marta (22-year-old lesbian), is somewhat more sanguine about the matter. She believes that the buying power, and concurrent boycott power, of the gay consumer culture is significant indeed. If gay-friendly is trendy, she's ready to embrace that. She states:

> I don't know if I would call it an obligation [for the media to portray gay characters]. I think it's more of a—they know if they don't, they're not gonna get good media, they're not gonna get good ratings, someone's going to come along and say oh well this channel or whatever is homophobic. And then they're afraid that something's gonna happen like with the whole—what was it, Coors Light or something, one beer a long time ago, it came out that they were homophobic and then, all of the gay and lesbian people stopped drinking their beer. So I think that they're afraid that something like that will happen it's like they want to be seen as being forward-thinking and progressive and open-minded and so I think that everyone is trying to you know have that token gay person and show that you know they're with it that, they are trying to be . . . open and to show everyone that they're trying to you know at least acknowledge their presence and not try to hide it or anything. I think it's great but I don't think their intentions are completely altruistic . . .

In contrast to Debbie, Marta welcomes a token gay character as a well-intentioned representation of social diversity. She expresses some suspicion of the true motives of media programmers—they might be doing it just for show, a clear recognition that conspicuous representation takes place for profit-driven reasons. However, regardless of motive, the increase in diversified portrayals occurs. Also, Marta does not hesitate to indicate that gay consumers can send a significant statement to companies. Specific companies need to decide whether or not to seek the gay consumer, and will profit or be punished accordingly by gay consumers. Ultimately, Marta implies, the gay consumers wield no small measure of control over media outlets. She does not reference the other side of the coin: the possibility of groups/organizations that are not friendly to the LGBT community may stage a boycott of their own against companies that have chosen to court the gay community. In Marta's view, the presumed mindset of advertisers is a liberal one.

Meanwhile, Alan (21-year-old gay man) returns us to a rather dispirited notion of how consumer culture may guide but ultimately may overshadow any potential societal gains of more varied media portrayals. His view comports with Debbie's; he clearly believes that motive greatly matters when assessing or endorsing gay depictions. Alan says:

> [programmers] have no obligation whatsoever [to portray gay characters in the media]. And the reason why I say that is because—they do whatever they can to get the money. And if this was an ideal society, I would say yes, they deserve to show us because we're here just like anyone else. But because mass media is controlled by patriarchy, they have a very clear set agenda. If they know they can get money from us, or make money off of us, they're gonna do it. And it makes me sick to my stomach, and I actually am upset with myself that I had to say they had no obligation to show us. . . . They're choosing to . . . I feel that because the people in charge know that they can get money from the culture, they're gonna do it, and then the other part of me that says yes, they—they should show us because we are here, we are essentially consumers of their products, we do give them money in return, essentially we hold more money than most heterosexual persons, therefore, they should show us because if they show us, we'll reward them with our money, and that unfortunately is not how the business of our society works, our business in society is more like, hey, we found a new trend. And—that hurts me.

Alan's view is that money won by programmers through their portrayal of gay characters comes at a price; conspicuous representation is ultimately a zero-sum game for the gay community. The gay audience as profitable audience niche diminishes the value of whatever portrayals are on offer. Conspicuous representation is a response to a trend and not an integration of gay portrayals into the fabric of media representation and such exposure may be as short-lived as the trend itself. Alan, like Doug, invokes the familiar if dubious notion that gay consumers have more to spend than others. In Alan's view, no significant social ground is really gained through the media's carpet-bagging tactics.

In comparison with Alan, Greg (23-year-old gay man) offers a more upbeat assessment of the buying power of the gay community serving to provide incentive to media programmers. He notes a figure related to gay buying power that is $128 billion less than the figure stated by Iwata (2006), but again the specific numbers are of little concern. Greg states:

> I think they should [depict gay characters in the media] because it would be smart business move um, it would be smart for so many reasons, I mean, there's the gay and lesbian chamber of commerce now, five—what is it, 513 billion dollars was it—something—they gave me some really large number that, that gay people spend a year and it's just smart business not to, to try to just I guess not to a . . . I'm trying to think of a nice word and I can't really come up with the word I'm looking for but, it would be smart business for them to, to appeal to us, to uh, to have a gay character and then hey, look, well now our advertisers realize that we have gay characters and gay people are watching and guess what, now we can target them, something to buy, it's smart business.

Like Marta, Greg does not begrudge programmers from recognizing a "smart business" move that leads to greater gay social visibility. Even if done mainly for appearances—Greg implies that such depictions would be illuminating to advertisers, not specifically that they would be illuminating to audiences—it is a foolproof move. More diverse programming content, even if created for/as conspicuous representation, serves as a conduit to well-remunerated advertisers and represents an acceptable blend of cultural and business interests.

Brenda (23-year-old lesbian) agrees that media outlets would be amply rewarded if they were to increase the portrayal of gay characters. The specific reasons she offers resonate with those stated by others discussed here. Brenda states:

> The business end, yeah [television does need to portray gay characters], because we're paying customers too. We buy the shit that—that the advertisers put on television. You know, we, we're just like everyone else and then at the same time we're not, um . . . so it's, it's like yeah, they have a responsibility, anybody who they want to watch television you know or, you know, we're—we're out there. We have televisions and stuff like that, so yeah.

In very simple terms, Brenda invokes the most basic elements of participation in television culture—gay people own televisions and buy the advertised products. In this sense, they are exactly like all other viewers. Her statements position conspicuous representation as a self-serving ploy to court gay audiences on the part of programmers. Even so, appealing specifically to them will curry favor and, presumably, loyalty. The responsibility to offer representation applies to any other group programmers would like to have as part of their audience, though; the portrayal of gay characters is one of any number of responsibilities the media has.

Television ratings are broken down into demographic categories, but rarely, if ever, is there any assessment of top shows among gay audiences or estimates of how many gay viewers are watching a particular program. While the Logo channel has gain significant carriage on various cable systems around the country and it available to 35 million viewers, the channel is still not ranked by the Nielsen rating service (Hampp 2009). Nonetheless, Derek (21-year-old gay man) sees gay viewers as a demographic that should be coveted. In fact, he believes the gay demographic is capable of enhancing or diminishing overall ratings levels for specific programs. In speaking about television ratings, Derek approaches from a different angle than other interviewees, but still strikes some of the same chords in his ideas. Derek offers this:

> Um, well I think it's in their [media outlets] best interests to [portray gay characters] because uh we are out there, we are consumers uh we are viewers of their shows and without us their ratings would suffer, so I think it's in their best interest to and as for an obligation um . . . I think so yeah, because I feel they have an obligation to provide um entertainment that can appeal to anybody whether it's a common theme or um whether it's specific character selection. Um, they cater to other minorities, why not to us?

Derek opines that gay viewer defection from programs would be substantial enough to dent ratings. As a societal minority group, the gay audience has clout. He indicates how media can "cater to minorities" while, apparently, at the same time, provide entertainment "that can appeal to anybody." This represents another instance of a viewpoint noted by other participants: that everyone, gay and non-gay audience segments, programmers, and advertisers, win when gay portrayals are present. He echoes other interviewees quoted earlier in regard to how gay viewers are consumers too and how it's in the "best interest"—presumably business interest—of programmers to offer varied depictions. Derek indicates an expectation of both a universal and more personal appeal from entertainment programming. He implies that perhaps conspicuous representation is already available for other societal groups.

Paige (37-year-old lesbian) also positions money-making as the top priority of media outlets. Paige immediately moves, as did others, to a business paradigm for entertainment media. However, in her view the realm of profit and the consumer commitment to be won from the gay community extends well beyond entertainment-oriented media outlets. Paige comments:

> I would like to see it [more media portrayals of gay characters]. Um, I think they're probably obligated to make money. Y'know, it's a business, that's what TV is about. Um, if they want to make money certainly the gay and lesbian um community is a place where they can, they can look for some substantial a-, assets and certainly the city of Philadelphia has recently figured that out . . . Um, but, so if, if their obligation is to make money, then they would be foolish to turn their backs on the gay and lesbian contingent. You know, we have a lot of money to spend you know most of us don't have children, some of us, but most of us don't have children, oftentimes we're talking about dual-income households. Um, we, and we spend money in a, um, in a very—I, I deal with travel a lot, as a leisure activity. And um P-town [Provincetown, MA] as a travel destination is based upon the gay—is based upon a gay economy and there are hundreds of thousands of dollars that tri- that are um available for discretionary income. That um, so if the goal of TV is to make money they would be foolish to not pay attention to the gay and lesbian community, from, to—if they want to be more altruistic and they want to look at y'know humanity as a whole I think it would certainly be nice and certainly if promoting humanity is, is, is their goal then to ignore this lar-, this you know demographic which is, permeates every county, every state, every nook and cranny of this country as well as throughout the rest of the world, to ignore us would be to ignore part of what it is to be human. So um, y'know, it depends on what the TV producers think their goal in life is about.

Extending her comments beyond media portrayals, Paige invokes the recent efforts of various cities to specifically advertise themselves as gay-friendly destinations, and also reiterates the notion that the gay population has a larger-than-average amount of discretionary income. It would be foolhardy of companies to miss the boat on such a lucrative potential audience. Ultimately, though, Paige gestures to much broader potential motives for media outlets. Media programmers should carefully ponder what their "goal in life" is, presumably as far as entertainment programming is concerned. Like other interviewees, she is not convinced that the media actually has her best interests at heart. However, an increase in diversified media depictions can't be all bad. Presumably even dubiously-intentioned portrayals that might be a profit-driven calculation to appeal to gay consumers are preferable to the alternative: conspicuous representation is more attractive than the invisibility of gay identities in the media.

DISCUSSION

As exemplified by the excerpts in this study, many interviewees drew a direct line between the availability of more diversified media portrayals of gays and profit potential on the part of programmers and advertisers. The theme of conspicuous representation discussed here reflects a clear recognition on the part of interviewees of several major trends in the present-day consumer market. What is untapped in their comments, and should be explored by further research, is whether any correlation exists between gay visibility in the media and the real-life experience of gay Americans in regard to anti-gay discrimination, violence, or sentiments. Naturally, the consumer culture discussed here is part of a larger movement with different political ends besides the exertion of marketing clout. Links between media visibility, flexing of consumer muscle, and real political gains toward equal rights and the ability to live a life free of discrimination need to be explored.

There is further evidence that gay consumers potentially do indeed wield the type of clout in the marketplace suggested by many interviewees. Complaints from organizations like the Gay and Lesbian Alliance Against Defamation (GLAAD) in response to dubious media portrayals of gay themes have had significant impact, such as a bizarre 2007 Super Bowl ad (Horovitz 2007). In 2009, Absolut Vodka placed a lot of marketing muscle behind the Logo television show "Rupaul's Drag Race," and even used the show as a launching pad for a new flavor, Absolut Mango (Hampp 2009).

It should be noted that the number of specifically-identified gay and lesbian characters on network television scripted series declined in the last several years (Where we are on TV, 2007), but then had an upswing in the 2008 to 2009 television season, according to statistics compiled by GLAAD (Where we are on TV, 2008). So while the gay consumer culture is supposedly continuing to mature and solidify in American society, the prevalence of non-heterosexual characters on scripted programs is still very limited. For the 2008 to 2009 television, a small 2.6 percent of characters on American network television series identified as gay, lesbian, bisexual, or transgender (Where we are on TV, 2008). While GLAAD's assessment is somewhat discouraging, it should be recognized that the study does not include "reality" television shows, a genre which is recognized as perhaps more inclusive of gay or lesbian participants than scripted programming. To be sure, LGBT characters on network television are more prevalent currently than in the 1980s or 1990s (Streitmatter 2009). Still, the wishes of interview participants to see more and more diverse portrayals of the gay community are not realized in trend lines for American television shows.

An additional notable factor for this study is that no interviewee voiced the idea that media outlets courting gay viewers or customers could, at least theoretically, raise the ire of conservatives that might have substantial buying power of their own to bargain with. Publicly associating one's company as gay-friendly may carry as much risk in the general realm as it does cachet in the gay community. A gay-friendly company may experience both an organized "buy-cott" from gays and an organized boycott from a conservative organization. Nothing can be assumed regarding what interviewees might have said in relation to this. However, it can be reasonably assumed that certain companies would see more benefit in courting rather than ignoring gay customers (or the opposite) due to the nature of their products or services. Many companies with broad-based customers would not find it in their best interests to court either gays or conservatives. Just like estimates of gay buying power are dubious at best, conservative buying power is an indefinable commodity, so no definitive conclusions are possible.

Of course, interviewees struck the theme of conspicuous representation completely independently of each other; the interviews were conducted separately and one-on-one, and no suggestion of entertainment as business was suggested by the interviewer when posing the question about the media's responsibility to provide gay portrayals. I do not believe that the theme bespeaks so much a sense of personal entitlement on the part of the individual gay viewers as much as it represents the rather well-informed observation that media outlets that do not provide content that will appeal to gay audiences are missing opportunities that would simultaneously further increase the visibility of gays in the media and enhance their bottom line as a business entity. By and large, interviewees said that media programmers do not have to represent gay characters, but they would be somewhat crazy not to.

CONCLUSION

As these interview excerpts suggest, gay media audiences assume that business and financial interests are likely to be paramount in the process of generating entertainment programming. Time and again, participants implied that it would be in the best financial interests of entertainment media to recognize the buying power of the gay community and tailor entertainment options that will appeal to them. This idea of conspicuous representation was sometimes questioned and sometimes viewed as cynical, but was recognized and endorsed by many participants. The statements resonate with a suggestion by Bob Witeck, who heads a marketing firm that directs its efforts to gay and lesbian households, that when gay viewers seek "truthful stories about our lives" and when such stories are found, "we give a higher degree of confidence and support to a program that reflects us" (quoted in Bernhard 2009, C5).

But again, we must ask if any real political gains are to be found in celebrating gay consumer culture. While it may represent a notable measure of mainstream acceptance for the gay community to be sought out as a market niche, any real benefits to their lives and experiences in society may be negligible. Conspicuous representation may ultimately be as vacuous as the concept its name was adapted from.

Concurrent with—or perhaps as an undercurrent to—their suggestion of the profitability of gay media portrayals, interviewees directly or indirectly endorsed the notion of an increase in television and media portrayals of gay experience. While they differed in the amount of cynicism they showed for the motivations of media outlets, interviewees indeed desired to see the landscape of media portrayals grow and expand. Regardless of the motives of programmers, there is reason to hope that if more and more varied portrayal of non-heterosexual characters appears in the media in the future, there is potential for programmers to profit financially. Should the media landscape further and better recognize the existence of gay, lesbian, and other non-heterosexual people? Many interviewees say yes. Just maybe there are non-financial profits to be gained as well.

NOTE

Matters of nomenclature are challenging for researchers studying people who are members of the non-heterosexual population of society. Because of its simplicity, the term "gay" is used in this paper as a generic term that refers to all male and female homosexuals, unless otherwise noted. For the sake of variety, "gay" and "non-heterosexual" are generally used interchangeably. While the term "queer" has become more accepted in recent years, the term is not frequently used by gay, lesbian, or bisexual people or television characters to self-identify. However, references including "gay" such as "gay identity" resonated with all gay male, lesbian, and bisexual interview participants in this project.

REFERENCES

Battles, K., and W. Hilton-Morrow. "Gay Characters in Conventional Spaces: *Will and Grace* and the Situation Comedy Genre." *Critical Studies in Media Communication, 19 (2002)* 87–105.

Berger, P., and T. Luckmann. *The Social Construction of Reality: A Treatise in the Sociology of Knowledge*. New York: Doubleday and Co., 1966.

Bernhard, L. "Love That Dares to Tweet Its Name Sparks New Web Series." *New York Times*, August 25, 2009, C1, C5.

Capsuto, S. *Alternate Channels: The Uncensored Story of Gay and Lesbian Images on Radio and Television*. New York: Ballantine Books, 2000.

Chasin, A. *Selling Out: The Gay and Lesbian Movement Goes to Market*. New York: St. Martin's Press, 2000.

Dow, B. J. "*Ellen*, Television, and the Politics of Gay and Lesbian Visibility." *Critical Studies in Media Communication, 18* (2001): 123–140.

Fejes, F. "Making a Gay Masculinity." *Critical Studies in Media Communication*, 17 (2000): 113–116.

Fejes, F., and K. Petrich. "Invisibility and Heterosexism: Lesbians, Gays, and the Media." *Critical Studies in Media Communication*, 10 (1993): 396–422.

Gross, L. "Minorities, Majorities and the Media." In *Media, Ritual and Identity*, edited by T. Liebes and J. Curran (1998): 87–102. London: Routledge.

Gross, L., and J. D. Woods. "Up from Invisibility: Film and Television." In *The Columbia Reader on Lesbians and Gay Men in Media, Society, and Politics*, 291–296. New York: Columbia University Press, 1999.

Hampp, A. *Absolut Pours Good Chunk of Marketing Dollars into "Drag Race."* (accessed January 28, 2009), http://adage.com/madisonandvine/article?article_id=134902.

Hecht, M. L. "2002—A Research Odyssey: Toward the Development of a communication Theory of Identity." *Communication Monographs*, 60 (1993): 76–82.

Hernandez, G. "Logo Turns 1." *The Advocate*, July 4, 2006, 50–51.

Horovitz, B. "Snickers Maker Drops Super Bowl Ad." *USA Today*, February 7, 2007, p. 1B.

Iwata, E. "More Marketing Aimed at Gay Consumers." *USA Today*, November 2, 2006, B3 (accessed February 1, 2007, from Proquest database).

Kama, A. "The Quest for Inclusion: Jewish-Israeli Gay Men's Perceptions of Gays in the Media." *Feminist Media Studies*, 2 (2002), 195–202.

Kates, S. M. *Twenty Million New Customers!: Understanding Gay Men's Consumer Behavior*. New York: The Haworth Press, 1998.

Keller, J. R. *Queer(Un) friendly Film and Television*. Jefferson, NC: McFarland, 2002.

Lacroix, C., and R. Westerfelhaus. "From the Closet to the Loft: Liminal License and Socio-Sexual Expression in *Queer Eye for the Straight Guy*." *Qualitative Research Reports in Communication*, 6 (2005): 11–20.

Leff, L. "Firms No Longer in Closet during Gay Pride Parades." *Houston Chronicle*, June 26, 2005 (accessed February 1, 2007, from Proquest database).

Lukenbill, G. *Untold Millions: Secret Truths about Marketing to Gay and Lesbian Consumers*. New York: Harrington Park Press, 1999.

Mason, R. *The Economics of Conspicuous Consumption: Theory and Thought since 1700*. Cheltenham, UK: Edward Elgar Publishing, 1998.

Rich, F. "Gay Kiss: Business as Usual." *New York Times*, June 20, 2003, section 2, 1, 7.

Sender, K. *Business, Not Politics: The Making of the Gay Market*. New York: Columbia University Press, 2004.

Shugart, H. A. "Reinventing Privilege: The New (Gay) Man in Contemporary Popular Media." *Critical Studies in Media Communication*, 20 (2003), 67–91.

Strauss, A., and J. Corbin. *Basics of Qualitative Research: Grounded Theory Procedures and Techniques*. Newbury Park: Sage, 1990.

Streitmatter, R. *From "Perverts" to "Fab Five": The Media's Changing Depiction of Gay Men and Lesbians*. New York: Routledge, 2009.

Svetsky, B. "Is Your TV Set Gay?" *Entertainment Weekly*, October 6, 2000, 24–28.

Tropiano, S. *The Prime Time Closet: A History of Gays and Lesbians on TV*. New York: Applause Theatre & Cinema Books, 2002.

Veblen, T. *The Theory of the Leisure Class*. New York: Penguin Books, 1994.

Walters, S. D. *All the Rage: The Story of Gay Visibility in America*. Chicago: The University of Chicago Press, 2001.

Weinraub, B., and J. Rutenberg. "Gay-Themed TV Gains a Wider Audience." *New York Times*, July 29, 2003, A1, C5.

What Is Conspicuous Consumption? (accessed February 8, 2009, on Wisegeek Web site at http://www.wisegeek.com/what-is-conspicuous-consumption.htm).

Where We Are on TV: GLAAD's 12th Annual Study Examines Diversity of the 2007–2008 Primetime Scripted Television Season (September 24, 2007). Press release accessed September 25, 2007 on the GLAAD Web site at http://www.glaad.org/media/release_detail.php?id=4054.

Where We Are on TV: 2008–2009 season. The overview and analysis was accessed August 25, 2009 on the GLAAD Web site at http://www.glaad.org/Page.aspx?pid=333.

Witeck, R., and W. Combs. *Business Inside Out: Capturing Millions of Brand Loyal Gay Consumers*. Chicago: Kaplan Publishing, 2006.

Chapter 5

Dropkicks, Body Slams, and Glitter: The Queer Image in North American Pro-Wrestling

Bryan Luis Pacheco

Pro-wrestling's lustful appetite for men in tights, obsessed lesbians, and tantalizing gyrations of anything queer has been a manipulation in invoking the darkest of homophobia, sexism, and unease. Pro-wrestling was gay before it intended to be: men in costume fondling in a ballet of grunts, women in intimate choke holds. It evokes the gayest of provocation. When discovered and uncovered that something queer could incite a crowd to a vocal frenzy, it cemented its place in pro-wrestling hysteria.

PRO-WRESTLING: AN OVERVIEW

Knocking out the competition, World Wrestling Entertainment (WWE) has been the most successful pro-wrestling company for at least the last 30 years. They have produced the biggest stars and have arguably garnered the most main stream attention for their antics. They have been around longer than both Extreme Championship Wrestling (ECW) and World Championship Wrestling (WCW), two companies that submitted to defeat and closed their doors in 2001. The WWE bought out WCW, and ECW declared bankruptcy.[1, 2] Underground, there is a slew of independent promotions where pro-wrestlers hone their skills, hoping to one day make it to the major leagues.

Popular culture is pro-wrestling's inspiration. In 2008, Hilary Clinton and Barack Obama were battling it out in the primaries to see who would secure the nomination for the Democratic Party for president of the United States. In an attempt to appear politically conscious, the WWE capitalized on the media scrutiny and featured pre-taped segments from the two candidates. Reminding fans they were watching a wrestling program, they showcased independent wrestlers portraying both Hilary Clinton and Barack Obama in a furry of takedowns and slams.[3]

Pro-wrestling does not mistakenly cause controversy. They play on sexism, racism, homophobia and any "ism" or phobia to elicit a reaction from their fans, provoke media attention and increase TV ratings. Negative or good press, pro-wrestling aims for it all. In the process, their characters have undoubtedly stereotyped and offended every group (marginalized or not) of people. In the WWE, a fierce duo of pissed off, irate Pretty Mean Sisters (P.M.S.) burned the hearts and heels of male wrestlers.[4] Based on the Mavericks of conservative thinking, a Right to Censor (RTC) stable was created to mock the multiple censorship groups that had focused in on the WWE's controversies.[5]

Even individual wrestlers/characters are exaggerated stereotypes. One of the biggest draws ever, Stone Cold Steve Austin, would stick his middle fingers up, humiliate and beat up on Vince McMahon (his boss and WWE Chairman) with defiant suplexes and clotheslines. Victorious, he would celebrate with a good ole' refreshing beer as an ode to all the *true American* men who wish they could do the same. He was a take on the trailer trash stereotype.[6] Or enter Eddie Guerrero, who was Mexican, and had the catch line of "I lie, I cheat, I steal."[7]

A wrestler's character is the foundation of his or her success. No subject matter is off limits and no stereotype left untouched. A good wrestler/performer uses every aspect of his/her gimmick to influence the character's performance; from the wrestling gear (or costume) to the wrestling moves and entrance. Never would one witness The Undertaker—a wrestling character, true to his name, based on the culture of death—have a high tempo entrance song, but you could expect to see a *gay* wrestler prance around in pretty pink to *It's Raining Men*. Pro-wrestling exposes and exploits gender, race, and all categories that box people in. It is wise to never take pro-wrestling too seriously, or you would exhaust yourself being offended.

A good story needs an antagonist and a protagonist. In pro-wrestling there is a heel (the villain) and the face (the hero). They feud against one another, either for a championship belt or bragging rights. As we move forward to discussing queer images in pro-wrestling, it is interesting to note that most queer characters have been heels or have at least started that way. They were the bad guys . . . or girls.

The actual matches at an event occur for different reasons. Often the matches reflect the current feuds, but sometimes a match could take place for other reasons and may serve no other purpose than being a combustible element. To win a match, typically one wrestler has to pin another, shoulders down, as the referee's hand hits the mat 1 . . . 2 . . . 3 . . . A wrestler can also win by locking in a submission while making his/her opponent scream in agony and tap. There are other more unique ways of winning, and specialty matches may have their own rules, but these two outcomes are the most common.

Pro-wrestling is a non-accidental circus hoopla of freaks, Adonises, side-show acts, and beauty queens. The fans, promoters, and all the wrestlers and crew are passionate about the product. They live for the adrenaline, the pulse of the cheer. A match or wrestler is only worth the reaction it receives. Everyone involved in the show works for that high, those moments when the audience is hypnotized by the dance raging inside the squared circle:

> We make our living on the vigorish. Most people have to cheer for either the [heel] or the [face]—it always comes down to that. Eventually, you have to be on one side or the other. As wrestlers, we want our [heels] to be reviled and hated as much as the [faces] are loved and revered. The real, true-blooded, honest-to-God people in our business, the best of us? We don't care who wins or loses or even how the game is played. We want a pulse—that's our vig. We want life . . . [8]

Pro-wrestling will do anything for that pulse; to get the crowd, the fans, you . . . *to react*.

THE INFLUENTIAL CHARACTERS

Gorgeous George

The affair between pro-wrestling and homosexuality, a team that would controversially entertain for years to come, began with the obnoxious and prissy Gorgeous George. Stirring insinuations, he would bestow himself with outlandish robes, prissy hand gestures and hold his head upright appalled by the lunacy of the world. The man with the golden curls would instruct a butler to disinfect the odors of the ring with a luscious perfume.[9]

Before the Gorgeous one, "Villains were necessary as plot devices but essentially existed to be conquered."[10] George reinvented that role, using homosexual references that "redefined the role of the bad guy . . . the villain grew to hero's size."[11] He was larger than wrestling life, and fans loved to hate him. He had become the biggest draw of his time: "In Buffalo, 11,845 fans had just jammed the Memorial Auditorium to see the outrageous performer in person. He drew 20,000 in Cleveland and 18,000 in Toronto, attendance figures unheard of for wrestling."[12] The portrayal of a male not conforming to gender had proved a success for fans to come out and display their disapproval.

During the time of George, promoters had used tools like television to draw fans, but the name Gorgeous George had garnered the same urgency and advertisements now read "GORGEOUS GEORGE, TELEVISION, HERE TONIGHT."[13] George was a one-man main attraction. With fame, George had to protect his character, which had become his meal ticket. The wife of Gorgeous George would tell "the press she was his personal hairdresser, Miss Betty. . . . "[14]

In the ring, the Gorgeous George character embodied the stereotypes of a "sissy." He would attack and hide, "he was a sniveling coward who ran away from conflict."[15] He used homophobia to evoke and force jeers from the fans. Despite the overt parallels to gay stereotyping, George denied it, " 'I am not a you-know-what,' he told an interviewer in 1951."[16] At the time, the 50s, maybe it was going too far to say "gay" and admitting to a gay character may have been too taboo, too scandalous.

In pro-wrestling history, the fame, success and notoriety achieved by Gorgeous George has inspired future generations of wrestlers, of all gimmicks. "I've been told by many people I was the next Gorgeous George, I take that to heart and every time someone says that or any other compliment. . . . It adds more desire for me to get more recognition."[17] One openly gay independent wrestler, Rick Cataldo, admits. The Gorgeous one influenced future wrestlers to do absolutely whatever it takes, to pull at the emotions of everyone watching in order to launch themselves into the spotlight.

Chyna

A young valet stands ringside supporting her client. She is Marlena, a conventionally beautiful, blonde hair, petite woman. She wears a tight fitting dress to accentuate her womanhood. Her role is to be T&A

(a wrestling term for tits and ass,) and give the male fans something to look at, drool over. She is smoking her cigar, the phallic symbol that is all too intentional. An unknown woman (man?) violently stalks in from behind, takes her well developed forearm and forces Marlena (by the hair nonetheless) into an embrace, a choke hold. Marlena, unsuspecting, is gasping for air, in desperate need of being rescued. " . . . Who is that?" ask the commentators. "Is that a woman?" they hope to clarify. Security rushes in and releases Marlena from Chyna's grip.[18] Chyna's assault on Marlena was offensive, abusive. They were not on equal playing fields; Marlena was the helpless female victim to this Amazon Chyna, who had strong physical parallels to men.

Not conforming to gender stereotypes, Chyna weighed in at 201 pounds and could bench press up to 365 pounds.[19] She was bigger than most male wrestlers. The fact that she was a woman was the only reason male wrestlers would challenge her; to protect their manhood. Physically she was intimidating and her appearance drew criticism and ridicule from fans and wrestlers alike. As a woman, she was not supposed to look how she did: huge defined muscles, tall (a threat). The other women in the WWE, at the time, were a direct contrast to Chyna: athletically thin, blonde hair, *Playboy* pin-ups. Chyna was "much more a part of the men's group, than the women's."[20] She began her career, usually interfering on behalf of Triple H and Shawn Michaels, two male wrestlers, who along with Chyna formed the team Degeneration X (DX). She was a force to be reckoned with, physically abusing any man that foolishly doubted her ability and power.

In retaliation to being different, Chyna got backlash: "They [the fans] threw batteries at me, spit in my face, power-flung beer into my chest, called me a cunt, chick-with-dick, dyke . . . "[21] She was labeled a lesbian, a dyke, because the perception is that no self-respecting straight woman would look or act like *that*. "You try to get beyond the girlie thing," Chyna said, adding, "you show 'em you're into the moves and counter-moves and that you can take a dive off the top rope as good as any of them, they start calling you a man, a dyke, a 'roid junkie, a muffin diver, all that crap."[22] Behind the scenes, Chyna (Joanie Laurer) was in fact straight. She had a well-documented personal relationship with teammate Triple H.

As time went on, the Chyna character changed. In pro-wrestling, wrestlers are constantly going through gimmick changes to reflect popular culture in their attempt to stay relevant. One could assume the pressure of the limelight and the unwritten rule of "sex sells" in wrestling and entertainment influenced the metamorphosis of Chyna. As

Chyna became more popular, she became more stereotypically feminine, altering the controversial aspects of herself that led to her popularity and the perception of her being a lesbian. In her words "The thing I did feel I could use was a little femininity."[23] Chyna had work done. Over time, noticeably, her jaw looked less defined, she discovered hair extensions, and make-up secrets. Completing the transformation, she had two breast augmentations.[24] Capitalizing on her new look and catapulting her into super stardom, "Chyna made history . . . by being the most muscular woman [to pose for] *Playboy*." (Today Chyna's first *Playboy* ranks in the top 10 of the bestsellers.)[25] The success of Chyna's *Playboy* issue had to do with the fact that no former playmate had looked like her before. There was an interest to see how she looked with her clothes off and would certainly help to dispel rumors that she was a man.

Chyna was never meant to be a lesbian nor was her character created from those stereotypes. Looking into Chyna shows the bias of the mainstream society (the fans) and how they turn queer words into oppressive language. Chyna, the character and person (Joanie Laurer), was boxed in and labeled for not conforming to gender stereotypes. Deviating from her assigned gendered role harbored consequences. She was met with hostility and reservation for being different. In an effort to insult, embarrass, and repress Chyna's independence and strength as a muscular woman, she was called gay (a dyke). She started her pro-wrestling career as a heel, and her transformation into a more feminine body narrated her role into a face. In this transition, the lesbian comments lost visibility, as she was celebrated for becoming more like the norm. However, it cannot be denied that Chyna helped to reinvent the role of women in pro-wrestling, to foster a new generation of women that dared to be strong.

Goldust

> I called for you in the night, yes I did, but you didn't want to come out and play anymore, did you? Are you sure you're up to it? Have you gotten your charge back? Or are you going to just lie there like a corpse again? C'mon dead man, let me light up the dark side with a magnificent golden shower . . . of sun light.[26]

Halloween, 1995, Monday Night RAW is on and millions of WWE fans are tuned in. "From Hollywood, California, weighing 260 pounds, Goldust!" Cue gold lights, gold glitter falling from the ceilings, gold stars on the entrance ramp. Cue outrageous wrestling character with gold face paint, long, gold wig, and a gold robe. Cue controversial gay character. Cue Goldust! " . . . If you are watching this bizarre entrance, what's going on in your mind. . . . You got to be intimidated, you got to be a little scared, you gotta' be a little bit spooked, don't you think?" The commentators discuss.[27]

The Goldust character began more as a campy mysterious Batman villain, but he quickly turned into an obsessive and manipulative flamboyant main attraction once the WWE saw how his over-the-top *gay* antics were getting over with the live crowd. Behind the scenes, "[They] would tell [Goldust] to rub against [the opponent] and do things to [the opponent] to incite the crowd."[28] Those creating and influencing the Goldust character were not thinking about being offensive or creating a positive figure for the queer community. They wanted to hear the crowd, provoke, excite, and enrage them so that they would remember the name Goldust.

Goldust never stated he was gay, and whether his character was intended to be or not, he used homosexuality and preyed on and pulled at the fan's homophobia to create a successful heel character. Dustin Runnels, the man who played Goldust, "was very proud of the fact that he was able to bring to life a character that was ahead of its time and accomplish something new and groundbreaking with Goldust. [He was] voted the #1 heel in wrestling that year."[29]

Not everyone held hands in unity over the Goldust character. The National Gay and Lesbian Task Force rose to action and stamped Goldust "a horrible example of homophobia." The backlash fell onto the WWE, and seeing the light Goldust transitioned to a man "with a wife and a daughter, which bored fans as if taking them in a somnolent sleeper hold."[30]

OPPOSITES ATTRACT

In pro-wrestling, in a feud, or a storyline, opposites attract. This aims to release fans from the sleeper hold and invest them in the characters. You need the hero (or face) to go against the anti-hero (or heel). If you have a blonde, you need a brunette. If you have the American hero, Hulk Hogan, you need the anti-American, Iron Sheik. When it comes to gay—or presumably gay—or queer characters, how would his/her opponent look?

Bout 1: Goldust Versus Razor Ramon

The sound of a car crash over the audio systems cues the entrance of Razor Ramon, a tall, good-looking, man's man. He struts into the arena, fans going crazy. Goldust is sitting on the sidelines, legs crossed, giving a polite seductive clap, admiring Razor's walk. They recap the night before: Razor receives a letter.

> Razor begins to read whatever the content of that letter was . . . you can see the look of the face of Razon Ramon, a look of revolution . . . disgust. [He] was appalled You have to wonder what Goldust wrote . . . [31]
>
> —*Vince McMahon commentates*

The Razor Ramon/Goldust feud was the first big feud that Dustin Runnels had in his career as this flamboyant character. Pro-wrestling uses feuds and storylines to gain interest in their wrestlers, to get fans to have an emotional investment in what they are watching. Goldust was beginning to get over as a heel; his outrageous homoerotic character had stirred much controversy and had certainly sparked interest, the WWE's goal. His opposition, Razor Ramon, was an already established fan favorite. He was a Latino stud who played into the machismo attitude; a great contrast to the gay-tinted Goldust and a stereotype on Latino men:

> **Backstage Interviewer:** How are you taking the way Goldust is somewhat interested in you?
> **Razor:** You know doc. Goldust sent me a letter. He tells me I'm so hot, I so handsome. Hey Chico, you're right, but I don't play that. Razor he only likes women. Goldust you can do your thing meng, just not with me.[32]

This promo illustrates many points behind the WWE's thought process. First, it is important to note that, like a movie, Razor Ramon and Goldust are characters. They do not reflect the individuals playing them; rather they more accurately represent the WWE writers and the WWE franchise. Razor's usage of "meng," meaning man, was to hint toward his Latino identity. Razor letting Goldust know that "you can do your thing . . . " was the WWE's way of avoiding liability and protecting the company and Razor's character. They can always point back to this promo and claim Razor was never anti-gay, he just was not gay himself. The opposition saw it differently though, stating "the whole Goldust character was ritualized fag bashing."[33]

Goldust began to become more controversial with his promos, insinuating gay sexual references and scenes:

> I just can't describe it, I just can't describe it in words . . . the real heat will intensify at the Royal Rumble. You and I, body to body,

hmmmm sweat to sweat . . . the thought alone sends . . . shivers up my spine. In one short week, that thought, that fantasy becomes a reality, oh yes. My hands on your body, I'm oozing already, are you? You remember the name and there is no way you'll forget . . . Goldust.[34]

The promo was an obvious conscious effort to illicit heel heat for the Goldust Character by using gay subtext to force out fan's homophobia. This would get the (mostly straight male) fans to be disgusted by Goldust and to want to see Razor Ramon beat him up, to silence him. Goldust continued to do outrageous things: sending suggestive pictures to Razor, seductively unzipping his suit to reveal a red heart with Razor's name. Razor would watch this behavior backstage and mutter "freak" under his breathe.[35]

The feud cumulated with an Intercontinental Title match at the Pay Per View "Royal Rumble." The feud had been based on Goldust using a gay and obsessive persona to get the fans (those intolerant) to hate him, to upset Razor Ramon, and to justify any violence Razor would inflict on Goldust. Now, fans could not look at Razor as a straight male attacking a gay character; rather they may view it as Goldust going too far and getting what he deserved. That night, Goldust confused the audience by introducing a female valet, Marlena.[36] Was Goldust not supposed to be gay? She was introduced as his director, allowing Goldust to keep his ambiguous sexual identity.

The match incorporated Goldust's flamboyant character into the spots and moves. The premise was that Goldust would have to resort to running around and using gay spots to demand jeers from the audience and frustrate Razor into retaliation. At one point in the match, Goldust licks his lips at Razor, gets on his knees, and assumes the position on all fours. The commentators would ask, "What kind of mind games is Goldust playing with Razor Ramon?"[37] The crowd ate it up, gasping and booing. The WWE was successful in its goal: Goldust was getting over, becoming a successful character (awakening homophobia).

Goldust "salutes" the crowd by caressing his body. The crowd boos heavily. Ramon throws his toothpick at him and the crowd cheers as if to say, *Get the gay boy!* Goldust taunts him the whole match, feeding into notion that gays harass the straight boys they like. Razor is forced to start the match and hit him. Continuing to use homosexuality as a novelty, Razor smacks Goldust in the face and, in an attempt to embarrass him, on his backside. Goldust is not embarrassed however; he begins to gyrate and smile; he likes it! Goldust hides behind Marlena and keeps running and hiding. He begins to annoy the crowd by continuing this cowardly behavior, enforcing the stereotype of gay men as cowards. This is unimportant to the WWE, as the fans are heavily engaged and that is the goal. Another male wrestler interferes, allowing Goldust to pin Razor in a compromising position, for the win.[38] This victory tells the viewing audience that gay men have to resort to soliciting help to be victorious in a fight.

Bout 2: Trish Stratus Versus Mickie James

Trish Stratus: How do I know that name, Mickie James?
Mickie James: Yea, I'm like your biggest fan![39]

Trish Stratus was a Canadian, blonde hair, Greek goddess who is arguably the most influential WWE female wrestler in the history of American pro-wrestling. Trish Stratus was one of the first divas (WWE's term for female personalities) to stir together a successful mix of sexuality and athletic ability. Women in wrestling are usually a side act, but Trish was a star. Trish was a huge draw for the company and was much beyond a novelty act; she was a headliner.

—WWE Women's Championship Match: Victoria vs. Trish Stratus ©—

Trish and Victoria had a storied past, full of chair shots, hair pulling, and hard slaps across the face. On November 10, 2005, their history was coming to a head and it was for the prized possession of the Women's division, the WWE Women's Championship. Holding that belt meant you were the absolute best among the divas. Sending a clear message to the power lifter Victoria, Trish started off strong with a stiff elbow to the face. Trish was in control, victory in her sight. A hard kick to the face of Victoria, and Trish was now ready to end the match. She flies through the air, clutching Victoria's neck in a headlock. Using her brute strength, Victoria reveres the momentum and slams Trish onto her knee. Crack! Victoria is toying with Trish now, lifting Trish over her head. The crowd is for Trish, hoping to motivate her to a victory. The end is near; Victoria has Trish set up for her finisher "The Widows Peak," a move that will guarantee victory. Trish flips Victoria over and bridges backwards into a pin. Trish wins. She's absolutely exhausted as an irate Victoria extracts revenge. Ashley, Trish's friend, comes to the rescue and gets slammed on her back by Victoria for interfering. It looks bleak for Trish. An unidentified woman rushes to the ring jolting across the ring to attack Victoria and save Trish.[40]

The Mickie/Trish love affair, like all love stories, started innocently enough, as Mickie revealed:

> These last few months hanging out with you have been amazing, I grew up watching wrestling with my grand papi. But then shortly after that, Grand papi passed way. He's looking down on us and he is smiling, because I get to hang out with you, my idol, my hero. After this match with Victoria, if I win . . . I could be in the ring with you![41]

Mickie had identified herself as Trish's biggest fan. She would accompany Trish to the ring and cheer her to victories. They were tag team partners, best friends. Mickie James always seemed a bit off, and any devoted wrestling fan knew what would transpire eventually.

Mickie James enters the arena for # 1 contender's match against Victoria. Trish Stratus accompanies Mickie, but sits at the announcers table to watch. "Wow, she's got spunk," says Trish. "Is that what you call it?" one of the commentators prods. Trish responds, "That's what I'm gonna call it . . . she [Mickie] likes to tell everyone we're best friends, well I'll say we're not best friends . . . we're acquaintances." Mickie James steals the victory, earning her chance for the Women's Championship and Trish Stratus.[42]

Building up to the match, and in an attempt to gain fan's interest, the WWE began to introduce lesbian undertones to the feud. A week before the match, Mickie James cleverly cornered Trish into a room and hung mistletoe above them. The fans encouraged the WWE's vision by cheering uncontrollably. Mickie stole a kiss from Trish, as Trish frustratingly pushed Mickie off. New Years Revolution would be the next time they saw each other.[43]

—New Years Revolution, WWE Women's Championship Match:
Trish Stratus © vs. Mickie James—

> "Ya' know Stylez, Trish Stratus and I came into the WWE 2 weeks apart, so I've been there since day one and I've never ever seen Trish Stratus as uncomfortable as she has been the last few weeks."[44]
>
> —*Jonathan Coachmen*

Mickie James extended her hand as a peace offering, and Trish pulled Mickie in closely and stared; she meant business. Homosexuality made a guest appearance when Trish had Mickie in a headlock and Mickie's hand purposely grabs Trish's chest. That was enough for Trish to push Mickie away and for the fans to then cheer at any intentional, or non-intentional, female-to-female contact that would follow. Mickie jumps on the turnbuckle and locks her legs around Trish's neck; the fans are absolutely insane as the WWE has stimulated their girl-on-girl fantasy. Trish ultimately leaves victorious.[45]

The storyline takes a turn for insanity. After weeks of repairing her relationship with Trish, Mickie decides to throw Trish a celebration, full of balloons and confetti littering the arena. A group of male cheerleaders cheer for Trish " ... and now it's time to say I love you too." Trish is visibly overwhelmed, not knowing how to stop Mickie. Ashley comes to her rescue. "If you're not gonna put this girl in her place, then I'm gonna do it for you. Mickie, Trish ... she does not love you. You got that? And you know what? She thinks exactly what everyone here thinks: Mickie James is a Psycho." The crowd begins the chant "She's a Psycho." Mickie James, distraught, starts crying and exits. She abrasively changes her mind and rushes back to assault Ashley. Trish gets involved to stop the brawl. This allows Mickie to take out Ashley. Mickie misinterprets: "I knew it! I knew it. I knew you cared about me Trish. You're the greatest ever!"[46]

Trish Stratus is now desperate. She introduces Mickie James to a new boyfriend, hoping an indirect sign would resonate loud and clear.[47] Retaliating, Mickie James plots a successful plan to get Trish's boyfriend arrested for sexual harassment.[48] Only a direct intervention will work and Trish builds up the courage. "You're just too much ...," she confesses. Mickie tries to interrupt, but Trish is empowered: "No, no! Everywhere I turn, you're there. I don't want any more of it, I think, you and I, we just need some time apart." Mickie pleads, "Trish, don't say that." But Trish is gone.[49]

After a victorious last tag match together, Mickie only wants to "say goodbye the right way." She extends her hand. Trish is hesitant. Mickie goes in for a kiss, and Trish pulls away, upset that she even considered Mickie could change, but not surprised. Mickie sets up her heel turn (turning into the villain) by slowing moving away and *jolting* back to kick Trish Stratus hard in her jaw.[50] This sets up their big match or, in wrestling terms, the blow off match.

—Wrestlemania 22, WWE Women's Championship:
Mickie James vs. Trish Stratus ©—

Trish aggressively takes the fight to Mickie. Mickie has embarrassed, harassed, and manipulated Trish into a woman with revenge on her mind. The divas are putting on an athletically sound match, showing that women can wrestle too. The crowd is entertained and it appears both women only want to destroy one another; their friendship is gone. Mickie James is the heel, the bad girl, but something unique is transpiring: Mickie James is getting cheered:[51]

> She was meant to be bad, a "heel" . . . she had an obsession with Trish Stratus, the uber diva, and the crowd ate her up and quickly took the side of the 'gay' and I think that is because, among other reasons, it was something they [the fans] could relate too, and that is to be loved especially by the person you want to love you.[52]

The positive reaction to Mickie James is astounding. She is injuring the baby-face diva Trish, and they are cheering for it. Never without controversy, Mickie James grabs the crotch of Trish Stratus, distracting her. Facing the crowd, she makes an obscene gesture; she forms one hand into a V and licks up the middle, insinuating female-to-female oral sex. This match/feud is a success to the WWE; the crowd is absolutely enthralled. Lesbian undertones and a "Psycho" persona have proven a successful concoction for the WWE. Mickie James is the new Champion. One commentator is shocked, "I think there are some fans here that got a hall pass from the home. They are actually cheering this psychotic woman. Mickie James used some very unique feminine strategy to take Trish Stratus mentally out of the game . . ."[53]

Goldust and the psychotic Mickie James stalked their ways into the hearts of pro-wrestling fans. Using homosexual subtext, both created characters that exploited the fans' craving forentertainment and stimulation. They, Goldust and Mickie, had an insatiable, uncontrollable sexual appetite for Razor Ramon and Trish Stratus, feeding on villainous gay stereotypes. Their lunatic obsessions crafted queers as people with no control, fixated on sex for gratification. Both played gay mind games, attempting to reveal the inner homophobia of their victims and their fans. For the storylines to work, the new heel queer characters needed a popular baby face to feed off of. If Goldust was the crazed gay stalker, he needed the machismo Razor Ramon to become the object of his desire. If Mickie James was the brunette love-stricken psycho lesbian, she needed to occupy herself with the blonde, bubbly model Trish Stratus. Societal views revealed its bias as Mickie James was cheered but Goldust was despised by the audiences, perhaps showing that it is more acceptable to be a sexualized lesbian than an obsessed gay man.

GAY SATIS(FACTION)

The West Hollywood Blondes

The feud between the Gay and Lesbian Alliance Against Defamation (GLAAD) and pro-wrestling began to heat up when GLAAD could no longer stand back and witness pro-wrestling's tyranny on gay stereotypes. World Championship Wrestling (WCW) was the first challenger to GLAAD when it introduced pink tights and pig tails in the form of Lenny Lane and Lodi, under the umbrella tag team name, The West Hollywood Blondes. They joined both Goldust and Gorgeous George in originating from Hollywood.

Kevin Nash, one of the creators and writers for Lenny and Lodi, claimed that they were supposed to be revealed as brothers, explaining "the closeness that they felt."[54] He continues, "'Who said they were gay? We aren't depicting these guys as gay. We're depicting different scenarios; you're the ones who said they were gay."[55] Nash closes in on the victory, but we flashback to a scene where the camera pans away from Lenny and Lodi to reveal the word "closet,"[56] which makes WCW's true intention clear.

GLAAD went on the attack, aiming where it would hurt WCW the most, with its advertisers. "It's hard enough to get advertising on wrestling,"[57] and so WCW eventually found themselves at the side of defeat, with GLAAD victorious. Lenny and Lodi "were faggots, playing up to every gay stereotype,"[58] and that was the problem. Their antics would prompt fans to scream profanities and promote homophobia, a phobia that could transcend beyond the arena: "If there is a 10-year old boy, whose classmates perceive him to be overly feminine, he has a good chance of being called 'Lenny' and being beat up. . . ."[59]

Billy & Chuck: The Gay Wedding

GLAAD took on their next opponents, a much bigger company, the WWE. This battle was more intense, as the WWE had played mind games, even getting GLAAD to believe the Billy/Chuck storyline would be positive. Before the commitment ceremony would be aired on national television, "Scott Seomin, an official with [GLAAD], went so far as to get Billy & Chuck a gravy boat from the Pottery farm."[60] They furthered embarrassed themselves, claiming the storyline "reaches a lot of potential bullies and gay bashers . . . what Billy and Chuck are saying is not only 'we're here,' but they also say 'Don't mess with us.'" [61]

Billy and Chuck were two bleach blonde, fake tanned, gay wrestling characters. They were managed by an even more stereotypical character, Rico, who was a spunky hyperactive gay male stylist. Channeling a rivalry with straight women, Billy and Chuck displayed their obnoxious antics, challenging WWE divas Stacy Kiebler and Torrie Wilson to a "Pose off." Torrie and Stacy used their feminine wiles to seduce cheers from the audience and displayed lesbian undertones by posing suggestively together. Billy and Chuck did the same, but sent the fans into an uproar of homophobic jeers.[62]

After proposing to Billy, Chuck would become excited for the commitment ceremony that would be engrained in pro-wrestling's history. Behind the scenes, the writers thought "a stunt like a gay wedding would somehow draw positive press and increase ratings because it was edgy."[63] Putting GLAAD onto a torture rack, The Godfather came out with "hos" to try and persuade Billy and Chuck away from their gay preference, insinuating it is a choice. Finally, Billy and Chuck succumbed and revealed it was just a "publicity stunt" and they were not gay.[64]

GLAAD was furious. "The WWE lied to us two months ago when they promised that Billy and Chuck would come out and wed on the air. . . . In fact, I was told (lied to) the day after the show was taped in Minneapolis that the wedding took place and all was well."[65] Like Lenny and Lodi, GLAAD was on the losing end, as the WWE had gone through with their storyline from start to finish, promoting negativity around gay marriage. The unfortunate tune here is that not only did they lie to GLAAD, but WWE officials themselves had ignorantly believed that somehow this would draw positive press for the company. The commitment ceremony between Billy and Chuck:

> did nothing to decrease the negativity surrounding gay marriage or gays in general. I think it increased it. Just listen to the amount of booing in the [live] crowd. And when Billy and Chuck profess their heterosexuality, the crowd cheers more loudly than they did for the last two hours of the show. The whole thing was absolutely stupid.[66]

Christopher Street Connection

Independent wrestling decided to get involved in the mayhem. Ring of Honor (ROH) introduced the Christopher Street Connection, an obvious play on the infamous Christopher St. (of Stone Wall Riots) in New York City. The faction's antics and glittered clothing and neon colored boas were staples of their gimmick. One unique element to the group was Allison Danger, the storyline lesbian/fag-hag of the faction. "I remember doing the one kiss with [another female wrestler] . . . that got such a pop . . . ," Allison gloats. Hinting at the desire for female wrestlers to fit in (backstage) with the frat party known as pro-wrestling, she recalls "I remember walking in the locker room . . . strutting in. I was like 'I made out with her, it was nice.' There was a little jealousy factor going on there too [from the male wrestlers]." Displaying her intentions and vision for her character motivated by lesbian stereotyping, she notes "It [the kiss] played really good into I'm the lesbian, I'm gonna' stalk you ha-ha."[67]

The male wrestlers of Christopher Street Connection "were openly gay wrestlers who would kiss at live events and come on to the other performers."[68] The group, including Allison, furthered the mindset that gay people have an uncontrollable sexual appetite and are crazed, except unlike most other gay characters fans were allowed and encouraged to cheer Christopher Street Connection. Unfortunately, the man who owned ROH, Rob Feinstein, was a closeted gay male himself and would later feed into that myth due to a well-publicized scandal where Feinstein was "caught by NBC 10 . . . attempting to solicit sex from what he thought was a 14-year-old boy."[69] Christopher Street Connection stopped appearing on ROH shows so as not to attract attention to the shameful event.

THE KISS OF DEATH

Two voluptuous blonde women are walking down the hallway; a sign on a dressing room door alerts their attention: "Lesbians." Hot Lesbian Action (HLA) is going to occur and the straight male fans are wild for it. "Don't you know who we are?" one of the lesbians asks a male wrestler, "We're the Lesbians!" In this bizarre storyline, WWE RAW General manager Eric Bishoff had hired the services of two women to perform HLA (WWE's way of causing controversy to get exposure from the mainstream media). In the ring, the Lesbians are eager to display their affection. "What about you? Do you want Jenny?" Bishoff teases the crowd. "My body aches all over for Jenny," she confirms. "Do you want to touch Tanya?" Bishoff asks the other lesbian. "Oh yea!" she replies, "I want to touch Tanya." After exciting the male crowd (mission accomplished) by slobbering all over each other, they are violently beaten down by two big Samoan wrestlers. One woman was kicked stiff right in her chest and the other pulled by her hair, thrown six feet up in the air onto the shoulders of one of the Samoan wrestlers and dropped down.[70]

Pro-wrestling and the WWE are intentionally ridiculous, but this was one of those examples where it is taken too far:

> What goes through the minds of those in the creative department when they think up something like this—Is there a set checklist? Degrading to women? Check. Degradingly Sexual? Check. Featuring a pervy, middle-aged madman brand owner? Check. Okay, cool, it qualifies—let's make it happen![71]

The images of the Lesbians in their underwear, making out and caressing one another was more fitting of a porno flick than a family show. Then, having the women beat down uncomfortably simulates violence against women and queer people. The beat down was for pure shock value, and some fans were in complete shock, not believing what they just witnessed. Other fans were cheering and enjoying the display, demonstrating why scenes like these are potentially harmful. Furthermore, it showcased Samoan men as women beaters and gay bashers. Being politically correct is never the WWE's goal, and it got the outcome it desired: everyone was talking, it left an impression, and it further got the Samoan wrestlers over as bad guys.

HLA also hints at society's obsession with lesbians in a sexualized role. Many television shows have inserted lesbian love storylines to increase ratings and create buzz. Pro-wrestling follows the trend, as seen with the Mickie James/Trish Stratus storyline. The sexualizing of women in pro-wrestling is not uncommon: "We all have to look enticing while getting the cellulite beaten out of us. You're expected to grimace and look gorgeous, you're supposed to pass out, land awkwardly but suggestively . . ."[72] The sexualizing of lesbians is just as common, most notably for the pleasure of straight men, further crippling the long battle to legitimize the love between two women.

Extreme Championship Wrestling (ECW) was notorious for using their women as T&A. ECW had one of the most memorable WTF moments, enticing straight men everywhere with a little three-way tonsil hockey. In television land, male wrestler Tommy Dreamer had suspicions that his on-screen (and real life wife) Beulah had been cheating on him. It reached its climax when Tommy forced Beulah into confrontation and asked, "Who is he?" Interrupting, another male wrestler gloated, "Oh it's not a he, Tommy Dreamer, it's not a he." Kimona, a female, rips the microphone from his hands and yells, "It's me!" to a rounding ovation from the male audience. The two women roll around the ring in a deep kiss. Tommy pulls them by their hair and with a mean glare becomes the envy of straight men everyone: "I'll take 'em both, I'm hardcore."[73] Not only does this put the man, Tommy, in control of the situation and the women's sexuality, it dehumanizes the women into pure sexual gratification.

WHAT A DRAG!

The art of drag has often been an avenue for comedic endeavors. Tyler Perry (of Madea fame) introduced himself into a very lucrative career impersonating women. Pro-wrestling has not been the exception. They have used drag to garner a cheap laugh or to get the male wrestlers involved with the women. Often, the male in drag has had his (her?) ability stripped and a wig, make-up, and gender performance has replaced their strength.

One of the more recent performances was by Santino Marella, under his stage name Santina. Santino pushed his way into superstardom by being a comedic Italian character who would romanticize English with an Italian twist. Santina, played by the same man, was the on-screen "sister" of Santino. Santina, like Santino, was a fan favorite, using comedy for approval. In one memorable segment, general manager Vickie Guerrero wanted to prove that Santina was in fact her brother Santino. She elicited the help of WWE diva Rosa Mendes to seduce Santina. "I want you to give Santina a good luck kiss before his match against Beth." Vickie demanded. Rosa reluctantly went for a kiss on the cheek and Santina forced Rosa into a full on lip lock. Vickie's assistant Chavo screamed, "I knew it! We all knew you couldn't resist a kiss from Rosa. Admit it, admit it . . . you're busted." Santina interrupted, "OK . . . fine! Fine! I admit it. OK. I am, how you say? . . . A lesbiana. It's true. I prefer the company of the womens. I always have."[74] Are lesbians big burly men with chest hair? Is this to be accepted at face value and appreciated as only a joke?

Harvina was a male in drag that claimed no woman could beat him. He stripped the petite Kat of the WWE Women's Championship, pinning her in a degrading "snow bunny match" for the title.[75] The Kat was a female personality who emphasized the T&A part of wrestling and was not a skilled wrestler. At the next show, Jacqueline challenged

Harvina for the title. This time, Harvina came out as his male self, Harvey. Jacqueline, who is a skilled wrestler, embarrassed him and won the WWE Women's Championship in under one minute.[76] Harvina, the character, was created by the WWE as a way for Jacqueline to win the title without pinning The Kat. The WWE wanted to get a struggling Jacqueline over as a face, and pinning the popular Kat would not aid in that direction. The WWE writers could have chosen another storyline to take the title off of the Kat, but "maybe the product of their shows get dull and slow, so they might add a form of homosexuality to see how crowds respond to it."[77]

In her autobiography *If They Only Knew*, Chyna recounts a time when she wrestled a man in drag in the independent leagues:

> "What the hell, Walter—I thought I was gonna wrestler a chick?"
>
> "You are," Walter insists, stuffing fake breast inside this poor guy's leotard.
>
> "A real chick. You said a real chick."
>
> "Never used the word real. I couldn't book anybody this late."
>
> "But he has stubble Walter—" Before I could finish Walter shoves this bizarre-looking latex mask in my face. It's for the guy to wear.[78]

Chyna made it acceptable for women to fight men, but early in her career, before the WWE, she had to work under the same oppressive system of wrestling: " . . . the only place people wanted to see a woman compete against a man was in a chili cook-off . . . "[79] Introduce drag and it becomes all right for a woman to beat a man. This not only says that a muscular woman cannot beat a non-drag man, but that an effeminate man cannot beat a muscular woman. This thinking places importance on size and gender performing, saying that he/she who is more masculine acting, is the one who is stronger. Of course, "his name was Raindrops. Don't ask."[80]

BACKSTAGE

Raindrop was not the only wrestler simulating homoeroticism. "And if you're not down with that, we've got two words for ya," and the crowd yells, "Suck it!"[81] Not a late night gay cable program, but a famous catch phrase from degenerates, and WWE tag team, Degeneration X. Pro-wrestlers have long found themselves throbbing against gay innuendoes encouraged by the irony of two straight men in short tights. The set-up has led to sticky situations, with male wrestlers finding themselves in a rather homoerotic locale:

Randy Orton: We got a lot in common . . . we're young . . . we're incredibly handsome. . . . You and I, guys like us, get treated like dirt and I won't take that lying down. Here is what I propose: tonight, you and I get together. We take out HBK, we take out Edge, and it leaves you and I standing alone in that ring. And then we see who the better man is. What do you say?

John Cena: See who the better man is? You really feel this way?

Orton: Yes I do.

Cena: So you really think I am handsome?

Orton: Wait a minute, that's not exactly what I meant.

Cena: You also said, that later on tonight you want to get together.

Orton: (backtracking) But I said that . . . like in the ring.

Cena: You said that you're not gonna' take this lying down, but your eyes tell a different story. Wait! Wait! Don't get mad. It's 2007, I'm not judging anybody . . . but that's just not my thing

Orton: (he is livid) You think you're funny Cena huh? The only pose you're gonna' be doing tonight is lying on your back, in that ring, with me on top![82]

Randy Orton and John Cena are main attractions, role models. Impressionable fans watch as the WWE stomps on and body-slams homosexuality into a mud-hole. Rejecting homophobia, Cena does not mind if Orton is gay, just not with him, "I'm not judging anybody . . . but that's just not my thing." He clarifies. Contradicting his statement, Cena intentionally ignites the homophobic in Randy Orton, sending him into a fury. Orton is offended and irate that Cena is insinuating he is gay; it is the ultimate offense to this machismo inspired wrestler. Now, ample oppressive opportunity is handed over to the fans to use homosexuality (slurs) to laugh at and direct derogatory comments at Orton. Orton being the heel, the villain, it also becomes acceptable.

That was not the first time a top star experimented with homosexuality. Announcer Michael Cole and pro-wrestling superstar The Rock had a turbulent relationship full of gay one liners.

Michael Cole: (knocking on The Rock's dressing room for an interview). Rock, excuse me, Rock Rock . . . (He walks in on the Rock nude) oh sorry Rock! Well we hope to find that information as soon . . .

The Rock: What in the blue hell is wrong with you Michael Cole? The Rock just got out of the shower; you want to barge in on the Rock? What's the matter with you?

[Cole looks down.]

The Rock: You looking at the people's strudel?

Cole: No no!

The Rock: To each his own Michael Cole, to each his own. Why don't you give The Rock one minute? The Rock just needs one minute. . . . Go frost your hair, do something like that . . .[83]

The challenge here is that homophobia is dressed comfortably in a non-confrontational way. This segment is entertaining. The Rock was very charismatic, a beloved fan favorite. The Rock comically imposes a gay identity onto Michael Cole, making him feel that being gay carries shame, "What's the matter with you?" The Rock asks. Cole stumbles to claim his heterosexual identity, losing the fight. The Rock mocks and pokes fun at Cole, locking him down into submission. Silenced, Cole is projected to the crowd as a homosexual. Presented as a joke, the crowd can view male homosexuality the same way. Additionally, do all gay men frost their hair?

Pro-wrestling has perpetuated all types of homophobia. In one segment, Charlie Hass tells his (tag team) partner Shelton Benjamin he needs to kiss his hand. Shelton refuses as Charlie reveals it was only a joke. They hug as Shelton laughs off the tension. The image of a shirtless Shelton and spandex-wearing Charlie ignites the very gay overtones of this segment. Farooq walks in and yells "Damn!" Both men push each other away, denying the insinuation. Cleansing himself, Shelton feverously dusts himself off.[84] Dramatizing the straight man's reaction to a gay accusation only says being gay is repugnant, straight men are insulated at such an accusation, and male-to-male intimacy can only be gay. Can straight guys not share a hug?

Deconstruct the meaning behind a body slam or the psychology of a suplex; is there such a way? Can The Rock telling Michael Cole to "frost his hair" or the portrayal of Santina truly be seen as offensive, or is it over-analytical to do so? Wrestlers and fans have long defended and protected the industry. "It's such a tongue-in-cheek industry as it is," states Kevin Nash, writer of Lenny and Lodi and a pro-wrestler himself. Continuing, he emphasizes "it would be one thing if it were a docudrama, and we were trying to depict something that was real life."[85] Wrestling is not real life, but homophobia is real and their depiction of Queers (intentionally or unintentionally) further promotes gay stereotyping, marginalization of Queers and gay-bashing.

THE CROWD SPEAKS

The GLAAD squared off in a rematch against the WWE CEO Vince McMahon when he said the masks of special guest Cirque du Soleil were "really gay."[86] GLAAD released a statement:

> McMahon wasn't implying the performers were gay, however, he used the term in a derogatory manner. It's just another example of how people throw around the word "gay" derisively. This came from the leader of a $500 million-plus organization who holds a lot of power in what he says and what he does. WWE programming reaches 16 million viewers each week. McMahon needs to understand that the words he uses and how he uses them can greatly affect people's lives.[87]

Fans were quick to react, claiming their love for Vince or telling GLAAD to "lighten up." Some poked fun at wrestling "cause oiled up musclemen grabbing each other's sack for ten minutes at a time isn't gay at all." The discussion allowed readers to access an unfiltered discourse, which presented all sides of the issue. One reader adamantly claimed "shut up with this oversensitivity and political bullshit. Unless they can establish that Vince McMahon made comments intended to provoke some kind of backlash against the gay community, their over analysis is full of shit." One fan outed himself, standing tall and saying "I'm gay and GLAAD needs to lighten the hell up. They find something wrong in everything and they're making me homophobic."[88]

Wrestling fans called GLAAD "gay" or agreed that the Cirque du Soleil was in fact "pretty gay." Other wrestling fans stood in the corner of GLAAD by saying "No . . . they don't need to lighten up" others elaborated, " . . . GLAAD is in the right here. Many people use the word 'gay' to mean 'stupid' or 'dumb.' It is really offensive to gay men and women around the country."[89]

The open forum, allowing fans to post their thoughts and views, illustrated that gay, straight, or non-identifying, wrestling fans, like everyone, are on all sides of the issue. McMahon, himself, stood in the corner of GLAAD and apologized, "My comment was not meant to be used in a derisive manner. [GLAAD's] point is well taken and I agree that people should be more cognizant about their usage of the word 'gay' "[90]

THE CLIMAX

The real tug-of-war begins as pro-wrestling aims to defend itself. "Stereotypes help us bring the characters into different storylines," explains [WWE] spokesperson Jayson Bernstein. "I don't think we're exploiting any individual group of people. It's just a matter of entertainment." [91] Entertainment at what cost? Does entertaining remove the responsibility of an organization to be conscious of what it perpetuates? There has to be a "balance between entertaining your audience and not inflaming stereotypes that are harmful to any particular group."[92]

Pro-wrestling is about response. If the fans do not react (negatively or positively), the WWE and other promotions would not follow through on an angle. Success is measured by the excitement of the audience. The WWE is not "afraid of provoking [the] fans. [Their] goal is to get reactions from them."[93] For the fans, pro-wrestling is "escapism"[94] where their thoughts are uncensored. They can boo the gay guy or, conversely, lust over the sweaty action in the ring. It's a safe haven where the ridiculous, or unspoken, becomes acceptable and unfiltered.

It is without question that pro-wrestling has bred, maintained, and fed off of homophobia, has sexualized the lesbian identity, and used gay identities to marginalize and shock those whose only interaction with queers may be the stereotypical images they see on a pro-wrestling show. They also started off most queer characters as heels, villains, showing the inflexibility to portray these characters non-stereotypically.

Pro-wrestling serves as a barometer of where society stands on issues of homophobia. (Remember the reaction to Chyna?) It would be interesting to see a gay wrestling character that begins as a face, is good looking and empowered, and the only knowledge of his/her sexual identity is his/her admittance and not subtle hints based on harmful gay stereotypes. However, it is only when that character is prominently embodied in mainstream society that pro-wrestling would introduce the proverbial said character into its programming. If Vince McMahon and the WWE feel they could make money off of it, they will try.

Pro-wrestling is a spectacle that can often, and usually does, offend. It invokes a reaction so strong that it pulls at your heart strings, your fears, your biases; it pulls at who you are. It upsets you, infuriates you, makes you cry, makes you proud. It makes you feel. Their influence on society is undeniably irrefutable, but pro-wrestling does not aim to be (or claim to have) a moral compass:

> Gays in wrestling, midgets in wrestling, women in wrestling, wrestling in general . . . is a fun strange and frustrating thing to try and make sense out of, and you probably won't. It will only mean something to you or it simply won't mean anything at all.[95]

NOTES

1. Tim Baines, "WCW Sale Has Plenty of Flair," *SLAM! Sports*, 25 March 2001, http://slam.canoe.ca/SlamWrestlingWCWSale/flair-sun.html.
2. "ECW's Stunning Money Woes Made Public," Gerweck.net. http://www.gerweck.net/ecwbankruptcy.htm.
3. WWE Superstars, WWE. *Barack Obama vs. Hilary Clinton Full video wwe*, 10:57; YouTube, MP4, http://www.youtube.com/watch?v=l2wiU-BNqYo (September 2009).
4. Jacqueline and Terri Runnels, WWE. Terri Runnels & Jacqueline join forces [PMS], 3:10; YouTube, MP4, http://www.youtube.com/watch?v=yAfHfpfzo5k (October 2009).
5. WWE Superstars, WWE. *Ivory Joins Right to Censor Group on RAW*, 2:44; YouTube, MP4, http://www.youtube.com/watch?v=01X6HZWtb_8 (November 2009).
6. Steve Austin and Vince McMahon, WWE. *Stone Cold vs. Vince Volume 2*, 10:01; YouTube, MP4, http://www.youtube.com/watch?v=pn82WUIC7sU (October 2009).
7. Jim Johnston, *Eddie Guerrero: "I Lie, I Cheat, I Steal" [Full]*, 3:31; YouTube, MP4, http://www.youtube.com/watch?v=JTgqotrwewg (November 2009).
8. Joanie Laurer, *Chyna, The 9th Wonder of The World: If They Only Knew* (New York: HarperCollins, 2001), 187.
9. John Capouya, *Gorgeous George: The Outrageous Bad-Boy Wrestler Who Created American Pop Culture* (New York: HarperCollins, 2008), photo captions.
10. Ibid., 74.
11. Ibid., 75.
12. Ibid., 136.
13. Ibid.
14. Ibid., 106.
15. Ibid., 226.
16. Ibid., 227.

17. Rick Cataldo, interviewed by Brian Pacheco, November 17, 2009, *Queers in American Popular Culture* interview, transcript.

18. WWE Superstars, WWE. *Chyna's Debut (In Your House: Final Four)*, 1:13; YouTube, MP4, http://www.youtube.com/watch?v=wfVmCY9_1ww (October 2009).

19. Joel Stein, "Chyna," *Time Magazine*, September 27, 1999, http://www.time.com/time/magazine/article/0,9171,992091,00.html.

20. *Sable Accuses Chyna of Steroid Use*, 2:59; YouTube, MP4, http://www.youtube.com/watch?v=Xcih1NRCtnk&feature=related (October 2009).

21. Laurer, Ibid., 230.

22. Ibid., 177.

23. Ibid., 75.

24. Ibid., 79–84.

25. "Marketing Chyna," alivingwonder.blogspot.com, 9 July 2009, http://alivingwonder.blogspot.com/2009/07/marketing-chyna.html.

26. Dustin Runnels, WWE. *WWF/WWE—Goldust Promo*, 1:00; YouTube, MP4, http://www.youtube.com/watch?v=lBF2lYhDSiU (October 2009).

27. WWE Superstars, WWE. *Goldust Debut in WWF*, 8:58; YouTube, MP4, http://www.youtube.com/watch?v=PbdHRe9eo_k&feature=related (October 2009).

28. Larry Csonka, "Dustin Rhodes Discusses Being Tully Blanchard's Last Opponent, Goldust, Cody, Dusty, TNA, His New Direction and More!" 411mania.com, 30 July 2007, http://www.411mania.com/wrestling/news/57777/Dustin-Rhodes-discusses-being-Tully-Blanchards-last-opponent,Goldust,-Cody,-Dusty,-TNA,-his-new-direction-and-More!.htm.

29. Ibid.

30. Vadim, "Grappling with Homosexuality, Professional Wrestling: Simultaneously Homoerotic and Homophobic," *Village Voice*, May 2, 2000, http://www.villagevoice.com/2000-05-02/news/grappling-with-homosexuality/.

31. WWE Superstars, WWE. *Legacy of the Intercontinental Championship—Part XXVI*, 43:00; WWE.com. MPEG. http://www.wwe.com/subscriptions/wweclassics/originals/intercontinental/ (November 2009).

32. Ibid.

33. Vadim, Ibid.

34. WWE Superstars, WWE. *Legacy*, Ibid.

35. Ibid.

36. Ibid.

37. Ibid.

38. Ibid.

39. WWE Divas, WWE. *Trish & Ashley Meet Mickie Backstage*, 0:46; YouTube, MP4, http://www.youtube.com/watch?v=Rfg0W8xY20A&feature=related (October 2009).

40. WWE Divas, WWE. *Trish vs. Victoria—Mickie James Debuts*, 6:33; YouTube, MP4, http://www.youtube.com/watch?v=efe4PdBb9xs (October 2009).

41. WWE Divas, *Mickie James vs. Trish Stratus Feud Music Video "Love Me,"* 4:51; YouTube. MP4, http://www.youtube.com/watch?v=L5MC0FqWFgo (October 2009).

42. WWE Divas, WWE. *Mickie vs. Victoria (# 1 Contender's match)*, 4:47; YouTube, MP4, http://www.youtube.com/watch?v=fPvUDjiPJo8 (November 2009).

43. Mickie James, Trish Stratus, WWE. *Trish & Mickie Kiss Backstage*, 1:15; YouTube, MP4, http://www.youtube.com/watch?v=6hX3bF1hh2A&feature=related (November 2009).

44. Mickie James, Trish Stratus, WWE. *Trish Stratus vs. Mickie James—NYR 2006 (Women's C. match)*, 10:16; YouTube, MP4, http://www.youtube.com/watch?v=D9dUK6uYzQ8 (November 2009).

45. Ibid.

46. WWE Superstars, WWE. *Mickie & Trish- Mickie Present the Trish's Celebration*, 8:30; YouTube, MP4, http://www.youtube.com/watch?v=q7WRNXuUtjw (October 2009).

47. WWE Superstars, WWE. *Trish Introduces Her Date to Mickie*, 1:00; YouTube, MP4, http://www.youtube.com/watch?v=kzSDPkYK7vI&feature=related (November 2009).

48. WWE Superstars, WWE. *Mickie and Trish Segment*, 3:10; YouTube, MP4, http://www.youtube.com/watch?v=jRP6lzCOcq8 (November 2009).

49. Mickie James and Trish Stratus, WWE. *Mickie & Trish Time Apart*, 1:21; YouTube, MP4, http://www.youtube.com/watch?v=qxKwJmSwqVE (November 2009).

50. WWE Divas, WWE. *WWE Divas Trish & Mickie vs Candice & Victoria*, 7:49; YouTube, MP4, http://www.youtube.com/watch?v=3exchzKQTcc (November 2009).

51. Mickie James, Trish Stratus, WWE. *Mickie vs. Trish Wrestlemania 22 UNCUT;* 5:43. YouTube. MP4. http://www.youtube.com/watch?v=obEVQJj-_IQ&feature=related (October 2009).

52. Cataldo, Ibid.

53. Mickie, *Wrestlemania*, Ibid.

54. Cyd Zeigler. Jr., "Kevin Nash: 'Wrestling's Gay Friendly Champion,' " *Outsport.com*, http://www.outsports.com/moresports/20061205nash.htm.

55. Ibid.

56. Leni and Lodi, WCW. *Lenny and Lodi Are in the Closet*, 0:43; Youtube, MP4, http://www.youtube.com/watch?v=Aom5t9XkWS8 (October 2009).

57. Zeigler, Ibid.

58. Vadim, Ibid.

59. Ibid.

60. John McClellend, "Billy and Chuck's Big Fat Wrestling Gay Non-Wedding," *Outspotr.com*, http://www.outsports.com/columns/20020913mcclellandwedding.htm.

61. Ibid.

62. WWE Superstars, WWE. *Billy and Chuck vs. Torrie and Stacy in a Posedown*, 7:15; YouTube, MP4, http://www.youtube.com/watch?v=xhOtwA6fR9M (October 2009).

63. Scott Keith, *Wrestling's One Ring Circus: The Death of the World Wrestling Federation* (New York: Citadel, 2004), 93.

64. WWE Superstars, WWE. *Billy & Chuck Wedding*, 7:06. YouTube, MP4, http://www.youtube.com/watch?v=0P5EFCuyyUc (October 2009).

65. Ashish, "GLAAD Upset over Billy & Chuck Smackdown Ceremony," 411mania.com, September 12, 2002, http://www.411mania.com/movies/film_reviews/17072/GLAAD-Upset-Over-Billy-&-Chuck-Smackdown-Ceremony.htm.

66. McClellend, Ibid.

67. Allison Danger, RFvideo. *Allison Danger Made Out with Mickie James!*, 1:44; YouTube, MP4, http://www.youtube.com/watch?v=HzBVL8oGDpE (October 2009).

68. Matt Barnes, "Not That There's Anything Wrong with That!," *Fighting Spirit Magazine*, http://www.fightingspiritmagazine.co.uk/article.asp?IntID=41.

69. Matthew Tremley, "Rob Feinstein of ROH Caught Attempting to Solicit Sex from a 14 Year Old Boy," *UGO*, March 4, 2004, http://www.lordsofpain.net/news/2004/articles/1078401154.php.

70. WWE Superstars, WWE. *Eric Bischoff Presents HLA*, 10:04; YouTube, MP4, http://www.youtube.com/watch?v=MmoEIGp0VKo (October 2009).

71. Barnes, Ibid.

72. Laurer, Ibid.

73. ECW superstars, ECW. *Beulah and Kimona Affair Exposed*, 5:45; YouTube, MP4, http://www.youtube.com/watch?v=lLb7v8A1lVQ (October 2009).

74. WWE Superstars, WWE. *Santina Marella Is a Lesbian*, 2:13; YouTube, MP4, http://www.youtube.com/watch?v=eFKryOthiS8 (November 2009).

75. WWE Superstars, WWE. *The Kat vs. Harvina (Snow Bunny Match)*, 5:39; YouTube, MP4, http://www.youtube.com/watch?v=uT2mzCWZ2jg (October 2009).

76. WWE Superstars, WWE. *Jacqueline Battles the Women's Champion Harvina*, 3:01; YouTube, MP4, http://www.youtube.com/watch?v=jYEGw-rNEXg (October 2009).

77. Cataldo, Ibid.

78. Laurer, Ibid.

79. Ibid, 158

80. Ibid., 159

81. Paul Lavesque and Shawn Michaels, WWE. *DX Suck It!!!*, 0:40, YouTube, MP4, http://www.youtube.com/watch?v=QfI5ddqyYsI (November 2009).

82. Randy Orton and John Cena, WWE. *John Cena Calls Randy Orton Gay*, 2:47; YouTube, MP4, http://www.youtube.com/watch?v=7pvu72p6g2Q (October 2009).

83. Dwayne Johnson and Michael Cole, WWE. *The Rock and Michael Cole Funny Segment*, 0:59; YouTube, MP4, http://www.youtube.com/watch?v=Z_3oAa5kBoY (November 2009).

84. Shelton Benjamin, Ron Simmons and Charlie Hass, WWE. *Ron Simmons DAMN Shelton & Hass*, 1:14; YouTube, MP4, http://www.youtube.com/watch?v=R8IROOxPhUk (November 2009).

85. Zeigler, Ibid.

86. Larry Csonka, "GLAAD Angry at Vince McMahon Over 'Gay' Comment on RAW," 411mania.com, August 26, 2009, http://www.411mania.com/wrestling/news/114546/GLAAD-Angry-At-Vince-McMahon-Over-%27Gay-Comment-On-Raw.htm.

87. Ibid.

88. Ibid.

89. Ibid.

90. "WWE Chairman Apologizes for Inappropriate 'Gay' Comments After GLAAD Outreach," glaad.org, August 31, 2009, http://www.glaad.org/Page.aspx?pid=929.

91. Vadim, Ibid.

92. Ibid.

93. Ibid.

94. Zeigler, Ibid.

95. Cataldo, ibid.

Chapter 6

Babylon Baseball: When the Pitcher Catches

Mark John Isola

In 2007, Outsports.com, which was created by Jim Buzinski and Cyd Zeigler Jr., celebrated its eighth anniversary with the release of a book titled *The Outsports Revolution: Truth and Myth in the World of Gay Sports.*[1] Michael O'Keeffe offers a descriptive overview of the site in the book's foreword: "Outsports is truly a community, with readers contributing story ideas and photos and making our discussion board the go-to destination for gay sports fans."[2] This description captures what is unique about the site, as it exists as a digital community that is by, for, and about the gay sportsman. Gays and sports are not readily compatible in the mind of many, but as Patricia Nell Warren's book *The Lavender Locker Room* reminds us, there has been something of a queer streak in sports since at least the funeral games Achilles ordered to honor the death of his beloved Patroclus.[3] Indeed, Warren's print collection of gay athlete profiles, which were originally featured on Outsports.com, aptly points out how much there is to say about the gay sportsman, and Outsports.com has become a successful high-profile site for such discussions. In fact, Outsports.com published the first full story about John Amaechi, the former NBA player whose 2007 coming out prompted Tim Hardaway to out his inner homophobe.[4] The publication of *The Outsports Revolution* is a celebration of a valuable and viable digital community that has provided a much-needed platform for a proscribed subject position—the gay athlete.

The productivity of Outsports.com culminates with a zeitgeist that is perhaps best summarized in the book's foreword, which was written by *New York Daily News* sports reporter Michael O'Keeffe, who writes:

> Jackie Robinson changed American history when he broke baseball's color line in 1947, but my guess is that things will be different for the big league's first openly gay athlete. He won't be an established player who rocks the world with an "I am gay" press conference. He'll be a gifted athlete who realizes he's gay at an early age. He'll be emotionally tough; he won't hide who he is as he climbs through the minor league ranks.[5]

Although O'Keeffe's sentiment is admirable, it is problematic on two levels, as it risks performing what could be considered a *digital dissociation*. O'Keeffe blurs virtual reality with actual—if not at least potential—reality, and by doing so he presumes an absence where there may well already be a silenced or coded presence, thereby unwittingly perpetuating the strictures surrounding gays in professional sports.

By positing a world where a major league gay player will not have to rock the world with an "I am gay" press conference, O'Keeffe overlooks several events in recent history, where major league baseball players have had to reinforce the hegemony of heterosexuality with an "I am NOT gay" press conference.

On May 20, 2002, the *New York Post's* Neal Travis's "Page Six" gossip column ran an item that suggested a New York major league baseball player was gay.[6] The rumors stuck to New York Mets player Mike Piazza, and Piazza established the defensive rhetorical strategy for a major league baseball player being identified as a homosexual. Piazza held a press conference to assert his heterosexual identity, and he set the record straight—this easy pun being wholly intended—by claiming, "I'm not gay. I'm heterosexual."[7] Piazza tempered his need to declare his heterosexuality by steeping it within a rhetorical position that refused the charge of homophobia by speculating about how the majors would respond to a gay player: "In this day and age, it [being homosexual] would be irrelevant. If the guy is doing his job on the field . . . I don't think there would be any problem at all."[8] Here, Piazza agreed with Mets former manager Bobby Valentine's comments in that summer's issue of *Details* magazine, where Valentine stated baseball is "probably ready for an openly gay player."[9] After Travis's gossip-driven interpretation of Valentine's comments, Valentine defended his original assertion by saying: "It's what I believe. I think we are all big boys, and I think the world has progressed enough to handle many different situations."[10] Apparently, the big boys of baseball can handle it—with denials gilded with liberalism.

Piazza's response can be interpreted as meeting the bar of *parrhesia*, the tactical use of speech that Michelle Foucault, author of *Fearless Speech*, contends strategically negotiates the potential for punishment—by comparing it to WNBA player Sue Wicks, who outed herself in an interview later the same month.[11] In response to a *Time Out New York* interviewer, who asked Wicks if she was a lesbian, Wick's responded:

> I am. Usually, I don't like to answer those kinds of questions because you worry the issue might become so much bigger than the sport. As an athlete, it's a little annoying when that becomes the point of interest. But I would never avoid that question, especially in New York. I think it's important that if you are gay, you should not be afraid to say who you are.[12]

So, the freeing air of New York City provides something of a cultural privilege and/or subcultural responsibility for Wicks; whereas, it translates into Piazza's queer performative heteroglossia of denial, declaration, and liberalism.

The cultural fulcrum that sourced Piazza's triangulated performative rhetoric can be detected behind sports and mainstream media's differing responses to Piazza's denial and Wick's admission. This difference is suggested by the media's fast and furious coverage of Piazza's denial. Outsports.com gave two dozen interviews and appeared on seven sports talk shows nationwide to discuss Piazza; whereas, they were not contacted about Wicks. Moreover, after searching the Dow Jones Interactive, Buzinski and Zeigler were only able to locate one media reference to Wicks's outing interview. Buzinski aptly explores this double standard in his article posted on Outsports.com.[13]

This difference is further delineated by the media response to a second "Page Six" blind item published later in the same year, which again suggested a major league baseball player was gay: "Which Hall of Fame baseball hero cooperated with a best-selling biography only because the author promised to keep it secret that he is gay? The author kept her word, but big mouths at the publishing house can't keep from flapping."[14] This time the gossip stuck to Sandy Koufax.

Just like the Piazza rumor and very unlike the Wick's admission, the suggestion of a gay major league baseball player provoked a media response that ran through several of the nation's major media outlets, including Keith Olberman's cable news show *Countdown*, and the popular news Web site Salon.com. This wide-ranging media coverage stands in even greater contrast to Wicks's lesbian admission, which relative to the Piazza and Koufax rumors was barely covered or commented upon. In addition to revealing the tendency toward sensationalistic news in the tabloidization of America's news media, if not also something of modern Western civilization's fetish for secrets, the differing media responses to the rumor of gay baseball players and the admission of a lesbian basketball player reveals something of the enduring double standard surrounding sex and sexuality in sports. Scratch the surface and you find the old familiar discourses: lesbians are athletic and gays are too prissy to play sports.

For the purposes of this chapter, it will suffice to note the differing responses to Piazza's denial and Wicks's admission is also informed by the fact that major league baseball receives much more media exposure than professional women's basketball. Therefore, Piazza is a famous professional sports figure, whereas Wicks is at best a sports figure of some renown. However, such formations are themselves crafted from the construction of difference and not from some anterior essential difference. Mike Piazza is a media celebrated sports personality precisely because he conforms to the central discourses and statistical configurations of professional sports, which prefigures and subjectifies males like Piazza as athletes for performing acts that are already socially, materially, and ideologically constructed as acts of athleticism, specifically male athleticism.[15] Therefore, Piazza needs to conform to heteronormativity, if not perform his heterosexuality—at least publically, but there is no denying the double play inherent in his public positioning as it also forces an awareness of private secrets.

The potential for gender, sex, and sexual non-conformity functions here as a fulcrum that explains the media's concern with Piazza's press conference in opposition to Wicks's admission, as cultural institutions and media mechanisms strive to restore or otherwise react to disruptions in the hegemony of heterosexuality in major league baseball and mainstream consciousness.

A constitutive component of O'Keeffe's digital dissociation occurs when he asserts that when the gay Jackie Robinson emerges he will "be judged like every other ballplayer—by his ability to hit, field, or pitch."[16] This may well be a premature impulse, however, for whether the gay Jackie Robinson pitches or catches, the social, material, and ideological forces that construct major league baseball will likely only permit the public record to reflect a heterosexual status—at least until the player's retirement, as has been the case with other professional sports figures like Dave Kopay, Glenn Burke, John Amaechi, Esera Tuaolo, and Billy Bean. The echo of Hardaway's homophobic rant goes a long way toward explaining why the legacy of the sports closet will continue for some time despite the productivity of Web sites like Outsports.com, and as Foucault suggests, this very same fact may incite sites like it into existence. Yet, for all we know, the *New York Post's* "Page Six" gossip column was correct both times, and the gay Jackie Robinson may well be warming up at next year's spring training. This possibility figures the anxiety behind Piazza and Koufax's sexual status, and in the era of the digital age, this anxiety appears to be growing, not diminishing.

Shannon Ragland's 2007 book *The Thin Thirty* reveals the secrets behind the 1962 Kentucky football team's role in a gay sex and game-fixing scandal with Rock Hudson nearly half a century after its occurrence.[17] The contemporaneous secrecy surrounding this scandalous story, despite how it trucks with the tabloid media demand for sensationalism, as well as the several decades long open secrecy surrounding Hudson's sexuality, was completely dependent upon the containment culture of mid-twentieth century America—the genesis of which was a function of this culture's technological and metanarrative limits. However, such secrets are becoming increasingly difficult to keep in the digital age. Between the surveillance of the digital panopticon and the metanarrative ruptures of the postmodern era, there is something of an increasingly fragile nature to the homosexual closet. Therefore, unless sexual secrets, especially homosexual secrets, are completely evacuated of their potential for scandal, new tactics will have to emerge to prevent the evidence of the digitized sexual scandal from morphing into a permanent stigma. Mike Piazza's "I am NOT gay press conference" can be interpreted as one of these developments, for even if the pitcher is caught "catching" on videotape, the stigma of homosexuality can be negotiated by the public performance of testifying, "I am now and have always been heterosexual."[18] This, of course, refers to the Cleveland Indians player, who asserted just as much in a 2004 press conference.[19]

With a very fast fastball and three quality secondary pitches, including the changeup Eepehus pitch, Kazuhito Tadano was expected to draft early in the first round of Japan's 2002 amateur draft. However, he was not drafted. This was surprising since an American major league scout, who commented on the condition of anonymity, asserted: "He should have been a top five pick over there [Japan]. He gets it up to 93-94 (mph), and he throws four different pitches for strikes."[20] Tadano was promising enough to make him a top draft pick contender in Japan and to receive attention from the Twins, the Padres, and the Braves in America, so the barriers to his success had nothing to do with his pitching; instead, it had everything to with his "catching." Kaz Tadano was not drafted or readily signed because of his involvement in a porn video that involved his playing the passive role during anal sex in the Japanese gay adult video series "Babylon."

"Babylon 34" was released shortly before the Japanese baseball draft in 2002. The video, which trades on the familiar gay porn narrative of coerced sex, features Tadano and three of his teammates literally rear-ending a Japanese gang member's car. In retaliation, the gang member forces Tadano and his teammates to have sex with one another at gunpoint. The scene includes elements of bondage and S&M when Tadano wears a leash and dog collar while playing the passive role in anal sex. This video was so problematic that when the Japanese news media began speculating about a top player, whose draft status was diminishing secondary to his appearance in a porn video, Tadano was forced to seek baseball employment outside Japan.

Following his failure to draft with a Japanese team, Tadano tried to sign with an American major league organization. However, despite his considerable pitching talent, he had difficulty finding a team to sign him. Eventually, the Cleveland Indians signed Tadano cheaply, and he began playing on their farm and minor league teams. Tadano had finally secured a position with a professional baseball franchise, yet his position was far from secure, and its tenuous nature required a series of rhetorical and public relation negotiations. Evidence suggesting this motivation can be found in Chris Kline's ESPN interview with Cleveland Indians General Manager Mark Shapiro, where Shapiro acknowledged the care Tadano's situation and signing would require:

> Signing him was not like the traditional minor league signing. The circumstances warranted support and management. As soon as we went forward with an attempt to sign him, we knew there were certain elements that differed from a typical signing. We knew we needed to support him not only culturally, but at some point we anticipated supporting him through all the extra focus, attention, and potential distractions that could come along because he was young and made this one-time mistake.[21]

In the same interview, Shapiro acknowledged that the Cleveland Indians management team had made certain Tadano's involvement with gay porn was indeed a "one-time mistake" before signing him:

> After we had chance to talk to him and watch his interaction with other players, we made the decision to sign him. It was our assessment that the event in the past was an isolated incident. It was not a pattern of current or future behavior. He was young and made a one-time mistake.[22]

Shapiro's admission that the team's management had observed Tadano interacting with other players before signing him evidences a concern beyond worrying over Tadano repeating his pornographic participation, and it suggests something of a surveillance of his sexuality. In other words, they made certain Tadano was a one-time switch hitter and not a gay player.

Signing Tadano to their farm league, the Cleveland Indians were buying Tadano cheaply and slowly investing in him before the possibility of his making a major league appearance. This awareness was clearly expressed by the Indians farm team director John Farrell when he stated:

> We have always anticipated there to be a media blitz at some point and the closer he gets to the major leagues, [the news] was bound to come out. We were more than willing to take that challenge on.[23]

Farrell was correct. The closer Tadano got to the majors the more he had to negotiate the scandal. This resulted in his making two separate apologies to his Kinston teammates in 2003 and to his Akron teammates later in the same year.

Then, in January 2004, before he made his major league debut with the Indians, Tadano held a press conference to apologize for his participation in the video. Tadano, who does not speak English, nevertheless managed a clearly and cleverly worded apology. He stated:

> I did participate in a video and I regret it very much. It was a one-time incident that showed bad judgment and will never be repeated. I was young, playing baseball, and going to college and my teammates and I needed money. Frankly, if I were more mature and had really thought about the implications of what I did, it never would have happened.[24]

Tadano concluded by taking a page from Mike Piazza's playbook by asserting: "I'm not gay. I'd like to clear that fact up right now."[25]

Tadano's short statement belies the complexity of his defensive rhetoric. Tadano's explanation includes the usual fast pitch in response to the evidence of pornographic photographs: "I was young and needed the money." This discursive defense invokes the clichéd rationale of naïveté and economic need. Given the potential stigma surrounding the nature of his particular pornographic pictures, however, Tadano threw a discursive eephus pitch by simultaneously subordinating his involvement in a gay porn video to the ideological pillars of professional sports. By claiming the impulse behind his participation in the video as an act of teamsmanship—"my teammates and I needed the money"—Tadano invoked a foundational discourse of team sports that managed to subordinate the motivations of sexual preference to fraternal practice. Moreover, by claiming heterosexuality, Tadano performed an identity that removed the implications of homosexuality from the homosexual act. The result was a change up discourse that provided all the familiar moves of homosociality and heterosexuality and left critics unexpectedly swinging at the air.

NOTES

1. Jim Buzinski and Cyd Zeigler, Jr., *The Outsports Revolution: Truth and Myth in the World of Gay Sports* (Boston: Alyson, 2007).
2. Ibid., v.
3. Patricia Nell Warren, *The Lavender Locker Room: 3000 Years of Great Athletes Whose Sexual Orientation was Different* (Beverly Hills: Wildcat Press, 2006).
4. Barry Jackson and Steve Rothaus, "Hardaway's Apology Fails to win over Critic: I Hate Gay People," *The National Post*, February 16, 2007, sec. Sports.
5. Buzinski and Zeigler, *The Outsports Revolution*, vi.
6. Neal Travis, "In and Out with the Mets," *New York Post*, May 20, 2002, Sec. Page Six.
7. Rafael Hermoso, "Baseball, Piazza Responds to Gossip Column," *The New York Times*, May 22, 2002, sec. D.
8. Dave Goldiner and Adam Rubin, "Mets Star: I'm STRAIGHT, Relaxed Piazza Quashes Rumors that he's Coming Out," *Daily News*, May 22, 2002, sec. News.
9. Mark Starr, "Starr Gazing: Is Baseball a Homophobic Bastion?," *Newsweek*, May 23, 2002, sec. Society.
10. John Smallwood, "Baseball Isn't Ready for Gay Player," *Philadelphia Daily News*, May 23, 2002, sec. D1.

11. Michelle Foucault, *Fearless Speech*, ed. Joseph Pearson (Los Angeles: Semiotext(e), 2001).

12. Jim Buzinski, "Double Standard Still Rules: Why Mike Piazza Got all the Attention While Sue Wicks Was Ignored," Outsports Columns. http://www.outsports.com/columns/suewicksmikepiazza.htm.

13. Ibid.

14. "Just Asking," *New York Post*, December 19, 2006, sec. Page Six.

15. Michael Butterworth, "Mike Piazza and the Discourse of Gay Identity in the National Pastime," *Journal of Sport and Social Issues* 30, no. 2 (2006): 138157.

16. Michael O'Keeffe, foreword to *The Outsports Revolution: Truth and Myth in the World of Gay Sports*, by Jim Buzinski and Cyd Zeigler, Jr. (Boston: Alyson, 2007), xii.

17. Shannon Ragland. *The Thin Thirty* (Louisville: Set Shot Press, 2007).

18. Buzinski offers a wider discussion of this trend as it involves pro athletes from other sports, who are also publicly declaring their heterosexuality, see Jim Buzinski, "Jeff Garcia: I'm Not Gay," Outsports NFL. http://www.outsports.com/nfl/2004/0204garcia.htm.

19. Ira Berkow, "Player's Tainted Past Stirs Little Commotion," *The New York Times*, June 17, 2004, sec. D.

20. Chris Kline, "Tribe Ignores Past, Reaps Reward," Baseball America. http://www.baseballamerica.com/today/news/030904tadano.html.

21. Ibid.

22. Ibid.

23. Ibid.

24. Berkow, "Player's Tainted Past."

25. Ibid.

REFERENCES

Berkow, I. "Player's Tainted Past Stirs Little Commotion." *New York Times*, June 17, 2004, sec. D.

Butterworth, M. "Mike Piazza and the Discourse of Gay Identity in the National Pastime." *Journal of Sport and Social Issues* 30, no. 2 (2006): 138–157.

Buzinski, J. "Double Standard Still Rules: Why Mike Piazza Got all the Attention While Sue Wicks Was Ignored." *Outsports Columns*. http://www.outsports.com/columns/ suewicksmikepiazza.htm

———. "Jeff Garcia: I'm Not Gay." Outsports NFL. http://www.outsports.com/ nfl/2004/0204garcia.htm.

Buzinski, J., and Cyd Zeigler, Jr. *The Outsports Revolution: Truth and Myth in the World of Gay Sports*. Boston: Alyson, 2007.

Foucault, M. *Fearless Speech*. Edited by Joseph Pearson. Los Angeles, Semiotext(e), 2001.

Goldiner, D., and A. Rubin. "Mets Star: "I'm STRAIGHT, Relaxed Piazza Quashes Rumors that He's Coming Out," *Daily News*, May 22, 2002, sec. News.

Hermoso, R. "Baseball, Piazza Responds to Gossip Column." *The New York Times*, May 22, 2002, sec. D.

Jackson, B., and S. Rothaus. "Hardaway's Apology Fails to win over Critic: I Hate Gay People." *The National Post*, February 16, 2007, sec. Sports.

"Just Asking." *New York Post*. December 19, 2006, sec. Page Six.

Kline, C. "Tribe Ignores Past, Reaps Reward," Baseball America. http://www.baseballamerica.com/today/news/030904tadano.html.

O'Keeffe, M. Foreword to *The Outsports Revolution: Truth and Myth in the World of Gay Sports*, by Jim Buzinski and Cyd Zeigler, Jr. Boston: Alyson, 2007.

Ragland, R. *The Thin Thirty*. Louisville: Set Shot Press, 2007.

Smallwood, J. "Baseball isn't Ready for Gay Player." *Philadelphia Daily News*, May 23, 2002, sec. D1.

Starr, M. "Starr Gazing: Is Baseball a Homophobic Bastion?" *Newsweek*, May 23, 2002, sec. Society.

Travis, N. "In and Out with the Mets." *New York Post*, May 20, 2002, Sec. Page Six.

Warren, P. N. *The Lavender Locker Room: 3000 Years of Great Athletes Whose Sexual Orientation was Different*. Beverly Hills: Wildcat Press, 2006.

Chapter 7

Communitarian Considerations for the Coverage of "Outed" Athletes

Richard Kenney

The way we construct and communicate our lived experiences has become intertwined with the lives, loves, and liaisons of celebrity entertainers and athletes. They lead the evening news and dominate the daily discourse of the papers, the Internet, the water-cooler talk. Audiences wait anxiously to hear word of O. J. Simpson's or Scott Petersen's guilt or innocence and agonize over the breakups of Brad and Jennifer, of Ben and Jennifer, of Kobe and Shaq. When Princess Diana died, many among the millions who mourned said they had felt a close "personal relationship" with her, just as President Bush and other modern evangelicals describe their religious devotions. Celebrity worshippers pilgrimage to Althorp Park to pay honor to Diana, just as others go to Graceland to visit the shrine to Elvis Presley.

Despite all this implied reverence, however, the culture of celebrity neither guarantees not promotes ethicalor even equaltreatment for all who enter the media spotlight. Paparazzi hound the photogenic incessantly, even to death, as in the case of Diana; private investigators in the employ of tabloid publishers snoop through the garbage of even pseudo-celebrities, such as Henry Kissinger; and Web site operators post the latest private pornographic video of ingénues like Paris Hilton. Neimark (1995) argues that as fame grows, celebrities and their fans are diminished: "a certain cynicism has set in among us all, and a rabid fascination not only with the false beauty of the glorified, sterilized celebrity, but also with the dark and seamy underside" (57). We "both elevate and destroy our celebrities," who "are worthy of our slavish devotion, attention, and respect" yet "are just like us . . . people with problems [who] drink too much or hit their wives or have bad relationships."

> Today we shuttle routinely between Ivory-soap versions of celebrities—their perfect marriages, perfect children, and perfect careers—and genuine slander. Cindy Crawford and Richard Gere become the golden couple when they first marry, only a few years later having to take out full-page newspaper ads to protest that they are not homosexual and that their marriage is real. Soon after, they divorce. (57)

This wicked dichotomy applies not only to Hollywood celebrities, but also to those who play professional sports. Athletic Arthurian archetypes who enjoy the hero worship of millions and reap financial windfalls in the hundreds of millions are hardly immune to speculation about their vices as well as their virtues. From Paul Hornung to Jose Canseco to Kobe Bryant, players are placed upon a pedestal by fans and sports media willing to temporarily turn a blind eye to their heroes' hubris, only watch them fall from grace at the whim of gossipers and the whiff of a scandal. Whether exposed honestly in possibly legitimate news stories about gambling, substance abuse, or sex crimes, or whether inaccurately wronged by news accounts grown from gossip, athletes—like other entertainers—often endure invasions of their private lives that sometimes leave them subject to harm greater than just to their reputation.

In recent years, two superstars, one a major-league baseball slugger and the other a Pro Bowl quarterback, suffered the slings and arrows of outrageous publicity—not to mention the taunts and threats of teammates and opponents—after mistakenly being "outed" as gay. Although neither New York Mets catcher Mike Piazza nor then-San Francisco 49ers quarterback Jeff Garcia was outed initially by credible mainstream media, and the utilitarian paradigm of traditional, objective news media practice ensured that these disclosures—despite the principals' vehement denials—would receive wider circulation and gain in currency. Although the U.S. courts have decided that calling someone "gay" isn't *ipso facto* defamatory, society's ingrained cultural animosity toward gays suggests that athletes who risk full contact on the playing field are particularly jeopardized when outed by the media. Their health and well-being are threatened when the scarlet G becomes a bull's-eye on their uniform.

True, gay athletes have endured social inequalities and public prejudices since long before the current outing trend; those problems are not produced by media discourse alone. But longstanding media practices contribute to such hegemonies through the traditional reproduction of ideas and construction of social realities. Some journalists and gay activists have argued that disclosure and debate about outings serve a greater social good. For example, post-hoc attempts at justifying the publication of information about Arthur Ashe's AIDS infection framed it as a vital discussion of public health policies and attitudes—all at the expense of his and his family's privacy (Black, Barney, and Steele 1999). But when it comes to the reporting of gossip, rumors (whether founded or unfounded), or any legally private facts about celebrity athletes as news, traditional values of media practices are inadequate. The utilitarian dependence on amoral craft values—among them: timeliness, prominence, conflict, and controversy—simply does not meet fundamental ethical obligations of truth, justice, and equality. Outing gay athletes singles them out in ways that violate Aristotelian concepts of virtue, Kantian ideals of dignity, and Rawlsian notions of social justice and thus represents a callous and amoral disregard for the potential harmfulness of unwanted publicity.

I suggest in this essay that when it comes to the reporting of gossip and unfounded rumors about celebrity athletes as news, traditional values of media practices are inadequate. They are amoral in the sense that they do not protect human dignity and well-being: the mutual interests of every member in a society. In contrast with popular ethical foundations that underlie traditional news media practice, however, communitarianism offers a distinctive and normative approach to coverage of gay/lesbian/transgender issues in general and to the outing of gay athletes in particular. Using communitarianism as the ethical framework for critique, my study of the outing of gay athletes in contact sports examines serious issues of privacy and harm.

In this essay, I focus on two particular cases—Piazza's and Garcia's—thatare illustrative because of the way falsehoods about each became "known" truths, first through entertain or alternative media and then through mainstream media.

OUT IN SPORTS

The Origins of Outing Athletes

Among the earliest athletes in modern U.S. sport known to be gay was Bill Tilden, the tennis great who, in the 1920s won seven U.S. Open titles, three Wimbledon championships, seven U.S. clay court titles, and six U.S. doubles championships (Deford 1975). Tilden's homosexuality became generally known in the 1930s, when, as his skills faded, he was eventually ostracized and banned from major tournaments. He was arrested in 1946 and 1949 and jailed on charges involving teenage boys; he died broke and alone in Hollywood a few years later. But for all the damage to reputation and livelihood done to Tilden by the gossiping about his sexual orientation, his physical presence and performance as an athlete was never in danger because tennis is not a contact sport. For the purposes of this study then, in which I examine the implications of potential physical harm to outed athletes, I consider athletes in only two major contact sports in America: football and baseball.

Football: Down and Out

The first such professional athlete from a contact sport to come out as homosexual was David Kopay, a running back for the Washington Redskins in the 1960s and 1970s who came out in 1975 after he had retired from playing (Kopay and Young 1977). His disclosure was triggered by the anonymous outing by the *Washington Star* of three of his teammates. Although Kopay did not identify him in his book, Redskins tight end Jerry Smith was Kopay's first lover (Buzinski 2002). Kopay now says that Smith was one of the anonymous sources in the *Star* article (Provenzano 2003). Kopay also says that teammates may have known Smith was gay and that some tried to bully Smith, who was known as one of the NFL's toughest players, while others defended him. Kopay also says Smith had lovers among other NFL players. Smith died from AIDS-related causes in 1986, shortly after disclosing he had contracted the disease, but Smith never disclosed that he was gay.

Since then, two other NFL players have come out, both in retirement: Roy Simmons, a New York Giants and Washington Redskins offensive lineman from 1979 to 1983 who came out as a bisexual on a 1992 episode of *The Phil Donahue Show* and who disclosed he was HIV-positive in a *New York Times* article (Orth 2003), and Esera

Tualo, an offensive lineman for several NFL teams in the 1990s who came out on the October 29, 2002, episode of HBO's *Real Sports* (Provenzano 2002).

> Simmons would never have dreamed of declaring himself gay during the four seasons he played for the New York Giants and the Redskins, for fear of destroying his career. "The N.F.L. has a reputation," he said, "and it's not even a verbal thing; it's just known. You are gladiators; you are male; you kick butt." (sect. 9, 1)

Tualo (2002) came out on a broadcast episode of HBO's *Real Sports* in October 2002 and in an *ESPN The Magazine* essay that same month. He wrote that he could never talk about it for fear of being released by his team or injured intentionally by another player. "I was sure that if a GM didn't get rid of me for the sake of team chemistry, another player would intentionally hurt me, to keep up the image. Because the NFL is a supermacho culture. It's a place for gladiators. And gladiators aren't supposed to be gay." In response to Tualo's disclosure, Garrison Hearst, a San Francisco 49ers running back, told a reporter: "Aww, hell no! I don't want any faggots on my team. I know this might not be what people want to hear, but that's a punk. I don't want any faggots in this locker room" (Bryant 2002). Hearst was forced to apologize, and the 49ers issued statements deploring what he said.

Hearst's remark struck more deeply within the 49ers organization that either he or most of his employers first realized. The team's trainer, Lindsy McLean, came out publicly two years later, after nearly a quarter-century of working in fear of "being terrorized by players he'd kept on the field and in the money" (Bull 2004, 90). McLean's sexual orientation was at best an open secret; he had taken his partner to a team Christmas party in 1982. For more than two decades he endured verbal putdowns. McLean described how he kept his head down or stared at walls around naked players and kept them covered in the training room. Still, he recalled a player grumbling within earshot, "That faggot trainer's not taking care of me" (93).

The 49ers won a record five Super Bowls with McLean as their trainer. After Hearst was injured in 1999, fracturing his fibula, McLean spent part of the next two years helping him heal and rehabilitate his leg for a successful comeback. A year later, he read the "faggots" quote from Hearst. The team's owner, John York, spoke with Hearst, and the team induced Hearst to apologize publicly. McLean says he was never angry with Hearst, who says he learned McLean was gay when he joined the team in 1997 and didn't have a problem with it. Still, Hearst "can't bring himself to say the word gay" (95). The two have never broached the subject but maintain a cordial relationship.

Other NFL players have endured publicized rumors about their sexuality and have felt compelled to deny they were gay as a way to defend themselves and pre-empt backlash, including being abandoned by their front office, abused by fans, ostracized by teammates, and injured by opponents. Kordell Stewart announced publicly that he had met with his Pittsburgh Steelers teammates the previous season to assure them that rumors stemming from a *Sports Illustrated* story that referred to fan speculation about his sexual preference had not affected his play (Harlan, 2004). *Sports Illustrated* and Stewart addressed the sexuality issue:

> some Steelers admit they were fazed by rumors that Stewart was gay, until he called a meeting before the 1999 season and issued a denial that included graphic descriptions of heterosexual acts he enjoys. "I could see the humor in the situation," Stewart says, "so I decided to have some fun with it. At one point I said, 'You'd better not leave your girlfriends around me, because I'm out to prove a point.' A couple of guys said, 'F— you, Kordell,' and we all cracked up." (Silver 2002, 40)

More recently, Atlanta Falcons quarterback Michael Vick went on local radio to defend himself against a bizarre and intentionally spurious rumor that he was gay (Buzinski 2004). A news-hoax Web site, Global Associated News, had briefly allowed the posting of a fake story that began, "He's here, he's queer, and his name is Michael Vick. Shocking sports fans around the globe, NFL representatives for Michael Vick issued a public statement today confirming rumors that began circulating earlier this week about his sexual preferences and homosexual lifestyle." A Web site disclaimer read: "If you are reading this page, it's likely that you read a 'fake' story from the 'global associated news" – a totally bogus news source. This news story was dynamically generated by someone who visited the site. It was created by dynamically inserting a name into a template on this Web site." Still, Vick addressed the issue with Atlanta radio station V-103 and issued a non-denial denial: "I won't even feed into that . . . Everybody who knows me, knows how I get down. It's not even an issue."

Potential for Harm

Hearst and his 49ers teammates were not the only ones who have helped create an unsafe environment for gays in football. At times, the climate has been made uncomfortable by epithets used as insults. In December 2003, Detroit Lions president Matt Millen, a former 49er played while McLean was the team's trainer, called the Kansas City Chiefs' wide receiver Johnnie Morton a "faggot" during a post-game rant (Sylvester 2003). Morton apologized for his own remark, which prompted Millen's outburst, but added: "What he said is demeaning and bigoted. Jeremy Shockey got in trouble for saying it about a coach, and now we have a president of a team making statements like that. It's totally unacceptable" (C1). He was referring to an incident in 2004, when New York Giants tight end Jeremy Shockey made headlines by calling former head coach Bill Parcells a "homo" ("Shockey," 2004). Both Millen and Shockey apologized for their remarks without admitting wrong.

Other reactions to players' homosexuality have been regarded as more ominous. In 1998, former Buffalo Bills and Green Bay Packers player Reggie White, a fierce defensive end and pass rusher who was elected to the NFL Hall of Fame, declared the nation has retreated from God by allowing homosexuality to "run rampant." Other statements attributed White, who died in late 2004: "Let me explain something when I'm talking about sin, and I'm talking about all sin. One of the biggest ones that has been talked about that has really become a debate in America is homosexuality;" "I'm offended that homosexuals will say that homosexuals deserve rights;" "Homosexuality is a decision, it's not a race. . . . " (Zeigler 2004). Tualo's former Green Bay Packers teammate, Shannon Sharpe, typified what many felt was the view among NFL players. "Had [Esera] come out on a Monday, with Wednesday, Thursday, Friday practices, he'd have never gotten to the other team. He would have never gotten to the game on Sunday" (Zeigler 2004). And Simmons' former teammate, Butch Woolfolk, who played for the Giants and also with the Houston Oilers and Detroit Lions, acknowledged that if Simmons had disclosed his sexual orientation earlier, it would have wrecked his career: "You can be a wife-beater, do drugs, get in a car wreck and the team will take care of you. But if you're gay, it's like the military: don't ask, don't tell" (Orth 2003, sect. 9, 1).

Former 49ers trainer McLean can testify to the potential for physical abuse and harm generated by homophobic attitudes in the NFL. The verbal putdowns he endured eventually turned to physical abuse. In the early 1990s:

> a 350-pound lineman would chase him around, grab him from behind, push him against a locker and simulate rape. Get over here, bitch. I know what you want. The lineman . . . reprised his act whenever he could, even after he was traded to another team, he'd sneak up on McLean in the locker room or alongside the team bus. (Bull 2004, 93)

McLean's coming out in the magazine had a ripple effect that turned the private life of 49ers quarterback Jeff Garcia public and led to media prying into his sexuality. Asked by a reporter for a small California newspaper for his reaction to the McLean story, Garcia replied that he himself had been "the subject of inaccurate speculation for years. 'I've heard the rumor myself that I'm gay' " (Maiocco 2004, C3).

The rumors to which Garcia alluded had previously circulated about two married NFL quarterbacks who had won Super Bowls. Garcia maintained that such gossip came with the territory.

> "Part of it is the label," Garcia said, "being successful, being single, being the quarterback of the San Francisco 49ers, speaking properly, having a sense of style. A combination of those things gets you categorized as being gay. Just because an individual in his 30s hasn't found true love . . . " Garcia . . . said he has learned of the rumors from friends who have been approached by others who do not know him. (Maiocco 2003, C3)

A combination of the endless rumors and Garcia's own admission that "I've heard the rumor myself that I'm gay" may have fueled the firestorm of controversy that flashed in summer 2004 when a former teammate hinted that the rumor about Garcia, who was subsequently traded to the Cleveland Browns, was true.

The Garcia Case

The first media reports about Garcia in Cleveland supported the idea he was demonstratively heterosexual.

> New Browns quarterback Jeff Garcia has yet to throw one touchdown pass for Cleveland, but the former San Francisco 49er is

> certainly scoring well in making new (and interesting) friends here. Word is Garcia is dating Avon Lake native Carmella DeCesare, *Playboy* Magazine's current Playmate of the Year and tongues are wagging that the Browns QB has ALREADY become a major, popular celebrity on the local social scene. (Brown 2004a)

Later, a reporter for *Playboy* magazine asked another former 49ers player whether he thought Garcia was gay. The player, Terrell Owens of the Philadelphia Eagles, who had feuded publicly with Garcia when the two were teammates, replied: "Like my boy tells me: If it looks like a rat and smells like a rat, by golly, it is a rat" ("Twenty," 2004), implying that Garcia was gay. Given the opportunity to clarify, Owens did not disavow his statement.

> "It was just some loose conversation and they asked me about it," Owens said. "I just told them that my boy always told me that if it looks like a rat and smells like a rat, obviously, by golly, it must be a rat.
>
> "I didn't say he was gay. Like I said, the conversation and interview was loose. And from my knowledge, I'm not sure if Jeff is gay or not. He had a girlfriend when we were in San Francisco, and there have been recent reports that he has a girlfriend now.
>
> "Everyone is going to make a big deal about it," Owens said, "but like I said, it's not like I came out and said Jeff is gay. People asked me similar questions about Steve Young, so everybody is going to have their rumors." (O'Rourke 2004, C1)

In Cleveland, Garcia was quick to dismiss Owens' comments as "ridiculous": "It is really a waste of my time to sit here and to have to answer to such ridiculous, untrue comments that are made out there in the world today" (Windhorst 2004, C1)

Ridiculous or not, the story would not go away. Although Owens's initial remark appeared in an issue of *Playboy* that had not even reached newsstands yet, sports-talk radio and the Internet took up the topic; the mainstream media then pounced on it and made it front-page news in some sports sections. ESPN devoted coverage to the story, including it in a story about homosexuals in the NFL. A Google search revealed that more than 150 media reports repeated the remark, amplifying it and framing it to assert that Owens was, indeed, outing Garcia. As the regular season of play began, Garcia remained an easy target for cheap shots even in mainstream media.

> During a recent conference call featuring Fox network football commentators, we asked pregame studio analyst Terry Bradshaw (and others) for comments on Garcia. With a laugh, Bradshaw responded, "If it looks like a rat . . . " before letting his voice trail off and leaving the sentence unfinished. Asked to explain what he meant, Bradshaw would only add, "Ah, I don't know about Garcia"—but made no other comment on the Browns QB. (Brown 2004, C2)

Two months later, when Owens and his new team, the Philadelphia Eagles, traveled to Cleveland to play Garcia's Browns, the conflict resurfaced, manufactured for news by mainstream media in coverage during the week preceding the game. Owens sought to evade reporters' questions, at one point insisting that they, and not he, were guilty of bringing it up again and again. Still, Garcia felt compelled to defend himself against Owens.

> "I don't know why he can't let it go," Garcia said. "I mean, it's unfortunate because I've never looked at T.O. as being an enemy of mine. I don't know where the anger or the negativity or the criticism comes from, and why certain comments have been made, because he's known my situation in the past."He's always known my girlfriends, things like that, and to have the things said that have been said, I just don't know where it comes from." (Withers 2004)

The story followed Garcia into the locker room for the post-game interviews.

> The questions about Terrell Owens weren't going anywhere on Sunday, not after a long day in which Owens and the Eagles had the last—albeit delayed—laugh against the Cleveland Browns, a 34-31 win in overtime. Not after a long week in which Owens continued to slyly rip his former teammate. The questions weren't going anywhere and neither was Jeff Garcia until he addressed them.
> "I really wasn't paying attention," Garcia said when someone asked how he thought the Cleveland defense handled itself against Owens. "I was thinking about what I had to do."
> . . . Somewhere in the back of his mind, whether he admitted it or not, there was the distraction of knowing his personal tormentor also was on the opposite sideline. (Ford 2004)

Even after that game was played out, the Garcia-is-gay story played on.

Baseball: Out at Home

Major-league umpire Dave Pallone, who was fired in 1988 after rumors began to circulate about his sexual orientation, says you could field an all-star team with the gay players in baseball (Pallone and Steinberg 1990). In reality, only two gay baseball players have come out, both in retirement. Glenn Burke, who played outfield for the Los Angeles Dodgers and Oakland Athletics, came out in 1982 and maintained for years that he was blackballed from baseball (Burke and Sherman 1995). Burke died from AIDS-related complications in 1995. Outfielder Billy Bean played for the Detroit Tigers, Los Angeles Dodgers, and San Diego Padres from 1987 to 1995 and came out in 1999. Bean, whom Dodgers manager Tommy Lasorda described as "the boy of every girl's dream," lost his partner to an AIDS-related death—an incident he kept secret from his team—the same day the Padres sent him down to the minor leagues for the last time. Bean has become a successful restaurateur in retirement and is an active speaker about gay causes who says he hopes someday a gay will pioneer acceptance in baseball but thinks the challenge is daunting and one he was unwilling to accept himself. "After my incidental outing, fans and sportswriters rushed to anoint me the gay Jackie Robinson. Let me make one thing perfectly clear: I'm no Jackie Robinson" (Bean and Bull 2003, 233).

A gay Jackie Robinson seemed to be just what New York Mets manager Bobby Valentine was calling for when, near the end of a long article in the June/July 2003 issue of the men's magazine *Details*, he said baseball was "probably ready for an openly gay player," adding, "the players are diverse enough now that I think they could handle it" (Litke 2003). *New York Post* gossip columnist Neal Travis (2003) called Valentine's comments a "preemptory strike" designed to more easily allow one of his known gay players to come out: "There is a persistent rumor around town that one Mets star who spends a lot of time with pretty models in clubs is actually gay and has started to think about declaring his sexual orientation" (6).

The Piazza Case

By noon the next day, sports-fan radio talk shows were abuzz with gossip and guessing about the player's identity (Acee and Finley 2003). The speculation calculus added up to the name of Mets star catcher Mike Piazza. Some stations aired a rumor that Piazza was involved with a local male TV personality. Factoring into the equation was a previous anonymous outing of a major-league baseball star by the editor-in-chief of *Out*, who reported that he was having an affair with a major-league baseball player from "an East Coast franchise . . . not his team's biggest star but a very recognizable media figure all the same" (Lemon 2001). The journalistic irony was that the editor of the nation's largest-circulation gay magazine devoted to outing chose not to identify the player but let the broad brush of gossip paint many indiscriminately.

Piazza's name had been bandied about only by alternative media of sports-talk radio and blogging. He had not yet been outed in mainstream media, but newspaper and broadcast reporters also were beginning to listen to the pervasive messages that were outing Piazza in alternative media. Piazza called a press conference, and a crowd of mainstream media representatives was waiting for him at the batting cage before the Mets' next game at Shea Stadium in New York. "So Mike," a reporter asked as journalists jockeyed for position, "are you gay?" He replied, "I'm not gay. I'm heterosexual. That's pretty much it. That's pretty much all I can say" (Acee and Finley, D1). "I can't control what people think. That's obvious. And I can't convince people what to think. I can only say what I know and what the truth is and that's I'm heterosexual and I date women. That's it. End of story" (Litke 2003).

One journalist in particular, however, *New York Post* sports columnist Wallace Matthews, did not think it the end of the story. Matthews wrote a column critical of his own newspaper for reporting the rumor in the first place.

> Valentine's comments to *Details* sparked an irresponsible 'blind' item in Monday's *Post*, in which a gossip columnist reprinted a scurrilous rumor concerning an unnamed Met. The gossip columnist then acknowledged he was unable to substantiate any part of the rumor. He printed it anyway. The Mets' reaction, and Piazza's statements avowing his heterosexuality, were in direct response to that item. But in truth, there was no reason to respond to the item and even less reason to print it. (Matthews 2003)

The *Post* spiked Matthews' column, but Matthews posted it on the Internet the next morning. Fired that same day, Matthews later told ESPN Radio that the initial rumor—the blind item on the tabloid's gossip page—couldn't have run in the sports section of the newspaper because the ethical standard was too high.

Piazza was not the first athlete anonymously and indirectly outed by the *Post* who felt compelled to defend himself. In February 2003, Page Six:

> suggested that a former baseball player who was the subject of a recent biography was gay. Sandy Koufax, who was the topic of a book released in 2002, thought the *Post* implied he was gay. The Hall of Famer broke ties with the Dodgers, the only team he played for, because team owner Rupert Murdoch also owned the *Post*. (Buzinski 2003)

Potential for Harm

That both players responded in such a way to rumors about their sexuality "speaks to the media's power and the sensitive nature of such allegations" (Buzinski 2003). Both took drastic actions to quell rumors that never named them specifically. Consider the following quotes from major-league baseball players reacting to questions about gays in general, hypothetical teammates in particular:

> **John Smoltz**, Atlanta Braves pitcher, 2004, to the Associated Press when asked about gay marriage: "What's next? Marrying animals?" (Cosgrove-Mather, 2004). Smoltz claimed the quote doesn't accurately reflect his views (Anti-gay, 2007). He also said he wouldn't have a problem having a gay teammate "unless it compromised the team."
> **Eddie Perez**, Atlanta Braves catcher, 2004: "If I knew a guy was gay, then I could work it out. I could be prepared. I could hide when I'm getting disrobed. It would be hard to play with someone all year and then find out they're gay." (Cosgrove-Mather, 2004) Perez claimed he was misquoted by an AP reporter (Anti-gay, 2007).
> **Todd Jones**, Colorado Rockies pitcher, 2002: "I wouldn't want a gay guy being around me. It's got nothing to do with me being scared. That's the problem: All these people say he's got all these rights. Yeah, he's got rights or whatever, but he shouldn't walk around proud. It's like he's rubbing it in our face. 'See me, hear me roar.' We're not trying to be close-minded, but then again, why be confrontational when you don't really have to be?" (Anti-gay, 2007)

It cannot be lost on any prospective gay Jackie Robinson contemplating his future or fate that all three players quoted are directly involved in the calling of pitches directed toward batters at varying velocities, angles, and trajectories.

WHAT THE MEDIA ETHICISTS HAVE TO SAY

Media ethics codes provide little guidance for journalists trying to decide how to handle gossip about an athlete's sexual orientation. In addressing privacy issues, ethicists and practitioners tend toward utilitarian justifications in the abstract.

The Associated Press Managing Editors Statement of Ethical Principles (2005) is touted as "a model against which news and editorial staff members can measure their performance." Yet its prescriptions are broad and either ill-defined or undefined. For example, it describes a "good newspaper" as one that "avoids practices that would conflict with the ability to report and present news in a fair, accurate and unbiased manner," but it doesn't define, for instance, fairness. APME adds that a good newspaper "should respect the individual's right to privacy," but the ethics statement does not define that ambiguity either.

In his semantic analysis of the wording of a draft of that code, Merrill (1997) characterized the principle of guarding against invading a person's privacy as "part of a basic respect for others" (186). Acknowledging privacy's complexity, he advised journalists to "take care not to intrude into the lives of private individuals." Merrill does not, however, differentiate for public figures or public officials, a step that one must assume leaves them not a target for fairness, but rather, fair game.

Englehardt and Barney (2002) did not directly address outing or coverage of a person's sexual orientation, but they do seek to answer a question they pose themselves from a clearly teleological perspective: "Does invasion of privacy serve the public?" (179). Weighing competing interests—the individual versus society—the authors tipped the scale in favor of "more public information rather than less" on the "assumption that 'to publish is good' and the equally troubling assumption that "secrecy (withholding information from audiences) is inevitably more damaging than disclosure." The utilitarian face of this prescription is hardly hidden behind a thin veil of deontology.

Black, Barney, and Steele's (1999) *Doing Ethics in Journalism* handbook, which grew out of the Society of Professional Journalists' ongoing discussion of ethics, followed this same utilitarian curve. Most of the book's prescriptions center on the SPJ Code of Ethics, which comprises four major principles and their underlying guidelines. Although several principles and guidelines could be construed to relate to outing, the second principle, "Minimize Harm," addresses privacy—and, thereby, outing—most clearly:

> Recognize that private people have a greater right to control information about themselves than do public officials and others who seek power, influence or attention. Only an overriding public need can justify intrusion into anyone's privacy.
>
> Show good taste. Avoid pandering to lurid curiosity. (7)

The phrase "overriding public need," however, opens the door to the utilitarian rationale that somehow the greater good may be served by disclosing private and potentially embarrassing and damaging facts about a person—a clear violation of the harm principle. One of the book's case studies, " 'Outing' Arthur Ashe?" includes a thoughtful discussion of the competing interests in the "precarious balance between the principles of maximizing truthtelling and minimizing harm" (243). The outcome of this debate over deontological principles still hinges on the utilitarian calculus of "whether the benefits outweigh the anguish" (244). To this, however, the authors added at least an element of moral reasoning beyond mere cost-benefit analysis: justification by publicity, which one might perceive as a nod to communitarian conversation.

Under the subheading "Homosexuality" (2003, 139), Day treated the ethics of news coverage of sexual orientation as largely descriptive. He refers to news organizations' unease in reporting, first, on the incident in 1975, in which a secretly gay ex-Marine named Oliver W. Sipple foiled an attempt to assassinate President Gerald Ford; and then, on a 1977 fire at a homosexual club in Washington, D.C. in which eight men died. Day notes that "until the 1980s, references to homosexuality were virtually taboo." Here, though, Day also attempted to articulate a normative ethic for outing:

> At times, the labeling of someone as gay or lesbian can still be harmful. In terms of news coverage, the key test for the moral agent is whether a person's sexual orientation is *relevant* [original italics retained] to the story, such as when a police officer is fired for being homosexual or a service member is discharged from the military because of his or her sexual orientation. (139–140)

Day identifies "*relevance*" [original italics retained] as alternately a key "ingredient" or "requirement" of "newsworthiness"—thus mistaking an amoral traditional news value for an ethical value.

Smith (2003) covered the same ground but more extensively, adding historical perspectives on the Sipple and fatal fire stories as outings and including a 2002 case. Additionally, Smith examined the opposite of outing: "inning" (221) —a term he applied to news organizations that "purposefully" hide the fact that people are homosexual. It is just this sort of descriptive ethics to which gay activists in general and Queer Nation in particular object.

Patterson and Wilkins (2008) forwent descriptions of how news media have handled outing. Instead, they offer in a framework that may be applicable to outing a theoretical discussion of normative "distinctions between secrecy and privacy" (124) and the concept of "discretion" (125). In the former section, the authors describe philosopher Louis W. Hodges's explanatory concept of "circles of intimacy" (124) and include a diagram (125). The diagram, as the authors interpret it, illustrates that as an individual's intimacy—her willingness to disclose—spreads, so does she progressively lose control over information; invasion of privacy occurs when people or institutions wrestle control over circles of intimacy from individuals and invade those circles. Here, Patterson and Wilkins offer normative advice that acknowledges the reality of traditional news values:

> Awareness of the concept will allow you to consider the rights of others as well as balance the needs of society in critical ways, particularly when the issue is newsworthy. Under at least some circumstances, invasion can be justified, but under other circumstances invading privacy constitutes usurping an individual's control and stripping him or her of individuality and human dignity. (124–125)

Clearly, this is a Kantian norm. Immediately following in the discussion of discretion, however, the authors abandoned the importance of individual human dignity in favor of a balance between "private information . . . and a public that might need the information or merely want the information" (125). The resolution to this apparent conflict of theories and its possible utilitarian leaning, the authors suggest, is "to rely on moral reasoning to decide if he is feeding the voyeur or the citizen in each of us" (126). The discursive strategy that comes next, though, speaks most loudly about the competing ideals:

> Kantian *theory* [italics added for emphasis] would suggest that the journalist treat even the indiscreet source as the journalist

> would wish to be treated, making publication of the indiscretion less likely. Yet many journalists claim that, in practice [italics added for emphasis], everything is "on-the-record" unless otherwise specified. (126)

This clearer delineation between the normativity of Kantian ethics and the descriptive prevailing journalistic ethic as utilitarian stresses the gap between theory and practice. Still, Patterson, and Wilkins (2008) offered moral guidance here, too, suggesting a return to Ross's list of prima facie duties. The result of this moral reasoning: "Which duties emerge as foremost to the journalist should make such decisions more consistent" (126).

Patterson and Wilkins (2008) turned to an idea suggested by media ethicist Deni Elliott, that one mass media function was "to provide information to citizens that will allow them to go about their daily lives in society, regardless of political outlook" (127). Following this notion, Patterson and Wilkins bolstered the overarching idea of the public need to know:

> Need to know is the most ethically compelling argument of the three. Need to know demands that an ethical case be constructed for making known information that others wish to keep private. Need to know also demands that journalists present the information in a manner that will make its important evident to a sometimes lazy citizenry. (127)

Embedded in this paragraph is a key to an emerging and potentially superior ethical construct: the triumph of pure moral reasoning over the presumption of traditional news practice based on a vague public right to know. The very phrases "most ethically compelling" and "demands that an ethical case be constructed" leave no doubt that the normativity of "ought" must prevail. Moreover, this normative argument advances the ethic by demanding Aristotelian excellence: to present the information in a way that makes its importance evident.

Patterson and Wilkins (2008) overlaid John Rawls's theory of social justice and the concept of the veil of ignorance against the privacy issue. The value of the "veil" here is that "how one retains both becomes a debate to be argued from all points of view without the bias of status" (128). Where the argument in favor of this rationale weakens, however, is when it is acknowledged that consensus need not exist behind the veil. This explanation of reflective equilibrium falters temporarily into a utilitarian imbalance of the needs (here, characterized as "betterment") of "most individuals in the social situation" outweighing either the individual or a minority number of individuals. Yet, Patterson and Wilkins acknowledged utilitarianism's failure by hastily adding:

> Reflective equilibrium summons what Rawls calls our "considered moral judgment." Decisions would be based on the principles we would be most unwilling to give up because we believe doing so would result in a grave wrongdoing for all. (129)

This consideration finally begins to hint at the communitarian ideal that will be the centerpiece of an alternative ethical construct toward which I am moving in this essay.

AN ALTERNATIVE ETHICS

Communitarianism, a radical social ethic based on notions of justice, covenant, and empowerment, presents a morally useful alternative to traditional libertarian and utilitarian press practice. In *Good News: Social Ethics and the Press* Christians, Ferre, and Fackler (1993) argued that neither persons nor their communities are paramount, but that their relationship to one another is (49). Communitarian ethics requires more of journalists than merely being fair in covering newsworthy events. "Under the notion that justice itself—and not merely haphazard public enlightenment—is a *telos* of the press, the news-media system stands under obligation to tell the stories that justice requires" (93). This prescription has special relevance in the case of athletes who in contact sports face the threat of real physical danger when singled out for their sexual orientation.

The communitarian perspective also demands that journalists acknowledge that reporting on whole communities, including otherwise marginalized groups, is not only a professional duty but also an ethical value. Not engaging the whole story of gay athletes—instead ignoring or avoiding telling stories about any particular person or group in a community—is journalism devoid of ethics. By not covering the oppression of gay athletes as fully as possible but instead choosing to ignore their plight, journalists are at least tacitly supporting a xenophobic ideology. The choice to concentrate coverage on constituents who "matter" socially represents a simplistic—but typically journalistic—utilitarian choice: favoring the greatest good for the greatest number. Choosing to ignore any segment of the community is a form of tacitly supporting an ideology of dangerous and harmful "-isms:" racism, sexism, or ageism, for example. Conversely, a thorough and ongoing discussion of such issues—or rather, the public conversation about them on the conversational commons that journalism could represent—is a way of challenging the dominant social ideology. Hence, communitarian journalism confronts morality and centralizes it in an alternative exercise of craft skills.

Communitarianism identifies an act as morally right when it is intended to "maintain the community" (Christians et al. 1993, 73). The focus is not on individual right, but the well-being of all humans. The primary duty, for journalists and others, is to treat others with dignity and care; the secondary duty is to readers (81). This last statement is significant in that it places care, or minimizing harm, ahead of truth-telling in the case of competing interests. That is a radical departure from other contemporary arguments for normative ethics, most of which maintain that, all things considered, the primary duty of journalism is truth/information.

The authors argued for the Kantian principle of "the sacredness of human dignity" (178). Journalists driven by a utilitarian ethics of traditional amoral news values are prone to leaving out those people who face obstacles: economic, racial, gender, physical, or emotional. Such obstacles leave them marginalized, powerless, and largely invisible—except in conflict.

CONCLUSION

Richard Greenberg's *Take Me Out*, which won the Tony for Best Broadway Play in 2003, dramatized a New York City baseball hero who announces that he is gay. That in itself represents a hopeful fiction, but the plot reveals—spoiler alert! —a revenge tragedy. The symbolism should not be lost on us. Outing itself is a revenge tragedy. Those who, like Signorile (1993), practice it, and those who, like the National Gay and Lesbian Task Force, tacitly condone it in the case of public officials and public figures, because "you can't be publicly attacking and hurting gay people and privately courting them" (Marech 2004) are Hobbesian characters acting in a war drama of all against all. Outing "uses sexual orientation as a weapon, which is everything we try to fight against," says Mark Shields, spokesman for the Human Rights Campaign. Assemblyman Mark Leno, D-San Francisco, however:

> views loss of privacy simply as the price of becoming a public figure—like it or not. "If you don't want (a secret) to come out and think it's no one's business, then don't enter into public life," said Leno, who is gay. "The public believes that everything is fair game. That's a fact of life." And the public has the Internet—enemy of secrets—at its disposal. (Marech 2004, A1)

Those who encourage outing in the name of political warfare, or journalistic objectivity, or competition for the scoop simply cannot justify their own amoral practices as moral. So what are the ethical rules of engagement for journalists in the practice of outing? Communitarian reporting on gay issues must include context and background that explains the harm of oppressive practices and policies. Communitarian journalists must do this prominently in the same story in which any episodic news is reported, rather than relegate the background to the "bottom" of the story as the traditional craft value of writing in inverted pyramid style demands. Communitarian journalists must provide stakeholders who are most affected the opportunity to make their claims and counterclaims in those episodic news accounts.

Rather than follow journalism's craft value of objective, "on-the-other-hand" reporting, communitarianism demands that journalists actively counter false claims or inflammatory statements with actual fact. In the episodic nature of gossip narratives, this would require a cultural sea change. Communitarian journalists would demand that those who make claims produce evidence and be accountable. Each statement would be contextualized and countered if necessary, regardless of market-driven considerations about timely publication. By communitarian standards, the traditional craft value of timeliness, which may further individual interests in the marketplace where media businesses compete for news, carries less weight when measured against a community value of, say, completeness or compassion. By communitarian standards, business competition—the game of "scoop"—is not an ethic, neither moral nor immoral. Unable to produce evidence, specious claims as well as potentially harmful invasive claims offer nothing substantial to offer in the community debate of issues. They bring nothing to the conversational commons—in this case, the metaphorical press box. Sports journalists in all media must elevate the ethics of their game. Until such time, in a "bewildering panorama spread out upon the green plain below" (Rice 1925), gay athletes in contact sports may continue to be caught in the crossfire of the chattering classes.

REFERENCES

Acee, K., and P. Finley. "Call it Sports' Last Taboo." *The Union-Tribune*, September 1, 2003, D-1.

Anti-gay slurs. (2007). Retrieved Sept. 20, 2009 at http://www.outsports.com/antigay/antigayrockerslist.htm.

Associated Press Managing Editors. (2005). Statement of Ethical Principles. http://www.apme.com/ethics/.

Bean, B., and C. Bull. *Going the Other Way*. New York: Marlowe & Co., 2003.

Black, J., B. Steele, and R. Barney. *Doing Ethics in Journalism* (Third Edition). Boston: Allyn & Bacon, 1999.

Brown, R. "Garcia's First Pass a Winner." *Plain Dealer*, July 21, 2004, C2.

Brown, R. "Vicious Hits don't take Respite when Garcia Leaves Field." *Plain Dealer*, September 12, 2004, C2.

Bryant, M. F. "Life Still Tough for Gay Male Athletes." *The Fresno Bee*, November 1, 2002, D1.

Bull, C. "The healer." *ESPN The Magazine*, February 16, 2004, 90–95.

Burke, G., and E. Sherman. *Out at Home*. Manchester, England: Excel Publishing Co., 1995.

Buzinski, J. "Dave Kopay: Still Going Strong." September 3, 2002 (accessed at http://www.outsports.com/nfl/2002/kopay0902.htm).

Buzinski, J. "What's Wrong with Being Gay?" February 23, 2003 (accessed at http://www.outsports.com/columns/koufax02242003.htm).

Buzinski, J. "Vick is Gay Story a Hoax." April 24, 2004 (accessed at http://www.outsports.com/nfl/2004/0426vicknotgay.htm).

Day, L. A. *Ethics in Mass Communications: Cases and Controversies*. (Fifth Edition) Toronto: Wadsworth/Thomson Learning, 2003.

Christians, C. G., J. P. Ferre, and P. M. Fackler. *Good News: Social Ethics and the Press*. New York: Oxford University Press, 1993.

Cosgrove-Mather, B. (2004, July 8). Mixed signals for gay athletes: gays try to find their place in sports world. Retrieved Nov. 30, 2004 at http://www.cbsnews.com/stories/2004/07/08/national/main628303.shtml.

Deford, F. *Big Bill Tilden: The Triumphs and the Tragedy*. New York: Simon and Schuster, 1975.

Englehardt, E. E., and R. D. Barney. *Media and Ethics: Principles for Moral Decisions*. Toronto: Wadsworth/Thomson Learning, 2002.

Ford, B. "For Owens, Just Another Day at the Office; for Garcia, Another Loss." *Philadelphia Inquirer*, October 25, 2004, C1.

Harlan, C. "Stewart puts Pittsburgh Experience in Perspective." *Pittsburgh Post-Gazette*, December 24, 2004, B1.

Kopay, D., and P. D. Young. *The David Kopay Story: An Extraordinary Self-Revelation*. Westminster, MD: Arbor House Publishing, 1977.

Lemon, B. Letter from the Editor. 2001. (accessed at http://out.com/html/edletter90.html).

Litke, J. "Piazza Denies Rumor as Gay Player Issue Resurfaces." May 2, 2003. (accessed at January 5, 2004 at http://espn.go.com/mlb/news/2002/0522/1385446.html).

Maiocco, M. "Garcia Shrugs off Rumors about being Gay." *The Press Democrat*, February 4, 2004, C3.

Marech, R. "Activists Consider Ethics, Efficacy of Outing." *San Francisco Chronicle*, November 11, 2004, A1.

Matthews posts disputed column on Internet. (accessed at http://espn.go.com/mlb/news/2002/0522/1385611.html).

Merrill, J. C. *Journalism Ethics: Philosophical Foundations for News Media*. New York: St. Martin's Press, 1997.

Neimark, J. "The Culture of Celebrity." *Psychology Today*. (29:5) (1995): 54–60. O'Rourke, L. "T. O. not saying whether or not Garcia is gay." *The Morning Call*, August 11, 2004, C1.

Orth, M. "Out of the Locker Room, and the Closet." *The New York Times*, November 30, 2003, Sect, 9, Page 1.

Pallone, D., and A. Steinberg. *Behind the Mask: My Double Life in Baseball*. New York: Viking Press, 1990.

Patterson, P., and L. Wilkins. *Media Ethics: Issues & Cases*. (Fourth Edition) Boston: McGraw Hill, 2002.

Provenzano, J. "The Gay Gridiron." 2002. (accessed December 16, 2005, at http://www.qsyndicate.com/SportsComplex.htm).

Rice, G. "Titanic Struggle of the Ages." *New York Herald Tribune*, October 18, 1924, 1.

"Shockey calls Parcells "homo" in magazine interview." 2003. (accessed at http://sports.espn.go.com/espn/print?id=1592493&type=news).

Signorile, M. *Queer In America: Sex, Media, and the Closets of Power*. New York: Random House, 1993.

Silver, M. "In Control." *Sports Illustrated*, 96(2), January 14, 2002, 40–46.

Smith, R. F. *Groping for Ethics in Journalism* (Fifth Edition). Ames, IA: Iowa State Press, 2003.

Sylvester, C. "One Sorry Lion: Players Left to Answer Questions Millen Wouldn't." *Detroit Free Press*, December 2003, C1.

Travis, N. "Page Six." *New York Post*, April 30, 2003, 6.

Tualo, E., and L. Cyphers. "Free and Clear." *ESPN The Magazine*, October 30, 2002.

"Twenty Questions. The Terrell Owens Interview." *Playboy*, 51(8), August 2004.

Windhorst, B. "Garcia Stands Up to Owens." *Akron Beacon-Journal*, August 12, 2004, p. C1.

Withers, T. "Garcia Wishes Owens Would let Bygones go." October 20, 2004. (accessed at http://web.lexis-nexis.com/universe/document?-m=461780f28333b62f08bbce2d8118af61&_docnum=115&wchp=dGLbVzz-zSkVA&_md5=cc14d2a3f81670ef5eb77858914a0628).

Zeigler, C. "How to not treat your closeted boyfriend." 2001. (accessed at http://www.outsports.com/review/review051501.htm).

Chapter 8

"It Is Just Something Greek; That's All": Eugen Sandow—Queer Father of Modern Body Building"

Jim Elledge

> Sandow is the most wonderful specimen I have ever seen. He is strong, active and graceful, combining the characteristics of Apollo, Hercules and the ideal athlete. There is not the slightest evidence of sham about him. On the contrary he is just what he pretends to be.
>
> —Dr. D. A. Sargent[1]

Although virtually unknown today, Eugen Sandow earned international acclaim during the first decade of his 35-year career in "physical culture," now called bodybuilding. Considered "the most remarkable example of perfect physical development and prodigious human strength ever seen," "the most powerful man of the century," and "one of *the* icons of the nineteenth century," he was also "a dangerously handsome young man" and "the first great male pinup in modern history." One contemporary journalist succinctly described the "fad" that Prussian-born Sandow became almost the instant he arrived in the United States:

> Wherever he went mobs paid . . . to see [him], and after the mobs had looked their fill there were private séances to which nice people went; first in secret, then in brazen bravado. . . . It booted little how much he could lift, or whether he could lift anything at all; one attended his exhibitions to look and be exalted by pure beauty . . . [2]

Sandow guaranteed his universal acceptance as the father of bodybuilding when he debuted at the Trocadero Music Hall in Chicago on August 1, 1893. However, what is far less acknowledged, but whispered about, is his sexual orientation.

Sandow revealed his private life, not just his body, publicly through a brilliant strategy that was as simple as it was effective. He embraced ambiguity in ways that no public figure had before, sporting it as if it were camouflage at the same time that, paradoxically, he was virtually nude on stage before hundreds, posing in imitation of various classical statues then lifting weights, other men, and even horses. The gay codes of the time that were steeped in ambiguity allowed him to highlight clues about his gay life to those aware of the codes while they simultaneously veiled his life against those who weren't.

In Sandow's day, notions of gender were black-and-white and not debatable. If men and women mused about gender at all, they thought of polarities: maleness at one extreme, femaleness at the other, with each defined in exacting detail. However, by the close of the 1800s, reports of the existence in large metropolitan areas of groups of individuals who were physically male but who sought out other men for sexual relationships were confronting medical and legal authorities. There was no place for such individuals in the gender polarization of the time.

The men called themselves belles, queens, queers, pansies, temperamentals, fairies, andro-gynes, and so on. They often cross-dressed (at home, at parties, in clubs, or when they cruised the streets at night), wore makeup, assumed the "submissive" or "passive" role in oral and anal sexual activities, adopted female names, referred to one another using female pronouns, and sometimes worked in "women's occupations" (e.g., counter help in department stores or stenographers). Medical authorities of the time believed belles had inverted their gender roles, rejecting the male role and adopting the female. Initially, the medical profession called them "inverts" and their state "sexual inversion." Some may have engaged in sexual activities with other inverts, but many sought what they called "normal" men for sexual liaisons.

Unlike inverts, "normal" men, who had sex with inverts, were invisible to medical professionals because they looked and acted like heterosexual men. Blending into the mainstream, they were virtually unknown and rarely discussed in the medical literature. "Normal" men engaged in same-sex sexual relationships, often playing the active, assertive *male* role to the inverts' passive, penetrated *female* role. Inverts created small communities of like-minded individuals, marginalizing themselves to some degree while also affording one another support, safety, and a sounding board for ideas about themselves and their place in the world. "Normal" men camped in the mainstream, typically marrying women, fathering children, holding male-identified jobs (police officer, store owner, doctor, member of the armed forces), growing facial hair, and dressing appropriate to their gender. Meeting society's expectations, their activities, especially those with other men, were virtually above suspicion.[3]

Sandow wasn't simply aware of the polarities that governed men's lives. He understood the trappings of heterosexuality and how he could manipulate them to allow him to enjoy sexual relationships with whomever he chose, especially other men, without consequence. He was especially expert at employing codes that inverts and "normal" men knew in order to communicate one message to them while telling others something completely different. McDonnell reminds us that

> For artists and writers, musicians and dancers who lived and worked before the gay rights movement . . . acknowledgment of their sexual sides needed to remain private. This situation promoted the invention of codes, of discrete vocabularies that could simultaneously reveal and conceal. Only then could the average viewer pass over gay content without notice, while viewers sensitized to the signs of a gay aesthetic could read it effectively.[4]

In Sandow's case, the codes appeared in the photographs of him that circulated widely, in his public and private performances, and even in his writings.

"A FINE PIECE OF NUDE"

Eugen Sandow, who was born Friederick Wilhelm Müeller on April 2, 1867 in Königsberg, Prussia and who later changed his name, offered distinctly different versions of various important experiences in his life.[5] He first claimed that as "a child he was healthy and well-formed, but there was nothing of the prodigy about him, physically or mentally; nor were either of his parents of anything but normal physique." His father took him on his first vacation, when he was ten to Rome where "he liked most to frequent the art-galleries, and there to hang about and admire the finely-sculptured figures of heathen deities and the chiseled beauty of some Herculean athlete. . . ."[6]

Three years later, Sandow offered a very different scenario of the same situation and experience:

> As a child, I was myself exceedingly delicate. More than once, indeed, my life was despaired of. Until I was in my tenth year I scarcely knew what strength was. Then it happened that I saw it in bronze and stone. My father took me with him to Italy, and in the art galleries of Rome and Florence I was struck with admiration for the finely developed forms of the sculptured figures of the athletes of old.[7]

The three points that are identical in both accounts are very revealing: Rome, his age, and his reaction to nude, male bodies.

The Mediterranean world had a special appeal for U.S. and northern European homosexuals during this period: "the homoeroticism of the [classical] statues remains . . . an example of beauty and virility for all, [but] . . . a representation with a special meaning to homosexual viewers."[8] Things Greek took on a special meaning for homosexuals because of the budding realization during this period that Greece had been what they thought of as a homosexually-inclined culture. In fact, any item associated with Greece—such as sandals, temple columns, garlands, togas, lyres, etc.—became associated with homosexuality even if, like togas, they were also common to other cultures.

During the 1800s and early 1900s, several homosexuals recorded how, as boys or adolescents, they were attracted to the classical statuary they studied in school or saw during visits to museums. One of England's most prestigious literary figures, Sir Edmund Gosse, admitted in his memoir, *Father and Son*, that "the sculpted classical nude body" had aroused him when he was a boy.[9] Sir Edmund's

> eroticised interest in the nude . . . does not . . . make him an exceptional spectator in the mid-nineteenth century, but in some senses a representative one, a typical Victorian viewer whose desire to behold the nude risked being described and even experienced in terms of ideas of sodomy.[10]

Any museum might provide homosexuals with titillating sculptures, including the British Museum, which had been

> a favorite amongst homophile Victorian gentlemen who could get an eyeful of flawless male beauty in the Greek statue room without fear of arrest. The historian Matt Cook quotes one gay man who got a completely carried away looking at the statues: "I revelled in the sight of pictures and statues of the male form and could not keep from kissing them.[11]

In his late twenties and becoming a "fad," Sandow declared his boyhood admiration for classical, nude, male statues, and doing so echoed an experience common to homosexuals, employing a gay code to signal his identity to other like-minded men.

Sandow spent his late teens and early adulthood traveling throughout Europe, touring with circuses, taking part in wrestling matches, giving exhibits of strength. At eighteen, he left Königsberg and traveled for two years with a circus to Russia then throughout Europe to evade his military responsibility. In the early months of 1887, the circus went bankrupt, and Sandow was stranded in Brussels jobless. He became a nude model for art students, some of whom were also physical culture students of Professor Attila (Louis Durlacher), a famous strongman in local music halls and the founder of his own bodybuilding school. They introduced Sandow to Attila who, once he saw "Sandow stripped down, . . . decided to take him on as a prize pupil at once"[12] At the same time, Sandow also began modeling nude for photographers as well as for well-known artists who could afford to pay.[13] He posed as Satan in Charles Van der Stappen's sculpture *Michael Vanquishing Satan* and for Joseph Maria Thomas Lambeaux's sculpture *Le Denicheur d'Aigles*, among many others. Edmond Desbonnet, who knew Sandow during this period of the Adonis' life, wrote that Sandow trained with Attila between each "posing session."[14]

He went to London with Attila, then to Paris on his own, where he modeled for Gustave Crauck's *Combat du Centaure*, posing as the Lapith. After Paris, he traveled across France, and stopped in Italy in 1888, earning his keep as a circus performer. In Rome, he became a wrestler, won the first of a number of wrestling contests, and modeled for artists and photographers: "There are some early photographs of him at this period which show a finely developed, though still immature, athlete swinging an Indian club and striking heroic poses."[15] One of Sandow's early biographers, William Pullum, questioned the Adonis' modeling activities, suggesting that he was paid for sexual favors by at least one homosexual artist, E. Aubrey Hunt. Pullum noted that Hunt had "discovered he had engaged a model who could do much more with his muscles than a painter might suppose."[16]

Sandow and Hunt met on the Lido, a well-known cruising spot for homosexuals.[17] As with other important events, Sandow offered two distinctly different versions. The first appeared in his book *Sandow's System of Physical Training* (1894):

> It was at Venice, shortly after his recovery, that Sandow made the acquaintance of the English artist, Aubrey Hunt, R. A., whose admiration of the fine physical development of the great athlete led him to paint the now well-known picture of Sandow in the Coliseum at Rome, in the character of a gladiator.[18]

Sandow published the second version of this event thirteen years later in the memoir, "My Reminiscences," after his empire of bodybuilding schools, lecture tours, inventions, and publishing venues were netting him large profits. The second is decidedly more revealing, and probably more honest, than the first. Walking from the ocean across the beach, beads of water dripping from his hair, slipping across his glistening chest and down his abdomen, he was unaware of "the state of physical symmetry" his body exhibited (i.e., how buff he was), until he noticed that he

> had become the particular attraction for a gentleman sauntering by. As I apologized in passing him he stopped to compliment me upon what he was pleased to term my "perfect physique and beauty of form." That casual critic proved to be none other than Aubrey Hunt, the famous artist, with whom I afterwards became on terms of close friendship, and to whom I had the pleasure of posing in the character of a Roman gladiator, and my eyes never rest upon that picture but it recalls the many happy days we spent together.[19]

Queers would have read the snippet as a pick-up. Hunt was cruising the beaches. Sandow was available. He knew he had caught Hunt's eye and acknowledged that fact, while at the same time he indicated to Hunt that he was available by speaking first. This allowed the gentleman to respond (if he were attracted) or not (if he were not). The thirty-four year-old Hunt did, complimenting the Adonis on his body—"perfect," beautiful—thus declaring his desire for the 22-year-old.

Over the years, those who knew Sandow or biographers who had access to Sandow's contemporaries, published innuendos about the fateful meeting between the artist and the Adonis. All seem too invented to be believable, yet each acknowledges, if subtly, the sexual nature of the meeting. In 1926, the year after Sandow's death, William Pullum described the incident in more detail than others:

> Aubrey Hunt, an Associate of the Royal Academy, . . . had journeyed to Italy in search of a suitable subject for depiction as a Roman gladiator. [At the same time,] a young German (. . . Eugen Sandow), who by physical culture had developed a physique which was coveted by sculptors and showmen. Camping on the trail of these, his quest of the period had brought him also to Italy.
>
> One day strolling along the Lido of Venice in musing mood, Hunt saw emerging from the sea just the figure that he had pictured in his imagination. The sight moved him at once to act! Addressing the bather, he introduced himself and explained his mission, inviting the former to pose for the painting he had in mind. The terms he offered made the assignment an attractive one, so it was agreed to on the spot.[20]

Pullum added the realistic detail of payment, something that was hardly unique: "It had become almost traditional for many working-class men and boys [of the time] to be sexually available to any 'toff' with a disposable income."[21] Eleven years later, one report claimed that the "words that were first uttered by . . . Hunt, when he gazed upon that beautiful figure at Lido near Venice," were "The Non-pareil.'"[22]

Hunt painted Sandow as a gladiator wearing a "leopard-skin costume," but oddly, the gladiator neither carries a weapon nor faces an enemy, as we would expect. Instead, he "merely stands there heroically, his handsome blond head gazing pensively to one side."[23] Just as strangely, Sandow is not standing in an arena full of gawking Romans, which we would also expect in a painting of a gladiator. The background is only a blur of colors without a single person being discernable. Sandow is the painting's sole object, with nothing to detract attention from him. We note his highly-muscled body, his beauty, his youth, but nothing else because nothing but his body exists in it. We cannot discern even the slightest narrative fragment in which he might have a role—or the slightest movement. His purpose in the painting is simply to offer his body for viewing: to be considered, to be envied, to be adored, to be ogled.

"In patriarchal mainstream culture," Healey reminds us, "positioning a man in front of a camera [or an easel] is inherently problematic, as it entails an unmanly passive acceptance of objectification."[24] He continues:

> The male object resists the authority of the gaze by displaying contempt or superiority in refusing to look at, or decisively staring through, the spectator; whereas conventionally female models are required to display an obsequient acknowledgment of the (male) spectator even when they do not meet his eyes. Potential passivity is also compensated for by demonstrative activity: men are usually photographed doing something. Whereas women must passively appear, men must actively act.[25]

Hunt has so thoroughly imbibed the painting with passivity that it is not a slogan for Sandow's masculinity at all, but offers clues for his feminization. Queers would have "read" the painting as a coded report of Sandow's willingness to have sex with other men.

Making the painting even more coded is the fact that, for the popular culture of the time, the gladiator was considered to be a passive sex object for both men and women, and as such it had found its way into numerous popular novels:

> Romances . . . between patrician women and gladiators . . . were commonplace in Victorian historical novels . . . for instance, in Whyte Melville's *The Gladiators* . . . [and in] Bulwer-Lytton's *The Last Days of Pompeii* . . . [in which] the dialogue stresses the women's sexual excitement as they see the gladiators entering the arena. One of the characters asks her companion, "But who is yon handsome gladiator, nearly naked—is it not quite improper? By Venus! but his limbs are beautifully shaped!"[26]

Simeon Solomon's painting *Habet!* depicts "Women—desiring the fallen gladiator who is under their inspection."[27] A reporter drew a parallel between the gladiatorial code and one of Sandow's private soirees, noting that "The scene at [Sandow's private] exhibitions recalled those that were enacted in Rome when the nobles of both sexes visited the gladiators in their quarters and admirably examined their brawn and sinews . . . "[28] The homosexual aspects of the "exhibition" were not lost on the reporter.

Despite, or perhaps because, the painting emphatically placed him in a queer context, Sandow had a strong attachment to it. At one time, he kept it at home:

> In Mr. Sandow's dining-room is a very fine portrait, by Mr. Aubrey Hunt, of the athlete attired as a Roman gladiator, standing in the Colosseum [*sic*] at Rome. The work is an admirable likeness, and shows off the enormous muscles of Mr. Sandow's body to great advantage. £500 has been offered for the painting, but, naturally enough, its owner refuses to part with it.[29]

Three years later, he moved it to his school: "Mr. Hunt painted me in the character of a gladiator in the Coliseum at Rome. This picture, which I prize very highly, is to be seen in the reception room at my St. James' Street school. I am told that it is a very striking likeness."[30]

In the same year that Hunt painted Sandow in Venice, another Englishman, Edmund Gosse, bought copies of a series of photographs of Sandow in a London shop that had been taken a few months earlier.[31] They were "a beautiful set of poses showing the young strongman clad only in a fig leaf"[32] Now a rising celebrity in London who was beginning to get minor but important notices in U.S. newspapers, Sandow had begun to replicate then market his body. The profits he reaped were not simply financial. More important, they afforded him a great deal of free publicity, especially among queer men. While the black-and-whites "were sold legally for educational purposes" (i.e., as anatomical studies) "this did not cancel their erotic appeal."[33]

Gosse was so enthralled with Sandow's photographs that he not only snuck them into the funeral of poet Robert Browning at Westminster Abbey to peak at during the service, he shared them with other queer men, including John Addington Symonds, another important man of letters. In acknowledging his friend's gift, Symonds was as circumspect as the times required, although his prurient exuberance comes through loud and clear: "The Sandow photographs arrived. They are very interesting, & the full length studies quite confirm my anticipations . . . The profile & half trunk is a splendid study. I am very much obliged to you for getting them for me."[34] Symonds was one of a large group of queer men who exchanged nude photos of adolescents and men. The group included Oscar Wilde's lover, Alfred Douglas, and other British literati.[35]

Sandow's photos weren't simply passed from one hand to another, but were also distributed in journals that catered to queer men:

> one of the numerous quasi-homosexual German magazines of the era, *Mannerluff*, had photographs of Sandow in almost every issue, always stressing the harmony and joy of the male body, man and boy *Mannerluff*, published with the contention it was homosexual "in spirit," but not gay, a distinction best left to academicians.[36]

Sandow was not the only physical culturalist to be photographed, but he was unique. His rivals had not admired classical statues when they were 10-year-old boys as Sandow had, and their goal was to develop their bodies into machines that could lift incredible amounts of weights, nothing more. Because Sandow sculpted his into an icon of male beauty, he could take his career a step farther than they. His performances included weight-lifting extravaganzas as theirs did, but he also *posed* to show off his body and to titillate his audience. Audiences might be in awe of the number of pounds that, for example, Luis Cyr could lift, but the barrel-shaped Cyr's sex appeal was nil.[37] When the buff Sandow stripped down to nothing but a fig leaf in photographs and to tiny, tight-fitting boxer briefs and a tank top on stage, audiences lapped it up, caring "little how much he could lift, or whether he could lift anything at all" because they, like Hunt, Gosse, Symonds, and countless other "normal" men, "attended his exhibitions to look and be exalted by pure beauty."

"WHEN THE MAINSTREAM REMAINS BLISSFULLY IGNORANT, BUTCH QUEENS SIMPLY PASS"

By April 1893, Sandow had become an extremely well-known and highly-respected strongman in the United Kingdom and across Europe. In fact, he had achieved so much notoriety that Henry S. Abbey of the New York firm Abbey, Schiffel and Grau, a group of vaudeville impresarios, had invited him to perform in the Big Apple, an offer that Sandow eagerly grabbed. The *New York Times* announced the bodybuilder's imminent arrival: "Sandow is coming here from England. Sandow's special line is strength and activity."[38]

Despite its best efforts, Abbey, Schiffel and Grau had little success in promoting Sandow's act. During the 1893 season, audiences at all of the vaudeville houses and even in the legitimate theater establishments were small, due in large part to a heat wave then engulfing Gotham, which kept people out of sweltering, crowded buildings, and to the stock market crash that spring, which had sunk "the economy into a deep depression."[39] Complicating matters was the fact that Sandow had also "arrived at the close of the theatrical season,"[40] when audiences would've been small at any theater regardless of who was performing. Abbey approached Rudolph Aronson, the manager of The Casino Theater, hoping that Aronson would hire Sandow. He suggested that Aronson "place [Sandow] between the two acts or at the finish of [the] operetta at the Casino," which was the operetta *Adonis*.[41] To Abbey's amazement and relief, Aronson agreed. Aronson slated Sandow to appear at 10:30 nightly beginning June 12, 1893 as a sort of epilogue to the play, his act commenting on its lead performer's role as Adonis. Sandow was an immediate sensation.

William Gill's *Adonis* had already been one of the season's biggest hits. The role of Adonis was played "by a handsome, trim matinee idol named Henry Dixey" who was very "successful at embodying [the] popular theatrical ideal of physical perfection."[42] The play parodied the Pygmalion and Galatea myth:

> A sculptress has created in her statue of Adonis a "perfect figure." Indeed, he is so beautiful and alluring that she cannot bear to sell him as promised to a wealthy duchess. Seeing Adonis, the duchess, together with her four daughters, is instantly and passionately smitten as well. The daughters try to conceal their ardor [but fail].
>
> To resolve the question of ownership, an obliging goddess brings the statue to life.—The pursuit of Adonis [by the women] rapidly [ensues]. . . . Ultimately, Adonis is cornered by all his female pursuers, who demand that he choose among them. Instead, he beseeches the goddess who gave him life, "Oh take me away and petrify me—place me on my old familiar pedestal—and hang a placard round my neck:—'HANDS OFF.' " Thus, exhausted by his stint as a flesh-and-blood object of desire, Dixey as Adonis reassumed the pose of a perfect work of art as the curtain fell.[43]

That Adonis preferred to return to his stony state rather than succumbing to the lust of a woman would have delighted queers in the audience. Adding to the humor, the operetta also lampooned gender roles. In his role as Adonis, Dixey "ludicrously" donned a women's dress and becomes "a village maid" to escape the lusty women after him only to be "courted" by a man.[44] Again, the queers in the audience must have loved Dixey as an invert.

On June 12, when the curtain fell, the audience applauded appreciatively then waited for the curtain to rise and cast members to return to center stage for ovations. Instead, when the curtain rose, Sandow was standing in the same pose that Dixey had been in when, as Adonis, he was returned to stone. The audience was stunned, it gasped, then it went wild. One reporter summarized the event:

> New York has come to look upon Dixey as a fairly well-made young man. When New York has seen Sandow after Dixey, however, New York will realize what a wretched, scrawny creation the usual well-built young gentleman is compared with a perfect man. Sandow posing in various statuesque attitudes is not only imposing not only because of his enormous strength, but absolutely beautiful as a work of art as well.[45]

Hereafter, Sandow represented the ideal of male beauty throughout the U.S. for decades.

Beginning with his tour of the English countryside in the summer of 1890, when he posed for photographer Warwick Brooks, throughout his first tour of the U.S. (Dec. 16, 1893-July 1894), Sandow posed for a number of photographers, all for public distribution. Most of the photographs present one message to the mainstream—that is, heterosexual—audience, while offering a different, coded message to inverts and "normal" men.

First, the obvious: Sandow is nude in many of them, posing in each one before a male photographer. In some cases, he is actually wearing a fig leaf while he poses, the band holding it in place plainly visible around the Adonis' waist. In other cases, however, the photographer added it during the developing process, the Adonis naked during the shoots. The intimacy of the relationship between photographer and model was no less erotic in the imaginations of the photographs' audience (especially those queers who saw or owned them) than that between painter and model. Even the style of the fig leaf, how the photographer or Sandow positioned it, how the photographer arranged the studio light to strike it, and even its size fueled queer men's fantasies.[46]

Such manipulation reveals that either the photographers were aware of the sales potential of such eroticized images to a queer audience or, more likely, that Sandow and the photographers were in cahoots, creating a series of poses that offers, on one hand, the ideal, male physique that a heterosexual man engaged in bodybuilding might emulate, but which, on the other, was a highly erotic spectacle for queers.

Sandow's erotic appeal in the photos isn't simply a matter of his good looks and muscles, nor of the teasing fig leaf. The actual poses Sandow undertook in the photographs were also a coded message. In one pose called "The Dying Parthian" (1893), Sandow recreates a scene in which, for a mainstream audience, a valiant and vanquished warrior is defending himself with his last breath. He's nude, on the ground, obviously weakened by the fight he's just lost, but which he heroically tries to continue. In fact, he's raised his sword with his right hand in an attempt, against all odds, to continue fighting, while in his left, he hangs onto his shield in a last-ditch effort to protect himself.[47] For a queer audience, however, the pose is as erotic as it is heroic. His raised sword is undeniably phallic, extending from his crotch as if it were an erect penis that he offers to the soldier he's fighting—a distraction, perhaps a peace offering, or a bargaining tool.[48]

In two others, which Sandow included in *Sandow on Physical Training*, he performs a simple pushup, his muscles knotted under the strain, to instruct his readership how to perform the exercise for best effect. In the first, the naked Sandow raises himself to arm's length above a bearskin (or lion-skin) rug, which is on top of a leopard-skin rug. In the second, he has lowered himself inches above the rugs. Queer viewers could easily imagine the Adonis' body's thrusting downward into a writhing body, and the fact that his genitalia were airbrushed away wouldn't detract from the fantasy.[49]

In yet a third photo, a pose often called "The Dying Gaul," a fig-leafed Sandow lies on his left side, looking up. His thighs are spread, his right arm up, his right hand open palm out, as if imploring the gods to spare him from his impending death while his face suggests utter acceptance of his rapidly approaching fate. Or so, given the pose's title, a mainstream viewer might interpret it. A queer man, on the other hand, would see a "normal" man in a state of sexual ecstasy reaching for his lover, his thighs spread in invitation. He isn't in the last throes of life, but in an erotic swoon. If a queer man saw any suggestion of dying in the pose, it was the *petite mort*, a euphemism from the Renaissance for "orgasm," that he noted.[50] Indeed, even in the late twentieth century, the sexuality of any bodybuilder who posed as "The Dying Gaul" was immediately suspect:

> The goal [of a bodybuilder's routine] is to play by the audience's accepted rules, and then to shock them within the form, not

> venturing outside it. [Posing as] Michelangelo's *David* and the Farnese *Hercules* are one thing, but, as professional bodybuilder Bob Paris learned, *The Dying Gaul* is quite another. From the Capitoline Museum in Rome to Columbus, Ohio, Paris concluded his posing program with *The Dying Gaul* at the 1989 Arnold Classic. It was met with an uncomfortable silence and angry suspicion, the latter confirmed months later when he revealed his marriage to his "husband," male model Rod Jackson.[51]

At the same time that Sandow was camouflaging himself with the trappings that disguised him as heterosexual in his photographs, he was able to live openly in "happy domesticity" with another man—Martinus Sieveking, his "great and inseparable friend' "—without compromising his masculinity or his career.[52] One reporter disclosed that:

> Sandow is living now at No. 210 West Thirty-eighth Street. With him there lives a friend, Mr. Martinus Sieveking, who is a very able pianist. Mr. Sieveking is a Dutchman. His musical compositions have already attracted considerable attention in London, and he is an unusually brilliant artist. He and Sandow are bosom friends. He thinks that Sandow is a truly original Hercules, and that no one has ever lived to be compared to him. Sandow thinks that Mr. Sieverking [*sic*] is the greatest pianist in the world and that he is going to be greater. It is pleasant to see them together. Mr. Sieveking, who is a very earnest musician, practices from seven to eight hours a day on a big three-legged piano. He is decidedly in earnest. He practices in very hot weather, stripped to the waist. While he plays Sandow sits beside him on a chair listening to the music and working his muscles. He is fond of the music and Sieveking likes to see Sandow's muscles work. Both enjoy themselves and neither loses any time.[53]

"Bosom friends" was often used to indicate a same-sex sexual relationship from the 1800s into the early 1900s. Most queers would've been delighted to learn that Sieveking "practices—stripped to the waist" as Sandow "sits beside him on a chair—working his muscles," that the musician "likes to see Sandow's muscles work," and that "Both enjoy themselves and neither loses any time"—a wonderfully ambiguous line that would have raised the eyebrows, and a few chuckles, of anyone in the know.

They had known one another since Sandow's "years in Belgium and Holland," when they were 19, and the "two men had been living together for some time" before Sandow's debut at The Casino.[54] Their relationship was an open secret among London's hoi polloi. Even the staid *Dictionary of American Biography* reported their living arrangement.

Caroline Otéro, called "La Belle Otéro," an infamous Spanish courtesan and lover of "many of the rich, famous, and titled men of her era," including "King Leopold of Belgium, Prince Albert of Monaco, the future Kaiser Wilhelm of Germany, Prince (later King) Edward of England, and many others" had set her sights on Sandow.[55] As she explained:

> I had heard about Sandow for a long time and was anxious to meet him—I sent him a note, but he never answered, even though he certainly knew who I was. When I didn't hear from him I assumed he was one of those rare animals, a man who remained faithful to his wife. Then I found out he wasn't married, and supposed he had a mistress who wouldn't let him out of sight.[56]

She continued, " 'I made up my mind that if Sandow wouldn't come to me, I'd go to him.' "[57]

She caught his act at London's Alhambra Music Hall—" 'What a physique! What muscles! My God! I never saw anything like it before in my life' "—and hurried to his dressing room as soon as he finished his act:

> I told him I thought his act was marvelous and that I'd like him to join me and a few of my friends at a small supper party I was giving that evening in my hotel. He said he was happy to accept and would be along just as soon as he was dressed. I nearly told him he needn't bother.[58]

She had not planned a "supper party" at all, but a seduction. Her efforts were ill-fated:

> It was all over very soon. I should have taken the cue when Herr Sandow refused to drink my fine champagne and asked for milk. Faugh! But hindsight is so superior to foresight. Poor fellow! He must have had a bad hour or two with me before I sent him back to the young man he was living with.[59]

As La Belle Otéro discovered, it was not a mistress' charms that held Sandow's rapt attention, but Martinus Sieveking's.

When Sandow moved to New York at Abbey, Schiffel, and Grau's invitation, he brought Sieveking with him. They arrived on the *Elbe* a few weeks before Sandow's debut at the Casino. Safe in his "normal"-man camouflage, Sandow felt free to discuss Sieveking in his second book, *Strength and How to Obtain It*, four years later:

> An old friend and famous pianist, Martinus Sieveking, whom I knew years before in Belgium and Holland, accompanied me to the New World. Sieveking was a brilliant artist, but as a man he was exceedingly weak and delicate. He had no powers of endurance, and it was difficult for him to remain at the piano long at a time.
>
> "If I had only your strength," he used to say, "I think I might become almost the greatest player in the world."
>
> I suggested that he should come with me as my guest to America, guaranteeing that in nine months or a year, under my personal supervision and training, he would grow so strong that his best friends would scarcely recognise him.[60]

Sieveking worked with Sandow, performing music as the Adonis strutted across the stage. One reporter noted that Sieveking gave Sandow's act a touch of class: "the environments of [Sandow's] unique act, including the music composed for it by Martinus Sieveking, place the act on a much higher plane than would be otherwise possible."[61] Sieveking even composed music for Sandow's performances, including "March of the Athletes" and "Sandowia." Throughout Sandow's first tour of the United States, Sieveking was his constant and inseparable companion city after city. "From New York I went to Boston, where my system of physical training became very fashionable; and after the Boston visit came Chicago, Mr. Sieveking always accompanying me."[62]

Legend has it that, in the summer of 1893, Flo Ziegfeld, Jr., who would make his mark in theatrical history with his well-known series of *Follies*, had scoured New York City in search of talent for this father's Trocadero Music Hall in Chicago. According to the story, Ziegfeld, Sr. had sent his son to Gotham to hire highbrow acts—symphonies, opera stars, or Shakespearean-style monologists. Instead, Junior made the round of burlesque theaters, a long-standing craze in entertainment. Lowbrow in its fare—acrobats, comedians, women who whistled lavish songs, men who lifted both inanimate and animate objects, and erotic *tableaux vivants*[63]—burlesque attracted rabble that filled theaters to the rafters and made some owners of the theaters in which it was presented rich. During the search, he serendipitously discovered Sandow and hired him on the spot. However, the facts reveal nothing serendipitous about Ziegfeld's hiring Sandow at all.

Sandow's exploits as a strongman had been publicized four years earlier on the front page of the *Chicago Daily Tribune*, when he won the title of the strongest man in the world from Charles A. Sampson in London, then again two years later in a list of strongmen and their talents, and a third time two months before he arrived in New York. D. E. Flannery, a member of the Trocadero's board of directors was first to see Sandow's money-making potential for the Trocadero, not Ziegfeld:

> When Sandow's fame as a strong man sped across the Atlantic to this country one of the first men to call the attention of the Board of Directors to the necessity of securing the muscular phenomenon was D. E. Flannery, attorney for the company and a member of the board. Sandow was a high-priced attraction, but Mr. Flannery told the board the Trocadero could make money on him.
>
> "By persistent kicking I managed to win the directors over to my way of thinking," said Mr. Flannery, "and we authorized Dr. Ziegfeld to secure Sandow at a salary of $1,100 a week. That was the figure set by Sandow's manager, H. E. Abbey."[64]

Ziegfeld père sent his son to New York for the expressed purpose of hiring the Adonis.

Sandow debuted at the Trocadero on August 1, the theater's headliner. Although Ziegfeld cannot be credited with foreseeing Sandow's profit-making potential, once he recognized it, he protected his investment in several different ways. To deflect rumors about his protégé's obvious relationship with Sieveking, Ziegfeld created a number of other rumors to underscore the Adonis' he-man image. He linked several women romantically to Sandow, among them the alluring beauty/actress Lillian Russell. He also had an extremely important suggestion for beefing up Sandow's act that, in turn, generated free and wild-fire publicity, increased their profits, and catapulted Sandow into superstardom.

Before his opening at the Trocadero Music Hall, Sandow typically appeared on stage in a pink leotard that covered him head to toe and either a blue shirt or vest over it. Beginning with his premiere at the Trocadero, Ziegfeld had Sandow dress in nothing but a pair of "small white silk trunks."[65] Illustrations from the time show him in a pair of skin-tight boxer briefs and almost always from behind, suggesting that the briefs revealed so much that a frontal view would be too scandalous to publish. In the few frontal views that do exist, his trademark "small white" boxers are usually blackened in to blot out offending bulges. One newspaper drawing of him was obviously traced from a nude photograph of the Adonis, with lines added to suggest the waistband and thigh hems of Sandow's skin-tight boxer briefs.

Sandow's was the last performance each night. He appeared sharply at 10:45 and typically performed for an hour. Nevertheless, after the curtain fell, his performance was just beginning. When on August 1, 1893, Sandow finished his act:

> Ziegfeld Jr. walked in front of the footlights and made a daring proposal. Any woman willing to donate $300 to charity would be allowed to come to the strongman's private dressing room and feel his muscles. Mrs. Potter Palmer and Mrs. George Pullman immediately stood up and made their way backstage.[66]

That was not the first of Sandow's private exhibits. At least as early as the previous December, Sandow modeled for a British army physician's lecture on physical education at Aldershot, a military school. While the physician spoke, Sandow "applied the hands of some of the bystanders to the skin over the chest . . . and other parts of the trunk of his body."[67] By the time he joined the *Adonis* company, his private soirees had become a substantial part of his act:

> Five minutes after the curtain went down, Sandow, clothed only in his muscular development, was found crouching in a rubber bath tub in his drawing-room, while an attendant with a rubber pipe doused him with cold water. That was the chance to study Sandow.
>
> * * *
>
> Taking his visitor's hand, he placed it on his heart . . . and called attention to the fact that there was no violent beating. In fact the action of the heart could not be felt at all through the thick coating of muscle.[68]

The ambiguous "That was the chance to study Sandow," who was bathing naked, would not have been lost on a queer readership. That the writer was male would have made the scene that much more tantalizing to them.

Sandow included the private show during his entire run at the Trocadero, and after his engagement there ended, he repeated it night after night in every U.S. city in which he performed. What had begun as a supplement to his act became a major performance. The following report, published at the end of his first U.S. tour, shows that even during the tour's last days he was inviting strangers' caresses:

> after the show is over and the public has departed and the big building is almost deserted, carriage after carriage rolls up to the door. Men in dress suits and women in opera cloaks alight and pass quickly into the big, empty play-house.
>
> There are whispered greetings, and the visitors are taken in hand by an attendant, who conducts them through the darkened theatre up a long, narrow staircase on to the stage and into Sandow's reception-room. The room is decorated with flags of all nations. From the ceiling at the upper end hangs a chandelier of electric lights whose glare is thrown downward and under which Sandow presently stands.
>
> Around three sides of the room are arranged settees, and the handsomely dressed men and women seat themselves in silence. They gaze at the big dumbbells and the rugs on the floor, the portraits on the wall and the sparkling sandals and tights which lie on a chair.
>
> At last the curtains that hide the inner room are parted, and Sandow appears before his visitors in all his physical beauty fresh from the bath. A thin pair of flesh-colored tights fitted closely to his well-formed legs, a small pair of white satin trunks and light slippers complete his wardrobe. There is a buzz of conversation on the part of the men and an enthusiastic murmur from the women.
>
> He bows with easy grace as he is introduced to each of his visitors, and gives them a giant grasp with both hands. Then stepping under the chandelier, where the light throws into sharp relief the lines of his perfectly moulded figure, Sandow stands erect.[69]

As Sandow began his discussion of the muscles of his body, "The men look interested. The women gaze at him in wonder." The reporter notes that there was a far larger contingency of men than women at this private soiree, as was also the case for all of his performances, public or private. As Sandow moved among his audience, he said,

> "I want you to feel how hard these muscles are. As I come around I want you to pass your right hand flat across my chest." He approaches the first man, takes the outstretched hand and rubs it over the hard muscles of his iron-ribbed chest.
> An expression of astonishment on the part of the man heightens the expectation of others. Sandow moves along the line, taking hand after hand, until he approaches the first woman in the party.[70]

As Sandow's most recent biographer admits, "One thing seems certain . . . : while his admirers were fondling Sandow's muscles, they were satisfying feelings other than mere curiosity."[71]

While Sandow's private performance was not Ziegfeld's idea, having both Mrs. Palmer and Mrs. Pullman, grand dames of Chicago's high society set, give $300 each to charities in order to "feel" the "absolutely beautiful" Sandow was. In fact, it was his most brilliant publicity ploy, assuring that the very next day and for many weeks after, Sandow's name was on the lips of every society lady of the Windy City—as well as on the lips of numerous society men—"normal" men, inverts, and perhaps even others.

"JUST WHAT HE PRETENDS TO BE"

Chicago marks the turning point in Sandow's career, his first step, under the direction of Flo Ziegfeld, to becoming an international star. Once his run at the Trocadero ended, Sandow and Sieveking hurried back to Gotham, where Sandow signed a contract to perform at Koster and Bial's, one of New York's best-known venues, in mid-December. According to Ziegfeld, Sandow set sail, probably with Sieveking, for Germany a few days later "on the steamer *Columbia* with the intention of settling up his European affairs and returning permanently to this country."[72] The report was likely more of Ziegfeld's hype. Sandow also returned to England to visit photographer Warwick Brooks in Manchester. Brooks had photographed Sandow four years earlier. At the same time, Sandow met Brooks' daughter, Blanche with whom he had begun corresponding. A newspaper reporter once described her in terms that also suited Sieveking: "tall, slender, exquisitely beautiful," "eyes— large and soft, black as night, and very sensitive," "hair—just as black."[73] Sandow returned to New York with Sieveking to begin their first tour of the U.S., opening to a highly successful engagement which lasted twice as long as the contract specified.

When the tour opened in December, Ziegfeld adjusted Sandow's act again. They would limit the number admitted to his private soirees to caress the Adonis' body to fifteen, the small number allowing each person to linger over Sandow's muscles far longer and more intensely than ever before. The publicity was also more intense than ever before.

Throughout the tour, Sieveking was at Sandow's side, and strangers eagerly lined up for their turn to caress his flesh. They closed the tour in late July. Ziegfeld, Sandow, and Sieveking headed East. Ziegfeld stopped off in Chicago, while the others continued to New York, from which they sailed to London. Sandow had triumphantly conquered the hearts—and other parts of the bodies—of his audiences wherever he performed. Then on August 8, 1894, shortly after his twenty-seventh birthday, "normal" man Sandow married Blanche Brooks.

Most biographers claim this was unexpected, but their engagement had been announced nearly eight months earlier in the *Chicago Daily Tribune*: "Eugene [*sic*] Sandow, the strong man, announces his engagement to Miss Blanche Burns [*sic*] of London. She is not on the stage."[74] Thirteen days later, the *Tribune* ran another story, outlining the details of Sandow and Blanche's meeting, a fairy tale that was certainly one of Ziegfeld's finest creations and meant to protect his investment. Undoubtedly, Ziegfeld is the unidentified "gentleman in this city:"

> A gentleman in this city tells a romantic little story about how Eugene [*sic*] Sandow, the strong man, met Miss Blanche Brooks, the young lady to whom it as recently announced he is engaged to be married, says the New York *Herald*. While Sandow was performing at the Crystal Palace in London a couple of ears ago the platform of which he was supporting horses on his breast broke and it was only his presence of mind that saved him from being crushed to death. As it was he escaped unhurt and crowds of people rushed forward to shake hands with him and congratulate him. In the midst of this excitement a lady, who was sitting in a box, threw him a bunch of violets.
>
> A few moths later a runaway truck horse came near rushing into a coupe occupied by a lady. Sandow, who chanced to be passing, saw the danger, and boy this great strength saw the danger, and by his great strength succeeded in diverting the course of the run-away horse, and so saved the life of the young lady.

> She proved to be the same who had thrown him the bunch of violets, and Sandow now learned that her name was Miss Blanche Brooks. They subsequently became engaged, and expect to be married this summer.[75]

Regardless of whatever else it may have provided him, Sandow's engagement camouflaged his travels with Sieveking and their "domestic happiness."[76] With his fiancée thousands of miles away, the Adonis could have his cupcake and eat him, too. Yet, the two appear to have called it quits at the end of the first tour, on the eve of Sandow's marriage, and almost immediately, the Sandows and Ziegfeld put together Sandow's second U.S. tour, this one without Sieveking.

It is obvious that Blanche wielded some power in their marriage because the bodybuilder changed his performance drastically. It is not difficult to imagine that Ziegfeld was not happy about the changes, either. When he left London and returned to New York for his second U.S. tour, Sandow sailed with wife in tow and he had axed the private, flesh-caressing sessions that had been such an integral and important component of his act. By most accounts, the second tour was a lackluster series of performances lasting seven and a half grueling months. At the end, Ziegfeld and Sandow were barely speaking, and Blanche, who left the tour early, was pregnant with the first of her and Sandow's two daughters.

Following Sandow's lead, Sieveking also married, in 1899, and he fathered a son, who died in childhood. He and his wife eventually divorced. He toured the United States on his own several times (as he had before arriving as Sandow's protégé), giving concerts with good-to-lukewarm reviews at Carnegie Hall and other venues across the United States. He eventually moved to Los Angeles, and when he died on November 26, 1950, his body was placed in a grave, the whereabouts of which is still a mystery.

Sandow's marriage fared only slightly better. He and Blanche remained married, raising their daughters, Helen and Loraine. After decades of touring many countries, of creating an empire of bodybuilding journals and schools, of inventing several physique-training devices, and of endorsing products, all of which made him quite wealthy, he died on October 14, 1925. Sandow's body, which had given him fame and fortune, had been *ooohed* and *ahhhed* over by thousands, had been caressed by hundreds of trembling hands, and had been photographed in every pose imaginable, was buried without a stone or any identifying marker—then immediately ignored. Blanche's "forgetfulness" suggests retaliation, and it appears that her husband had not abandoned his cavorting with men at all. From 1914 through at least 1918, rumors that Sandow engaged in same-sex sexual relations circulated widely in London and in France:

> Cabaret acts and stage revues often featured performers who imitated Sandow with satirical intent. One skit in the musical pastiche *L'Amour* is especially revealing. An actor representing what is obviously Sandow impersonating a statue, is standing on a pedestal in a park. A bevy of young beauties cross in front. No reaction. Finally a sailor passes, and the figleaf [*sic*] begins to rise and rise, until it stands straight out supported, obviously, by an erection.[77]

When a young American female fan tired to explain why she owned one of Sandow's photos, she blurted, "Some people think it is terribly indecent—I don't. It is just something Greek; that's all"—a rationalization, not an explanation. The photo in question was a shot of Sandow's "torso, with muscles—like that of the Vatican over which the aged Michael Angelo passed his hands."[78] With one word, *Greek*, she unknowingly pinpointed the key to Sandow's success. His photos' columns, the sandals he typically wore, even the fig leaf so expertly positioned alluded to classical statuary, the same ones that the 10-year-old Sandow had admired in Rome and that other men like him had also admired during their boyhood and adolescence. The classical accoutrement gave Sandow's photos a distinctly artsy characteristic, which the young girl, and others of her time, identified as "Greek." However, had a queer man said, "It is just something Greek; that's all," his use of *Greek* would not have been only to suggest an artiness to the photos but, more pointedly, to indicate an erotic overtone for him: in gay slang, *Greek* has been a code for anal intercourse between men since the late 1800s. With one word, the young woman unwittingly and succinctly revealed Sandow's use of ambiguity by the props that appeared in many of his photos. Using *Greek*, the young woman unlocked Sandow's secret when she explained his photograph as his queer audience would have when they looked at his photos, but without ever knowing what she had done.

NOTES

1. The quote in the title is from Bourget, Paul. *Outre-Mer: Impressions of America* (New York: Scribner's, 1895): 60–61. The epigraph is from Buck, Josh. "Sandow: No Folly with Ziegfeld's First Glorification." *Iron Game History* 5

(May 1998): 31–32. The sources of the titles for sections one and two are from Callen, Anthea. "Doubles and Desire: Anatomies of Masculinity in the Later Nineteenth Century." *Art History* 26 (Nov. 2003): 688; and Healy, Murray. " The Mark of a Man: Masculine Identities and the Art of Macho Drag." *Critical Quarterly* 36 (Mar. 1994): 89, respectively.

2. The quotes are from, respectively, "Sandow To Be at the Schiller," *Chicago Daily Tribune* 1 Apr. 1894, 25; "Strength of Sandow" *Chicago Daily Tribune* 20 August 1893: 15; H.P.M. "The Latest Society Fad: Fashion Pays Court to Sandow, the Strong Man, at His Private Levees," *Frank Leslie's Illustrated Weekly* March 29, 1894: 206; John F. Kasson, *Houdini, Tarzan, and the Perfect Man: The White Male Body and the Challenge of Modernity in America* (New York: Hill and Wang, 2001): 68; and "How the World Went Mad Over Sandow's Muscles." *Literary Digest* 87 (31 October 1925): 46, 48.

3. One of the best discussions about gender polarity and homosexuality in the late 1800s and early 1900s can be found in George Chauncy's *Gay New York: Gender, Urban Culture, and the Making of the Gay Male World, 1890–1940.* New York: Basic, 1994.

4. Patricia McDonnell, 'Essentially Masculine:' Marsden Hartley, Gay Identity, and the Wilhelmine German Military," *Art Journal* 56 (Summer 1997): 65.

5. Sandow's birth information is from Sandow, Eugen. *Sandow on Physical Training*. Ed. G. Mercer Adam. New York: Tait, 1894. 23. Although Adams is identified as the book's editor, it is probable that he actually wrote it. Except where otherwise noted, facts about Sandow's life and career is from Chapman, David L. *Sandow the Magnificent: Eugen Sandow and the Beginnings of Bodybuilding* (Urbana, IL: University of Illinois Press, 1994).

6. Sandow. *Sandow on Physical Training*. 23, 24.

7. Eugen Sandow, *Strength and How to Obtain It* (London: Gale & Polden, 1897), 87.

8. Robert Aldrich, *The Seduction of the Mediterranean* (New York: Routledge, 1993), 160.

9. Jason Edwards, "Edmund Gosse and the Victorian Nude," *History Today* 51 (November 2001): 34.

10. Edwards 35.

11. Kate Smith, "Untold London," www.untoldlondon.org.uk/news/ART53498-.html (accessed January 25, 2008).

12. Chapman 9.

13. www.ironmagazineforums.com/gallery/showphoto.php/photo/7085 will take the reader to a copy of the photo. Taken in 1886, when Sandow was beginning to document the development of his body, the 19-year-old Adonis is wearing only a loincloth and none of the classical allusion that were typical of "physical culturists" of the time, not even his trademark sandals. Note the "V" that the loincloth makes, drawing the viewer's

attention to Sandow's penis, something that would not go unnoticed by queer viewers.

14. Chapman 11.

15. Chapman 16.

16. Chapman 19.

17. Few homosexuals who cruised Venice for sex partners left actual records of their experiences, but Frederick Rolfe, better known as the author "Baron Corvo," recorded his meeting with a young hustler in a letter ("Frederick Rolfe to C., November 28, 1909, from Venice," in *Nineteenth-century Writings on Homosexuality: A Sourcebook*, ed. Christ White (London: Routledge, 1999), 337–339).

18. Sandow, *Sandow on Physical Training* 41.

19. Eugen Sandow, "My Reminiscences," *Strand Magazine* 39 (March 1910): 147.

20. W. A. Pullum, "The Arrival of Eugen Sandow," *Bodybuilder Magazine* (January 1954), www. sandowplus.co.uk/S/bodybuilding%20mag%20jan%2054/sandow%20arrival.htm.

21. Gardiner, James. *A Class Apart: The Private Pictures of Montague Glover.* London: Serpents Tail, 1992. Excerpted at www.walnet.org/csis/biblios/monty_glover.

22. "Eugen Sandow: The Non-pareil," at www.sandowplus.co.uk/S/s&h-june1937/np.htm.

23. Chapman 19.

24. Murray Healy, "The Mark of a Man: Masculine Identities and the Art of Macho Drag," *Critical Quarterly* 36 (March 1994): 86.

25. Healey 87.

26. Michael Hatt, "Physical Culture: The Male Nude and Sculpture in Late Victorian Britain," In *After the Pre-Raphaelites: Art and Aestheticism in Victorian England*, ed. Elizabeth Prettejohn (New Brunswick, NJ: Rutgers UP, 1999), 165.

27. Hatt 165.

28. M., H. P., "The Latest Society Fad: Fashion Pays Court to Sandow, the Strong Man, at His Private Levees." *Frank Leslie's Illustrated Weekly*, March 29, 1894: 206.

29. Sandow, *Sandow on Physical Training* 135.

30. Sandow, *Strength and How to Obtain It*, 93.

31. www.ironmagazineforums.com/gallery/showphoto.php/photo/7086 will take the reader to one of Henry Van der Weyde's photos of the 22-year old Adonis. Sandow still has not yet grown his trademark mustache nor has he yet disguised his intent with classical accoutrement. Note the fig leaf. Because the light strikes it more brightly than it does any other spot on Sandow's body, our attention is drawn to it, and its raised position suggests an erection, fueling a queer viewer's imagination.

32. Chapman 34.

33. Alison J. Smith, *Chicago's Left Bank* (Chicago: Regnery, 1953), 58.

34. John Addington Symonds, *The Letters of John Addington Symonds: Volume 3, 1885–1893*, ed. Herbert M. Schueller and Robert L. Peters (Detroit: Wayne State University Press, 1969), 436.

35. The network of men with whom Symonds shared nude photographs was extensive and international and can be tracked in his letters.

36. J. Moriarty, "Sandow: Gay Strongman of the Gay 90s," *Advocate*, March 14, 1973: 30.

37. www.sandowplus.co.uk/Competition/Cyr/gallery.htm leads the reader to a gallery of various photos of Cyr. Not anyone's idea of "pure beauty," Louis Cyr was one of Sandow's best-known rivals in the late 1800s. He could lift extraordinary amounts of weight and was a superstar on the weight-lifting circuit. In the top/first photo, note Cyr's "fig leaf" and its decidedly vaginal appearance.

38. "Minor Sporting Matters," *New York Times*, April 2, 1893, 3.

39. John F. Kasson, *Houdini, Tarzan, and the Perfect Man: The White Male Body and the Challenge of Modernity in America* (New York: Hill and Wang, 2001), 23.

40. Sandow, *Sandow on Physical Training* 106.

41. Rudolph Aronson, *Theatrical and Musical Memoirs* (New York: McBride, Nast, 1913), 82.

42. Kasson 24.

43. Kasson 25.

44. Kasson 25.

45. "The Strongest Man in the World," *New York World*, June 20, 1893, 8.

46. http://lcweb2.loc.gov/cgibin/query/D?ils:20:./temp/~pp_capR::@@@mdb=fsaall,brum,detr,swann,look,gottscho,pan,horyd,gethe,var,cai,cd,hh,yan,lomax,ils,prok,brhc,nclc,matpc,iucpub,tgmi,lamb,hec,krb leads the reader to a photo of Sandow illustrating the effects of lighting on the fig leaf he wore.

47. www.stanford.edu/group/SHR/6-2/html/guttmann.html leads the reader to a photo of Sandow in the "Dying Parthian" pose.

48. Ibid.

49. www.sandowplus.co.uk/sandowindex.htm leads the reader to an electronic version of *Sandow on Physical Training*. Nude photos of Sandow performing push-ups are on page 217.

50. http://lcweb2.loc.gov/cgi-bin/query/D?ils:1:./temp/~pp_6Tcn::@@@mdb=fsaall,brum,detr, swann,look,gottscho,pan,horyd,genthe,var,cai,cd,hh,yan,lomax,ils,prok,brhc,nclc,matpc,iucpub,tgmi,lamb,hec,krb leads the reader to a photo of Sandow in the "Dying Gaul" pose.

51. Samuel Wilson Fussell, *Muscle: Confessions of an Unlikely Bodybuilder* (New York: Poseidon, 1991), 191.

52. Chapman 51. www.bach-cantatas.com/Lib/Sieveking-Martinus.htm leads the reader to two photos of Sadow's "bosom friend."

53. "The Strongest Man in the World."
54. Chapman 51.
55. Chapman 51.
56. Arthur H. Lewis, *La Belle Otero* (New York: Trident, 1967), 102.
57. Lewis 103.
58. Lewis 103–104.
59. Ibid.
60. Sandow, *Strength and How to Obtain It*, 121.
61. "Music Again at the Trocadero," *Chicago Daily Tribune*, September 10, 1893, 28.
62. Sandow, *Strength and How to Obtain It*, 130.
63. They inspired the way Sandow posed on stage. Alison Smith has informed us that "*tableau vivant* or *pose plastique* was a popular form of entertainment in which a group of actors clad in 'fleshlings' [i.e., tights] would impersonate a famous work of art. Despite differences of context and audience expectation, life modeling, and the *pose plastique* were construed as similar activities" (Alison J. Smith, *Chicago's Left Bank*. Chicago: Regnery, 1953, 25).
64. "Exit of Trocadero," *Chicago Daily Tribune*, January 25, 1894, 1.
65. "He Is a Man of Mighty Muscle," *Chicago Daily Tribune*, August 11, 1893, 9.
66. Chapman 60.
67. Chapman 46.
68. "The Strongest Man in the World."
69. "The Ladies Idolize Sandow," *National Police Gazette*, January 27, 1894, 6.
70. "The Ladies Idolize Sandow."
71. Chapman 75.
72. "Sandow Sails for Germany," *Chicago Daily Tribune*, November 5, 1893, 25.
73. Chapman 92.
74. "Gotham Brevities," *Chicago Daily Tribune*, January 14, 1894, 3.
75. "Thrilling Romance of Strong Man," *Chicago Daily Tribune*, January 27, 1894, 16.
76. Chapman 51.
77. Moriarty 31.
78. Bourget 61.

Chapter 9

RuPaul: Fashioning Queer

Alison Bancroft

RuPaul is an American drag artist whose creative output has included film, television shows, music, and club/cabarets, and he is well-known for his ambivalence toward gendered personal pronouns, declaring that he does not much care whether he is referred to as "he" or "she." Most interestingly, though, he is the only drag queen to have been given "supermodel" status, an accolade usually reserved for the world's most beautiful women. He has been the face of MAC cosmetics and has appeared on runway shows in Paris fashion week for the couturier Thierry Mugler.

This chapter will present a psychoanalytically inflected queer reading of fashion. It will interrogate in particular what happens when what is usually seen as unequivocally feminine— fashion—accommodates the equivocal erotic visuality of a biological man masquerading as the very acme of femininity. Usually drag "plays the game," as it were, and adheres to the security of gender codes even as it plays with them. It works because both masculinity and femininity retain their distinctness within the artist, and the act is successful precisely because of this duality. RuPaul transcends drag inasmuch as, in his fashion work at least, both masculinity and femininity are shown to be inherently unstable, and the very categories of gender themselves are problematized. On television, in films, in clubs, and in sound recordings, RuPaul is a drag artist. It is only in fashion that he becomes more than a drag queen. Arguably, fashion itself, by virtue of its inherent femininity, provides the possibility of transgression that other media and art forms do not, and RuPaul evidences this with abundant clarity.

Fashion is not necessarily a matter of expressing one's "identity," nor is it merely about trends or a matter of business, products, branding, and economics, although there are many instances when these issues are very much in evidence. Fashion is instead largely concerned with innovation in the surface decoration of the body and the wider social and cultural responses to this innovation. Moreover, it is the wearer, and the act of wearing, that are central to fashion. Fashion is not a discreet or enclosed collection of fixed objects. A garment is not an independent, fully formed object that is superimposed on the blank canvas of a woman's body. On the contrary, it exists only when it is in the process of being worn, and when fashion is encountered in contexts other than the act of being worn, it can often invoke a sense of disquiet. As Elizabeth Wilson has said, "Clothes without a wearer, whether on a second hand stall, in a glass case, or merely a lover's garments strewn on the floor, can affect us unpleasantly, as if a snake has shed its skin."[1] This unease that wearer-less garments can induce is explored in the fashion/art installation *Spring Summer Collection 1770–1998* (1998), by Lun*na Menoh, which demonstrates the processual nature of fashion with a linear depiction from left to right of consecutive changes in style through time.[2] More interestingly, though, it demonstrates how imperative the wearer is to the operation of fashion. These ghostly garments, devoid as they are of any corporeal relation, are suggestive of a sinister otherworldliness that Freud calls 'The Uncanny.' They are simultaneously familiar, almost mundane, in the way that only something as ubiquitous as clothing can be, and also alienated, following their removal from their expected context. As Freud puts it, " . . . the uncanny is in reality nothing new or alien, but something which is familiar and old-established in the mind and which has become alienated from it."[3]

Besides its relation to the human body, fashion is also closely associated with femininity and with art. It was Baudelaire's 'The Painter of Modern Life' that first distinguished this association and that tied this relationship to modern culture. In this essay, Baudelaire identifies a shift in fashion, from its role in revealing social distinctions predicated on class to distinctions predicated on gender instead.[4]

He sees fashion as synonymous with the feminine and suggests that the woman and the dress are inseparable from one another.[5]

In "The Painter of Modern Life," Baudelaire uses the words fashion (*mode*,) costume (*costume*), and dress (*robe*) to talk about a particular mode of dress that he describes as the historically specific aspect of beauty, and that renders beauty of a particular type, and in doing so makes it all together more human than it might otherwise be. He sees beauty, femininity, and fashion as bound together, contingent upon one another, and at once a product of its time and a-historically classic.[6] The mid-nineteenth century, when Baudelaire wrote "The Painter of Modern Life," is also the point in history when what J. C. Flügel calls "the Great Masculine Renunciation" occurs, when rational men renounced their right to adornment and chose useful work as an alternative means of gaining and maintaining status. Thorstein Veblen tells us too that the need of the new middle class to differentiate themselves from other social classes of the time led to the positioning of women as a vehicle for the vicarious display of her husband's wealth, a display that was conducted through the physically restrictive and heavily ornamented fashion worn by women at the time. A shift occurred, then, at around the time fashion became distinct from mere clothing in the mid-1800s that led to the association of fashion with the feminine.

This association remains even today. Anne Hollander reminds us that men's fashion is still a minor subsidiary of fashion and carries hardly any of the resonances of fashion that is associated with women.[7] Fashion is unique in this. Usually, where cultural forms (literature, art, film, music) are gendered, they tend to default to the masculine, with the feminine as a subset within the form; there is literature, and there is women's writing, for instance. There are artists, and there are women artists. Fashion alone defaults to the feminine.

Femininity is usually understood to refer to the attributes of woman, whatever they may be. Certainly that is the context in which Baudelaire uses it. In terms of its relationship to fashion, however, I suggest that it can be understood in rather broader terms; as pertaining to feminine subjects, usually but not exclusively women, as pertaining to and contingent upon the body, in particular the female body, and, in a specifically Lacanian idiom, as following an impossible and contradictory logic. These three definitions of femininity anchor fashion to the category of the feminine, while also rejecting any notion of that category as in any way either biologically or anatomically determined, or reliant on social structures for its resonances and its meaning.

Besides becoming associated with the feminine in the mid-nineteenth century, fashion simultaneously became associated with art. Baudelaire's "The Painter of Modern Life" has been acknowledged as the place in aesthetic discourse where fashion is isolated from history of costume, clothing or dress itself.[8] By suggesting that fashion has a place in artistic discourse, Baudelaire effectively identified fashion as a classification distinct from the operation of clothes, and advocated the centrality of fashion to modern aesthetic practice. This is not to say that fashion is art. Fashion relies on being worn by the human subject for its actualization in a way that art does not, and fashion can and should retain its identity distinct from art because of this. However, there are instances when fashion can be talked about in the same terms as art, and it is those instances that are of interest here. The premise that fashion is distinct from dress and that it creates this distinction through its aesthetic properties is central to the definition of fashion used in this paper. It allows fashion to enter into artistic and critical discourses while still retaining its disciplinary precision, and to simultaneously show up the limitations of existing gender specificity in art theory and practice.

Fashion is too dependent on existing social and psychic structures to ever present a realistic or viable challenge to them, and it is therefore difficult to claim that fashion is radical or revolutionary. Fashion is not likely to change the world. I do believe, however, that it is inherently seditious and can and does "subvert from within," offering profound challenges to existing structures in the terms that are available to it. The point where fashion manifests most clearly the concepts that this paper seeks to address—queer subjectivity and notions of the feminine and the masculine—is also the point where fashion is at its most innovative, provocative, and challenging, and the moments that demonstrate its disruptive potential.

FASHION, DESIRE AND A DRAG QUEEN

John Galliano is the design director at Christian Dior, part of LVMH (Louis Vuitton Moet Hennessy,) the most dominant luxury goods corporation in the world. For Galliano fashion must be a tangible commodity that exists in the here and now with the sole purpose of generating a financial profit. He is quite clear though that despite this economic imperative, eroticism is fashion's primary consideration, and, within that eroticism, heterosexual masculine desire is prioritized. Thus, he once famously suggested that the purpose of fashion is to make a man look at a women and think, "I have to fuck her."[9]

The appearance on fashion runways and in fashion magazine and billboard advertising of RuPaul thus raises questions for both fashion and for the operation of desire. What happens when what is usually seen as unequivocally feminine accommodates the equivocal erotic visuality of a biological man masquerading as the very acme of femininity? I propose that fashion itself, by virtue of its inherent femininity, provides the possibility of transgression of sexed identity and desire that other media and art forms do not, and that RuPaul evidences this with abundant clarity.

While much has been written about drag, and it is not my intention to review these debates in detail here, very little has been written about RuPaul himself. One article complains that he is letting down black gay men by dragging, and the practice of "tucking," where the penis and testes are tucked between the legs to give the impression, if not the authentic appearance, of female genitalia, is seen as symptomatic of his betrayal of black gay men.[10] Another complains that drag is a manifestation of the misogyny of gay men and provides a study of drag acts in Atlanta, including RuPaul early in his career, as evidence of this.[11] In terms of his involvement in fashion particularly, the well-known feminist critic Sheila Jeffreys has described his work again in terms of misogyny. She sees Thierry Mugler's employment of RuPaul as a model in his runway shows as evidence of misogyny in fashion and argues that this is evidence of the marginalization of what she calls "real, live women" in the representation of feminine sexuality.[12] The fashion critic Caroline Evans describes RuPaul's appearance in fashion in quasi-psychoanalytic terms, arguing that it is evidence of a masculine power, the "symbolic power of the phallus," lurking beneath the surface decoration of femininity.[13]

The problem with all of these ideas is that they are predicated on the idea of either masculinity or femininity or both as fixed or stable entities, when, as I will show, what RuPaul evidences in fashion is that *all* sexed identities are at best unstable, or, more likely, a conceptual impossibility. RuPaul is a model drag act, in every sense of the word: model as ideal and also model as mannequin. Thus he suggests an instance where queer interacts within fashion to problematize sexed identity, and, from this, sex and desire themselves.

PERFORMATIVITY AND PERFORMANCE

The continuum between life and art, or, more particularly, between the artist as subject in their own right and as creative producer, is the basis of Gavin Butt's analysis of the lesser-known post-war American painter, Larry Rivers. Butt starts his review of Rivers with a reading of a photograph of Rivers in a magazine, which showed him in a variety of roles (saxophonist, sculptor, nightclub host) in front of his painting of a number of human faces, all shown as different, but sharing the commonality of montage. The corollary between the many talents of the artist and the multiple fragmentary images of people in his paintings is made in this photograph. This leads Butt to argue that there is in fact little division between the artist as subject and artist as creator, and that the two segue into one another to such an extent that they are indivisible. By drawing attention to "the aporetic tensions between the way Rivers *is* and the way Rivers *acts*," Butts suggests that it is performative enactments that make both the artist and the art. There is no difference between "self "and "work" here. Instead, they are "continuous with the performative being of Larry Rivers, who can no more stop posing than he can stop being an artist since the very 'being' of his artistic self *is* the posing."[14]

This argument is clearly derivative of Judith Butler's profoundly influential 1990 publication *Gender Trouble: Feminism and the Subversion of Identity*. In this volume Butler cites drag acts as indicative of the impossibility of a core gender identity, saying that these very specialized performers and performances mock "both the expressive model of gender and the notion of a true gender identity."[15] Drag, for Butler, is a paradigm of the failure of gender in real life, which illustrates in parodying gender how gender is itself a parody. Drag shows the emptiness of the original it ostensibly copies. What is of particular note in Butler's thesis is her use of the term "performative." Following from her analysis of drag, she argues that:

> Gender ought not to be construed as a stable identity or locus of agency from which various acts follow; rather, gender is an identity tenuously constituted in time and space through a *stylised repetition of acts*. The effect of gender is produced through the stylization of the body and, hence, must be understood as the mundane way in which bodily gestures, movements and styles of various kinds constitute the illusion of an abiding gendered self. This formulation moves the conception of gender off the ground of a substantial model of identity to one that requires a concept of gender as a constituted *social temporality*. Significantly, if gender is instituted through acts which are internally discontinuous, then the *appearance of substance* is precisely that, a constructed identity, a performative accomplishment which the mundane social audience, including the actors themselves, come to believe and to perform in the mode of belief.[16]

While there is little with which we would wish to argue in Butler's efforts to denaturalize gender and at the same time remove it from any notion of substantive social truth, her thesis is problematic for a number of reasons. Tim Dean, for instance, highlights the way in which her account of the body evacuates both desire and the subject from sexuality, while Joan Copjec argues for the necessity of the real and its irreducibility to either materiality, language or social structure.[17] In a consideration of RuPaul, in particular, Butler's idea of the performative falls short for several reasons. The first issue is the conflation of performance with performative. Butler derives the latter from the former, although there is no direct or automatic connection between the two. Indeed, there is a strong case to be made for their being entirely separate entities. Performance is entirely and knowingly artificial, and there is a clear disjuncture between the performance and the performer doing the performance. The performer, at the end of the performance, takes off their costume and make-up and goes home. Even in the more radical instances of performance art, such as Orlan or Leigh Bowery, there is no suggestion that the performance is an artistic articulation of the artist themselves. Rather, these artists use performance conceptually, to question the very notion of selfhood or subjectivity itself. These performances are more concerned with the audience than they are with the artist. What is more, these performances take place within certain charmed enclosures, environments in which performance is possible, or indeed expected—art galleries, theatres, and nightclubs in major international cities. These performances are very much an urban cultural form, and it is therefore reasonable to suppose that if these performances were to take place outside of the charmed enclosures in which they are permissible, the performer may well be subject to hostility and opposition, as the Coober Pedy scene in the 1996 film *The Adventures of Priscilla, Queen of the Desert* suggests. Here, a drag queen from Sydney (played by Guy Pearce) goes out in full drag in a small mining community in the Australian outback and is violently assaulted by several men of the town as a consequence. His performative parody of gender is very badly received by a group of miners, who have their own very clear ideas about gender.

To extrapolate from the idea of a particular mode of performance that directly addresses questions of gender, to the claim that that the knowing artificiality of performance is something fundamental or common to all people in all circumstances, is a connection that is, in my view, untenable. Quite apart from anything else it disregards any suggestion of the psychic processes by which gender is constituted, which I have discussed at length throughout this thesis. Also, to commute performance to performativity, that is, "repetitive and stylized acts," posits a model of the subject that does not account for the many and complex psychic and social processes which shape and influence the subject and their interactions. While Butler is quite right to suggest that there is no core gender identity, and that there is no direct connection between what we understand as gender identity and any anatomical or biological distinction of the categories of man and woman, to understand gender in terms of a performativity that is derivative of performance instead is problematic.

Gender, to my mind, is not "instituted in an exterior space through a stylized repetition of acts"[18] but is instead constituted at the level of the unconscious, which has little or nothing to do with either anatomy or social mores. It is, in fact, all about the subject. Without the subject there is no gender, normativized or otherwise, and we can say that without suggesting that gender is in some way a "core" to the subject themselves.

In fairness to Butler, she addressed many of the concerns that arose following the publication of *Gender Trouble* in her next book, *Bodies That Matter* (1993).[19] Here she seeks to address the materiality of the body, something that was conspicuous by its absence in *Gender Trouble*. Unfortunately, this book follows *Gender Trouble* in that although she mentions various psychoanalytic concepts they do not underpin her arguments in any meaningful way. In the chapter "Arguing With The Real," for instance, she actually argues with Zizek and his take on the real, rather than the concept of the real itself. She is also particularly concerned with the ways in which the sexed subject is constituted in relation to their own body, and again does not make any reference to the psychic processes that are in psychoanalytic terms essential to any consideration of sex.

For the purposes of this chapter, then, the way in which RuPaul's life and work reflects on the concept of sexual desire and sexuated subjectivity will be central. We will not be speculating on the man himself, nor will we consider him as paradigmatic of a human commonality. If there is a continuum between the man and his work, such as the one suggested by Gavin Butt in his analysis of Larry Rivers, it will be considered in terms of the articulation of particular psychic processes and phenomena, and not as a voluntarist continuum between performance and subjectivity of the kind suggested by Butler and her followers. Where the word performativity is used in this chapter, it will be used in the sense of art criticism, and not in the Butlerian sense.

In art criticism, the term performativity has been used to describe the process by which external influences become a part of the subject's own thoughts. This is, in fact, how Peggy Phelan uses the term when she says:

> The interaction between the art object and the spectator is, essentially, performative—and therefore resistant to the claims of validity and accuracy endemic to the discourse of reproduction. While the art historian of painting must ask if the reproduction is accurate and clear, Calle [the artist under discussion] asks where seeing and memory forget the object itself and enter the subject's own set of personal meanings and associations.[20]

Here, Phelan is making the case for the dynamic and active exchange that is the viewer's encounter with an artwork, suggesting that it is a process of ongoing engagement rather than a static and temporal encounter.

FASHION

John Galliano is on record as saying that "when a man sees a woman in my dress, I want him to think, 'I have to fuck her,' " while his contemporary, Alexander McQueen, produces garments that make men look at the woman and think, "I wouldn't dare!" In Lacanian terms these two design philosophies are paradigmatic of the different ways in which the feminine relates to the masculine in the Symbolic, as *objet a*, which offers the potential for both merely phallic jouissance and the disruptive, anarchic feminine jouissance There is a sense in which RuPaul preempts this debate, as it is played out in Galliano's and McQueen's collections. In particular, RuPaul appearances in fashion seem to resist the structural logic of sexuation and desire, especially as it pertains to the feminine, and this can be explained under the rubric of two key terms from Lacanian psychoanalysis: the *hommosexuelle* and *transgression*.

Lacan refers to the homosexual as the *hommosexuelle*, a pun on homme (man) and sexuelle (the feminine form of the word sexual). It is clear from his wordplay that conflates man and the feminine sexual that Lacan sees homosexuality not as same-sex desire between men but as an attestation to an extreme love of the feminine. For Lacan, a homosexual (*hommosexuelle*) is a man who occupies a feminine-sexuated subject position and who loves women differently, indeed who loves rather than desires. Lacan suggests that the *hommosexuelle* is a man who loves Woman as an ideal and who is defined by both this ideal love and (Lacan departs from Freud here) the wish to keep this ideal distinct from sex. Where Lacan has argued that (the ideal and idealized) Woman does not exist, the *hommosexuelle* nevertheless believes that in fact she does.[21] The *hommosexuelle* retains the belief of Woman as Ideal and idealizes woman by refusing in his unconscious to acknowledge her representation of lack. This idealization is maintained through a refusal of desire for woman. Unlike a heterosexual man who is quite happy to seek phallic jouissance from woman, the *hommosexuelle* believes that such jouissance is impossible to attain from the ideal without destroying the ideal. The *hommosexuelle*, then, manifests a "pure" love, as distinct from heterosexual desire.[22]

It is worth noting that there is nothing one can do about either love or desire. They cannot be reined in or controlled. They are their own masters and operate in and through the subject, making a mockery of any notion of agency or free will. The mode of desire that emanates from this *hommosexuelle* love is of a very different order to love as it is defined within the normal heterosexual matrix and can be seen as the manifestation of the disruption of the real in the order of the symbolic.

The word jouissance has no direct translation into English but is generally taken to mean some kind of powerful orgasmic joy. How this is experienced depends on the subject and their circumstances, but in terms of desire, the masculine subject will experience merely phallic jouissance (something Slavoj Zizek calls "stupid") while the feminine subject will enjoy a "jouissance of the other," an altogether more intense, ecstatic, and troubling experience.[23] The jouissance of transgression offers another model of jouissance, one that is not contingent on sexed subjectivity necessarily, but one that arises from breaching the social contract.

RuPaul uses fashion in two ways; firstly to articulate the *hommosexuelle* and the occupation of a feminine subject position by a biological male and so disrupt masculinity and heteronormativity, and secondly to introduce the impossibility of feminine jouissance, and, more importantly, the disorder of transgressive jouissance, into the symbolic order.

The question of performance arises at this point, and the extent to which RuPaul's modeling can be considered performance. I suggest that although it might not be deemed performance in the usual theatrical or artistic sense of the word, his work in fashion can be talked about in the same terms as performance for several reasons. They take place, for the most part, in environments where performance is anticipated, and that are at one remove at least from domestic or working environments; fashion runways during fashion week, or professional photographer's studios, where unusual and non-normative characterization of the self is encouraged, and that are quite literally and figuratively several thousand miles away from RuPaul's industrial home town of San Diego, California. There is an immediacy to the garments that suggests that once they are removed from the wearer they become, in the words of one magazine editor, "a wardrobe of wilted relics."[24] This immediacy is shared by the MAC advertising campaigns, in that photography is the capturing of a moment in time. In this regard we can see that fashion and performance share the feature of immediacy, they can only exist in the moment. There is the sense that in appearing as a model, he is presenting an artistic piece of work to an audience, in the same way that his video and sound recording performances can be seen as artistic or creative output.

By virtue of their having an ongoing quality, with the images still in circulation, RuPaul's fashion work fits in with the definition of performativity set out by Peggy Phelan, which suggests that an encounter between viewer and art is an ongoing process of engagement and a dynamic and active exchange. Despite the apparent marginality of drag acts, RuPaul was sufficiently well-known for him to be invited to participate in some remarkably high-profile fashion events, and his presence in the feminine world of fashion disrupted absolutely any idea that the feminine is in any way either biologically or anatomically determined, or reliant on social structures for its resonances and its meaning. All of this can be seen as indicative of the performance inherent in his appearances in fashion.

More importantly for our purposes, though, Phelan's idea that the body in performance is metonymic will be helpful in interpreting the many aspects of RuPaul's fashion work. The body in performance, her argument goes, is a metonym, but for some aspect of the performance (a character, for instance, or movement or sound, or art), rather than the performer themselves. The performer's subjective presence is lost, thus suggesting the disjuncture between the body and subjectivity. Moreover the body itself can only appear in performance through an addition of some other aspect or element, it can never appear in its own right.

This raises two questions regarding RuPaul's fashion work that we are discussing here. Firstly, if RuPaul's body is functioning metonymically in the performance for some aspect of the performance (and not for RuPaul himself), what is it that his body is standing metonymically for? Secondly, if the body can only appear in performance through an addition or supplement, what is that addition or supplement that makes the body appear here, if indeed it can be said to appear at all? RuPaul's body in these performances, I suggest, stands for the feminine body as emblem of the lack, the lacuna, that psychoanalysis has identified as being at the heart of subjectivity and that is obscured by dress. This lack is what is central to RuPaul's modeling, it is this lack that he is articulating through his engagement with fashion, and it is this lack that his body stands for metonymically in his runway and photographic performances. And what is the addition that enables the body to appear? I suggest it is the addition of fashion. The costume and make-up of fashion, then, serve a double and contradictory purpose—they allow the metonymic function of the body in performance, and they also allow the body to elide this metonymy and appear in its own right. This radical and contradictory dualism is what makes RuPaul's modeling such a unique and iconic phenomenon.

Psychoanalysis tells us that it is the feminine body that stands for the lack that is at the heart of human subjectivity and so must be covered. Fashion, arguably, is an essential aspect of the veil that is femininity, and following Joan Rivière's influential 1929 essay, "Womanliness as Masquerade" the association between femininity and masquerade has become a widely accepted critical position.[25] Rivière argues that femininity is not covered or hidden in some way, but rather is itself the cover, the mask. The question of what it is that femininity masks is precisely what makes the condition of femininity so problematic; it masks that which cannot be represented. There is, moreover, hostility within patriarchy to femininity that emanates from the perception of its duplicity. There is a sense in which the masquerade that is femininity is seen as a willful act of treachery, that women don a mask in order to deliberately mislead men. Examples abound in Western culture of the inherent deceitfulness of women, from the biblical myth of Eve onwards. (The myth of Eve is particularly instructive, as it is she who first insists on clothing to cover the symbolic lack that is central to human subjectivity.) Curiously enough, there is no suggestion that women benefit in any way from this deceit, nor indeed that men are disadvantaged by it, but nevertheless the assumption that there is a degree of agency in it is basis enough for continued suspicion of the feminine as inherently untrustworthy.

Michelle Montrelay describes this masquerade in terms of the materiality of fashion (it "takes shape in this piling up of crazy things, feathers, hats and strange baroque constructions which rise up like so many silent insignias") and observes further that "man has always called the feminine defenses and masquerade *evil*."[26] For Jacques Lacan, the term *semblance* is key here and refers to the requirement placed on women to don the colors, as it were, of the Other's desire, the better that they may be, as they are required to be, the phallus. The masquerade serves to demonstrate how the woman's lack (of a penis) leads to her instead becoming the phallus. "Such is the woman behind her veil: it is the absence of the penis that makes her the phallus, object of desire."[27] Referring to fashion as a paradigm of the veil behind which feminine sexuality must operate is a common device among critics, and the contribution of fashion and bodily adornment to the inherent masquerade that is feminine sexuality is well established.[28] Adornment is, then, the woman in the symbolic order because she represents lack and lack "is never presented to us other than as a reflection on a veil."[29]

Crucially, though, what we see in RuPaul's fashion modeling is that the *hommosexuelle*, because of his sexuated subject position, is able to allow the masculine body to stand for lack too. The adoption of seemingly feminine corporeal characteristics in conjunction with the maintenance of the masculine aspects of the body, in particular his height, suggests also that masculinity is not as secure as it might wish to be. In presenting the artifice of the feminine at the same time as disrupting the masculine, as RuPaul does in fashion, heteronormativity is also challenged. Its reliance on stable, oppositional gender identities is shown to be an edifice built on sand.

What we see coalescing around the figure of RuPaul are instances of *hommosexuelle* transgression that can be understood in terms of both psychoanalysis and performance. RuPaul as model can be seen as enacting a performative manifestation of transgressive jouissance, and that is contingent upon a negation of the self. Performance ceases to exist immediately when it comes into being. It must do this in order to be performance. If RuPaul constitutes his queer subjectivity as performance art, which, arguably, his modeling did, this means that RuPaul is enacting in his own work the very dissolution of the subject. His performances suggest the obsolescence of the subject, and specifically the masculine subject.

The fact that RuPaul's performances self-consciously engage with visual signifiers of the feminine merely augment this by demonstrating the inherent instability of masculinity, and gender more generally, in the symbolic. Central to any understanding of RuPaul is the idea that he not only transgresses social mores but that he goes further, that he rides roughshod over the underpinnings of sociality itself, as they are constituted through sexed subjectivity.

When masculine subjectivity is rendered obsolete, as it is by RuPaul, questions of meaning arise. It is an instance of metonymy not least because although the failure of the masculine is unthinkable in the symbolic, the masculine is in fact on much shakier ground than it realizes. Metonymic slippage in both performance and language is a way of circumventing the ego, the censorship that would have us believe that masculinity is more fixed and stable than is in fact the case. RuPaul's fashion work is just such a metonymic slippage precisely because they foreground the problems with masculinity that are habitually repressed.

Thus, RuPaul's unique appearances as a model, on the runway and in cosmetics advertising, evidences two decidedly queer concepts. They show that gendered subjectivity is an area of contestation, and that the occupation of feminine (and by extension masculine) subject positions are contingent upon the operation of the psyche rather than either an anatomical actuality or a cultural construct. The hostility that greeted his appearance on the runway, of the kind that we saw in Sheila Jeffrey's response mentioned earlier, indicate just how disturbing his fashion work can be. Far from being misogynist, RuPaul shows how *all* gendered identity is problematic. They also show how such anti-normative positioning can be a source of both feminine and transgressive jouissance, and that they are instances of a profound and troubling disruption of the symbolic order. The discomfort that viewers may feel looking at the images of RuPaul as a model is perhaps a jouissance of a sort, and it is the sort of jouissance that is intense and disquieting rather than reassuring and enjoyable. RuPaul reminds us that our comforting assumptions about men, women, sexuality, and the body are precisely that, assumptions, and his foray into the charmed enclosure of fashion made it possible for him to relay that reminder with abundant clarity, and in impeccable style.

NOTES

1. Elisabeth Wilson, *Adorned in Dreams: Fashion and Modernity* (London: I. B. Tauris, 2003) 2.

2. An image of this installation can be seen in *Addressing the Century: 100 Years of Art and Fashion* (London: Hayward Gallery, 1998) 63.

3. Sigmund Freud "The Uncanny" (1919) in Sigmund Freud, *An Infantile Neurosis and Other Works*, trans. by James Strachey and Anna Freud (London: Hogarth Press, 1955) 363.

4. Prior to the mid-nineteenth century fashionable dress was used as a marker of rank, with gender as only a subset within that. In particular, the Sumptuary Laws, vestimentary codes that were common across Europe until the Renaissance, dictated who could wear what fabrics, colours, and so on, so that social rank was clearly visually discernable. For a full description of them, see Marjorie Garber, *Vested Interests: Cross-Dressing and Cultural Anxiety* (London: Penguin, 1993) especially 32–35.

5. Charles Baudelaire, *Selected Writings on Art and Literature* (London: Penguin, 1992) 424.

6. Baudelaire, *Selected Writings on Art and Literature* 392.

7. Anne Hollander *Sex and Suits: The Evolution of Modern Dress* (Brinkworth: Claridge, 2004) 11.

8. Leila Kinney "Fashion and Figuration in Modern Life Painting" in *Architecture: In Fashion*, ed. Deborah Fausch and Paulette Singley (New York: Princeton Architectural Press, 1991) 291.

9. Michael Specter, "Le Freak, C'est Chic," *The Observer*, 30th November 2003, Magazine section, 17.

10. Keith E. McNeal, "Behind the Make-Up: Gender Ambivalence and the Double-Bind of Gay Selfhood in Drag Performance," *Ethos*, 27:3 (1999) 344–378.

11. Paul Outlaw, "If That's Your Boyfriend (He Wasn't Last Night)," *African American Review*, 29:2 (1995) 347–350.

12. Sheila Jeffreys, Beauty and Misogyny: Harmful Cultural Practices in the West (London, Routledge, 2005) 100.

13. Caroline Evans, *Fashion at the Edge: Spectacle, Modernity & Deathliness* (New Haven; London: Yale University Press, 2003) 124.

14. Gavin Butt "The Greatest Homosexual? Camp Pleasure and the Performative Body of Larry Rivers", in *Performing the Body/Performing the Text*, ed. Amelia Jones and Andrew Stephenson (London: Routledge, 1999) 108, 120–121.

15. Judith Butler, *Gender Trouble: Feminism and the Subversion of Identity* (New York, London: Routledge, 1990) 137.

16. Butler, *Gender Trouble*, pp. 140–141.

17. See Tim Dean and Christopher Lane, ed., *Homosexuality and Psychoanalysis* (Chicago; London: The University of Chicago Press, 2001) 174–214 and Joan Copjec, *Read My Desire: Lacan against the Historicists* (Cambridge, Mass.; London: MIT Press, 1994) 7–24.

18. Butler, *Gender Trouble*, p. 140.

19. Butler, Judith, *Bodies That Matter: On the Discursive Limits Of "Sex"* (New York, London: Routledge, 1993).

20. Phelan, Peggy, *Unmarked: Politics of Performance* (London: Routledge, 1993) 147.

21. Jacques Lacan, *On Feminine Sexuality: The Limits of Love and Knowledge (the Seminar of Jacques Lacan; Book XX)*. trans. Bruce Fink (New York; London: Norton, 1998) 72.

22. Lacan, *On Feminine Sexuality* 85.

23. Slavoj Zizek, *Interrogating the Real: Selected Writings* (New York; London: Continuum, 2005) 307.

24. Mariuccia Casadio, in her introduction to Fergus Greer, *Leigh Bowery: Looks* (London: Violette Editions, 2002).

25. Reproduced in *Formations of Fantasy*, eds Victor Burgin, James Donald and Cora Kaplan (London: Methuen, 1986) 35–44.

26. Michèle Montrelay, "Inquiry into Femininity", *m/f*, 1:1 (1978) 91–116, 93.

27. Jacques Lacan, *The Écrits: A Selection*. trans. Sheridan, Alan (London: Routledge, 2004) 322.

28. See Ellie Ragland Sullivan and Mark Bracher, *Lacan and the Subject of Language* (New York, London: Routledge, 1991): Suzanne Barnard, and Bruce Fink, eds., *Reading Seminar XX: Lacan's Major Work on Love, Knowledge, and Feminine Sexuality* (Albany, N.Y.: State University of New York Press, 2002) (particularly "Feminine Conditions of Jouissance" by Geneviève Morel and "What Does the Unconscious Know About Women" by Colette Soler): Caroline Evans, "Masks, Mirrors and Mannequins: Elsa Schiaparelli and the Decentred Subject," *Fashion Theory*, 3:1 (1999) for examples of this.

29. Jacques Lacan, *The Seminars of Jacques Lacan Book II: The Ego in Freud's Theory and in the Technique of Psychoanalysis*. trans. Tomaselli, Sylvana. (Cambridge: Cambridge University Press, 1988), 261.

REFERENCES

Addressing the Century: 100 Years of Art and Fashion (London: Hayward Gallery, 1998).

Barnard, S., and B. Fink, eds. *Reading Seminar XX: Lacan's Major Work on Love, Knowledge, and Feminine Sexuality*. Albany, NY: State University of New York Press, 2002.

Baudelaire, C. *Selected Writings on Art and Literature*. London: Penguin, 1992.

Burgin, V., J. Donald, and C. Kaplan, eds. *Formations of Fantasy*. London: Methuen, 1986.

Butler, J. *Gender Trouble: Feminism and the Subversion of Identity*. New York and London: Routledge, 1990.

Copjec, J. *Read My Desire: Lacan Against the Historicists*. Cambridge and London: MIT Press, 1994.

Dean, T., and C. Lane, ed., *Homosexuality and Psychoanalysis*. Chicago; London: The University of Chicago Press, 2001.

Evans, C. "Masks, Mirrors and Mannequins: Elsa Schiaparelli and the Decentred Subject." *Fashion Theory*, 3:1 (1999) 117–139.

Evans, C. *Fashion at the Edge: Spectacle, Modernity & Deathliness*. New Haven; London: Yale University Press, 2003.

Fausch, D., and P. Singley, eds. *Architecture: In Fashion*. New York: Princeton Architectural Press, 1991.

Flügel, J. C. *The Psychology of Clothes*. London: Institute of Psycho-analysis, 1930.

Freud, S. *An Infantile Neurosis and Other Works*, trans. by James Strachey and Anna Freud. London: Hogarth Press, 1955.

Garber, M. *Vested Interests: Cross-Dressing and Cultural Anxiety*. London: Penguin, 1993.

Greer, F. *Leigh Bowery: Looks*. London: Violette Editions, 2002.

Hollander, Anne. *Sex and Suits: The Evolution of Modern Dress*. Brinkworth: Claridge, 2004.

Jeffreys, S. *Beauty and Misogyny: Harmful Cultural Practices in the West*. London, Routledge, 2005.

Jones, A., and A. Stephenson, eds. *Performing the Body/Performing the Text*. London: Routledge, 1999.

Judith, B. *Bodies That Matter: On the Discursive Limits Of "Sex."* New York and London: Routledge, 1993.

Lacan, J. *The Seminars of Jacques Lacan Book II: The Ego in Freud's Theory and in the Technique of Psychoanalysis*, trans. Sylvana Tomaselli. Cambridge: Cambridge University Press, 1988.

Lacan, J. *On Feminine Sexuality: The Limits of Love and Knowledge. The Seminar of Jacques Lacan; Book XX*. Trans. Bruce Fink (New York; London: Norton, 1998).

Lacan, J. *The Écrits: A Selection*. Trans. Alan Sheridan. London: Routledge, 2004.

McNeal, K. E. Behind the Make-Up: Gender Ambivalence and the Double-Bind of Gay Selfhood in Drag Performance. *Ethos*, 27:3 (1999) 344–378.

Mestrovic, S., ed. *Thorstein Veblen: On Culture and Society*. London: Sage, 2003.

Montrelay, M. "Inquiry into Femininity" *m/f*, 1:1 (1978) 91–116.

Outlaw, P. "If That's Your Boyfriend (He Wasn't Last Night)." *African American Review*, 29:2 (1995) 347–350.

Phelan, P. *Unmarked: Politics of Performance*. London: Routledge, 1993.

Ragland S., and Ellie and Mark Bracher, *Lacan and the Subject of Language*. New York, London: Routledge, 1991.

Specter, M. "Le Freak, C'est Chic," *The Observer*. November 30, 2003, Magazine section.

Wilson, E. *Adorned in Dreams: Fashion and Modernity*. London: I. B. Tauris, 2003.

Zizek, S. *Interrogating the Real: Selected Writings*. New York; London: Continuum, 2005.

Chapter 10

Boi's Story

Barclay Barrios

This is a story about boi. Not about *a* boi, but about boi. And not about boy but very specifically about *boi*. Though homonymically related, boi and boy differ greatly in meaning. What's more, there are several different understandings of what this new version of boy means, and who gets to claim it as a marker of identity. In this chapter, I want to explore these competing meanings of boi as well as the various genealogies behind the term. I am interested not simply in what the several meanings of boi have in common, but even more so in the ways in which certain subcommunities have come to police the term. In other words, while personally fascinated with the story of boi, I am critically interested in mapping who gets to tell that story.

To place this development in context, the emergence of boi is only one manifestation of a larger linguistic liberalization in LGBT communities. As Rona Marech (2004) explains in the *San Francisco Chronicle*, "With the universe of gender and sexual identities expanding, a gay youth culture emerging, acceptance of gays rising and label loyalty falling, the gay lexicon has exploded with scores of new words and blended phrases that delineate every conceivable stop on the identity spectrum—at least for this week." Marech goes on to offer as examples terms such as "polygendered," "bi-dyke," "stud," "stem," and, of course, "boi" (2004). But while this lexical explosion would seem to be one benefit of greater acceptance of LGBT individuals, since it opens the possibilities for identity, it is actually a dangerous development, for these terms are what Tony Thorne of the English Language Center at King's College London calls "unstable" (2004). Jonathan Duffy quotes Thorne as saying "They're liable to change their connotations and meanings depending on who is saying them, to whom, in what circumstances, sometimes even depending on their tone of voice" (2004). Given this instability, literacy is crucial. You need to know not simply how to read the term but how to deploy it as well.

So what exactly is a boi? That all depends on who you ask. One location for the emergence of the term is within the lesbian community. And yet even within that one community there are various meanings for the term—"it's a fluid identity," writes Arial Levy, "and that's the whole point" (2004). But Levy also identifies a key common denominator: "What all [lesbian] bois have in common is a lack of interest in embodying any kind of girliness, but they are too irreverent to adopt the heavy-duty, highly circumscribed butch role," a description supported by one self-proclaimed boi dyke who claims that "boi dyke is simply an extension of the butch community" (2004; What am I?, n.d.). Levy goes on to locate several possible genealogies for this understanding of boi, ranging from gay male SM relationships to the increasingly visible transgender and transsexual communities.

Certainly, the term has strong roots within the transgender community, where it is used to describe a female-to-male or FTM transsexual. Thus veganboi writes on his homepage, "I'm not a girl, not really a boy, but somewhere in between, but I identify more as a boi, so the label would actually be FTM" (n.d.). In terms of the genealogy of boi in the trans community, Jes Kraus (2003) relates the altered spelling to feminist reclamation of words like "women" through spellings like "w-o-m-y-n." Interestingly, then, the trans and lesbian senses of the term seems to reference each other for the term's origin. For boi dykes, the term emerges from the FTM community. For trans bois, it is related to the kind of feminist practices traditionally associated with the lesbian community.

Of course, boi dykes also reference, in part, gay male sadomasochistic (SM) relationships—Daddy/boy configurations in which "boy" refers not to age but to mindset and in which the relationship is characterized by dominance, submission, and affection. Gay male leather thus functions as another milieu for the circulation of this term. A search through screen names on America Online, for example, would yield any number of boys and bois. Other Web sites devoted to gay male SM similarly are populated by both boy spellings. On the site World Leathermen, for example, Beardadmaster (n.d.) advertises for a "Son & boi" and CigarDaddy (n.d.) seeks "likeminded Boiz." But, curiously, within this particular community, the terms seem to be, at times, interchangeable. Thus on the same site LordFalconJock69 (n.d.) seeks a "boy/boi" and ROPEDBOI (n.d.) refers to himself as a boy. This makes some sense since boi is neither a new term nor a new identity within this community, just a new spelling.

One possible genealogy for gay leather bois has to do with a contiguous sexual community, gay skinheads. Submissive gay skinheads sometime use this spelling as a way to mark both their boy and skin identities. "Oi!"—named by Gary Bushell—is a kind of skinhead music, and so boi, in this sense, specifically marks a gay male submissive as a skin. Skinhead bois often intermingle with the larger gay male leather community, which helps explain the circulation of boi out of the skin community and into gay male leather in general. The aforementioned World Leathermen site, for example, is only one site of several run by a single company. These sites are all interlinked and include a site devoted to gay skinheads. Thus, while boi has a very specific meaning for gay skins, because that meaning is analogous to boy for gay leathermen, the two terms intermingle as the two groups do.

There is, too, a more general understanding of boi in the gay community. Reacting to Levy's description of boi dykes, Towleroad (2004) blogs that "Gay men have adopted the term as a way to give off the impression of youth and innocence while still retaining enough of a masculine sensibility to not be considered effeminate. It's the anti-bear." Yet while "confused" by the adoption of the term among lesbians, his description of the gay boi is remarkably similar, in some ways, to the dyke boi (Towleroad 2004). Just as boi is counterposed to the more "grown-up" butch for lesbians, boi is here set against the more "grown-up" bear of the gay community.

We might assume that these gay bois are white, based on the general perceived racial composition of the gay male community, but boi also circulates specifically within the gay African-American community. There is, for example, a very specific black gay male understanding of boi in the leather community. Lolita Wolf (2004), posting to the gl-asb mailing list, writes that Rodtney Ross used boi because "He felt that as an African American being called 'boy' was inferior but being called 'boi' was a term of endearment." Phil Ross (2004) adds to Wolf's observation: "so far as I know, I created this spelling as the 'familiar' of boy to distinguish it's [*sic*] use in the African-American community as a term of endearment. It has NOTHING whatsoever to do with gender. It's an oral language and so the spellings are 'made-up'; but All [*sic*]

African Americans recognize the difference of use by inflection." Ross's claim that "all" African Americans recognize the difference is, perhaps, unsupportable, and yet boi clearly circulates in a larger African-American gay community. The homepage for Club Boi, a gay bar in Miami, explains that "The name CLUB BOI speaks for itself. Run by bruthas with years of club experience who created an environment especially for the 'bruthas' in the South Florida area. The Kids have their clubs, the girls have theirs, but this is **OURS**" (n.d.). In this usage, boi seems to be specifically African-American but not specifically gay. One of the two men who make up the singing group OutKast goes by the name Big Boi.

There are other bois as well. Singer Avril Lavigne's hit debut was the song "Sk8r Boi," which led blogger Towleroad (2004) to comment "Apparently there are straight bois as well." And, in the discussion of boi on the gl-asb mailing list, Steve Scofield notes that the emergence of boi can also be explained by the limitations of identity on the Internet, specifically the limitations of various screen names. He notes the creation of "Musc, musl, mscl for muscle; bare, ber, behr for bear. So [he] suggest[s] that boi and boyz and boiz are used by many simply as alternative spellings without any awareness of the cultural context" (2004).

It is perhaps in part *this* usage of boi—divorced from specific meaning—that has prompted a certain policing of the term. While boi is a term with multiple meanings for multiple communities, and while across its usages it seems to reflect a renegotiated masculinity, there are isolated stirrings to restrict both its meaning and circulation. This is the very instability Thorne warned of, and this is precisely why having a fine-tuned literacy is crucial when using the term boi. In his World Leathermen profile, for example, BullKiser writes: "Please note: if you spell boy as boi, then don't bother to contact me . . . you obviously don't know leathersex and its history well enough to create trust with me. A boi is not of male gender in Old Guard Leathersex" (n.d.). MrKevin's profile has a similar tone in reference to boi: "I have been in the BD/SM community long enough . . . to know the term 'boi' was coined to describe a biological female who identified as a 'boy'. Even though pop culture has now taken on the term. It should make sense that I find it odd and somewhat telling about ones experience level when a biological male describes himself as a 'boi'" (n.d.). MuscleCubAOL seems even more adamant: "If you REALLY KNEW what the term 'boi' meant, you'd never EVER use it. Ever. Ask a sociopolitical historian" (n.d.). Not being a sociopolitical historian myself, and not having one handy to ask, I can't help but wonder what the term really does mean.

And yet again, I'm not sure how to read this policing. While certain segments of the gay male leather community seem to be vehemently rejecting the usage of the term in their community, what remains unclear is why. Is there, for example, a kind of transphobia in operation here, where the masculinity of the biologically male leather community needs to be protected from FTM intrusion? Or is the opposite true? Is this a way to protect and respect female leather boys and FTMs? Or, perhaps, is this simply a reactionary response from older members of a community? After all, with his 18 year history in the BD/SM community, MrKevin's response to boi seems similar to the response of some butch/femme lesbians to the term. Levy quotes Deborah, an out femme dyke for fourteen years: "And the whole b-o-i business. I'm like, what the fuck? What does that mean? In one respect I thought it meant a little bit butch of center, slightly more andro, with this whole tweezed-eyebrow business that makes me want to puke" (2004). These questions are a crisis in my own literacy: I just don't know how to read these reactions to boi. But they are part of boi's story, as surely as any of its meanings or origins.

And so boi is a story without an ending. For now. Language, after all, never remains unstable. Ultimately, perhaps, boi will have a clear meaning, one that will, most likely, erase other meanings and one that will, we might suppose, have a single if metaleptically constructed genealogy. In other words, some day boi will grow up. For now, though, boi's just a boi—mischievous, playful, energetic, and wild. And that is quite a story.

NOTE

This chapter originally appeared in *MEAT JOURNAL.COM*, Vol. 1.1 (Spring 2005). Reprinted with permission.

REFERENCES

Beardadmaster. (n.d.). beardadmaster. Retrieved October 27, 2004 from http://www.worldleathermen.com/beardadmaster.

BullKiser. (n.d.). BullKiser. Retrieved October 12, 2004 from http://www.worldleathermen.com/bullkiser.

CigarDaddy. (n.d.). CigarDaddy. Retrieved October 21, 2004 from http://www.worldleathermen.com/cigardaddy.

Club Boi. (n.d.). clubboi.com. Retrieved March 14, 2005 from http://www.clubboi.com/gay_black_miami.html.

Duffy, J. (2004). "The terms they are a-changin". Retrieved March 4, 2005 from http://news.bbc.co.uk/go/pr/fe/-/1/hi/magazine/3554684.stm.

Kraus, J. (2003). Defining ourselves. Retrieved March 4, 2005 from http://www.uusociety.org/sermons/define.html.

Levy, A. (2004). Where the bois are. Retrieved March 4, 2005 from http://www.newyorkmetro.com/nymetro/news/features/n_9709/.

LordFalconJock69. (n.d.). LordFalconJock69. Retrieved December 14, 2004 from http://www.worldleathermen.com/lordfalconjock69.

Marech, R. (2004). Nuances of gay identities reflected in new language. Retrieved March 4, 2005 from http://sfgate.com/cgi-bin/article.cgi?file=/chronicle/archive/2004/02/08/MNGKO4RNJP1.DTL.

MrKevin. (n.d.). MrKevin. Retrieved September 30, 2004 from http://www.worldleathermen.com/mrkevin.

MuscleCubAOL. (n.d.). MuscleCubAOL. Retrieved October 17, 2004 from http://www.worldleathermen.com/musclecubaol.

ROPEDBOI. (n.d.). ROPEDBOI. Retrieved October 12, 2004 from http://www.worldleathermen.com/ropedboi.

Ross, P. (2004, February 9). Re: "boi", boy, boyz; etc, etc. Message posted to gl-asb mailing list, archived at http://groups.queernet.org/cgi-bin/mj_wwwusr?user=&passw=&func=lists-long-full&extra=gl-asb.

Scofield, S. (2004, February 9). Re: "boi", boy, boyz; etc, etc. Message posted to gl-asb mailing list, archived at http://groups.queernet.org/cgi-bin/mj_wwwusr?user=&passw=&func=lists-long-full&extra=gl-asb.

Towleroad. (2004). Boi crazy. Retrieved March 4, 2005 from http://towleroad.typedpad.com/towleroad/2004/01/who_are_the_rea.html.

Veganboi. (n.d.). Coming out: again and again. Retrieved March 4, 2005 from http://www.angelfire.com/folk/veganboi/comginout.html.

What am I? (n.d.). Retrieved March 4, 2005 from http://boidyke78.tripod.com/id4.html.

Wolf, L. (February 8, 2004). Re: "boi," "pig" and the evolution of language. Message posted to gl-asb mailing list, archived at http://groups.queernet.org/cgi-bin/mj_wwwusr?user=&passw=&func=lists-long-full&extra=gl-asb.

Chapter 11

He's My Gay Mother: Ballroom Houses, Housework, and Parenting[1]

Marlon M. Bailey

In November of 2005, the National Black Justice Coalition (NBJC)[2] held a State Wide Town Hall Meeting in Oakland, California to discuss their national campaign for marriage equality. A political comrade of mine suggested that I go to this meeting to get a better sense of what members of the black LGBT community think about same-sex marriage. For much of the meeting, it was clear that although the gathering was said to be designed to allow for people in the community to express their views on the issue, the executive director of the NBJC was aggressively promoting "coming out" and marriage as the most important ways to improve the lives of black LGBT people. These sentiments seemed to be shared by most of the members of the panel as well as members of the audience. Some people at the meeting even suggested that marriage is an effective way to decrease HIV/AIDS infection rates among LGBT African Americans, it will raise our economic standing, and it is a central means through which we can resist and eradicate the various forms of gender and sexual inequality that we face.

While listening to this litany of so-called virtues of marriage in general, and the direct benefits that same-sex marriage supposedly offers black LJBT people in particular, I became disheartened and confused. Fortunately, one of the panel members expressed concern that we were not subjecting marriage to scrutiny and that marriage may not be "our" issue. Having felt uneasy about expressing my strong opposition to same-sex marriage in the midst of such fervent support for it, the reservations expressed by the panel member was an opportunity for me to raise questions regarding the narrow identity and class-based assumptions that formed the basis of the discussion. I suggested that some of the members of black LGBT communities are ambivalent about this promotion of marriage because it ultimately gives the State the license to intrude in our lives and regulate black gender and sexual relations, while rights and privileges that should be accessible to all people/citizens are cordoned off and circumscribed within the regulatory institution of marriage. Chiefly, I was concerned about people who are marginalized in multiple ways, those of us who do not enjoy race and class privileges and those of us who do not have the option of making open claims of nonnormative gender and sexual identities due to the often violently homophobic environments and conditions in which we live. When I raised these concerns, I was rebuffed by the executive director who suggested that we all have choices, and we should all *choose* to "come out" as a form of resistance, just as our foremothers and forefathers of the civil rights movement chose to fight racial segregation. He added that there are those of us who have class privilege and many of us are the ones who do not come out and that it is essential that we do so. For him, "coming out" and marriage equality are analogous to civil rights struggles against racial discrimination even though the oppression that black gender and sexual marginials experience often comes from within black communities. Thus, the homophobia that many black LGBT people experience within black communities (as well as in society at large) is joined with the racism that we face in overall society, make for a very complicated set of conditions under which black, primarily working-class, LGBT people live on the daily basis, conditions for which same-sex marriage is not a solution nor a desire, at least for most of the people with whom I work and socialize.

In light of the experience I described above, I am concerned about the hastening move toward a politic and logic of what Lisa Duggan refers to as the *new homonormativity*. *Homonormative* logics do not contest dominant heteronormative assumptions and institutions, but rather uphold and sustain them, while pushing for a depoliticized gay constituency that aims to be included within gender and sexual normativity.[3] And what is more disturbing is that a small number of black LGBT people purport to represent and speak for the entire community, and in most cases, subordinating and excluding the positionalities and experiences of working-class black LGBT people. How can one organize one's life differently within this hegemonic discourse of marriage? Can we conceive of forms of kinship that are not based on heteronormativized notions of family? It is within these questions and contexts that I situate Ballroom Culture as an alternative that many black working-class LGBT people have taken up. The members of the Ballroom community create and sustain a queered form of kinship that revises normative gender and sexual relations, notions of family, and community.

This chapter delineates the dimensions of Ballroom Culture in two main points. First, I examine how, through a reconstitution of gender and sexual identities, Ballroom houses revise the gender and sexual relations of the familial structure. While in some ways, houses reify the gender hierarchies and social arrangements characteristic of the biological families from which they have been excluded, I am more interested in the necessary labor or what I refer to as "housework" that the members take up that sustains the community. Second, in order to enact the labor of care that is necessary to the maintenance of the house, Ballroom members forge parental bonds based on friendship and partnership rather than romantic and sexual ones. This form of parenting exists in tension with the roles that parents play in dominant configurations of family and kinship. I see the social maintenance of the Ballroom house through "house work" and parenting based on friendship as cultural labor. This cultural labor points to the ingredients per se to the building of a community within collective marginalization that has not only material and social dimensions, but psychic and spirituals ones as well.

BALLROOM CULTURE

Notoriously underground in most places, Ballroom culture, sometimes called "house culture," is a national black and Latino/a queer phenomenon where gender and sexual performativity, kinship, and community coalesce to create an alternative world. My overall study focuses on the Ballroom community in Detroit, Michigan and highlights two inextricable features upon which the entire culture depends: flamboyant competitive ball rituals, and houses, the family-like structures that produce these rituals of performance. Ballroom gender and sexual identities and familial roles are based on system that offers more gender and sexual identities from which to choose than available to its members in the "outside" world. What members of the Ballroom community refer to as the "gender system" consists of the following:

Gender Identity System

1. Butch Queens (gay men)
2. Femme Queens (male-to-female transgender people at various stages of reassignment)
3. Butch Queen up in Drags (gay men that dress and perform as women)
4. Butches (female-to-male transgender people at various stages of reassignment)
5. Men (males born as male and that live as men but do not identify as gay)
6. Women (females born as female and live as female and are straight, lesbian, or queer)

This gender system is an important form of labor and is the social machinery of Ballroom Culture. This system structures the performance criteria at the balls as well as the members' roles in the houses. Houses are led by "mothers" (Butch Queens, Femme Queens, and Women) and "fathers," (Butch Queens and Butches) who, regardless of age, sexual orientation, and social status, provide a labor of care and love with/for numerous Black LGBT people who have been rejected by their blood families, religious institutions, and society at large. This presents distinct challenges in Detroit, a place known as both the "chocolate city" and the "motor city," signifying its unique racial and class character. Many of the LGBT people that I interviewed described Detroit as considerably homophobic. I might add, Detroit is not unique in this sense given the marked increase in homophobic violence cases reported throughout the country.

The intense, often collectively competitive, performances within the ball rituals create a space of celebration, affirmation, and critique. Thus the ball combined with the social relations within the houses outside of it are mutually constitutive and, taken together, make up the world of Ballroom Culture. Members of the Ballroom community undertake a labor of care and love that Black communities fail to provide for people who occupy the lowest realms of society, socially, economically, and politically.

Similar to gender and sexuality, for Ballroom, houses are performative. Not able to rely on fetishized biological/blood bonds to define them, the naming of and the identification with the house function in tandem with the work behind it. In other words, the existence of the house depends on its members, the relationships in which they are engaged, and individual and collective performances at the balls. For instance, Kali from the now defunct House of Ford described a house:

> A house is a clique of friends that got to know each other within the gay life. The establishment of our house was a result of us being friends for 6–7 years. Most of us were just a group of friends and then the year of 1998 decided to become a house. According to my understanding, there were about 5 of my friends who were coming back from a trip to Atlanta during Black Gay Pride, and they came up with the idea to start a house. We've been together every since.

Kali somewhat downplays the kin-making component to the house, but foregrounds the role of friendship. Thus, such friendship within the context of the house as a family-like structure is an important element to Ballroom members' reconstitution of the experience of kinship. Offering a slightly different view, Prada Escada elaborates:

> First of all, a house is a collection of like minded-individuals that share common interests, who for the most part can agree on different issues and ideas . . . or they can just agree to disagree. It is born from groups of good-good friends. The house structure is geared specifically towards the ball scene (particularly in Detroit). As far as its purpose, houses provide a source of family nurturing that often times a lot of kids don't get at home. It gives kids a sense of pride in saying a member of such-a-such house or that Miss Thing is my mother, particularly if the house or parent is thought of as sickening[4] in Detroit.

Prada speaks to the function of houses beyond "just a clique of friends" to suggest that they serve multiple functions, including a space of friendship, nurturing, conflict, affirmation, and belonging. Further on in Prada's response, he suggested, in some cases, that houses serve as an actual physical shelter for "those lost souls to craft and cohabitate."

Lovely of the House of Mohair, only 20 years old, articulates the need to earn the right to be a part of a house through commitment:

> My house is a place of refuge. Here, we do not have a lot of balls. We focus on family, community, and togetherness . . . Some people jump from house, to house, to house, but in my house, once you jump out you can't come back. I am not going to play that. That is no respect . . . So yeah they jump around here, but I tell them in the beginning, "once you leave here, do not think about coming back. And whatever happens don't look for my protection because it was your choice."

As participants in the production of a new social sphere, one that provides the kind of support, recognition, and critique that many members do not get in the outside world, Ballroom members are always marking and reconciling the difference between just being a member of a house *and* distinguishing themselves from others within the house through commitment and deeds. All of my interlocutors' explanations rest on the notion that Ballroom house members, for whatever reason, decide to participate in the "doing of family." Thus, in deciding to be family, one has to be committed to what the *doing* of family entails. This is an implicit critique of their biological family's failure to perform the labor that the concept of *family* signifies. Ultimately, in Ballroom, the house and house chapters only exist as long as the members do the work.

BALLROOM PARENTING

Even though many gay people are vigorously engaged in a struggle for marriage equality, marriage is a failing institution in the United States. This is in large part due to the perceptions of marriage as an inadequate institution among the national citizenry. Many people are finding it difficult to adhere to rigid heteronormative constraints associated with marriage. As E. Patrick Johnson notes, the pervasive heteronormative logic of marriage sees two loving heterosexuals nesting together as the ultimate sign of family wholeness.[5] Actually, this does not vibe with many people's lives. I have written elsewhere that historically, the United States has always sought to violently attack, aggressively undermine, and ultimately delegitimize black cultural institutions. Black people have had to do whatever they could to sustain the entire community by creating a variety of kin structures to care for our children and ourselves and to, as a community, struggle against sexualized, gendered, racial forms of oppression. For black people, then, such rampant practices have instantiated a vexed relationship with the State and its sanctioned institutions like marriage. This is a far different scenario for our white, especially male, counterparts. Thus, marriage, parenting, and family in actual practice have meant something very different to black people than what can be gleaned from current discourses on these topics.

As a product of both American culture and black culture, Ballroom's kinship system is, in part, an outgrowth of both dominant and alternative forms of kinship. As a dissidentifactory strategy, the Ballroom house structure both reinscribes hegemonic gender and sexual hierarchies within the house unit while recasting what bodies actually engage in the domestic labor of the house. For example, foundational to Ballroom kinship and the community in general is a form of parenting that is nonheteronormative and non-romantically/intimate. I argue that Ballroom members emphasize the actual practice of parenting as opposed to a mere title or an entitlement based on biological ties. Ballroom parenting brings into focus how mothering (as socially configured domestic labor) bears the brunt of the work of parenting and thus is an integral aspect of the friendship and partnership that leads the Ballroom household.

It is worth mentioning that many house mothers and fathers are single parents. Most mothers are Butch Queens, although increasingly there are more Femme Queens and Women running houses. Masculinity, whether it is attached to and/or performed by male, female, or transgender bodies, to some degree, enjoys privilege within the Ballroom scene as it does outside of it. This element influences how members chose to be referred to as either fathers or mothers depending what "kind" of masculinity or femininity they embody, perform, and represent.

Having said that, as one can guess, in the house, mothers do most of the work. For instance, Danny of the House of Galliano stated that:

> Housemothers are recognized for mostly her performance experience. They are usually femme and usually walk femme categories. 90% of housemothers are older and have been around for awhile. They are usually into mothering . . . doing the things that mothers do. . . . If they are good, they are sometimes asked to start other houses in other places. The most important thing for a house to have is a legendary mother.

As Danny further states, mothers are into the "mothering." House mothers do the labor of what Evelyn Nakano Glenn describes as the social, rather than biological, construct of "mothering."[6] All of my informants state that the mother performs most of the labor of care on which the house depends. "She arranges all of the events and makes most of the decisions," says Danny.

Let me offer another illustration of this point. In a brief exchange between Ariel, a Femme Queen, and Grandfather Reno, a Butch, Ariel expresses her realization that being a mother is difficult:

Ariel: Reno I never knew that being a mother of a house would be this hard but it is and when I see that things is going well, it keeps me going and pressing on.

Reno: Yes Mother, it is tough being a parent. If I may give some sound advice . . . remember our job is to help the kids learn to help themselves. We are guides, not "getovers." You are a natural nurturer, like a "real mother" should be.

This exchange, along with the identities involved, demonstrates how complicated gender and parental roles are in Ballroom Culture. In most cases, house mothers are Butch Queens; therefore, the division of labor that makes the mother the worker, the domestic laborer, to be performed by a woman, in Ballroom houses, it is assumed by a gay man. In the case of Ariel and Reno, Ariel is a Femme Queen and Reno is a Butch, two identities that have primary coherence in the Ballroom scene. (Femme Queen is an identity that was created by Ballroom and does not exist outside of it, and Butches exist outside of Ballroom but not in the same way.) As a biological female but living as a man, Reno takes on the role of the "fatherly" advisor. Contrary to most Ballroom experiences with their biological fathers, as a biological male, now living as a woman, Ariel is the "mothered" mother, the nurturer, the caretaking and the socially configured domestic of the house. In specific ways, masculinity still trumps femininity, yet Ballroom allows for more flexible and elastic masculine and feminine roles and performances.

This reconstitution of gender and parental roles directly influence the parental relationship in houses. Again, by and large, parental relationships in houses are built on platonic relationships rather than a romantic/intimate one. In some cases, they are more like what we call "judies" in Ballroom to signify hanging buddies. In general, although they have conflicts, intimate/sexual struggles and politics do not dictate house parents' relationship, at least not in the same way that they do in the outside world. Parents are enthralled in building and sustaining the house, to make sure its members can compete, and to make sure all the kids are emotionally, morally, and in some cases spiritually provided for.

For example, the house parents of the House of Galliano have been running the house together, as friends, for six years (at the time of the interview). Danny says that typically parents are not "together" nor do they always reflect a butch/femme binary. Sometimes, both the mother and the father are Butch Queens and feminine but sometimes not.[7]

Friendship underpins *most* relationships in Ballroom. When I asked Richy Rich (a Butch Queen) house mother of the Detroit chapter of the House of CMB (Cash Money Boys) what influenced him to be a mother and to choose his mother he said: friendship (Mother Goddess the Overall Mother of the House of Rodeo, shook his head in agreement). In 2002, the House of Prodigy's Detroit Chapter was led by a masculine Butch Queen father and a biological woman who is queer and their relationship was based on friendship.

Within the Ballroom social sphere, where its members do not enjoy a diverse range of intimacy within their biological families, Ballroom houses offer a space for love, care, and critique between people who share similar life experiences. It is important to understand that not only is this bond drawn on characteristics of kin, it is also based on a common competitive drive to "slay and snatch" trophies for the house and its individual members to gain legendary acclaim throughout the Ballroom scene. Again, the focus is on the work involved in parenting, in bonding, in slaying and snatching, and in building a kin unit as a part of an overall minoritarian sphere.

CONCLUSION

Ballroom exemplifies the transitive nature of culture that directly deconstructs itself and illustrates that just as diaspora is never finished, never an accomplished fact, the tasks of self-fashioning, creating and sustaining social configurations such as houses, and in effect building a community is ongoing. Even when this cultural labor is steeped in the structures of oppression that it purports to stand against, the productive space in-between full hegemony and full transformation or the interstices is where possibilities and hope exist. Ballroom houses offer an alternative perspective to the same-sex marriage debate, if its members are ever asked, that takes into account the very complex realities that structure black queer lives. I do not mean to suggest that

Ballroom has all the answers; instead, I want to reveal how its member "make do" with what they have in order to survive.

NOTES

1. A version of this paper was presented at the 2005 American Anthropological Association's (AAA) Annual Conference in Washington D.C.

2. In the National Black Justice Coalition brochure, the organization describes itself as "the only national civil rights organization of concerned Black, lesbian, gay, bisexual, and transgender individuals and our allies. Our organization and its programs address the problem of gay inequality in America with a goal to increase African American support for gay and lesbian equality."

3. Lisa Duggan, *The Twilight of Equality? Neoliberalism, Cultural Politics, and the Attack on Democracy* (Boston: Beacon Press, 2003), 50.

4. In black queer lingo, "sickening" means that one is so good or that one's clothing is so exceptional that it is difficult to accept. One has a hard time looking at it.

5. E. Patrick Johnson, *Appropriating Blackness: Performance and the Politics of Authenticity* (Durham: Duke University Press, 2003), 79.

6. Evelyn Nakano Glenn, "Social Construction of Mothering: a Thematic Overview," In *Mothering, Ideology, Experience, and Agency,* ed. Grace Chang, Linda Rennie Forcey, and Evelyn Nakano Glenn (New York: Routledge, 1994), 3.

7. Parental couples usually consist of two Butch Queens, or a Butch Queen and a Femme Queen, or a Butch Queen and a Butch.

Chapter 12

From the Margins to the Mainstream: Communication about Travel and Tourism in the Gay Community, 1960–2000

David R. Coon

Giving a speech at the 2006 convention of the International Gay and Lesbian Travel Association (IGLTA), Mark Elderkin, founder of the popular Web site Gay.com, said that "the evolution of the gay travel market [had] been 12 years in the making."[1] He made his comment in response to the perceived overnight development of what is now a $54 billion industry in the United States.[2] The perception is understandable given that in 2004, just two years before Elderkin's speech, cities like Philadelphia, Pennsylvania, and Bloomington, Indiana, made headlines because of their attempts to attract gay and lesbian travelers.[3] Though these seemingly radical moves initially drew skepticism, they were very lucrative for the cities involved, and soon other cities and resorts across the country were clamoring to construct their own promotional campaigns to lure gay and lesbian travelers. Jeff Guaracino, the marketer behind Philadelphia's gay-friendly campaign, notes that 2005 and 2006 were "pivotal years in gay tourism, with a record number of destinations coming out as gay friendly."[4]

Cities like Boston, Dallas, Atlanta, Washington D.C., and Phoenix launched campaigns targeting gay and lesbian tourists. Membership in the IGLTA grew to over a thousand members, as airlines, hotels, resorts, travel agents, and rental car companies saw the possibilities offered by this market.[5] Gay and lesbian travel periodicals like *The Out Traveler* began appearing alongside other travel magazines in mainstream bookstores. In essence, gay and lesbian tourists came to be seen as a viable target market, and cities and companies large and small were quick to pitch their products and services to this highly desirable group.

Although gay tourism went from being a risky marketing experiment to a booming growth market in a very short time, Elderkin's comment that the market had been 12 years in the making suggested that it was not quite the overnight success it appeared to be, and that tourism professionals should recognize the years of work involved in developing the market. However, Elderkin's timeline is still too short. While the 12 years before 2006 may account for the recent work of marketers trying to identify and appeal to gays and lesbians as a market, it is a mistake to think that gay tourism did not exist before marketers recognized it, or that it was in fact created by marketers. The true development of the gay and lesbian tourism industry has a much longer and more complicated genealogy, generally mirroring GLBT struggles and successes over the years, including secrecy and fear in the pre-Stonewall1960s, the growing gay rights movement in the 1970s, and the AIDS crisis in the 1980s. In addition to being too short, the 12 year timeline suggested by Elderkin also ignores the efforts of the men and women who were excluded by the mainstream travel industry for decades, and thus took it upon themselves to develop their own means of exchanging valuable travel information. Filling the gaps left by traditional travel agents, gays and lesbians provided a subtle yet significant form of resistance to the oppressive conditions placed upon them by heteronormative society.

This chapter traces the development of gay tourist promotion over the second half of the twentieth century, showing the many years of growth and change that created the huge market only recently discovered by the mainstream.[6] Gay tourism's evolution from near invisibility in the 1960s to a multi-billion dollar industry in the 2000s raises a number of questions. For example, during these developmental years before gay travel magazines, Web sites, and high-profile ad campaigns, how did travelers know where to find gay or gay-friendly establishments and other safe spaces? Who made such information available? How was this information collected and distributed? How did the exchange of information change over the years, and what did those changes signify within the broader context of identity politics and the social struggles faced by gays and lesbians in American society?

Through the analysis of a series of texts dealing with travel, including gay-oriented periodicals and travel guides written for homosexuals, this chapter answers the above questions to reveal how gays and lesbians communicated about tourism in the years before becoming a prized target market.[7] Without the aid of large promotional budgets, publishing houses, or national networks of communication, gays and lesbians found ways to exchange information about travel and tourism, often relying on underground channels. The tactics employed in this endeavor display the creativity and ingenuity that have become vital survival tools for a group frequently ignored or ostracized by mainstream heteronormative society. As the materials examined in this chapter demonstrate, the current boom in gay tourism—driven by mainstream marketers and large corporations—is founded upon four decades of development by individuals within the gay and lesbian community.[8]

FOUNDATIONS: THE 1960S

The 1960s are known for their political turbulence and upheaval. The Civil Rights movement and Vietnam protests gave voice to racial minorities and a youthful counter-culture. Homosexuals, however, remained largely invisible and silent despite the efforts of homophile organizations like the Mattachine Society, ONE, Inc., and the Daughters of Bilitis, all of which worked to raise awareness and protect the rights of homosexuals in the United States.[9] Writing about the social atmosphere in the 1960s, journalists Dudley Clendinen and Adam Nagourney note that most homosexuals "kept their feelings inside, identifying themselves only to each other, if they did so at all."[10] Historian John D'Emilio suggests that, "Since the power of homophobia in post-World War II America was so strong, it necessarily forced things gay into the background" for most of the 1960s.[11] Homosexual behavior was criminalized, as evidenced by the regular police raids in gay bars and the confiscation of gay materials sent through the postal service.[12] This does not mean, however, that homosexuals did not communicate with one another or find ways to congregate and meet other homosexuals. They simply had to be more careful and secretive about their activities. It was in this environment that the first recognizable traces of homosexual travel appeared in significant numbers.

A notable example of this is the series of trips organized by ONE, Inc., a homophile organization based in San Francisco. The first trip, a tour of Europe, was organized in 1964 by the Social Services Division of ONE, Inc., which had previously been devoted to assisting homosexuals facing difficulties with regard to housing, employment, the law, or other troubles. The trip was "available to Friends of ONE (Associate class) only," and was primarily publicized through *ONE Confidential*, a periodical distributed only to the Friends of ONE (those who paid dues or gave donations).[13] As noted by the editors in the December 1964 issue of *ONE Confidential*, it was "not the Social Service Divisions' intention to open the doors wide to any save those whose support of ONE has been demonstrated."[14] In addition to running articles to attract travelers in the months leading up to the trip, *ONE Confidential* published a wrap-up of the trip, including letters from some of the men who had gone, and describing the hospitality of the various homophile organizations who had acted as hosts in the countries visited. Noting that this was the "first such enterprise ever undertaken by a homophile organization," the editors declared it a success and announced plans for future trips to Europe and other destinations.[15] Yearly European tours were eventually joined by a Caribbean cruise and a Mediterranean Holiday.

As the pre-tour and post-tour articles in *ONE Confidential* demonstrate, these early tours were intended for, and in the end involved, a small, select group of individuals. Only dues-paying Friends of ONE were notified, and only those paying enough to qualify as "Associate class" were allowed to participate. The trip was essentially coordinated by a network of friends, a model that would dominate homosexual tourism for the next couple of decades.

ONE Confidential was not the only periodical to discuss gay travel in the 1960s. The *Los Angeles Advocate* launched in 1967, initially targeting the gay community of southern California, and eventually becoming national in scope as *The Advocate*. Although not specifically a travel publication, it featured gay travel and tourism information early and in a number of ways. Preeminently, discussions of travel appeared in columns and feature stories. Early issues featured a column called "The Gay Traveler," which included personal accounts of trips to various cities and offered tips about interesting attractions, gay bars in the area, and the best places to meet people, find a date, or engage in an anonymous sexual encounter.[16] Along with occasional columns, *The Advocate* sometimes ran standalone stories about travel, such as the February 1969 article "Holy Toledo: Midwest Swings," about the gay scene in and around Toledo, Ohio.[17] Moreover, early issues of *The Advocate* occasionally offered updates on laws, regulations, and civil rights issues in various cities, states, and countries, providing helpful information for travelers to better understand the social climate of destinations that they might visit.[18]

Furthermore, *The Advocate*'s 1960s advertising specifically promoted gay travel. One ad in the August 1968 issue announced "Tours exclusively for guys. To every major area: Europe, Caribbean Mexico, Orient, etc. Beginning with a Christmas Tour to Hawaii."[19] The ad did not say who was organizing the trip, but gave Los Angeles contact information for anyone interested in more details. Another ad the following spring announced "Trip '69' to Europe," which was organized by Jackson Travel Service in San Francisco and described as "a leisure tour of Europe for businessmen visiting London" and included "experienced guides to assist you in searching out the gay life!"[20] These advertisements show that there were multiple groups arranging excursions specifically for gay travelers in the late 1960s, and unlike the trips organized by ONE, Inc., these ads did not mention membership restrictions and were seemingly open to anyone who could afford the trip. The majority of the ads in early issues of *The Advocate* were for Los Angeles bars, restaurants, bathhouses, and book stores, which would have been helpful not only to those living in Southern California, but also to visitors. In addition to the local ads, early issues occasionally ran ads for establishments in other cities, most likely aimed at Los Angeles residents traveling to places such as Reno, Seattle, or Vancouver.[21] The other notable references to travel in early *Advocate* issues were the advertisements for gay travel guides (discussed in more detail below). The most commonly advertised guide was *Barfly,* a guide assembled, at least in part, by *Advocate* staffers, and eventually published under the *Advocate* umbrella. Additional ads trumpeted the arrival of the *69 Gay Directory* and *Carl Driver's Gay Europe '70.*

The Advocate may be the most recognizable and significant gay periodical of the era, but other publications also provided information about gay travel. *The Homosexual Citizen*, published by the Mattachine Society of Washington, D.C., focused on "news of civil liberties and social rights for homosexuals."[22] As part of this discussion, the journal often included reports on the progress of rights in certain locations, such as Illinois, Russia, and Yemen. As with similar reports in *The Advocate*, these articles were not written as tourist guides, but they would have been helpful for gays traveling to the destinations discussed, letting them know where it was or was not safe to express their sexual identity openly.

In June of 1965, *The Cruise News and World Report* made its debut. Produced in San Francisco, *Cruise News* was a tabloid-size publication, usually about eight pages long, providing news of interest to homosexuals, including updates on rights and civil liberties as well as entertainment and humor. *Cruise News* had a limited circulation and was only published for a few years, but it exemplifies the small-scale, underground publications that allowed members of the gay community to communicate in the 1960s. Sent by mail to those who paid for a subscription (in "plain, sealed envelopes" according to the editors), this small publication also included detailed information about select cities of interest.[23] The first issue, for example, featured a fold-out map of San Francisco with listings for tourist spots, restaurants, clubs, news stands, and "places to go and not to go" when cruising for sex. The second issue featured a similar map of Los Angeles (referred to as "Gomorrah, a sleepy Mexican village 450 miles south of Sodom") with the same general information that was offered for San Francisco.[24] The editors did not get so involved with cities outside the state of California, but future issues contained short articles describing the gay scenes of other American cities, based on writers' personal experiences. In addition to the articles and maps, *Cruise News* ran ads for a number of travel guides, including the *Lavender Baedeker, Lavender World*, and *The Gray Guide*, all of which were published by Strait and Associates, the publishers of *Cruise News*.

Beyond these periodicals were the many gay travel guides produced during the 1960s, most of which were simply lists of gay or gay-friendly establishments in various parts of the world. The first known guide of this type, *Gay Guide to Europe*, was printed in Paris in 1960 by Ganymede press. This 14-page guide was clearly an amateur production, printed with a ditto machine on standard letter-size paper, folded and stapled. The guide offered a broad introduction to European culture in general, along with a few comments about the status and behavior of homosexuals in each country listed. The section on France, for example, noted that the French (gays and straights alike) almost never invited strangers home because of "the lack of privacy due to the housing shortage and the feeling that the home is reserved uniquely for the family."[25] Beyond the brief descriptions of each country and its culture, the guide merely listed the names and occasionally addresses of gay bars, restaurants, and other places where homosexuals could meet.

Many of the early guides were similar to *Gay Guide to Europe* in terms of content and quality. *World Report Travel Guide* was slightly more extensive than the *Gay Guide to Europe*, covering all parts of the world and offering minimal indications of the quality of establishments. According to a note on the first page, an asterisk "indicate[d] good" and two asterisks "indicate[d] very good."[26] Maintaining its presentation, the guide grew quickly in just a few years, expanding from 27 pages in its first edition to 114 pages by the fifth edition in 1965.[27] *The Lavender Baedeker*, from the publishers of *Cruise News and World Report*, announced itself as "A Guidebook to Gay, Interesting, Hysterical & Historic Places in the U.S."[28] Moving beyond the U.S. focus of *The Lavender Baedeker*, two other publications from Strait and Associates, *Lavender World* and *The Grey Guide*, worked to cover the rest of the world.[29] These publications were hardly a wealth of information, offering little more than names (and sometimes addresses) of gay establishments. But without any more formal means of collecting information about gay-friendly establishments, even these minimal booklets would have been valuable resources for gay travelers in this era.

Some publishers produced smaller guides for particular cities rather than attempting to cover entire countries or the world. The publishers of *Gay*, a Canadian magazine, produced the *Gay Guide to New York*, an eight page, pocket-sized pamphlet offering information about bars, baths, beaches, clothing stores, night clubs, and restaurants. Covering a more confined area and fewer establishments, this guide offered more detailed descriptions of each location listed, including prices, the type of clientele to expect, and the general feel and quality of the location.[30]

The editors of *The International Guild Guide*, which first appeared in 1965, prided themselves on being better than the competition, noting in the introduction to the second edition, "The great success of the 1965 Guild Guide has confirmed us in our belief that a guide of quality will ultimately prevail over those inferior items which have flooded the market."[31] The 210-page, professionally-produced, paperback edition offered names, addresses, and occasionally phone numbers for bars, restaurants, and other gay establishments throughout the United States and a few major cities in other countries. Another higher-quality guide, the inconspicuously titled *Directory 43*, was produced by a Minnesota-based company called Directories, Inc. Like many of the guides, the pocket-sized, hard cover *Directory 43* was a basic list of bars, restaurants, and baths, with no descriptions or codes of any kind to identify clientele or quality. Unlike most publications, however, *Directory 43* explained why descriptions were not included. "No attempt has been made to comment on the furnishings, location, or clientele of places listed in this Directory. No two persons would evaluate a place in the same way."[32] This comment emphasizes the nature of these early guides. They were informative, not promotional, letting gay travelers know where they *could* go, rather than telling them where they *should* go. Although the listings remained simple, *Directory 43* contained two helpful elements left out of most guides: phone numbers for every establishment listed and population estimates for the cities included.

The most significant guide to appear during this period was *Bob Damron's Address Book*, commonly referred to as *Damron's*, which is the only early guide that survives to this day. The first edition, published in 1965, was 48 pages, pocket-sized, stapled together, and with a heavy-stock paper cover. Boasting "more than 750 places to go in 220 cities," the book offered names and addresses of bars, restaurants, and clubs, along with the occasional bit of added advice.[33] The 1968 listings for Columbus, Ohio, for example, contained the following: "Some bars turn neon signs off and appear to be closed. Don't let this fool you."[34] Certain listings were given code letters, explained by a key at the beginning of the book. Moving in the opposite direction of *Directory 43*, which specifically avoided categorizing establishments, the early *Damron's* offered these codes as a way of identifying the activities, mood, and clientele that one could expect. For example, "D" indicated dancing, "PE" meant "pretty elegant," and "M" referred to a crowd that was "mixed, and/or tourists."[35]

The end of the 1960s saw the appearance of *Barfly*, the guidebook advertised so heavily in early issues of *The Los Angeles Advocate*. A close relative of the early *Damron's*, *Barfly* was produced by Advocate Publications, Inc. and came in two editions, one for the Eastern states, Canada, Mexico, and Puerto Rico, and the other for the Western states. Like the early versions of *Damron's*, *Barfly* was pocket-sized, less than 100 pages, and offered names, addresses, and codes to designate the types of crowds, atmosphere, and activities to expect at various venues.[36]

The gay travel guides of the 1960s all had similar goals and shared many common traits, but they also varied significantly in a number of ways. All of the guides remained very simple in appearance, with no color printing or illustrations beyond an occasional logo. They were basically lists of establishments with varying levels of detail, occasionally offering simple descriptions, usually in the form of a code. The earliest gay guides included little or no paid advertising, though they were essentially providing a form of publicity for the establishments listed within their pages. Most of the guides were completely ad free. *The Lavender Baedeker* contained a few simple ads, usually just highlighting the name of an establishment, perhaps with a logo or directions.

Gay Guide to New York contained a single pitch for the magazine that published the guide, but nothing more. By its 1968 edition, *Damron's Address Book* had added a single ad for a bookstore, an early sign of a trend that would eventually become the norm.

In general, the production quality of these early guides was fairly low. Some, like the *Gay Guide to Europe, World Report Travel Guide, The Lavender Baedeker, Lavender World,* and *The Grey Guide* were clearly produced in homes or offices by amateurs. Others, like *The Gay Guide to New York, Directory 43, The International Guild Guide, Barfly,* and *Bob Damron's Address Book* offered a more professional appearance, though they were still produced by small-scale printers, not national or international publishing houses.

Reflecting the lack of acceptance of homosexuals in this pre-Stonewall, pre-liberation movement era, most of the guides remained very discreet. Because many of the users were closeted, most of these guides remained largely in the closet themselves. The two primary exceptions were the *Gay Guide to Europe* and the *Gay Guide to New York City.* If their titles did not give them away, the repeated references to homosexuality in their country overviews (in the case of the former) or brief establishment descriptions (in the case of the latter) left little doubt as to the specific nature of these guides. *Lavender World* announced itself as a "guidebook to gay bars, baths, and beaches," making it pretty hard to misunderstand.[37]

The rest of the guides remained more subtle. *The Lavender Baedeker* and *The Grey Guide* announced themselves as guidebooks to "gay, interesting, historical and hysterical places."[38] In the absence of any other references to homosexuality, the word "gay" here might be interpreted to mean something other than homosexual—perhaps lively, or merry. *The Lavender Baedeker* contained a few ads for gay catalogues and gay Christmas cards that would likely give it away, but *The Grey Guide* offered no further indication of any connection to homosexuality. This was also the case with the early editions of *Damron's Address Book, World Report Travel Guide, Barfly, International Guild Guide,* and *Directory 43,* all of which made their gayness essentially invisible to anyone who was not already in the know. *Directory 43* offered this intentionally vague introduction: "This directory has been compiled to help you know where to go on your travels when seeking entertainment or new acquaintances."[39] The others remained similarly vague in their introductions, referring to their publications and others like them simply as "guides," without ever specifying a particular type of guide. With their nondescript titles, plain front covers, and simple lists of establishments, these guides could easily have been left on a coffee table or bookshelf with no threat of revealing their owner's sexual behaviors or identities. This level of secrecy was also important to the establishments listed inside, since gay and lesbian bars were no more acceptable than gay and lesbian individuals. Many of these bars were owned and/or protected by organized criminals, and most owners paid off the police and public officials in order to avoid harassment.[40] Minimizing public visibility was necessary to the survival of these establishments, and the lack of detail in the guides of this era aided in this process.

The early travel guides were compiled and written primarily by individuals and small groups, and the work involved in putting the guides together was often mentioned in the book itself. The editor of *The Lavender Baedeker* invited guests to visit the editorial offices, but suggested calling first, "to assure that the editor is not out, asleep, or cruising for news or for some other reason."[41] This revealed the small size of the operation responsible for the guide book. The introduction to the first edition of *Damron's Address Book* said that Bob Damron himself "personally visited some 200 cities in 37 states and crossed Canada in the Spring of 1965" to obtain the information in the book.[42] While the other guides did not present a heroic compiler like Bob Damron, many of them did emphasize the process involved in assembling their own guides. *Directory 43* claimed that "No place pays for its listing. All listings are from recommendations made by our customers and thru staff research."[43] Highlighting the improvements made since their first edition, the editors of *The International Guild Guide 1966* noted that they had "made every effort to verify the accuracy of the information received. Where there were states and areas not well represented, we wrote to friends and customers in these areas and corrected the deficiencies."[44]

Recognizing the need for additional help (in part because of the underground nature of most gay establishments as well as their often rapid turnover), most of the guides made appeals to their readers, asking for updates, corrections, and additions. Editors of *The International Guild Guide* noted that their attempts to list all possible establishments had not been enough. They noted that there was "much room for improvement and we must rely upon our readers to provide the information which will close the gap."[45] *World Report Travel Guide* went so far as to include a tear-out form for readers to send back to the publishers with information on establishments that had been left out of the guide, or which had changed or closed since the last printing. This particular guide was apparently updated so frequently that the purchase of one guide included "one year's revision service (all corrections, additions, and revisions issued)."[46]

The early guides were distributed primarily (and in some cases exclusively) by mail order. Almost every guide contained information about how to order additional copies, with the *Gay Guide to Europe* and the *World Report Travel Guide* including notes saying that this was the only way to order the guides. The *Gay Guide to New York* was most likely distributed to subscribers of the magazine that published it. According to an ad in *Cruise News and World Report*, *The Lavender Baedeker* was available at a number of gay bars and book stores on the west coast.[47] Other guidebooks were available at gay establishments in or near the cities in which they were printed. Given the importance of readers in the production/updating of the guides, the publishers likely depended on those same readers to publicize the guides and their availability by word of mouth.

The vast majority of travel information circulating in this period was aimed primarily at gay men, with lesbians either included as an afterthought or excluded entirely. Damron's included lesbians as part of their coding process. Just as a "D" next to a listing indicated dancing and an "R" indicated a restaurant, a "G" identified establishments where one might find "Girls, but rarely exclusively."[48] From the travel articles in *The Advocate* to the listings in *Directory 43* and *Barfly*, there was very little acknowledgement of the possibility that women might have different interests or concerns from men.

On the whole, the early gay travel guides represented a network of homosexuals sharing information with one another. The guides were not produced by outsiders trying to attract gay travelers, but were assembled by insiders as a way of establishing and identifying a network of spaces that could help create a sense of community. The exchange of information took place largely underground, reflecting the status of the majority of gay establishments and a large proportion of gay individuals at the time. As historian Les Wright notes, gay businesses began to come together in the 1960s, "creating an economy parallel to the social mainstream, but still invisible, or downright incomprehensible, to outsiders."[49] By making this parallel economy visible to those who wanted to find it, the guidebooks of the era aided in the early development of the GLBT community.

Through the creation and use of these travel guides, gay and lesbian individuals generated a discourse that, in turn, created what Michael Warner describes as a "counterpublic." Warner notes that "a counterpublic comes into being through an address to indefinite strangers," and he goes on to suggest that the individuals addressed by such a discourse, "are socially marked by their participation in this kind of discourse; ordinary people are presumed not to want to be mistaken for the kind of person who would participate in this kind of talk or be present in this kind of scene."[50] Counterpublics are clearly marked as different from the mainstream, and the gay travel guides of the 1960s helped to nurture the development of a queer counterpublic from a group of marginalized individuals within American society.

GROWTH AND VISIBILITY: THE 1970S

Sparked by the highly publicized Stonewall Riots of 1969, many gay and lesbian organizations, publications, and individuals decided to move away from the secrecy and invisibility of the 1960s. Increasing numbers of gays and lesbians fought openly for civil rights, strengthening the movement's organization and achieving national visibility. In 1971 the National Organization for Women passed a resolution endorsing lesbian rights, thus aligning the gay rights movement with the more established feminist movement.[51] In 1972, Democratic presidential candidate George McGovern invited gay and lesbian activists Jim Foster and Madeline Davis to the Democratic National Convention to speak about gay rights.[52] In 1973, gays and lesbians formed the Lambda Legal Defense Fund to help fight gay civil rights cases, and the American Psychiatric Association voted to remove homosexuality from its list of psychiatric disorders.[53] These and other advances in political, legal, and medical arenas set the stage for increasing openness and visibility in the realm of gay travel and tourism.

The defining characteristic of *The Advocate* during the 1970s was growth. The original press run was just 500 copies, but by 1976 *The Advocate* had become one of the nation's fastest-growing magazines, with a circulation of 60,000 nationwide.[54] Through the early 1970s, the publication was supported primarily by advertisements for gay establishments in Los Angeles and classified ads, many of which were rather explicit, showing partial nudity and referencing sexual activities. In the mid 1970s, the editors redesigned *The Advocate*, moving classifieds and more sexually explicit ads to a separate pullout section. Katherine Sender notes that explicit content was removed from the main body of the magazine "so that mainstream advertisers might find *The Advocate* a more hospitable context for national ads."[55]

As *The Advocate* grew and changed as a publication, much of its connection to gay travel remained the same. The magazine still ran feature articles about travel, such as the 1975 article "Breckenridge Holds Special Attraction for Gay Skiers," which highlighted the resort town's gay establishments and overall friendliness.[56] Also continuing from the early days were paid ads for Southern California establishments like bars and bathhouses, as well as ads for various gay travel guides, including *Douglas Dean's Gay Mexico II* and *Skipper's Gay Guide*.[57] The primary change from the earliest issues was the significant increase in the number of classified ads appearing throughout the magazine in the early 1970s, and in the pullout section beginning in the mid 1970s. These ads, sometimes in a special "Travel" section of the classifieds, promoted specific destinations and establishments around the world, sought travel companions, offered places to stay and guided tours in particular cities, and sold guides and maps to specific cities and unusual attractions, like California's gay nude beaches. The growing number of classifieds indicated an increased flow of communication between members of the gay community as the growing readership of *The Advocate* allowed those who ran such ads to reach larger and more dispersed audiences. Although the volume of communication was increasing, the majority of the ads were placed by individuals and small businesses, and they were placed in the less expensive classifieds section, as opposed to larger ads mixed in with editorial content. The role of these notices was more informational than promotional.

As *The Advocate* matured and grew, a handful of new gay-oriented periodicals made their debut. *Gay* and *Gay Scene* were both published in New York and focused largely on the city that was their home, covering gay rights news, entertainment reviews, and personal interest stories. The biweekly *Gay* (not to be confused with the earlier Canadian publication of the same name) ran a regular section called "Where Will You Go Tonight?" which served as a directory of gay establishments and special events in the city—a handy reference for locals as well as visitors to the city.[58] The monthly *Gay Scene* more commonly ran travel features, including stories about foreign countries, significant American cities, and interesting resort towns.[59] Both publications also featured ads for New York establishments as well as display ads and classifieds for various resorts and travel guides, including *Damron's Address Book*, *Skipper's Guides*, *Gay Ways 1972*, and *EOS's Gay Guide*.

The Los Angeles and New York publications may have reached the largest audiences, but they were by no means the only gay periodicals making an impact in the 1970s. Gay newspapers appeared in cities across the country, including *Gay Chicago*, *Seattle Gay News*, *G. Milwaukee*,

Philadelphia's *Gay News*, Houston's *Montrose Star*, and Atlanta's *The Barb*. These papers connected local gay readers with news of the larger gay world, but their ads for local establishments and news of local events also acted as references for gay visitors. As the number of cities with gay papers increased, it became easier for gay travelers to acquire accurate, up-to-date information on the gay scenes in the cities they visited.

As periodicals grew, changed, appeared, and disappeared in the 1970s, so did gay travel guides. By its 1977 edition, *Bob Damron's Address Book* had expanded from its original 750 listings to "approximately 3,575 listings."[60] The explanation of listings had been expanded to include a notation for "Cruisy Areas" where visitors could likely find public sex. The listings also sought to specify crowds based on race and age. Notes included "B" for "blacks frequent," "OC" for "older/more mature crowd," and "YC" for "young/collegiate types."[61] *International Guild Guide* also continued into the 1970s, changing very little over the years. The guide's parent company, Guild Press, Ltd. closed its doors in 1973 ("after a decade of uninterrupted harassment from the Post Office and the FBI"), but in 1976 a new edition of the guide was released.[62] The guide remained a simple list of establishments and their addresses, sometimes with phone numbers, along with occasional code letters to indicate clientele or atmosphere. *Barfly* also continued well into the 1970s, in its eastern and western editions, providing a basic list of gay bars and clubs in a handy, pocket-sized booklet.

A handful of new guides appeared during the 1970s, the most significant of which was *Spartacus International Gay Guide*. As *Damron's* became the dominant guide to the United States, *Spartacus*, produced in the Netherlands, became the dominant international gay guide. It offered a coding system similar to *Damron's*, eventually offering information not only about clientele and atmosphere, but also the quality and safety of the establishments listed. The guide also offered overviews of individual countries' laws and social mores as they applied to homosexuals. *Spartacus* was first published in 1970, but it was not made available in the United States until 1975.[63] Many other new guidebooks, including *Gay Times' International Gay Guide*, and *The Golden Key for Gay Swingers*, followed the basic "list of establishments" approach, but none were as successful as the long-running *Spartacus*.

Meanwhile, other publications began moving away from solely listing bars and clubs, opting instead for more varied and/or detailed information. One such publication was *Skipper's Guide*. While most of the guides originated in large cities such as Los Angeles or New York, *Skipper's Guide* was published in the small town of Danville, Kentucky, suggesting a further expansion of gay networks beyond large urban centers. *Skipper's Guide* was joined by *Skipper's Newsletter* ("News about products and services for gay guys"), Skipper's Mates (a pen pal club for gays), and *Skipper's GUYS GUIDE* (personal ads).[64] According to its own introduction, *Skipper's Guide* offered "names and addresses not only of bars, baths, etc., but also of gay magazines and newspapers, other gay guides, mail order dealers, and gay-liberation groups."[65] Still aimed at those traveling away from home, *Skipper's Guide* provided a broader range of information than most other guides.

This expanded focus also characterized the *Gayellow Pages*, which first appeared in the early 1970s and continues to be available. Early editions announced coverage of bars and restaurants, places to stay, health clubs, gay movement and counseling services, publications and newsletters, radio programs, theater groups, businesses and commercial enterprises, all of which specifically welcomed gay patrons.[66] Entries were arranged as they would be in any phone book, grouped together based on the type of establishment or the type of service provided.

Another guidebook that went beyond bars and clubs was *A Gay Person's Guide to New England*, which described itself as "a practical guide to living gay in New England."[67] It covered everything from bars, bathhouses, and cruising areas to churches, clothing shops, and gay rights organizations. Moreover, this guide offered brief descriptions of every establishment listed as well as feature articles of interest to gay readers and maps of various towns and cities. Like the *Gayellow Pages*, this guide listed information that would have been helpful to residents of the area as well as visitors.

While some guides offered expanded depth and breadth in their coverage, others targeted a segment of the homosexual population that had previously received little attention: women. As previously mentioned, the majority of travel materials aimed at homosexuals over the years have been produced primarily for men. Although most of the guides in the 1970s made occasional references to establishments catering to lesbians, the main focus of the guides was gay men. *The Girl's Guide* and *Gaia's Guide*, both started in the mid 1970s, were written specifically for women. Despite their shift in focus, both followed the model made popular by *Damron's*, *Barfly*, *Spartacus*, and others, offering little more than lists of establishments. *Gaia's Guide* included an elaborate system of coding, with the number of stars indicating the proportion of lesbians likely to be found in the establishment. More stars indicated more lesbians, while fewer stars indicated more gay men or heterosexuals.[68] Aside from these two publications, most of the available information about tourism continued to be directed at gay men.

The sources of information about gay travel headed in a number of different directions during the 1970s. The production of gay-oriented periodicals increased in number, quality, and circulation, providing easier access to the various kinds of information included in such publications—travel articles, ads for local establishments and travel guides, and classified ads to connect individuals with one another, despite geographic separation. While some, like *The Advocate*, attempted to move toward the mainstream by eliminating explicit sexuality, others, like *Gay* and *Gay Scene*, made no such attempt, regularly including nudity and blatantly sexual advertisements in their pages.

Travel guides also moved in different directions. Some, like *Damron's*, *Spartacus*, and *International Guild Guide*, greatly improved their production quality with glossy covers, photographs, and professional-quality binding, while others, like *The Girl's Guide*, *Skipper's Guide*, and *Barfly*, still exhibited the amateur feel of most of the 1960s guides. Many of the guides continued to favor basic lists of bars, baths, and clubs, while others went broader to cover additional services and attractions, and still others went deeper to provide more detailed information about the locations covered within their pages.

While very few of the guides in the 1960s featured advertising, very few of the 1970s guides went without it. *International Guild Guide* remained ad free, as did *Skipper's Guide* and *The Girls Guide*. Other publications, however, embraced the support of those willing to contribute advertising dollars, representing the growing level of cooperation between individuals and establishments within the gay community. *Damron's*, for example, which contained no ads in its early days, increased its ad content significantly during the 1970s. While the number of ads increased, they were limited to establishments listed in the book, such as bars, book stores, and bath houses. *Spartacus* also featured ads for listed establishments, placing them among the listings for the countries that were home to the establishments. The sections for some countries, such as France, Germany, and the Netherlands, were filled with advertisements, while others, like New Zealand, Ghana, and Italy had no ads. In general, this reflected the acceptance of homosexuality in various countries, as indicated by the brief country descriptions given by the guide's editors. The countries with the most ads tended to be those that were the most tolerant of homosexuality. Countries where gays had to be particularly careful and discreet were less likely to feature ads at all. Proprietors in these countries were unlikely to feel safe officially declaring the gay-orientation of their business, which a paid advertisement would certainly do.

In the 1960s, most of the guides essentially remained "in the closet," keeping their gayness subtle or invisible so as not to out their owners. A few guides continued this trend to varying degrees into the 1970s, including *Skipper's Guide, Gaia's Guide,* and *The Girls Guide,* all of which featured non-descript covers, but included references to gayness in either their introductions or their specific listings. *International Guild Guide,* which had offered no obvious traces of gayness in the 1960s, remained discreet on its cover and in its listings, but included a photo of a shirtless young man and the tagline "The most complete guide to the gay scene ever!" on its first page.[69] (One could potentially tear this page out and erase the book's gayness, as it made no other explicit references.) The other guides, however, appeared to be out and proud, reflecting the increasing visibility and political activism of the growing liberation movement. *A Gay Person's Guide to New England* clearly announced and openly referred to gayness in its name, listings, and ads, but not in a sexually explicit manner. *Damron's, Spartacus, Barfly,* and *Gayellow Pages* featured ads that included either photos or drawings of full or partial nudity and explicit references to sexual activities. *Gay Times' International Gay Guide* featured a naked young man on the front cover and erotic illustrations of hypermasculine, hypersexualized, semi-nude men throughout the book. There was no mistaking these guides for anything other than what they were.

In terms of information collection, the guides generally continued to stress the importance of reader contributions, often thanking readers for their suggestions and letting them know how to contribute updates for future editions. *Skipper's Guide* stressed the personal effort and cooperation that had made the guide possible. "None of the information has come to us from any newspaper, magazine, or other gay guide; the information has come to us from more than three thousand men who have responded to our numerous gay scene survey questionnaires."[70] *The Girls Guide* emphasized its dependence on user contributions—along with its focus on women—by saying, "if we've guided you to a place that was so bad it almost sent you rushing back to your dangerously violent husband—why not write and tell us so that we can strike it off in future years?"[71] *Spartacus* highlighted the cooperative nature of the project, saying "*Spartacus* is really a huge information exchange—and we emphasize the "exchange" part of this! One of the keys to the Guide's success is the large contribution made by readers."[72] The emphasis on a sense of grassroots cooperation reflected the values of the gay liberation movement, which sought to bring homosexuals together to achieve rights and visibility.

Gayellow Pages took a different approach to information collection. Rather than listing establishments and organizations based on personal research or reader recommendations, *Gayellow Pages* based its listings on applications submitted by proprietors. The application form gave business owners the chance to describe the type of product or service they provided, the clientele they typically served, hours of operation, and other basic information, and required that they sign a statement confirming that "the enterprise detailed in this form welcomes the patronage or participation of gay people."[73] Although it gathered its information in a slightly different way, *Gayellow Pages* still took an approach that depended on participation by members of the increasingly visible gay community.

Distribution of the travel guides did not change significantly from the 1960s. Travel guides in the 1970s continued to be available primarily by mail order, with ordering information and/or forms included in the guides themselves and in *The Advocate*, *Gay*, *Gay Scene* and other gay-oriented periodicals. Bars also continued to distribute the guides, particularly those in which they advertised. Some of the higher-quality guides were increasingly available at gay book stores, primarily in large cities.

Overall, the trend in guide books in the 1970s was one toward increased visibility. Unlike most of the guides from the previous decade, which often concealed their very gayness through vague language and lack of detail, the guides of the 1970s were more explicit, both verbally and visually. The increased visibility of these guides reflected the gay liberation movement's idea that homosexuals should no longer have to hide and should be able to openly come together to create change. The counterpublic generated in part by the travel guides of the 1960s became more visible and outspoken during the 1970s. While *Gayellow Pages* and *A Gay Person's Guide to New England* followed *The Advocate* in avoiding, minimizing, or marking off sexually explicit content, many of the guides emphasized sexuality as a part of their identity. Through their descriptions, ads, and other illustrations, many of the guides explicitly highlighted the sexual differences that set homosexuals apart from the mainstream. The liberation movement brought homosexuality out into the open, but the publications still gave the impression that information about gay travel and tourism in this period was distributed by gays, for gays, and among gays, reflecting their continued marginalization in society.

MOVING TOWARD ACCEPTANCE: THE 1980S AND 1990S

The attention generated by the gay rights movement in the 1970s led to more than just increased visibility—it also generated a backlash. The outspokenness of gay rights advocates evoked responses from antigay groups and individuals. Those speaking out against homosexuality in the late 1970s and early 1980s included politicians like California State Senator John Briggs, who fought to remove gay employees from public schools, as well as religious leaders Jerry Falwell and Pope John Paul II, who argued that homosexuality was a sin.[74] The HIV/AIDS epidemic that first gained national attention in the early 1980s continued to demonize homosexuals as the disease was framed by many as a punishment for homosexual activities. After a brief period of fear and silence, the gay community came together stronger than ever, as they united to raise awareness of AIDS and to fight for gay rights.

The remainder of the 1980s and the 1990s were defined by a constant struggle for acceptance, marked by both defeats and victories. Court decisions like *Bowers vs. Hardwick* (1986), which protected the constitutionality of state anti-sodomy laws; legislation like the 1996 Defense of Marriage Act, which legally defined marriage as one man and one woman; and hate crimes like the 1998 torture and murder of gay college student Matthew Shepard all presented setbacks in the fight for equality and acceptance. President Clinton's "Don't Ask, Don't Tell" military policy generated a mixed response, but his appointment of out lesbian Roberta Achtenberg to a high-level cabinet position paved the way for other gay and lesbian federal appointees. *Kentucky vs. Wasson* (1992) and similar cases and legislation in other states turned against the precedent of *Bowers vs. Hardwick*, declaring that consensual acts of sodomy should not be considered criminal behavior.[75]

As John D'Emilio argues, gay rights in the 1990s moved from marginal status to mainstream status, as major corporations regularly offered domestic partner benefits, mass media outlets featured openly gay performers and characters, advertisers targeted gay consumers, and gay/straight alliances appeared in schools across the country.[76]

During the same period, gay and lesbian groups struggled with internal conflicts, as some (like ACT UP and Queer Nation) took an aggressive, in-your-face approach that highlighted sexual difference, while others tried to argue that homosexuals were not that different from heterosexuals. The changes and struggles within the gay community and society at large led to similar changes in the realm of gay tourism.

Building on the 1970s increase in visibility, periodicals and travel guides in the 1980s and 1990s worked toward an increase in acceptance, respectability, and even mainstreaming. Leading the charge was *The Advocate*. Having distanced itself from sexually explicit ads and content in the 1970s, the magazine continued to position itself as a lifestyle magazine similar to mainstream magazines—aside from the fact that its readership happened to be gay. As Sender points out, the early 1980s onset of the AIDS epidemic frightened away some mainstream advertisers who were afraid to associate themselves with the community that was most publicly associated with the disease.[77] This slowed the magazine's bid for mainstream acceptance, but it did not stop the publishers from producing a magazine with the look and feel of a mainstream publication.

The magazine continued to feature stories about travel, presented glossy color photos of exotic locations around the world, and occasionally included an ad for one of the more popular travel guides like *Damron's*. Increasingly, the magazine ran ads for all-gay resorts, guesthouses, and travel agencies around the nation. No longer forced to settle for the one yearly gay vacation adventure planned by an agency otherwise geared toward heterosexuals, readers now received information about agencies dedicated to planning vacations solely for gays and lesbians. For example, Hanns Ebensten Travel, Inc. advertised its Amazon cruises and other vacation packages through much of the 1980s and 1990s.[78] In 1985 RSVP Travel Productions (later to become RSVP Cruises, one of the biggest names in gay travel), announced their first event, "A seven-day, luxury 'Cruise to Remember.' "[79] By the early 1990s, Atlantis Events was sponsoring cruises for men and women, while Olivia Cruises and Resorts offered women-only vacation packages. *The Advocate* and other gay magazines gaining prominence in this period, such as *Out* and *Genre*, became primary sources of information about gay-owned and gay-operated travel resources. The International Gay and Lesbian Travel Association, founded in 1983, also provided more centralized information and assistance for both travelers and businesses associated with the travel and hospitality industries. With the availability of these resources, finding gay travel information became easier, but it still had not gone completely mainstream.

Most of the travel guides during the 1980s and 1990s also took on appearances similar to mainstream publications. By the end of the 1980s, *Damron's Address Book* had grown to 463 pages and "over 6,000 listings."[80] Changes in the explanation of listings represented changes in the times. In addition to the "B" for "blacks frequent," this edition contained a notation of "BWMT" for "black and white men together," while the 1980s fitness craze had led to the addition of entries for health clubs and gyms. The book also responded to the AIDS crisis by adding information about AIDS hotlines and other services. At 678 pages and containing "over 8,000 listings," the 1995 version of the guidebook made the pocket-sized travel guides of the 1960s a distant memory.[81] Reflecting an increasing awareness of diversity within the gay community, the explanation of listings had added notations for wheelchair accessible spaces as well as a number of multi-racial categories, including "multi-racial, mostly Asian-American," "multi-racial, mostly African-American," and "multi-racial, mostly Latino-American."[82] While early editions of the guidebook presented "cruisy areas" as acceptable locations for public sex, the AIDS-conscious 1990s editions offered an extensive notice about the dangers of these areas, adding that "Most police depts. in the USA have copies of the address book, beware."[83] The book also added information about sodomy laws in various states, as well as phone numbers for gay and lesbian legal services, youth services, and a hate crimes hotline.

Spartacus and *Gayellow Pages* also continued to follow their established formulas for success, while most of the other earlier travel guides faded from the scene. Most likely the success and dominance of *Damron's* (for bars, baths, and clubs in the United States), *Spartacus* (for similar establishments internationally), and *Gayellow Pages* (for more general, daily life listings) made the other guides unnecessary. Unable to compete, the old guides largely disappeared by the mid 1980s. New guides that appeared rarely lasted for long, and in some cases were intended as single volume guides, rather than publications that would issue yearly editions. In an attempt to gain respectability, many specifically tried to distance themselves from the traditional travel guides, which were seen as lists of places to find sex partners. Most of those that did appear during this time attempted to fill a specific gap left by the bigger, more established guides.

Places of Interest, for example, attempted to reach out to international visitors, offering information about cities in the United States and

Canada in English, French, Spanish, German, and Dutch.[84] *The Advocate Gay Visitor's Guide to San Francisco* offered a book-length, in-depth look at "the social and cultural opportunities offered to gay men and lesbians in America's most vibrant gay community."[85] The guide (library-ready with its ISBN and Library of Congress number) sought respectability by way of its connection to the magazine with which it shared its name. As the back of the book boasted, "This authoritative guidebook is brought to you by the editors of America's most respected gay magazine, *The Advocate*."[86] Covering far more than just bars and clubs, the book also featured chapters on shopping, cultural events, and gay history.

The editors of *Now, Voyagers!*, billed as "The Newsletter for Gay Travelers," specifically critiqued guides like *Damron's* in an attempt to distinguish their newsletter. A letter to potential subscribers lamented the failure of previous guides, suggesting that they often led to disappointing vacations. As the letter stated, "the only 'guide' for us has been various book-length listings of bars, baths and cruise areas—as if gay travel means nothing more than a sex hunt away from home."[87] The newsletter was intended as a remedy for the detail-deficient, sex-oriented guides of the past. *Out & About Gay Travel Guides* also attempted to separate themselves from guides like *Damron's* and explicitly stated a desire to be read as mainstream: "We think of our books as a mainstream travel series with a distinctly gay perspective. Most gay guidebooks have focused on sex, with travel being secondary."[88]

The most notable example of mainstream recognition came in 1996, when the popular *Fodor's* travel series began printing *Fodor's Gay Guides* to cities and countries around the world. These books offered extensive information about local culture, political climate, history, and traditions as well as locations and directions to various attractions, hotels, restaurants, and so forth. Unlike many gay travel guides, *Fodor's* excluded most sex-oriented businesses from its pages. In this way, the publication followed the path of gay periodicals like *The Advocate* and *Out*, which, as Rodger Streitmatter and Katherine Sender have demonstrated, eliminated sex-oriented advertising as part of their attempt to lure more "respectable" advertisers.[89] The inclusion of gay and lesbian travelers by such a prominent travel series was a significant moment in the shift toward making gay tourism more acceptable.

In general, the travel guides of the 1980s and 1990s went in one of two directions. Some, like *Damron's* and *Spartacus*, built on their past success, while most newcomers carved out space for themselves by offering formats and content that differed from previous guides. One trait they shared was a level of professionalism and quality. Guides were professionally produced, in some cases by large publishers, and had the look and feel of library-quality books. While the older guides continued to focus on offering lists of gay establishments, newcomers offered more detail about specific areas and included a wider variety of activities and points of interest that might appeal to the gay traveler. Advertising in *Damron's* and *Spartacus* increased not only in volume, but in variety, as national advertisers like Skyy Vodka and Holiday Inn began taking out ads that ran alongside those for bars, clubs, phone sex companies, and adult film studios. Most of the newer guides stayed away from advertising entirely, or reserved a few spaces for prominent national companies.

All of the guides of this era built on the increased visibility established in the 1970s and made no attempts to conceal their gayness, but their presentation of gayness varied. For *Damron's* and *Spartacus*, gay identity was driven by sex, and the guides continued to offer lists of places to meet potential sex partners. *Gayellow Pages* and most of the newer guides presented a different version of homosexuality by offering information and advice that would appeal to the social, cultural, political, and spiritual needs of gay travelers in addition to (or in some cases instead of) their sexual needs. This may have been, in part, a response to the AIDS epidemic, which equated gay sexuality with dangerous sexuality in the minds of many Americans. Minimizing the sexual aspects of gay travel allowed certain guides to move closer to the mainstream, in part by suggesting that gay travelers were just like any other travelers. Although they did not shy away from sexuality, *Damron's* and *Spartacus* did respond to the AIDS crisis, encouraging responsible sexuality and offering information related to AIDS and HIV.

The division between the two groups of guides carried over into production and distribution. *Damron's* and *Spartacus* continued to be produced by and for gays, and continued to reflect the notion of community members sharing information with one another. The newer guides, while written or edited by gays, often took on a more detached, corporate feel. They were written by editors of major magazines, or included in larger series of travel guides—in other words, they were produced by "experts" rather than average folks who decided to share information with others and needed the help of readers to stay current. The guides were still produced primarily by members of the gay community, but their move toward the mainstream hinted at the future of gay travel, when homosexuals would become a target market for outside businesses and mainstream tourist destinations. The older guides continued to be sold by mail order, and were often found in gay bookstores. The newer guides, however, appeared not only in gay bookstores, but also in some mainstream bookstores and libraries.

This split between the different sets of guides reflected the politics of the era. The gay community was split over the question of sameness versus difference. As Stevi Jackson argues, the assimilationist stance sought "to be included into heterosexual privilege, rather than to challenge it," while an argument based on difference "has always been seen as a challenge to institutionalized heterosexuality, a refusal to live within its boundaries."[90] These two views are represented respectively by the guides that minimized sexuality and difference and by those that foregrounded it. The argument over this division continues to this day, and the two sides of the argument continue to be reflected in communication about contemporary gay travel.

CONCLUSION: THE EVOLUTION CONTINUES

The earliest gay travel guides were simple, amateur productions, distributed by mail order or word of mouth, and containing information based on personal travel and/or knowledge passed along through friends and associates. But the significance of these guides goes well beyond their initial use as sources of information. The guides highlight the status of gays and lesbians as segregated, invisible outsiders, working to build a network of businesses and gathering spaces in the shadow of mainstream America. While local communities of gays and lesbians were developing in individual bars, neighborhoods, and cities, they remained very isolated. Much like a game of connect the dots, the early travel guides provided links between these isolated communities, sketching out a picture or map of the nationwide gay and lesbian community that was beginning to emerge.

The early travel guides also demonstrate the creativity, ingenuity, and subtle resistance that was essential for the development and maintenance of gay and lesbian communities at all levels. Ignored, ostracized, and persecuted by mainstream society, gays and lesbians—like many other minority groups before and since—had no choice but to turn inward and rely on themselves. They created their own guidebooks and built their own networks to share information and build a community under the noses of those who refused to accept them.

As time went on, these guides became more substantial in terms of content and attracted a greater number and wider variety of advertisers. Some continued to focus on simply identifying gay establishments, while others, like *Fodor's* and *Out & About*, focused on general travel concerns, including gayness as one of many components of a traveler's identity. While the earliest guides were circulated among the gay community and required a certain amount of effort to track them down, the more recent guides have moved more into the mainstream. Current *Fodor's* and *Damron's* guides can be purchased through Amazon.com and in mainstream bookstores. This evolution of gay travel guides parallels what Dereka Rushbrook identifies as a "transformation of gay culture, from an introverted, closed, private space epitomized by dark, unmarked bars to a space appropriated from the night and beckoning with neon signs and full-length windows open to the street."[91]

The gay travel guide's slow progression from the margins toward the mainstream laid the groundwork for the more recent developments in gay tourism—specifically the large-scale promotional campaigns attempting to lure gay and lesbian travelers to cities and resorts across the country. As this chapter demonstrates, this was not an overnight development, but a long, slow evolution. Mainstream marketers did not create gay tourism. This recognition by outsiders is only the most recent step in its evolution, as marketers tap into an industry that was initiated and cultivated for many years by the gay community itself. Now that cities and resorts are welcoming gay and lesbian tourists with open arms, we must not forget the hard work and creative methods that allowed gay and lesbian tourism to flourish long before the mainstream came calling.

NOTES

1. Jeff Guaracino, *Gay and Lesbian Tourism: The Essential Guide for Marketing* (Oxford: Butterworth-Heinemann, 2007): 3.
2. Guaracino, xvii.
3. Pia Sarkar, "Top Dog San Francisco Runs into Competition for Gay Tourist Dollars," *San Francisco Chronicle*, October 24, 2004, J1; Deborah Sharp, "More Cities Cast a Rainbow-Friendly Image To Lure Gay Travelers," *USA Today*, January 4, 2004, L6.
4. Guaracino, 4.
5. International Gay and Lesbian Travel Association, "IGLTA Facts," 2008, http://www.iglta.org/facts.cfm (10 May 2009).
6. This research is based primarily on materials housed in the archives of the Kinsey Institute for Research in Sex, Gender, and Reproduction. I would like to thank the librarians and staff at the Institute, particularly Liana Zhou and Shawn C. Wilson, for helping me to locate valuable resources and artifacts within the archive's vast collection of materials.

7. The analysis of texts such as these presents numerous methodological challenges. Gay travel guides, particularly in their early days, were largely underground publications, produced by and for a segment of the population that was forced underground by an intolerant majority. The individuals and small businesses who produced the guides were not keeping archives of their own products, and most of the guides never made it to libraries. Many of the individuals who purchased the guides did so in secrecy, and likely made an effort to keep them hidden or destroyed them when they were no longer useful. Due to the rapid turnover of many gay establishments, the guides were constantly being updated. Outdated guides were of little use, and therefore were discarded. As a result, a history of these guides must be pieced together from those that remain. My discussion is based on a collection of these guides housed at the Kinsey Institute in Bloomington, Indiana. Based on the commonalities and trends revealed by the guides that are available, one can reasonably read them as indicative of broader trends which would include those that are missing. I have attempted to fill in the gaps based on the evidence that is currently accessible.

8. I have broken the development of gay travel communication into decades primarily for the sake of convenience. I do not wish to imply that these periods are marked by firm or impermeable boundaries. Gay travel over the past forty years has been defined by gradual rather than abrupt changes, and it has responded to broad trends rather than distinct events. Therefore, the periods identified should be read as more suggestive than definitive.

9. Walter L. Williams and Yolanda Retter, eds. *Gay and Lesbian Rights in the United States: A Documentary History.* (Westport, CT: Greenwood Press, 2003): 72–80.

10. Dudley Clendinen and Adam Nagourney, *Out for Good: The Struggle to Build a Gay Rights Movement in America* (New York: Simon & Schuster, 1999): 12.

11. John D'Emilio, *The World Turned: Essays on Gay History, Politics, and Culture* (Durham: Duke University Press, 2002): 24.

12. Walter L. Williams and Yolanda Retter, 88.

13. "Social Services," *ONE Confidential* ix, no. 2 (1964): 3.

14. "Social Services," *ONE Confidential* ix, no. 12 (1964): 4.

15. "Social Services," *ONE Confidential* ix, no. 12 (1964): 3.

16. For example, "The Gay Traveler: Take a Cycledelic Trip," *The Los Angeles Advocate*, September 1967, 5.

17. "Holy Toledo: Midwest Swings," *The Los Angeles Advocate*, February 1969, 19.

18. For example: "Germany, Canada Pass 'Consenting Adults' Laws," *The Los Angeles Advocate*, June 1969, 3. "Connecticut Passes Sex Reform Law," *The Los Angeles Advocate*, August 1969, 1.

19. Tours. Advertisement. *The Los Angeles Advocate*, August 1968, 9.

20. Trip "69." Advertisement. *The Los Angeles Advocate*, May 1969, 13.

21. For example, Dave's VIP Club. Advertisement. *Los Angeles Advocate*, May 1969, 23. Also Dave's Steam Baths. Advertisement. *Los Angeles Advocate*, June 1969, 29.

22. *The Homosexual Citizen* 1, no. 1 (1966): front cover.

23. "Subscribe," *The Cruise News and World Report* 1, no. 2 (1965): 3. Kinsey Institute, Indiana University,Vertical File: Homosexual Publications— *Cruise News and World Report*. (Hereafter VF: CNWR).

24. *The Cruise News and World Report* 1, no. 2 (1965): 4–5, (VF: CNWR).

25. *Gay Guide to Europe* (Paris: Ganymede Press, 1960): 4.

26. *World Report Travel Guide* (New York: World Travel Guide Publishers, 1964): 1.

27. George A. Davis, Letter to WRTG Owner, August 12, 1965. Kinsey Institute, Indiana University, Vertical File: Homosexual Guide Books. (Hereafter VF: HGB).

28. *The Lavender Baedeker '66* (San Francisco: Strait & Associates, 1966): front cover, (VF: HGB).

29. *Lavender World* (San Francisco: Strait & Associates, 1965). Kinsey Institute: "Collection of pulp fiction, periodicals and travel guides of gay themes." (Hereafter KI: Pulp Fiction); *The Grey Guide* (San Francisco: Strait & Associates, 1965), (VF: HGB).

30. *Gay Guide to New York* (Toronto: Gay Publishing Co., 1965), (VF: HGB).

31. *International Guild Guide* (Washington, DC: Guild Press, Ltd, 1966): 3.

32. *Directory 43* (Minneapolis: Directory Services, Inc. 1965): Introduction–no page number given.

33. Bob Damron, *The Address Book* (San Francisco: Pan-Graphic Press, 1965): 1 (VF:HGB).

34. Bob Damron, *Bob Damron's Address Book 1968* (San Francisco: Pan-Graphic Press, 1967): 66.

35. Bob Damron, *The Address Book* (San Francisco: Pan-Graphic Press, 1965): 2 (VF:HGB).

36. *Barfly*, eds. Bill Rand and Bo Siewert (Los Angeles: Advocate Publications, Inc., 1973), (KI: Pulp Fiction).

37. *Lavender World* (San Francisco: Strait and Assoc., 1965): front cover, (KI: Pulp Fiction).

38. *The Lavender Baedeker* (San Francisco: Strait and Assoc., 1963): front cover, (VF:HGB). *The Grey Guide for 1965* (San Francisco: Strait and Assoc., 1965): no page number, (VF: HGB).

39. *Directory 43* (Minneapolis: Directory Services, Inc., 1965): Introduction–no page number.

40. Marc Stein, *City of Sisterly and Brotherly Loves: Lesbian and Gay Philadelphia, 1945–1972* (Chicago: University of Chicago Press, 2000): 50.

41. *Cruise News and World Report* (May, 1965): 4 (VF: CNWR).

42. Bob Damron, *The Address Book* (San Francisco: Pan-Graphic Press, 1965): 1 (VF: HGB).

43. *Directory 43* (Minneapolis: Directory Services, Inc., 1965): Introduction–no page number.
44. *International Guild Guide* (Washington, DC: Guild Press, Ltd., 1966): 3.
45. *International Guild Guide* (Washington, DC: Guild Press, Ltd., 1966): 3.
46. *World Report Travel Guide* (New York: World Report Travel Guide Publishers, 1964): front cover.
47. *Cruise News and World Report*, (May 1965): 2 (VF: CNWR).
48. Bob Damron, *The Address Book* (San Francisco: Pan-Graphic Press, 1965): 3 (VF:HGB).
49. Les Wright, "San Francisco," in *Queer Sites: Gay Urban Histories Since 1600*, ed. David Higgs (New York: Routledge, 1999), 177.
50. Michael Warner, *Publics and Counterpublics* (New York: Zone Books, 2002): 120.
51. Williams and Retter, 124.
52. Williams and Retter, 127.
53. Williams and Retter, 131–132.
54. Katherine Sender, *Business, Not Politics* (New York: Columbia University Press, 2004): 30–32.
55. Sender, 32.
56. Rick Hayes, "Breckenridge Holds Special Attraction for Gay Skiers," *The Advocate Pullout*, February 28, 1975, 5.
57. *Douglas Dean's Gay Mexico II*, advertisement. *The Advocate*, March 12, 1975, 44; *Skipper's Guides*, advertisement. *The Advocate*, February 26, 1975, 38.
58. "Where Will You Go Tonight?" *Gay* (February 1, 1972): 2.
59. For example, "If You're Going to France," *Gay Scene* 1, no. 8 (1971): 9; "Cincinnati – The Queen City,"*Gay Scene* 4, no. 12 (1974): 16; "Fire Island, Famous Gay Resort," *Gay Scene* 4, no. 12 (1974): 8.
60. Bob Damron, *Bob Damron's Address Book '77* (San Francisco: G. Howard, Inc., 1976): 3.
61. Bob Damron, *Bob Damron's Address Book '77* (San Francisco: G. Howard, Inc., 1976): 4.
62. Guild Book Services, Inc. Letter to "Friend." October 15, 1975, (VF: HGB).
63. *Spartacus International Gay Guide*, advertising flyer, (VF: HGB).
64. *Skipper's Guide* (Danville, KY: Skipper's Guides, 1972): 80 (VF: HGB).
65. *Skipper's Guide* (Danville, KY: Skipper's Guides, 1972): 3 (VF: HGB).
66. *Gayellow Pages* application, 1975, (VF: HGB).
67. David Peterson, ed. *A Gay Person's Guide to New England* (Boston: GCN, Inc., 1976): 3.
68. *Gaia's Guide*, seventh edition (Palo Alto, CA: Up Press, 1981): 2.
69. *International Guild Guide 1976 Bicentennial Edition* (Washington, DC: Guild Press, Ltd., 1976): 1.
70. *Skipper's Guide* (Danville, KY: Skipper's Guides, 1972): 3 (VF: HGB).
71. *The Girls Guide 1974* (San Francisco: Publisher Unknown, 1974): 1.

72. John D. Stamford, ed. *Spartacus International Gay Guide* (Amsterdam: Spartacus, 1979): 9.

73. *Gayellow Pages* application, 1975, (VF: HGB).

74. Williams and Retter, 144; 162–163.

75. Williams and Retter, 206.

76. D'Emilio, x.

77. Sender, 36.

78. Hanns Ebensten Travel. Advertisement. *The Advocate*, October 1, 1985, 14 and 31. Hanns Ebensten Travel. Advertisement. *The Advocate*, February 7, 1995, 21.

79. RSVP Travel Productions. Advertisement. *The Advocate*, October 1, 1985, 7.

80. Bob Damron, *Bob Damron's Address Book '89* (San Francisco: Bob Damron Enterprises, 1988): 21.

81. Gina Gatta, *Damron Address Book '95* (San Francisco: Damron Enterprises, 1994): Front Cover.

82. Gina Gatta, *Damron Address Book '95* (San Francisco: Damron Enterprises, 1994): 27.

83. Gina Gatta, *Damron Address Book '95* (San Francisco: Damron Enterprises, 1994): 28.

84. Marianne Ferrari, *Places Of Interest* (Phoenix: Ferrari Publications, 1983), (KI: Pulp Fiction).

85. *The Advocate Gay Visitors Guide to San Francisco*, revised 1982-83 edition (San Mateo, CA: Liberation Publications, Inc., 1982): 7, (VF: HGB).

86. *The Advocate Gay Visitors Guide to San Francisco*, revised 1982-83 edition (San Mateo, CA: Liberation Publications, Inc., 1982): back cover, (VF: HGB).

87. Robert Schirmer, letter to "Gay Traveler," n.d. [1982?], (VF: HGB).

88. Billy Kolber-Stuart and David Alport, *Out and About Travel Guides: USA Resorts and Warm Weather Vacations* (New York: Hyperion, 1997): 4.

89. Rodger Streitmatter, *Unspeakable: The Rise of the Gay and Lesbian Press in America* (Boston: Faber and Faber, 1995); Katherine Sender, *Business Not Politics: The Making of the Gay Market* (New York: Columbia University Press, 2004).

90. Stevi, Jackson, "Sexual Politics: Feminist Politics, gay politics and the problem of heterosexuality," in *Politics of Sexuality: Identity, Gender,Citizenship*, eds. Terrell Carver and Veronique Mottier (London: Routledge, 1998): 71.

91. Dereka Rushbrook, "Cities, Queer Space, and the Cosmopolitan Tourist," *GLQ* 8, no. 1–2 (2002): 193.

Chapter 13

Pride Translated: The Gay Carnival, San Francisco 2008

Christal Seahorn

Sunday, June 29, 2008, 8:30 A.M.—The parade begins in two hours. Figuring to work the early crowd, I arrive at Market Street on a brisk San Francisco morning (campy weatherman said 67 degrees for the high today, and with the clouds and the biting bay winds, it feels more like December than California June). Surprisingly, there are only a handful of people along the parade route. No indication of the estimated 1.2 million expected. If not for the police barricades and the procession of rainbow flags lining Market Street from Beale to 8th, I would worry I had the wrong date. No worries, a quick glance at my "Pocket Pride" confirms the 10:30 A.M. start time. I strike up a conversation with a young group of women sitting atop one of the barricades and ask about the sparse crowd. "Queens," says an athletic blonde wearing a purple Tootsie Roll t-shirt with the caption *The slower you lick, the longer it lasts*, "they're all still in bed. They'll show up fashionably late and want to squeeze in up front."[1]

9:15 A.M.—The streets are still pretty ghostly. Restaurant vendors are setting up tables in front of their stores, wafting smells of breakfast burritos and sausage sandwiches toward the noses of unprepared spectators who left home without food. I am one of those unprepared spectators and experience immediate buyer's remorse as I purchase my "Pride Special" breakfast: burrito and water, $11. Official Pride volunteers are busy posting "Keep Off" signs on the Muni Metro entrances. Apparently, the intoxicated or balance-challenged have a history of succumbing to the excitement of the day and falling into the tunnels. Sadly, the diligent volunteers would spend most of the parade shooing participants off the subway walls, many of whom were standing or sitting atop these same "Do Not Sit" signs.

10:45 A.M.—The parade starts on time (10:30 A.M.), and the opening contingent reaches my position in 15 minutes. I hear them long before I see them. A distant, low rumble progresses to a rib-shaking roar. The thunderous sounds of contingent #001: Dykes on Bikes. This iconic group marks the official start of the 2008 San Francisco Pride Parade (SF Pride).[2] The procession's largest contingent, Dykes on Bikes (officially, Dykes on Bikes/Women's Motorcycle Contingent) is a parade within a parade. Stretching more than five city blocks, this cavalry of Harley, Honda, and moped-riding women (and a few men comically crashing the women's party rather than riding with Mikes on Bikes) represent a legacy at SF Pride that spans more than three decades. In 1976, a small group of 20 to 25 female motorcyclists spontaneously joined the head of the procession, giving the parade its first motorcycle escort. One of these first women coined the phrase "Dykes on Bikes," and the *San Francisco Chronicle* picked it up and ran with it. For the next several years, riders simply showed up and rode the parade with no formal organization or registration. In the late 1980s, SF Pride became more structured and the riders' numbers swelled into the hundreds. The need to organize became necessary, and the Women's Motorcycle Contingent (WMC) was born ("Dykes on Bikes Women's Motorcycle Contingent History," 2007). This year, with the California Supreme Court's recent ruling to legalize same-sex marriage, some members of the normally leather-clad group have traded their jeans and vest for wedding dresses and veils.

The jubilant trail of exhaust fumes and lace announces a theme of nuptial equality that would pervade throughout the festival.

The ensuing nature of the procession becomes a river of carnivalesque revelry: wig-wearing unicyclists, acrobats on stilts, balloons in every color of the rainbow, marching bands, flag-covered police cars and fire trucks, go-go dancers, and rodeo riders. Impressively, the 2008 SF Pride coordinators keep the party on schedule: The parade runs about two hours with the Civic Center After-Party beginning around noon and running until roughly 6:00 P.M.What happens during this time, and what has taken over the city of San Francisco the entire week leading up to these final events, resists chronological confinement in its ordinary sense. The event becomes a nearly mystical time of celebration and merriment that transcends the societal constraints of daily life. Generally, in their expression of freedom, love, and self-identification, Gay Pride celebrations are a combination carnival, Mardi Gras, and Woodstock for the LGBT (lesbian, gay, bisexual, and transgender) community. The official SF Pride Web site identifies the San Francisco festival as "one of the last remaining pride events that can truly be called a rite of passage" (*San Francisco Pride*, 2008: "Celebration Info"). With over 200 parade contingents, 300 exhibitors, and 19 stages and venues, the San Francisco LGBT Pride Celebration, Parade, and Civic Center After-Party is the largest LGBT gathering in the nation. Life during Pride is pleasure-seeking and at times hedonistic, yet the festival is more than simply a huge gay block party. The following exploration of the 2008 SF Pride celebration considers some of the most meaningful elements of the festival and why it holds such a place of importance for the LGBT community. Specifically, the 39th annual SF Pride captures an apex of LGBT triumph, celebrating California's (short-lived) legalization of same-sex marriage and foreshadowing the tremendous success of Universal Pictures' *Milk* movie, set to be released in November.[3] A closer look at this celebration illustrates how the carnivalesque atmosphere of Pride in combination with the gay culture symbols represented throughout the event at once embody and complicate preconceptions of socio-political unity, group/individual identity, and community. Ideally, these representations, expressed and embraced during Pride, have the potential to transcend these complications and elevate the LGBT community to a feeling of true membership and inspiration.

SF Pride markets itself as a big, gay carnival. The festival culminates the last weekend in June with the official LGBT Pride Celebration. The days leading up to and immediately following the event reveal a month-long series of gay-friendly, official and unofficial Pride events. The National Queer Arts Festival hosts a series of art shows, readings, performances, and panels at more than a dozen city venues throughout the month ("*National Queer Arts Festival*," 2008). Frameline puts on the San Francisco International LGBT Film Festival—the world's premier showcase for lesbian, gay, bisexual, and transgender cinema—with more than 200 feature and short films playing at the historic Castro Theatre and other venues ("Film Festival," 2007). Exclusive to female participants, the San Francisco Dyke March occurs the day before the Pride parade with women of every shape, size, and haircut gathering at Dolores Park to celebrate the " 'Dyke Identity' to include women who are questioning and challenging gender constructs and the social definitions of women, and who are gender-fluid" ("The Dyke Identity," 2008). A 7:00 P.M. march and motorcycle ride follows the women's rights rally. Ultimately, the Arts Festival, Frameline's Film Festival and the Dyke March, though wildly popular and well-attended, are tame social gatherings compared to the lively pandemonium of the Pink Saturday Street Party.

Held on Pride parade eve (or Pink Saturday as it is know), this Castro District block party is a homosexual, Bacchanalian celebration, complete with hedonistic consumption of enormous pizza slices and ingestion of copious amounts of alcohol and various other mind-altering substances. The "block" party actually extends more than five blocks with bands playing and revelers dancing in the street. Affectionately called San Francisco's gay village, The Castro stretches from Market Street through the Noe Valley neighborhood. The historical area is home to many of the major LGBT night clubs and bars in the city. It has ties to the nearby Haight-Ashbury district made famous by the 1967 Summer of Love hippie rebellion and connections to the late Harvey Milk, who had a camera store there before he began his political career as a gay rights activist in the late 1970s early 1980s. Additionally, the area houses Twin Peaks, the nation's first ground-floor gay bar with expansive and clear glass windows; it is the site of the famous Castro Theatre and the place where the world-renowned AIDS Memorial Quilt got its start in 1987 (*San Francisco Study Center*, par. 2). More than a common street party, Pink Saturday occurs on land deeply rooted in the history of social activism.

Me? I did my homework. As I squeeze my way through the throngs of partiers and weave toward the Castro Theatre, I understand that I am on hallowed ground. Yet, most celebrants I speak with that night have little understanding of the historical importance of their party space. In fact, they seem a bit put off by my questioning, like making them think about the symbolism of Castro takes away from their "party-high." Notably, this feeling of a collective emotional "high" is a uniquely special moment in group settings. Psychologists Mihaly Csikszentmihalyi and John MacAloon refer to a similar sensation as the "flow experience." Like an athlete "in the zone," this feeling arises when a person/people are fully immersed in and invigorated by their activities. According to Csikszentmihalyi, participants risks losing this zone/high/flow if they become conscious of their state. "While an actor may be aware of what he is doing, he cannot be aware that he is aware—if he does, there is a rhythmic behavioral or cognitive break. Self-consciousness makes him stumble . . . flow becomes non-flow and pleasure gives way to worry, problem, and anxiety (qtd. in Turner 56)[4]. If Pride events occur in relatively sacred spaces (i.e., Castro District and San Francisco in general), then the sense of party high perhaps results from the free expression allowed by these spaces. My interview questions may seem like a sort of invasion that threatens to "break the flow" of the event.

Yet, even if Pride participants do not (and maybe dare not) focus too hard on the meaning behind the festival, the undercurrents of civil unrest and rebellion course visibly beneath the joviality of the celebration. Secular and irreverent, Pride is the Gay Carnival. The weekend gives voice to expressions of oppression and calls for more inclusive civil rights. During Pride, the LGBT community, having been pushed to the margins of society, claims the right to mock power rules in a completely Bakhtinian sense.[5] The playfulness and humor of Pride offers a chance for the "other" to reign—a brief moment where the world is turned upside down and gay is normal. The Pink Saturday Party of 2008 Pride provides a perfect example of the ways in which Pride participants thumb their noses at the prescriptive societal limitations that deem same-sex relationships offensive, unclean, and immoral.

After my initial attempts to interview the crowd, I do less questioning and more watching. A line wraps around the one pizza stand that is still open. Police outside instruct the owners to stop serving beer for fear that the crowd will get out of hand. Considering the large number of people, there is surprising room to move once I get passed the entrance. The atmosphere is, well, happy. I see friends hugging, partners holding hands. The dull thump of techno music pumps up from the distant stage at the bottom of the Castro Street hill. The cigarette smoke is thick at times and occasionally smells of an herb stronger than tobacco. To one side of the street, poetically juxtaposed directly beneath the Castro Theatre sign, stands a beautiful, Adonis-esque, thin young man with flowing blond hair and . . . absolutely no clothing. A small crowd has gathered. The man is standing, stark naked and simply chatting with friends. Frequently, he pauses to take photos with anyone who asks before returning to his conversation. A while later, he hugs his friends, hops on his bike, and casually cycles off.[6] I watch these events with a sense of wonder and amusement. The drugs, the alcohol, the music—all up to this point make this forum no different from many other festivals. But the nakedness, the nakedness stretches the margins even further and is a definite sign that Pride has unraveled normal social constraints. It is more than a fun testing of boundaries; it is a political statement. This young man's nakedness mocks social rules, invites conservatives threatened by homosexuality to take an unobstructed look at what they shun, and visually announces a claim for acceptance and freedom.

In *From Ritual to Theatre: The Human Seriousness of Play*, Victor Turner identifies two types of freedom: "freedom-from" and "freedom-to" (Turner 37). Pride participants experience a freedom from institutional prescriptions of heterosexuality and a freedom to create a new world where they can transcend structural limitations and prejudices. Many of the participants I speak with on Pink Saturday and during Sunday's parade and after-party identify Pride as a "safe" space. They describe feeling a freedom to do and have things they do not have in their everyday lives: holding hands, kissing, and wearing openly-gay paraphernalia and symbols. According to Rinda, a school teacher from Los Angeles attending her first SF Pride, the festival "means being free to feel safe in an environment where people can let their guard down and be themselves without any reservations, kick up their heels, and have a good time" [Lesbian, 37, Los Angeles, Teacher]. Others express feelings of trust and ownership, a sense of the parade as *their* space. Although gay-bashing and other homophobic hate crimes are less prevalent since the AIDS scare of the 1980s, this craving for a safe space expresses a collective reality for the practicing LGBT community. At some point, they each had to face the transition from the heterosexual world in which they were born to the homosexual one with which they now identify. To varying degrees, LGBT members experience an oppressive fear, unsure how their relationships will be received by the mainstream society. The Pride atmosphere again parallels the Bakhtinian carnival in that it releases this pressure and "takes away what is frightening in ordinary time" (Bakhtin 47). It inverts what is normal and expected of public behavior and allows time for being abnormal. Of course, freedom from conservative social norms is complicated in a Pride festival. LGBT members often wish for a broader acceptance of the sense of "normal" to include their lifestyles. While hand holding and kissing are common enough actions for homosexuals and heterosexuals, a sense of normalcy and worth for same-sex couples may not be available outside of the sacred grounds of a Pride festival.

Public nakedness speaks to the heart of what is threatening and "unnatural" about the homosexual world. The body is a display item that announces its difference from the heterosexual world while showing off its similarities. It is a physical freedom, sure, but it also challenges the limits of sexual taboo. The LGBT lifestyles challenge these limits on their own, but at Pride they become even more prevalent with nudity, sadomasochistic demonstrations, and overt displays of affection being the norm for the sacred festival space. It champions the "other" and destabilizes the control of the more conventional and "civilized." Nudity confronts the hegemonic belief that the homosexual lacks, and hence must be an object of scorn rather than envy (Gilbert 480). The dominant culture must maintain this perception of non-procreative gays as deficient or less than in order to frame its definitions of homosexual identity as inferior. The naked gay body, then, asserts strength and rebellious power. It makes sexuality undeniable and expresses confidence and a lack of fear that is a form of subversive social activism as well as a mark of festive playfulness.

Beyond the naked paraders, the dissidents of Pride are inevitably linked to LGBT socio-political issues. In 2008, equal rights are at the forefront as the festival theme announces itself as "United by Pride, Bound for Equality." By definition and tradition, Pride is a festival of politics. It was founded on a bed of political uproar. Historically, Pride Celebrations commemorate the three-day march of LGBT patrons following a police raid on the Stonewall Inn in New York City's Greenwich Village on June 27, 1969. The march was a civil but rebellious response to the injustice and cultural prejudice behind the raid. The year after Stonewall, the first "Gay-In" took place in San Francisco on June 27, 1970, and was the forebear to the current Pride festivals. Since 1972, the event has been held every year, though under various names: "Christopher Street West" in 1972, "Gay Freedom Day" from 1973 to 1980, then "International Lesbian & Gay Freedom Day Parade" from 1981 to 1994, and finally, its present title, "San Francisco Lesbian Gay Bisexual Transgender Pride Celebration" (*San Francisco Pride*, 2008: "FAQ"). The Stonewall riot gives Pride a calendrical importance, offering participants a chance to communicate cultural values and reflect on the seminal socio-political events in LGBT history.[7]

For San Francisco specifically, the 1978 assassination of Harvey Milk fuels the political bent of the Bay Area Pride festival. Milk became the first openly-gay person to be elected to the San Francisco Board of Supervisors in 1977. The outspoken Milk devoted his life to politics and freedom of expression. After only 11 months in office, Milk and then-Mayor George Moscone were assassinated on November 27, 1978. Feelings of anger and injustice mounted after Milk and Moscone's killer, former fellow Supervisor Dan White was absolved of charges and received only a seven-year sentence ("About Harvey Milk," par. 4).

The 2008 SF Pride celebrated a special tribute to Milk's legacy by naming as Celebrity Grand Marshals Milk's nephew, Stuart Milk, and the director (Gus Van Sant) and screenwriter (Dustan Lance Black) of the *Milk* movie.

Historically, Pride is inseparable from social politics. In this sense, the 2008 SF Pride becomes more than a jovial carnival and transitions into a strident political call for fairness and civil rights. Politics are part of the festival's evolution. Politician and celebrity representatives offer credibility through support and official recognition. San Francisco Mayor Gavin Newsom attends the celebration. Theresa Sparks, President of the San Francisco Police Commission and the highest-ranking transgender official in the United State, is the parade's Lifetime Achievement Grand Marshal ("Resolution No. 238-08," par. 6). Charo, Margaret Cho, and Leslie Jordan are Celebrity Guests of the event, and Cyndi Lauper joins Stuart Milk and the *Milk* contingent as Celebrity Grand Marshals.

Often, social politics come with the presumption of a relatively consistent political platform. Pride events propose this unity; however, the LGBT community is far too diverse to present uncomplicated agreement on whose agenda gets priority. In "Party with Politics," Kath Browne acknowledges that the Pride party is "negotiated and '(re) formed' through a multitude of individual and collective 'politics of performance" (64–65). These multitudes add to the richness of expression at Pride but can also dilute the message and limit the strength of possible reformations. Each year, the festival shouts demands for social change. Yet, in the years when major events or adjustments to legislative policies occur, the LGBT Pride voice sounds loudest: HIV/AIDS awareness in the 1980s, gays in the military/"Don't Ask, Don't Tell" in 1993/1994, and sodomy and civil union laws at the turn of the twenty-first century. Celebrants at San Francisco Pride 2008 experience another historical moment of unifying political focus for the LGBT scope. This year, the rebels again have their cause: the end of Proposition 22 and the legalization of gay marriage.

On May 15, 2008, the California Supreme Court ruled that barring same-sex couples from marriage was unconstitutional; this decision overturned the 2000 Proposition 22 ruling that marriage was only between a man and a woman. Beginning June 17, 2008, same-sex couples were free to marry in California. From 5:01 P.M. on June 16 (when the Prop 22 ban lifted) through June 23,San Francisco County reported 849 marriage license registrations.[8] The weekend of Gay Pride, the San Francisco county clerk had 259 marriage license appointments and 284 reservations for wedding ceremonies scheduled for that Friday alone (Vara-Orta, par. 5). At the parade, the liberation and vindication offered by the Supreme Court ruling takes over the procession as recently married men and women announce their wedding dates and march in favor of the change. The Civic Center honors the occasion with a first time venue: the "Get Engaged! Wedding Pavilion." Participants are invited to "Come celebrate the recent victory for marriage equality . . . Get all the answers you need about marriage rights, meet and greet civil rights leaders, and *get engaged* with the movement to defend marriage equality for all couples . . . *Can same-sex couples marry in California?* Yes" (*San Francisco Pride*, 2008: "Get Engaged! Wedding Pavilion," original italics). The acknowledgment of marriage to include same-sex couples infuses a feeling of accomplishment and progress into 2008 Pride. The ruling was lauded as a break-through for the LGBT community and upheld as a beacon of righteousness and liberation. The tributes to same-sex marriage where made more poignant by the fact that a mere three weeks earlier (June 2) opponents against gay marriage turned in enough signatures to add Proposition 8 to the upcoming November general elections.[9] The Pride celebrant marched knowing there was a real threat to their most recent legislative success. Like the symbolism of naked celebrants, marchers for marriage equality also demonstrate rebellion against social constraints; however, this group represents a more everyday reality where same-sex couples present a vision of family and commitment that is less morally condemnable than the public nudity.

Beyond declarations of socio-political cause, the 2008 SF Pride Celebration is decorated with distinct emblems of LGBT identity and community. Perennial Gay Pride symbols including pink triangles, rainbow flags, leather, and drag queens/kings pervade the parade route and after party. Each of these symbols[10] relates to freedom, politics, and the history of gay culture.

During the Holocaust, Hitler forced homosexual inmates to wear pink triangles on their clothes so they could be easily recognized and further humiliated inside the concentration camps. Between 5,000 to 15,000 homosexuals died in these camps (Schwatz par. 2). SF Pride honors LGBT members victimized by the Nazi reign with a Pink Triangle Installation and Dedication Ceremony. Early on parade-day morning, volunteers with Friends of the Pink Triangle construct a gigantic pink triangle on the Twin Peaks bar in the Castro. Elected officials and parade Grand Marshals attend the event; a champagne christening follows the installation. The ceremony has been a part of each SF Pride weekend since 1996. The triangle is said to serve as a "symbol of man's inhumanity . . . a [reminder] of the hatred and prejudice of the past to help educate others and try to prevent such hatred from happening again" (*San Francisco Pride*, 2008: "Official Pride Events"). Historically, there have been attempts to re-appropriate the pink triangle symbol as an affirmative sign of LGBT solidarity. Perhaps due to its negative origins, however, the pink triangle is a less common representation of gay unity than the rainbow flag.

Rainbow-striped flags flood the Market Street parade route and overflow onto the Civic Center's downtown buildings and most of the hotel entrances and department store windows lining the corners of Union Square. The rainbow flag debuted at the San Francisco Gay Pride Parade on June 25, 1978. It was created by San Francisco artist Gilbert Baker as a symbol of pride and support for the gay community. Originally, the flag had eight colors. In his piece "The Rainbow (Gay Pride) Flag," Ramon Johnson (par. 2) identifies the symbolic meaning of each original color [top to bottom]: pink (sexuality), red (life), orange (healing), yellow (sunlight), green (nature), turquoise (magic), indigo/blue (serenity), and violet (spirit). Although, hot pink and turquoise have since been removed, the multicolored flag still serves as a symbolic representation of the multi-facets of the homosexual population.

Leather, another staple adornment at Pride, shifts symbolism from an emblem of unity to a lascivious venture into the taboo sub-culture of leather sex. According to one informant, "There is no accidental leather at Pride. I made a conscious choice to wear these chaps. I'm saying 'tie me up and whip me, Baby' " [Leather Male, 41, San Francisco, Dispatcher]. As this quote exposes, the leather community is closely related to the S&M community. Members describe the style of wearing black leather clothing, like boots and vests, as important signatures of participation in the leather sub-group. In addition to the erotic component, the leather group has shared symbols and rituals: leather flags, leather competitions, and titles (Browne 65). Like many of the large contingents that represent a distinct LGBT sub-culture, the Leather Pride Contingent holds formal events throughout the week to honor Pride. SF Pride 2008 sees the First Annual Dirty Jock Strap Sale where Chaps Team Members[11] wear one jock for the week leading up to the final Pride weekend. On Pink Saturday, these jocks plus five others from Chaps celebrity go-go dancers are auctioned off with all proceeds going to STOP AIDS (*San Francisco Pride*, 2008: "Official Events"). Additionally, Sunday's Civic Center After-Party hosts "Leather Alley" as one of its pavilion venues. The venue advertisement reads "Do you think leather is hot? Curious about SM? Kinky? Got a fetish? Visit Leather Alley. Novices, curious people, and experienced players come together at Leather Alley to foster friendship and family in a safe and supportive environment. Check out our real life BDSM[12] demonstrations. Visit a variety of LGBT leather and SM groups" (*San Francisco Pride*, 2008: "Leather Alley"). The only after-party venue with an entry fee, "Leather Alley" is walled in by huge black fences. At the door, representatives offer information on the importance of trust and communication as a part of the leather environment. Inside the gate, spectators can witness demos and ask scene participants about the leather lifestyle. The leather culture is a private community, and this exhibit is a unique instance of taking what is normally a private encounter and opening it to the public. The invitation embodies the freedom of expression, taboo experimentation, and information-sharing that epitomizes the overall Pride experience.

The foundations of Pride as a homosexual festival and the existence of drag kings/queens as another major symbol of the celebration challenge notions of gender identity and preconceptions of what it means to be male or female. Drag kings/queens best capture the symbolic role reversal and blurring that occurs in same-sex couples. Like Bakktin's description of Carnival clowns and fools, drag kings/queens represent "a certain form of life, which [is] real and ideal at the same time. They [stand] on the borderline between life and art, in a peculiar mid-zone . . . they [are] neither eccentrics nor dolts, neither [are] they comic actors" (8). Drag kings/queens are often the glam and the fabulous of the Pride festival. Their outrageous costumes and enormous personalities make no apologies for their gender choices. They use parody to subvert what is perhaps most threatening about the homosexual lifestyle: its presumed feminization of men and masculinization of women. Cross-dressing is a common existence at pride, with feminine males or butchy females, but true drag divas/studs takes these stereotypes to an extreme. They revolt against the "thou shalt not's" (Babcock 21) of traditional hegemonic society. In their choice to live life so loudly, drag kings/queens engender the respect of the LGBT community in a way that the others do not.

Yet, gender-bending clothing is common at Pride, and the ways in which it problematizes gender assumptions do not stop at drag kings/queens. Referring to the occurrence of symbolic inversions in festival settings, Barbara Babcock notes that "inversion" is a common term for homosexuality. She goes on to clarify that during festival, the term denotes "ritualized 'role reversals' and *not* actual sexual practices"

(22, my italics). Yet, Pride festivals celebrate the very intertwining of role reversal *with* sexuality that Babcock attempts to separate. Unlike gender inversions in heterosexual celebrations (e.g., men dressing up like women), role reversal is part of ordinary non-festival time for the homosexual community. Inversion during festival is not a complete suspension of time, or "time out of time," as anthropologist and folklorist are prone to call ritual/festival periods. Rather, Pride inversions journey beyond playful cross-dressing into pronouncements of identity and group membership.

The LGBT community is less a singular community and more a collection of distinct cultural groups. Participant dress at Pride proves gender identity to be more fluid than conventionally assumed. The choice of "costume" is particularly important because the symbols of one's "uniform" often proclaim group affiliation. Each LGBT subgroup has its own unofficial code of dress. Women dress themselves to represent their categories: fem, jock, butch, stud, fish, professional, nature girl, grunge. Men do the same: twink, faerie, daddy, bear, queen, prep. Lamenting potentially negative media representation, one 2008 SF Pride participant identifies that "in some ways, everyone reverts to being a stereotype [at Pride] which always ends up on the news and perpetuates these stereotypes" [Lesbian, 38, Australia, Geologist]. Yet, at the risk of typecasting, categories remain important components of gay cultural expression. Everyone has a group, and the San Francisco Pride organizers attempt to recognize each one. The parade is a procession of affiliations: Bare Chest Calendar; San Francisco Leather Pride Contingent; Bears of San Francisco; Straights for Gay Rights; Transgender San Francisco; BABN—Bay Area Bisexual Network; Me, Not Meth, and so on. The Civic Center After-Party has multiple venues celebrating LGBT diversities: Women's and Transgender pavilions, Swing Block, Youth Space, Elder Space, Family Garden, Faerie Village, and so on.

With few exceptions (i.e., Leather-Alley, Faerie Freedom Village, Family Garden), each venue has pretty much the same activities. The music changes, but the course of events is the same—a stage, group-representative musicians or comedians, a crowd. Unlike more traditional culture festivals, visiting and remaining at a venue showcases one's identity. Usually, this is a conscious choice made by the spectator; however, the LGBT community is so attuned to labels that lingering at a venue too long can classify a person as one identity or another. In a sense, Pride is a formal way to "out" your LGBT identity and to explore or create new ones. Coming-out narratives are a personal part of gay folklore that is never a fully complete process. Coming "out" is certainly an occasion for a special celebration, but Pride spectators accept outing as a risk/benefit of the festival. The prohibitions that regulate gay life as unacceptable in ordinary time are reversed, as homosexuality becomes accepted and expected during the festival. Limey, a DJ from Los Angeles, explains it best when he clarified that "If you're not LGBT . . . in other words if you're straight [at Pride], you're assumed to be gay" [Gay male, 29, Houston, Disc Jockey.]. Unlike festivals that attract a large set of passive spectators, Pride refuses mere observation. Event participation is assumed as a declaration of LGBT membership. A desire to be viewed as anything else requires marching with PFLAG (Parents, Families, & Friends of Lesbians and Gays) and/or making some other obvious display of heterosexuality (e.g., public displays of affection with the opposite sex, t-shirts declaring sexual preference).

In many ways, Pride functions as a unified declaration of equality—a declaration as important for the participants to make as it is for the conservative, heterosexual mainstream to hear. Speaking to the merger of personal values with communal cohesion, one informant asserted that "Pride is all about defining who and what the gay community is about, both on a personal level and normally in larger groups" [Nathan, Female-To-Male Transgender, 37, Hawaii, Border Patrol Agent]. In day-to-day life, the mass collection of LGBT subgroups can make it difficult to sustain a collected identity. Somehow though, the disparate personalities of gay culture seem more collective during Pride events than at any other time.

One sense of this shared community of sub-groups is the transgenerational modeling that occurs at Pride. My experience at 2008 San Francisco Pride reveals a different perspective from the conclusions of Peacock et al. whose 2001 study found a "lack of connection, lack of shared values, and lack of shared aesthetics between young gay and bisexual men and the 'mainstream' [i.e., 'older'] gay community" (193).[13] Admittedly, most participants with whom I speak have put little thought into the fact that Pride might serve as a form of generational role-modeling; yet, it seems obvious that modeling occurs, even if subconsciously. At the Civic Center after-party, I meet Seth, a 20-year old male attending his first Pride celebration. The interview is a bit challenging because the young man had been dared by his female friends to spend 30 minutes completely naked. Intrigued by the sight of this small-statured, visibly embarrassed young man with none of the arrogant bravado of my previously-witnessed unclothed revelers, I meet up with Seth mid-dare. He willingly answers my questions. He is in town from Oakland. His parents do not know he is gay, but his friends all do. He is enjoying his Pride experience so far because he thinks it "cool to see so many people like [him]" [Seth, Gay Youth, 20, Oakland, Student].

Seth's comment indicates that young homosexuals look to Pride experiences as a way to find a sense of belonging. With much of the LGBT community accepting Pride as a rite of passage, new LGBT members inevitably learn what it means to "be gay" from the more versed members at the festival. All people are raised in a heterosexual world; *gay*, then, becomes a learned behavior.[14] Pride offers a grand-scale image of what the gay lifestyle encompasses and what it could be if free from the confines of societal pressure. The festival offers a venue for the transference of history and cultural lessons to younger members of the LGBT community; these early experiences are seminal moments in the development and sense of self for Pride novitiates. In many ways, the common voice of the celebration says to young/new Pride participants, "These are our values. These are our important causes. Welcome, and what are you going to do to help?"

Like other marginalized groups, the strength and socio-political success of the LGBT community depends on a unified message of purpose. Pride celebrations create a unique atmosphere of oneness often elusive outside of the festival. Members share the common experiences of isolation, ostracism, and discrimination within conventional social structures. Bonds of social togetherness are born from these trying conditions. The sharing of this restrictive existence in combination with the freeing atmosphere at a Pride festival allow for a spontaneous emotional connection among LGBT members that anthropologist, Victor Turner calls *communitas*.[15] According to Turner, if reached, this feeling, this *communitas* "has something 'magical' about it. Subjectively there is in it a feeling of endless power' . . . [when] compatible people . . . obtain a flash of lucid mutual understanding on the existential level, when they feel that all problems, not just their problems, could be resolved" (47–48). A Pride festival's greatest success comes when the separate LGBT affiliations merge into a shared group identity. If this happens, the community as a whole enlarges, hopefully creating a feeling of oneness reflexive of Turner's *communitas* and relating back to the sense of a "flow" or a collective "party high." Ultimately, however, Pride (like *communitas*) is an ephemeral experience, contained only in the space of the ritual/festival. Its true success may be measured on how well it refreshes and motivates LGBT members to continue their fight for free expression and equal legislative treatment once life's normalcy returns.

If only limited to one June week in San Francisco, the 2008 LGBT Pride Celebration, Parade and Civic Center After-Party accomplished what its spectators expected it to: a carnivalesque party, celebrating of the LGBT community, and offering a safe space for same-sex expression. The party holds intrinsic value for its participants beyond the publicity and media hype. A lack of conscious awareness about the lessons of Pride does not mean that these lessons are absent. Often complicated by warring political and cultural agendas, the meaning of a Pride festival can often be lost on its party-going participants. Quite honestly, the major politics of queer often take a subconscious backseat to the more enjoyable and fun actions of the event. Yet, the dancing, the drinking, the costuming, and even the subversive nudity—all embody the playful rebelliousness of Pride that challenges conventional norms, questions the politics of exclusionary social policies, allows for a free expression of individual identity and communal unity, and contests the confining bifurcation of gender and sexuality in mainstream American society. In illuminating some of the historic traditions and legacies present in the 2008 LGBT San Francisco Pride Celebration and Parade, I hope to foster the development of an audience that loves and better understands the event and its important symbols. Although a short-lived apex of socio-political accomplishment with the subsequent passing of Proposition 8, the true success of SF Pride 2008 was that it offered a chance to envision a world where love was accepted in all forms, where difference was celebrated, and inclusiveness was the status quo.

NOTES

1. To note, I did later see a very slightly built man clutching a camera and being body-surfed by his friends over this same group of young women. I can only assume that this was, in fact, an effort to "squeeze" him in up front.

2. SF Pride will be used throughout the paper to refer interchangeably to the pre-parade celebration, the parade itself, as well as the after-party.

3. *Milk* would go on to win two Academy Award Oscars: "Best Performance by an Actor in a Leading Role" (Sean Penn) and "Best Writing, Screenplay Written Directly for the Screen" (Dustin Lance Black).

4. Anthropologist Victor Turner notes that flow occurs in a structured environment. As such, it does not quite capture the spirit of Pride. Turner uses the term *communitas* to describe a more spontaneous feeling of group unity and connection.

5. For further information on the concept of Bakhtinian Carnival, see *Rabelais and His World* (1984) by the Russian Literary critic Mikhail Bakhtin.

6. This would be my first experience of nudity at Pride but not at all my last. At the parade, many Dykes on Bikes members rode topless. Other costumed women sprinkled with glitter, wearing heals and tights often had nothing but pasties covering their nipples. Some men's pants had cutouts where the back pockets should have been. Others (usually men) had nothing on at all but shoes and a hat.

7. On June 1, 2009, President Barack Obama formally proclaimed June as Lesbian, Gay, Bisexual, and Transgender Pride Month.

8. This 849 represents a 700% increase from the 120 license applications the same time the previous year (Vara-Orta, par. 5).

9. On Nov, 4, 2008 (during the month in which LGBT members would be remembering the 30th anniversary of the assassination of Harvey Milk), California voters passed Proposition 8, amending the California Constitution to eliminate the right of same-sex couples to marry. California Supreme Court decided to uphold Prop 8 but the court protected the more than 18,000 existing marriages that took place before the between May and the November election ("Marriage for Some," A24).

10. The symbols relate to what Rory Turner and Phillip McArthur term "reference points of identity" (83).

11. Chaps is a gay bar in San Francisco's SoMa ("south of market" street) neighborhood.

12. BDSM is muddled combo-acronym mixing bondage/discipline, dominance/submission, and sadism/masochism.

13. The Peacock et al. study focuses exclusively on the homosexual and bisexual male sub-communities in San Francisco, and does not purport female LGBT members. Since my informant is male, my example of Seth remains an appropriate counterpoint illustration.

14. "Gay" in this sentence refers to the cultural actions and expressions of gayness. It is not a comment on the nature vs. nurture debate on whether homosexuality is biological or environmental.

15. Turner's work in *From Ritual to Theatre* focuses mostly on sacred rituals and rites of passage as it relates to theatrical aesthetics.

REFERENCES

"About Harvey Milk." *The Harvey Milk City Hall Memorial*. Harvey Milk City Hall Memorial Committee, 2004. Web. December 5, 2008.

Babcock, B., ed. *The Reversible World: Symbolic Inversion in Art and Society.* Ithaca, NY: Cornell University Press, 1978. Print.

Bakhtin, M. *Rabelais and His World*. Trans. Helene Iswolsky. Bloomington: Indiana University Press, 1984. Print.

Browne, K. "A Party with Politics? (Re)making LGBTQ Pride Spaces in Dublin and Brighton." *Social & Cultural Geography.* 8.1 (2007): 63–87. Print.

"Dyke Identity." *The San Francisco Dyke March*. n.p., 2008. Web. August 15, 2008.
"Dykes on Bikes Women's Motorcycle Contingent History." *Dykes on Bikes Women's Motorcycle Contingent*. San Francisco Dykes on Bikes, April 9, 2007. Web. 4 May 2008.
"Film Festival." *Frameline*. n.p., 2007. Web. August 5, 2008.
Gilbert, R. " 'That's Why I Go to the Gym': Sexual Identity and the Body of the Male Performer." *Theatre Journal*. 46: 4 (1994): 477–488. Print.
Johnson, R. "The Rainbow (Gay Pride) Flag." *About.com: Gay Life*. About.com, 2009. Web. July 14, 2009.
Kugelmass, J. " 'The Fun Is in Dressing up': The Greenwich Village Halloween Parade and the Reimagining of Urban Space." *Social Text* 36 (1993): 138–152. Print.
"Marriage for Some." Editorial. *Los Angeles Times*, May 27, 2009 home ed.: A24. Print.
"National Queer Arts Festival." *The Queer Cultural Center Presents*. n.p., n.d. Web. August 8, 2008.
Peacock, B., et al. "Delineating Differences: Sub-Communities in the San Francisco Gay Community." *Culture, Health & Sexuality* Vol. 3.2 (2001): 183–201. Print.
The President of the United States of America. "Lesbian, Gay, Bisexual, and Transgender Pride Month, 2009." *The White House*. The Briefing Room, June 1, 2009. Web. August 14, 2009.
"Resolution No. 238-08." *sfgov.org*. San Francisco Board of Supervisors, May 9, 2008. Web. August 14, 2009.
San Francisco Pride. sfpride.org, 2008. Web. December 4, 2008.
San Francisco Study Center. "Pride." *Diverse Destinations San Francisco*. San Francisco Grants for the Arts/Hotel Tax Program, 2008. Web. June 14, 2009.
Schwatz, T. P. "Holocaust: Non-Jewish Victims." 1.1. *Holocaustforgotten.com*. The Holocaust Forgotten Memorial, 2008. Web. May 30, 2009.
Turner, R. and P. H. McArthur. "Cultural Performance: Public Display Events and Festival." The Emergence of Folklore in Everyday Life: A Fieldguide and Sourcebook. Ed. George H. Schoemaker. Bloomington: Trickster Press, 1990. 83–93.
Turner, V. *From Ritual to Theatre: The Human Seriousness of Play*. New York: PAJ Publications, 1982. Print.
Vara-Orta, F. "Same-Sex Unions Boost California's June Wedding Average: Survey Finds That More Than Two and a Half Times the State's Usual Number of Couples Are Issued Licenses." *Lesbian Dating & Relationships*. June 29, 2008. Web. December 8, 2008.

Chapter 14

A Thin Line Between Being Straight or Gay: Portrayal of Lesbian Women in Advertising

Malgorzata Skorek

Advertising can be seen as one of the most powerful visual forces shaping our society. Wherever we look advertisements "pop up" unexpectedly and want to be looked at: buildings, newspaper pages, bus stops, mailboxes, and Web sites. We can hardly hide from them and attempt to remain unaffected in our buying decisions. However, advertisements are not only selling products; they "sell" a great deal more: values, addictions, and concepts of success, love, and sexuality (Kilbourne 2000). They communicate information about ourselves and dictate our lifestyles. This happens partly because products are rarely presented in advertising alone; in fact, the majority of ads are accompanied by human models.

The roles that people portray in advertisements are powerful images that can influence how people act in real life. The problem is that they are not always presenting the roles of men and women that they really have, but instead they often show overly generalized and negative imagery. People may, in turn, start orienting themselves towards these outdated or simply fictional roles and introduce them into their everyday lives. In other words, advertisements cultivate a "reality'" that is not necessarily true, but viewers are likely to "buy into it" following repeated exposure (Gerbner et al. 1986). That is why the study of advertising content becomes so crucial. It reveals the major concepts, symbols, and images we are exposed to as well as the extent to which these are correct depictions of the real world.

Advertising has been criticized on this account especially for showing men and women in highly stereotypical fashion. The first critique of the portrayal of women in advertising was brought about in the late 1960s by the women's liberation movement in the United States. Women's concerns were soon after confirmed by content analyses that revealed that indeed advertisements tended to portray women in ways limited to unprofessional jobs, as housewives, and as sex objects (Courtney and Lockeretz 1971, Belkaoui and Belkaoui 1976, Pingree et al. 1976). Further studies have showed that men are presented in advertising in stereotypical ways as well, as dominant over women but also often objectified (Courtney and Lockeretz 1971, Rohlinger 2002, Skelly and Lundstorm 1981). Researchers continue to find gender stereotypes in advertising in more recent years (Hovland et al. 2005, Wiles et al. 1995).

Even though many content analyses of the portrayal of men and women in advertising have been conducted (for a review see Wolin 2003), their sexual orientation remained largely ignored. This could be due partly to the fact that portrayals of gay men or lesbian women in mainstream media used to be extremely rare. In the recent decade, however, the media have increasingly portrayed gay and lesbian couples, especially in advertising. There are two major reasons for this development. First, advertisers began to recognize that homosexual consumers constitute a market segment with above-average income and a willingness to spend (Lukenbill 1995), often referred to as the "Dream Market" (Oakenfull and Greenlee 2004). Second, more than half of these consumers do not read gay magazines (Poux 1998), and as Tharp (2001) reported, 90 percent of gay and 82 percent of lesbian consumers regularly read mainstream titles such as *Newsweek*, *Time*, *National Geographic*, *People*, or *Men's Health*. Hence, advertisers considered mainstream media to be the only possibility to reach this market.

Being more often portrayed in mainstream advertising, gay communities are likely to have similar concerns as women did four decades ago. Are the depictions of their lifestyle, activities, and behaviors reflective of reality? What positive or negative stereotypes are conveyed in those ads? What effect do these ads have on their homosexual and heterosexual audience? How do the portrayals of gay men and lesbian women differ? All these questions received very little attention in the literature so far. Content analyses are valuable investigations of how different groups are portrayed in advertising and they are a first step in providing information on the image promoted by the media.

Unfortunately, very little research has been done on the portrayal of gay men and lesbian women in the mass media. Rohlinger (2002) analyzed portrayal of men in ads from five U.S. mainstream magazines published in 1987 and 1997 and showed an increasing trend towards eroticizing men. Moreover, she reported more portrayals of men whose sexuality was unknown in 1997 than in 1987. These findings suggest that "sex sells" motto seems to apply equally to men as to women and that the rise of sexually ambiguous portrayals of men may indicate that gay men are becoming more present in advertising. Less literature exists describing the way lesbian women are portrayed in the media. One study by Vänskä (2005) provided an art history perspective on three ads of lesbian women found in a British *Vogue* and discussed new ways of looking at gender by using the concept of "femme-ninity."

Ragusa (2003) analyzed the content of business news articles published in the *New York Times* between 1970 and 2000 related to lesbian, gay, bisexual, transsexual, and queer groups. She found that gay men were twice as often covered in the business news as lesbian women in the studied period, but the discrepancy was smaller in the last two decades than between 1970 and 1990. In addition, a content analysis of *The Advocate*, one of the leading gay and lesbian magazines, reported that lesbian-targeted imagery accounted only for 3 percent of all advertising content in 1999 (Oakenfull and Greenlee 2000). In these two studies it becomes apparent that lesbian women are somehow forgotten in the mass media, in general. A possible explanation for why advertisers are not targeting lesbian women as much as gay men is their lower economic status as compared to gay men. Marketers are more focused on attracting money from gay male consumers (Schulman 1998) and therefore use more gay imagery in advertising.

Even though lesbian women are still rarely portrayed in magazine advertising, they are not portrayed in a simple or a uniform way. Instead, I observed a wide variety of their portrayals that range from very implicit portrayals of female friendship to sexually explicit depictions of a lesbian relationship. As suggested by previous research, overt portrayals remain a taboo even after the gains of the gay liberation movement (Clark 1995). Moreover, explicit and more overt depictions of lesbian women are likely to have different effects on the heterosexual public. Oakenfull and Greenlee (2004) exposed heterosexual participants to explicit or more implicit images of same-sex couples in advertising. A greater amount of intimacy depicted by the ads was considered indicative of a more explicit portrayal of homosexuality of the models. The study found that heterosexual men had more positive attitudes towards ads with overtly lesbian images than with less overt lesbian imagery. This was considered to result from the fact that lesbian relationships have an erotic value for heterosexual men. For heterosexual women, Oakenfull and Greenlee (2004) found an opposite effect; women had a more positive attitude towards implicit than towards explicit images of lesbian models.

To explain this relationship, Kite and Deaux's (1987) application of Freud's (1953 [1905]) inversion model was used. The model proposes that homosexuals are seen as more similar to the opposite-sex heterosexuals; homosexual women more similar to heterosexual men and homosexual men are more similar to heterosexual women. Therefore, heterosexual women in the sample were expected to consider overtly lesbian women as out-groups and identify with them less than with less explicit portrayals of lesbian women. The explanations provided by Oakenfull and Greenlee (2004) are not necessarily substantiated. It seems that men would be attracted by overt and intimate portrayals of any women, not only lesbians. Moreover, Freud's (1953 [1905]) model of homosexuality expects all gay men and lesbian women to be the same, which is a great simplification. Nevertheless, this study showed that the gender of heterosexual viewers might lead to very different preferences of lesbian portrayals in advertising.

Based on the above findings it is clear that we need to explore different types of portrayals of lesbian women, which were largely ignored in the previous research. This is important because different types of imagery are likely to have very different effects on the homosexual and heterosexual audience. In this chapter, I would like to cast more light on the ways advertising depicts lesbian women and their relationships and discuss implications of these different portrayals.

AN INVESTIGATION OF THE PORTRAYAL OF LESBIAN WOMEN IN PRINT ADVERTISING

Approximately 50 print ads presenting explicit or more implicit homosexual female couples were retrieved from a number of mainstream magazines published in the United States in the recent years,

Table 14.1
Indicators of different sexual relationships of women portrayed in the ads

	Heterosexual relationship	Homosexual relationship
Gaze	Non-seductive	Seductive
Touch	Absent	Holding hands, embracing, touching lips, face, hair, neck, breast, belly, buttock
Kiss	Absent	On the lips or cheeks (both the act of kissing or being about to kiss)
Nudity	Absent	Present (women wearing underwear, swimsuit, a revealing top, etc.)
Role-play	Absent, women are portrayed in a similar way (as equals)	Present (masculine and feminine role, a nurse and a patient, policewoman and a villain)

including *Cosmopolitan* and *Elle*, as well as ads from a Google image search.* The brands that portrayed lesbian couples in their advertisements found in this sample included Coors, Dior, Dolce & Gabbana, Dove, H & M, Jean Paul Gaultier, Sisley, Skyy Vodka, Versace, and a few others. The selected ads contained two or more female models, since an interpersonal relationship was needed to determine the sexual orientation of the models. Ads presenting single models were considered to convey too few cues to retrieve this kind of information. All ads were qualitatively analyzed and different cues served as indicators of a homosexual relationship. These cues were then used to create different portrayal categories. Please see Table 14.1 for an overview of these indicators.

After a careful investigation of the material, all collected ads fit into five categories of a lesbian relationship portrayal:

- *Sisterly friendship.* Women are shown as close friends but nothing more, there is no physical contact between them nor do they gaze at each other in a seductive way.

*English keywords were used in the online image search in order to find images posted by English-speaking Internet users. I selected only those advertisements that had slogans in English and that featured brands that are commonly advertised in the United States. Yet, I was not able to rule out the possibility that some of the ads were Canadian or British. The reason why I needed to resort to an Internet search is that there are very few portrayals of lesbian relationships found in mainstream print media, as suggested in the literature review section.

- *Innocent touch.* Women hold hands, embrace each other, or one of them touches parts of her partner's body, but these touches seem innocent and accidental; other cues of a homosexual relationship, for example, seductive gaze, are missing.
- *Role play.* Women do not necessarily touch or gaze at each other but they are presented in opposite gender roles (masculine and feminine) or other role play situations—e.g. a nurse and a patient, policewoman and a villain—and often involves dressing up.
- *Loving caress.* Women's touch is more sexually overt, and often both women touch each other and gaze at each other in a seductive way; some nudity may be also present.
- *Sensual kiss.* Women are shown kissing or about to kiss, and both fully clothed or nude portrayals are possible.

An example of a *sisterly friendship* ad would be a recent H&M ad in which two women advertising a new collection of dresses stand next to each other, one in the front, the other in the back. Both women gaze into the camera with a neutral expression on their faces. They are standing freely without any physical contact to one another and come across just as two models who happen to be in the same shot. Based on the facial expressions, body language, and the atmosphere of this ad there is no indication that these two models could be in an intimate homosexual relationship but friendship at best.

Dolce & Gabbana has created a series of advertisements of clothing and accessories that feature women lying in hay. One of them views from above two blond women lying in hay and facing each other. The blond on the right, dressed in a short lace dress, lies on her side and gazes into the camera. The women on the left lies on her belly and with her left hand touches the lace of the other woman's dress close to her breasts. Her gaze follows her action. The described scene in a subtle way depicts a very close and almost intimate relationship that may go beyond friendship. However, the viewer does not have enough evidence to know that there is more. This and similar ads were placed in the *innocent touch* category.

Women are also often shown as having opposite gender roles and at some occasions even are involved in stereotypical couple-games like the naughty nurse and a patient, policewoman and a villain. The portrayal of *role play* may reflect a sexual and intimate but playful relationship between two women. More importantly, taking up a masculine role by one of the women may be a further hint at the fact that the women are in a relationship that mimics a heterosexual gender role set-up. According to Butler (1993, 233), this performance of traditional heterosexual gender roles by lesbian women or gay men demonstrates a "critique of a prevailing truth-regime of sex." One example for this category could be a fashion ad by Jean Paul Gaultier. A long-haired blond women in a short black dress is sitting on a bar stool. She is touching her hair with the left hand and holding a handbag with the other. On her right stands a woman with a very short haircut. She is wearing knee-high army-like boots and pants, and a tight top with stripes. She is resting her left arm on the first woman's shoulder. Both women are gazing into the camera without a smile. When viewing this ad, the impression of a strong split between feminine and masculine roles is obvious and, even though still quite implicit, it hints at a close relationship between the two women.

More explicit scenes of a potentially lesbian relationship were contained within a *loving caress* category. Women were portrayed as touching each other and gazing at each other in a more sensual and intimate way that lead the viewer to doubt their innocence. For instance, an ad of Coors beer depicts two women in a public bathroom. One of them is a blond attractive woman sitting on the sink and smiling at the other one while looking into her eyes. The second model, to the right of the picture, faces the first woman and stands very close to her, grabbing her left knee with her left hand and applying a lipstick with another. Her right arm also seems to press against the blond woman's exposed breasts. The women in this scene are unlikely to be seen as close friends helping each other out, because too many cues dictate to think that these women are sexually attracted to each other.

An act of kissing or being about to kiss (*sensual kiss* category) was the most explicit relationship portrayed found in the sample of ads. It also conveys the most intimacy out of all five types of portrayals identified above. A kissing scene was found in ads by Sisley and Dior. The first one showed a close-up of women's faces only, while the latter also showed their bodies. More explicit scenes of a lesbian couple than the kissing scene were not found, and women were never portrayed in bed together or in a related overt depiction.

A *sisterly friendship* category was included in this categorization scheme, even though this portrayal would be most likely considered a heterosexual relationship. It is included because several portrayals of women's relationships are ambiguous. Sometimes very few cues exist that would indicate that the portrayed relationship is homosexual, but many others would speak for the heterosexual orientation. That is why

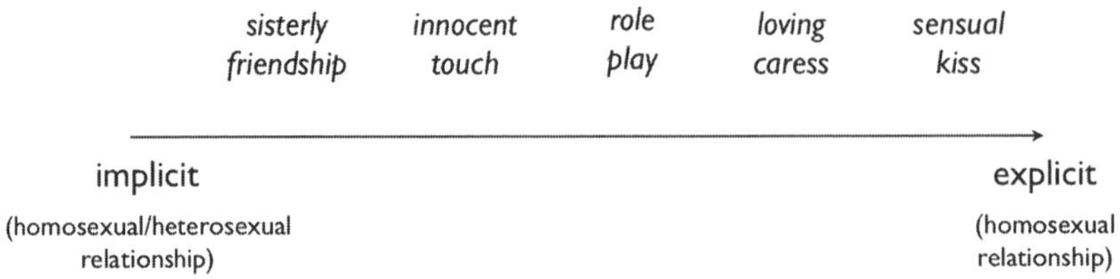

Figure 14.1 An implicit-explicit continuum of different types of lesbian portrayals.

I argue that advertising presents women's relationships on a *sexual continuum*, with portrayals ranging from explicitly heterosexual to explicitly homosexual and a grey area in between, rather than using a clear dichotomy of who is who. The diagram in Figure 14.1 maps the different lesbian portrayals on this continuum.

DISCUSSION AND CONCLUSIONS

This preliminary study of the portrayal of lesbian relationships provided some evidence that the media, advertising in particular, do not portray lesbian relationships in a uniform and clear way. Instead, they use subtle or more explicit cues about women's relationships that lead to a variety of different depictions of female homosexuality. These portrayals differ in their depictions of physical contact, gaze, and nudity. They suggest varying degrees of intimacy between women that could correspond to different stages in a relationship or the extent to which women may need to hide their relationship from the general audience. In fact, many of the distinguished portrayals, like the *sisterly friendship, innocent touch* and *role-play,* were considered implicit; that is, the women's sexual orientation was ambiguous. This suggests that advertisers are skeptical about the possible effects of using overt portrayals of lesbian couples and rely on the use of implicit imagery to attract gay consumers without alienating the mainstream. A possible explanation for it may be the fact that consumers' negative attitudes towards homosexuality are likely to translate into negative attitudes towards ads featuring gay models (Bhat et al. 1996). The strategy of using "dual messaging" is a way to target both homosexual and heterosexual consumers and avoid possible problems resulting from heterosexuals holding negative attitudes towards gays or lesbians. Advertisers can use a certain "language" which signs and symbols can only be meaningful by gay or lesbian consumers, whereas the heterosexual audience is unfamiliar with it and therefore their attitudes towards the product or brand remain unaffected by subtle homosexual language. In a way, these types of ads tell at least two possible stories and it depends on the consumers which one they will perceive.

A question that this essay has not answered is whether portrayals of lesbians in advertisements are true depictions of female homosexual relationships, or are these rather portrayals of what heterosexual marketers think homosexuality is like. This essay does not resolve this issue but encourages a further discussion and analysis of this topic.

This study's main limitation lies in that we looked only at ads portraying couples or multiple women. Would it be possible to determine sexual orientation of advertising models if only one model is present? My intuition is that it would be very hard. The fact that we tend to assume heterosexuality when looking at single women until proven otherwise seems to be a problematic issue that needs to be addressed. We also do not know the publication dates of the majority of ads analyzed. A comparison of prevalence of implicit-explicit portrayals over time would reflect important changes in social norms with respect to the acceptance and promotion of female homosexuality in mass media. Another drawback of this preliminary study is the inclusion of ads derived from an Internet image search, which might have contributed non-U.S. ads to the sample.

FURTHER RESEARCH

One of the further questions that come to mind is whether advertising portrayals of gay men are also as implicit as the portrayals of lesbians. Can we distinguish between different types of portrayals of gay relationships and are they likely to evoke different reactions in their viewers? Further research could also explore the level of generalization of this study's findings. Could we see a similar pattern of portrayals in other U.S. media, such as television commercials or online ads, and in other countries? Is the scale extended in the explicit direction in any media by including even more overt depictions of lesbian women than a kissing scene? Do advertisers in different countries use a similar array of implicit or explicit portrayals of homosexuality? An investigation of cross-cultural differences in the portrayal of gay and lesbian couples would reflect interesting differences in tolerance and promotion of homosexuality in advertising across the globe. It would be interesting to investigate what impact religion and a political climate of different nations have on the extent to which companies are willing to engage in creating ads featuring homosexuality.

Further content analyses of the portrayal of gay men and lesbian women are needed. The existing literature offers very little insights into the ways these two groups are presented and it does not provide answers to questions posed above. Researchers should also address the issue of positive and negative stereotypes conveyed by these different portrayals, whether they correspond to the reality and how harmful they might be. Investigating the portrayal of the gay community in the media is not only interesting for communication scientists and psychologists but also for future advertisers' practices.

REFERENCES

Belkaoui, A., and J. Belkaoui. "A Comparative Analysis of the Roles Portrayed by Women in Print Advertisements: 1958, 1970, 1972." *Journal of Marketing Research* 12, no. 2 (1976): 168–172.

Bhat, S., T. Leigh, and D. Wardlow. "The Effect of Homosexual Imagery in Advertising on Attitude Toward the Ad." In *Gays, Lesbians, and Consumer Behavior: Theory, Practice, and Research Issues in Marketing*, edited by D. Wardlow, 161–176. Binghamton, NY: The Haworth Press, 1996.

Butler, J. *Bodies that Matter: On the Discursive Limits of "sex"*. New York, NY: Routledge, 1993.

Clark, D. "Commodity Lesbianism." In *Gender, Race and Class in Media: A Text Reader*, edited by G. Dines and J. Humez, 142–151. Thousand Oaks, CA: Sage, 1995.

Courtney, A., and S. Lockeretz. "A Woman's Place: An Analysis of the Roles Portrayed by Women in Magazine Advertisements." *Journal of Marketing Research* 8, no. 1 (1971): 92–95.

Freud, S. "Three Essays on the Theory of Sexuality." In *The standard edition of the complete psychological works of Sigmund Freud*, edited by J. Strachev, 136–148. London: Hogarth Press, 1953 [1905].

Gerbner, G., L. Gross, M. Morgan, and N. Signiorelli. "Living with Television: The Dynamics of the Cultivation Process." In *Perspectives on Media Effects*, edited by J. Bryant and D. Zillman, 17–40. Hillsdale, NJ: Lawrence Erlbaum Associates, 1986.

Hovland, R., C. McMahan, G. Lee, J. S. Hwang, and J. Kim. "Gender Role Portrayals in American and Korean Advertisements." *Sex Roles* 53, no. 11/12 (2005): 887–899.

Kilbourne, J. *Killing us softly 3: Advertising's image of women*. Documentary, 2000.

Kite, M. E., and K. Deaux. "Gender Belief Systems: Homosexuality and the Implicit Inversion Theory." *Psychology of Women Quarterly* 11 (1987): 83–96.

Lukenbill, G. *Untold millions: Positioning Your Business for the Gay and Lesbian Consumer Revolution*. New York, NY: Harper Business, 1995.
Oakenfull, G., and T. Greenlee. "A Content Analysis of Advertising in Gay and Lesbian Media." Working paper, 2000.
Oakenfull, G. K., and T. B. Greenlee. "The Three Rules of Crossing Over From Gay Media to Mainstream Media Advertising: Lesbians, Lesbians, Lesbians." *Journal of Business Research* 57 (2004): 1276–1285.
Pingree, S., R. Hawkins, M. Butler, and W. Paisley. "A scale for Sexism." *Journal of Communication* 24, no. 4 (1976): 193–200.
Poux, P. D. "Gay Consumers MIA from Media Surveys." *Advertising Age* 69, no. 16 (1998): 26.
Ragusa, A. T. "Social Change in the Media: Gay, lesbian, Bi, Trans and Queer (GLBTQ) Representation and Visibility in The *New York Times*." Ph.D. dissertation, Virginia Polytechnic Institute and State University, 2003.
Rohlinger, D. A. "Eroticizing Men: Cultural Influences on Advertising and Male Objectification." *Sex Roles* 46, no. 3/4 (2002): 61–74.
Schulman, S. "The Making of a Market Niche." *Harvard Gay and Lesbian Review* (1998): 17–20.
Skelly, G. U., and W. J. Lundstorm. "Male Sex Roles in Magazine Advertising, 1959–1979." *Journal of Communication* 31, no. 4 (1981): 52–57.
Tharp, M. C. "Gay Americans: Sexual Orientation as community Boundary." In *Marketing and Consumer Identity in Multicultural America*, edited by M. C. Tharp, 213–241. Thousand Oaks, CA: Sage, 2001.
Vänskä, A. "Why are there no Lesbian Advertisements?" *Feminist Theory* 6, no. 1 (2005): 67–85.
Wiles, J. A., C. R. Wiles, and A. Tjernlund. "A Comparison of Gender Role Portrayals in Magazine Advertising: The Netherlands, Sweden and the USA." *European Journal of Marketing* 29, no. 11 (1995): 35–49.
Wolin, L. D. "Gender Issues In Advertising: An Oversight Synthesis of Research: 1970–2002." *Journal of Advertising Research* 43, no. 1 (2003): 111–129.

Chapter 15

"Seeing Is the Tithe, Not the Prize": Queer Femme Gender Expression in the 1990s and Current Decade

Anika Stafford

Queer counter-cultures are in the unique and *fabulous* position of being intrinsically influenced by the mainstream culture in which they take place and standing at a critical distance from it. This distance allows for expressions of sexuality and gender that are outside of popular cultural images and norms as to what is "correct" male and female behavior. However, an outsider status does not necessarily allow individuals to escape dominant hierarchies. This chapter looks at the position of femme-identified people within lesbian and queer women's communities. The position of femmes within these communities provides an excellent example of how counter-cultures can challenge mainstream hierarchies while simultaneously and unintentionally reproducing them. This chapter discusses how oppressive gender norms have been extended toward femmes within their communities. I examine how this speaks of the depths to which norms regarding gender and sexuality have become part of taken-for-granted cultural frameworks within dominant North American thought.

In order to demonstrate the active agency femmes employ to contest (and reshape) oppressive positions, I focus on how current art and activism by femmes attempt to extricate queer femme identity from historically demeaning views regarding femininity. I examine discourses surrounding queer femme cultural productions of photography, music, and narrative writing using contemporary queer and feminist theories.

I begin by over-viewing terms such as gender, femme, femininity, and misogyny as they apply to current queer women's and feminist contexts. From there I discuss the history behind misogynist conceptualizations of female bodies stemming from sexological and psychoanalytic discourses. I do this in order to better investigate how the meanings made regarding female bodies (and the following meanings made regarding "female homosexuality") can become part of both dominant and counter-cultural thought. Preceding queer and feminist thought of 1990s and current decade, "radical lesbian feminism" strongly influenced feminist discourse and community life. The rejection of Freudian psychoanalytic accounts of gender identity was a focus of this era of feminist and lesbian organizing. Current femme art and activism not only responds to sexological and psychoanalytic framing of gender identity and expression but also to radical lesbian feminism. The "historical context" section of this essay serves to provide a better understanding of the popular and alternative frameworks being addressed by recent queer femme action.

Drawing from theorists such as Judith Butler and Michel Foucault, I analyze femme counter-cultural production and provide useful tools for challenging misogynies embedded in notions as to what it means to occupy a feminine subject position. As much of the art and activism takes place in the context of third-wave feminism, I analyze trends within third-wave feminist discourses that at times re-inscribe masculinity as the source that makes femininity powerful. My paper investigates how this trend illustrates the insidious way in which misogyny has become part of both mainstream and alternative understandings of gender and sexuality.

KEY TERMS

In examining what the terms femme and femininity can mean, it is important to briefly talk about what gender and sex can mean. On February 2, 2007, Aaron H. Devor presented a lecture, "How Many Sexes? How Many Genders? When Two Are Not Enough," with the Institute for Critical Studies in Gender and Health at Simon Fraser University. Devor described how the dominant gender schema views sex as an intrinsic biological characteristic of which there are only two: male and female. According to this dominant schema, it is impossible to be both male and female and impossible to be neither male nor female. Gender, within this framework, comes to be seen as the cultural manifestation of sex of which there are also only two: masculine and feminine. Females are then expected to be feminine women and males, masculine men. If there is recognition that there are those who do not fit this description, it is generally seen as due to imperfect role of socialization or psychological pathology. The second wave feminism in the 1970s and 1980s sought to disrupt aspects of what Devor refers to as the "dominant gender schema."

During second-wave feminism, the general consensus came to be that sex referred to categorizing bodies as male and female whereas gender was the socialization of male and female into roles. As Eve Sedgwick states in *Epistemology of the Closet*, "The charting of the space between something called 'sex' and something called 'gender' has been one of the most influential and successful undertakings of feminist thought" (27). While this may have been useful in challenging the dominant gender schema, current queer theory often problematizes the concrete distinction between these two terms.

Repeatedly, in contemporary queer and feminist thought, the division between gender and sex is blurry. For example, in *Epistemology of the Closet*, Eve Sedgwick writes, "Sex, gender, sexuality: three terms whose usage relations and analytical relations are almost irremediably slippery" (27). Sedgwick contests the idea of a "natural sex" outside of social influences by asserting that "nature has a history" and that what constitutes sex often has taken place in a troubled and disputed terrain (5). She complicates the segregated and binary relationship of nature and culture by stressing how the two inform each other. Sedgwick writes, "The immemorial, seemingly ritualized debates on nature versus nurture take place against a very unstable background of tacit assumptions and fantasies about both nurture and nature" (40).

The assertion that biological sex is a gendered and socially constituted category does not deny that there are variations among human bodies. However, physical variations that do not fit concretely into either category, such as intersex bodies, are often overlooked within this schema. It is difficult to tell where the physical bodies begin and social constructions end; however, I chose not to engage with bodily differences as concrete in order to better analyze the social processes that inform the interpretations of bodies.

Within my theoretical framework, I use the term gender to delineate all the ways people are inscribed with bodily, psychological, and social differentiations of male and female, masculine and feminine.

I do this to facilitate an examination of the ways in which bodily investments, such as misogynist views of bodies categorized as female, blend into psychological and social constructions. When I refer to "female bodies," I use this terminology specifically to refer to what was seen as a female body and subsequent misogyny directed at those who occupied the social position of female. I do not use this terminology to deny the existence of transgender people who identify as female but who are not labeled as women in this context (or those labeled as women who do not identify as such). Rather, I refer to female bodies as a way to recognize a site upon which oppressive discourse takes place.

What "femme" can mean changes through generations. There is a cultural history of femme in relationship to the lesbian butch-femme bar scene during the middle of the twentieth century. While femmes in this context often appeared conventionally feminine, they exercised great risk in actively pursuing their desire within cultural expectations of mandated heterosexuality and passivity in women. Texts that were written about this period emphasize femme expression as taking place within an erotic exchange between butches and femmes as opposed to purely physical styles of appearance. Although I discuss femme counter-culture several decades after this period, I attempt to trace a lineage that shows a connection between these communities.

I do not use the terms *femme* and *femininity* interchangeably. I use the term femininity to describe cultural meanings made surrounding female-bodied people. Such meanings may be ascribed to physical, psychological, or emotional traits and are generally used prescriptively to construct what "women" should be or how they should behave. While femmes may reference traits that have been culturally positioned as feminine such as styles of dress or body language, these traits are generally adopted as something that has pleasure or significance for the individual as opposed to an inevitability of being female-bodied. Though femme is currently being discussed in contexts outside lesbian communities, my focus remains on femme in a lesbian framework.

As with the concepts of *femme* and *femininity, misogyny* means different things in different eras. When I use the term misogyny, I am referring to derogatory meanings read onto female bodies that are then credited as "causing" other negative qualities that are deemed feminine. This often manifests as contempt for those who are seen as "women;" however, the way in which ideas regarding female bodies are not separable from constructions of femininity creates a climate wherein misogyny can be reiterated in complicated ways and upon numerous sites (more below).

HISTORICAL CONTEXTS

In order to examine the misogynist meanings made regarding femme identity, femininity and female bodies, I draw from writing within sexology and psychoanalysis, whose discourses are part of the foundation to which my analysis responds. Often these discourses positioned the female body as a passive object of an active male subject (Buhle 73, Freud 138, Mitchell 73, Storr 17, Young Buehl 41). From Freud's claim that the "inadequacy" felt by females due to their lack of a penis gave them a psychological propensity toward neurosis (Freud 137), to Weininger's claim that this made women incapable of reason and development on par with men (Greenway 29), sexological writing from the turn of the twentieth-century tended to hold views of the female body and mind which they credit as cause for women's unequal status with men. This misogyny is focused on the female body; however, such ideology attributes the "lack" of the female body as part of an "essential" feminine psyche. This was differently applied to female-bodied people depending on how their genders were perceived—such as whether they are seen as masculine or feminine (Freud 79).

Desire was viewed as active and therefore masculine. Femme—or feminine—lesbian desire was somewhat unfathomable within psychoanalytic theory since those deemed feminine were understood to be, by definition, passive recipients of desire (not subjects who could possess desire). Because of the visual way in which butch—or masculine—lesbians disrupted gender norms for female-bodied people, they were often viewed as capable of desire. An extension of these biases was the view that butches were the "true" lesbians. As Merl Storr writes in, "Transformations: Subjects, Categories and Cures in Krafft-Ebing's Sexology," "Krafft-Ebbing's characterization of sexual inversion . . . insists that sexual inversion is not merely a desire for members of one's own sex, but such a transformation of one's entire sexual being that the latter no longer corresponds 'completely and harmoniously' with one's physical sex" (17). Though some sexologists, such as Havelock Ellis, viewed masculinity in female-bodied people as "grotesque" (Felski 5), there was a definite tendency to view the masculine lesbian as the true invert. In other words, the masculine lesbian's gender transgression was seen as her true inversion. It was her masculinity that caused her to be seen as an person capable of desire.

Not only was gender expression linked to notions of sexual orientation, lesbians positioned as feminine were seen as incapable of conscious desire. This was replicated within the bar culture where often femmes were viewed as suspect, fickle members of the community that would be as easily swayed back to heterosexuality by a man as they were swayed into homosexuality by butches (Nestle 143). In other words, they were seen as the objects of butch or male desire, but not subjects who were capable of active desire themselves. In this way, although the bar culture challenged many misconceptions regarding female passivity, it also simultaneously reproduced them through the treatment of femmes.

Sexologists such as Freud, Krafft-Ebbing, Ellis, and Weininger position "female homosexuality" differently according to the different ways in which they view the "masculine" and "feminine" lesbian. Their misogyny, though originally linked to the female body, became differently linked to what is seen as feminine and what is seen as masculine regardless of whether the bodies in question were both female. The idea that misogyny can be differentially iterated against female bodies disrupts the idea that misogyny is simply replicated by men against women.

The misogyny in sexology and psychoanalysis was the subject of much second wave feminist critique in the 1970s and 1980s, particularly by radical feminist theorists such as Andrea Dworkin, Sheila Jeffreys and Catherine Mackinnon. The rejection of Freud's ideas regarding the inadequacy of the female body and the way in which that shapes femininity and a "feminine psyche" was a primary focus in such theory. As Mari Jo Buhle states in *Feminism and its Discontents: A Century of Struggle with Psychoanalysis*, "The repudiation of Freud was a basic principle in second-wave feminism" (210). The ideology of the passive female body and its subsequent naturalization of a subservient femininity was attacked as creating a conceptualization of sex that was based in violence towards and repudiation of female bodies. As Catherine Mackinnon writes in, *Feminism Unmodified: Discourses on Life and Law*, " . . . the analysis of the social relation between the sexes is organized so that men may dominate and women must submit and this relation is sexual- in fact, is sex" (3). Andrea Dworkin further asserts that such conceptualizations of femininity takes away women's ability to give consent. In her book *Intercourse*, she states in heterosexual sex, women "do not have to have an orgasm; that terrible burden is on them. We are supposed to comply whether we want to or not. Want is active, not passive . . . " (134).

In her first book, *Woman Hating*, Andrea Dworkin described androgyny as a concept that rejects Freudian theory of feminine maturity necessitating repression in order to become "appropriately" passive. Dworkin writes, "Androgynous mythology provides us with a model which does not use polar role definitions, where the definitions are not, implicitly or explicitly, male=good, female=bad, man=human, woman=other . . . androgyny as a concept has no notion of repression built into it" (153). Dworkin further asserts that androgyny should be the "basis of sexual identity and community life" as it has no imperative to "discipline woman as the embodiment of carnality" (154). Similarly, when discussing oppressive gender norms, Mackinnon promotes "Androgyny as a solution," and claims that it gives people a "free choice of qualities of both roles" (118).

There were those within the feminist movement however, who still felt that butch and femme gender expressions were an integral part of their sexualities and selves, and did not feel that this was at odds with their feminist politics. Instead, they felt that the radical lesbian-feminist taboo against gender expressions other than androgyny was oppressive. Many have seen the work of such radical feminists as creating oppressively moralistic taboos concerning sexual practices and expressions of gender (Allison 105, Bright 38, Califia 161). The debates concerning taboos on gender expression, known as the lesbian "sex wars" (Healey 19) also inform my analysis as these debates often argued over the meaning of what is considered feminine.

CURRENT ERA

The activism and political idealism of the 1970s created a climate for a new generation of feminist activism in the 1990s that was distinct from previous generations. Many young women had grown up taking for granted the positive social changes won by second wave feminist activism such as increased access to career advancement and university education, as well as having a more established language to articulate the forms of discrimination and oppression they experienced. The "sex war" debates during the 1980s made it difficult for feminist theory and activism to operate as if there was political unity among feminists regarding tactics for social change. Feminists from differing social locations with respect to racialization, class background, disability and so on, consistently argued that conceptualizations of what constituted a "feminist concern" were complicated and multiple (Heywood and Drake 3). Many young feminists began to identify as "third wave," that is, to ascribe to a feminism that can be seen as building on but also departing from tactics of the second wave feminism of during 1970s and 1980s.

Often third wave feminist writings stress that they share much with second wave concerns but approach these concerns within a different framework and era as well as using different methods of activism. A departure point of third wave feminism from second wave feminism is often in the perception of the complexity of power relations. Current queer theory has complicated notions of solid identities and positions of power (Butler, Foucault, and Sedgwick). This is reflected not only in theory, but in narrative and community activist based writing as well. For example, in *Third Wave Agenda: Being Feminist, Doing Feminism* Leslie Heywood and Jennifer Drake write, "We define feminism's third wave as a movement that contains elements of second wave critique of beauty, culture, sexual abuse, and power structures while it also acknowledges and makes use of the pleasure, danger, and defining power of those structures" (3). This different approach and context is often said to complicate what activism will look like.

Feminist activism is often framed, in agreement with Butler's theory of gender performativity, as taking place when one simultaneously engages with and challenges oppressive norms. Contemporary feminist writers such as Heywood and Drake assert that this may make feminist activism manifest in ways that could appear to be confusing. Heywood and Drake write:

> Third wave feminisms must remain aware of the complex ways that power, oppression, and resistance work in a media saturated global economy so that what at first glance looks like progress might not be the change we most need, and what looks like regression might actually be progress. (23)

Heywood and Drake complicate the notion that there is one clear definition of what oppression is with a concrete path to a decisive liberation from that oppression. Not only does this type of feminist framework leave room for reclaiming "feminine" identity as a powerful place, but it has also complicated how sexuality and power are understood.

A Foucauldian understanding of power as taking place within an ever shifting matrix of privilege and oppression is reflected within third wave feminist writing. These shifting places of privilege and oppression are then explored as tools for pleasure, power, and subversion of dominant social hierarchies. Indeed, the role of pleasure and its complex relationship to power looms large in most writings on third wave feminism. Jennifer Baumgardner writes about this in *Manifesta: Young Women, Feminism and the Future*. She discusses how third wave feminists have successfully, "created a joyful culture that makes being an adult woman who calls herself a feminist seem thrilling, sexy, and creative (rather than scary, backbiting, or a one-way ticket to bitterness and the poorhouse)" (xx). Part of this sexy and thrilling approach in third wave feminism is an emphasis on reclamation not just of sexuality in general but of appropriating, for feminist purposes, terms and attitudes that had previously existed within an oppressive framework. As Baumgardner describes, "More and more women own . . . cunt (both the complex, odiferous body part and the wise, badass woman), and slut (the girl whose sexuality is owned by no one but herself)" (52). This kind of reclamation focuses on changing the meanings of social norms and opens dialogue around how performances of femininity can take place away from oppressive contexts.

Reclaiming terms that have previously been used in derogatory ways and questioning the context in which the derogatory meanings were created is characteristic of feminisms in the current era. This generation has examined the ways in which terms demarcating identities (race, gender, sex, and so on) have been interpolated by discriminatory constructions (racism, heterosexism, and sexism) (Sedgwick). For example, the construction of men and women as separate dualistic categories is seen as having been created in a sexist and misogynist climate. Therefore part of our understanding of the concepts of men and women is embedded in discriminatory ideologies. However, according to current feminist and queer ideologies, this does not mean that we need never make use of such terms when describing identity categories. Butler writes that it is "precisely because such terms have been produced and constrained within such regimes, they ought to be repeated in directions that reverse and displace their originating aims" (123). She states that this is because "one does not stand at an instrumental distance from the terms by which one experiences violation" (ibid.). This gives a person, "the occasion to work the mobilizing power of injury, of an interpellation one never chose" (ibid.). In other words, claiming an identity (even one created in the context of oppressive norms) can give a person the power to shift the meanings made about that identity.

Third-wave feminism is often skeptical of the idea that one can find a true gender expression that is separate from oppressive gender norms, or a sexuality that is not within the current structures of power. Such ideology is clearly prevalent in academic thought that currently shapes queer theory. For example, Butler engages with Foucault's conceptualization of sexuality being enmeshed with power. Butler writes, "Foucault, who, in claiming that sexuality and power are coextensive, implicitly refutes the postulation of a subversive or emancipatory sexuality which could be free of the law" (*Gender Trouble* 38). Butler concludes that this ideology does not leave room for an idealistic promise of a sexuality uncomplicated by societal norms such as those proposed by radical lesbian-feminists. As Butler describes, "if lesbian sexuality is no more and no less constructed than other modes of sexuality, then there is no promise of limitless pleasure after the shackles of the category of sex have been thrown off" (158). Such a framework does not necessitate denying that oppression exists within misogynistic and sexist constructions of sexuality that have been historically and culturally produced. Rather, the approach to contesting such power structures is changed from searching for expressions of sexuality and gender that are free from power dynamics and towards seeking ways to change the oppressive meanings within oppressive norms. For example in new anthologies on femme identity, such as *Brazen Femme: Queering Femininity*, Cloe Brushwood Rose and Anna Camilleri attempt to make a space for femme gender expression to exist in a way that is separate from historical constructions and positionings of femininity.

Brushwood Rose and Camilleri contest the way in which femme gender expressions are often positioned as passive and otherwise linked to stereotypically demeaning views associated with women in a misogynist and sexist culture. As part of these contestations they engage terms that are often positioned in negative ways and reassess them through a feminist lens. Brushwood Rose and Camilleri write about femme as:

> a way of being that cannot be described as quintessentially feminine. Instead, femme might be described as "femininity gone wrong"—bitch, slut, nag, whore, cougar, dyke, or brazen hussy. Femme is the trappings of femininity gone awry . . . Femininity is a demand placed on female bodies and femme is the danger of a body read female or inappropriately feminine (13).

The authors focus on reclaiming words that were previously seen as negative. In addition, they allude to historical and current cultural demands that prescribe meanings to bodies seen as female and the corresponding notions of what constitutes femininity. Instead of engaging in the "sex war" debates which argue *whether or not* femme gender expression can take place within a feminist framework, they explore *how* femme gender expression can engage with changing the meanings of misogynist and sexist norms. In this way, femme identities are seen not only as active, but also engaged in actions that challenge the status quo.

Brazen Femme further envisions an ability to challenge the position femme identified people have occupied within counter-cultures which have held demeaning views of femmes. Brushwood Rose and Camilleri write:

> Femme is inherently "queer" in the broadest sense of the word—as bent, unfixed, unhinged and finally unhyphenated. Released from the structures of binary models of sexual orientation and gender and sex. Released from a singular definition of femme. Released from the "object position" where femme is all too often situated. (12)

They assert that femme can be un-hyphenated, that is to say, not dependant on a butch-femme dyad. This challenges the concept of femininity as the site of absence, or the passive receptacle of masculinity. In doing so, they reframe the discourse around those with femme identities as having the potential to act as desiring subjects as opposed to solely being objects. Brushwood Rose and Camilleri challenge traditions of sexology and psychoanalysis through actively engaging with and building upon them.

Radical lesbian-feminism asserted that because women have been positioned as the feminine objects of masculinity, the solution is for all people to adopt androgyny. However, current third wave femme identified feminists argue that femme gender expressions can be reconstructed in a way that challenges the association of femininity with being an object (for those who choose such an expression). This helps to facilitate an examination of different ways misogynist, sexist and heteronormative views of gender can be recreated in different contexts.

Central to the ideology in *Brazen Femme* is the conceptualization of femme identity not only as independent from masculinity but also as dangerous to the status quo that has equated femininity with being "violable" (Mackinnon 118). This is clear from the front cover of *Brazen*

Femme in which Camilleri is photographed alone, wearing a short, low-cut dress, gripping a knife with the blade barring access between her legs. Camilleri narrates:

> I reached for the knife.
>
> This was not planned or pre-meditated. I had, however, lived this moment, imagined this moment many times over. The point of meeting—cold steel on warm skin, the utility of both (my) knife and (my) hand. The union of function and poetry, each functional, each poetic . . . I dared the viewer, the imagined viewer, to look. My legs spread apart, knife gripped tightly, mediating access. Seeing is the tithe, not the prize. A brazen posture? Yes. (11)

Camilleri intentionally employs an image generally associated with "feminine" sexual availability and then challenges the meaning of those associations by controlling the availability in the image. In the photograph, the knife comes to represent sexual power wherein the subject who possesses it is not the object of an active masculine gaze, but one who actively challenges the assumptions of the one who looks.

The location of the knife positions it as a replacement of the phallus. The femme subject holds a knife where convention would assume the phallus. This challenges the historical construction of the masculine subject being the one who possesses the phallus (which comes to stand for sexual subjectivity and power) with the feminine object embodying the receptacle of that power. In such a framework the concept of penis envy is refigured. Judith Butler writes about the way in which the phallus has come to symbolize male, or masculine, privilege that is invested in the penis and social meanings constructed around it, but that is not necessarily anatomy itself. Butler writes that with such recognition the site of such privilege can be challenged (*Bodies that Matter* 88).

The gendered meanings placed onto bodies and gendered expressions such as femme take place within social hierarchies. Such hierarchies are intertwined with notions as to what bodies are considered enviable and what bodies are deserving of contempt as well as who is seen as an object and who is seen as a subject. These notions have created gendered privileges wherein femininity comes to be associated with sites of domination. By mixing an image that has been associated with the feminine with an image associated with holding power and control, Camilleri challenges the ways in which power has been linked with masculinity. In addition, I argue, she challenges discourses that construct the penis as the site of phallic power. Thus, such an image can work to dislodge the cultural meanings of the phallus as inextricably linked to conceptualizations of male bodies and masculinity.

Reconceptualizing femininity as something that can come from an active, powerful and assertive place is often found within current third wave feminist, femme writings. However, writings such as Melanie Maltry and Kristin Tucker's "Female Fem(me)ininities: New Articulations in Queer Gender Identities and Subversion" at times position femme gender expression as active and powerful based on the way femmes often employ typically masculine characteristics along with those deemed feminine. While there may be subversive potential in such expressions of gender, I question whether the act of crediting "masculinity" as what makes "femininity" powerful can, however unintentionally, recreate discourses that deny the possibility for a feminine subject position as the feminine position is still defined as a site of "lack." In other words, recreate discourses which assume that "femininity" requires "masculine" signification. Butler describes the conceptualization of femininity being without agency as located in an historical context wherein the "mute facticity of the feminine [is] awaiting signification from an opposing masculine subject" (*Gender Trouble* 48). I use the following examples from Maltry and Tucker in order to illustrate how current era counter-culture can reproduce such ideology and therefore not fully investigate the ways in which oppressive norms can be recreated through conceptualizations of what makes particular gender expressions powerful.

In "Female Fem(me)ininities: New Articulations in Queer Gender Identities and Subversion" Maltry and Tucker discuss femme subversion of femininity in a way that is characteristic of the third wave, queer era. They discuss the specific gender expressions of some femmes and analyze why certain aspects of their appearance can be seen as subversive and feminist. For example, they discuss the gender presentation of author/performer Michelle Tea. They position her aesthetic presentation as "disrupting normative femininity," through creating "visual politics" that are subversive (100). They write that while Tea is:

> stereotypically feminine in many ways (Tea has glasses with sparkles, long hair in a pony tail, lipstick, and feminine looking clothing), she tweaks femininity to her liking. Her long ponytail is dyed blue, and her scant clothing reveals a number of tattoos. Both of these expressions are discordant with the idealized feminine. (100)

Maltry and Tucker's critique position Tea's femme gender expression as feminist based on the way she "tweaks" femininity through "alternative" aesthetics.

While I critique Maltry and Tucker's analysis of the subversiveness of Tea's gender expression based on the way it could potentially create new normative prescriptions of gender (as discussed below), it is not my intention to judge Tea's expression as "unsubversive." Rather my approach is consistent with Butler who writes, "I am not interested in delivering judgments on what distinguishes the subversive from the unsubversive. Not only do I believe that such judgments cannot be made out of context, but that they cannot be made in ways that endure through time . . . " (*Gender Trouble* xxi). On the contrary, what I wish to examine is the practice of using this type of criterion that judges specific aesthetics to determine what has feminist potential and what does not. As with lesbian-feminist investments in androgyny, I fear this practice also has the potential to create normative prescriptions of gender. This runs the risk of reproducing hierarchies that deny feminist agency to those who employ particular expressions of femininity. Rather than inquire as to which aesthetics are subversive and which are not, I find a more useful mode of inquiry would be to examine what limitations are placed on gender expressions and what ideologies perpetuate such limitations. For example, rather than defend a particular femme gender expression on the basis of specific aesthetics (e.g., hair color and tattoos), I question why the "feminine" attributes of gender expression were seen as reflecting a "lack" of ability to make an active choice in the first place.

Butler clarifies the differences between these two modes of inquiry and the importance this difference has for being able to challenge oppressive gender norms as opposed to create new hierarchies. Butler writes that it is difficult to critique current gender norms without creating a new set of norms. She warns that:

> positive normative vision . . . cannot take the form of a prescription: "subvert gender in the way that I say, and life will be good." Those who make such prescriptions or who are willing to decide between subversive and unsubversive expressions of gender, base their judgments on a description. Genders appear in this or that form, and then a normative judgment is made about those appearances on the basis of what appears. But what conditions the domain of appearance for gender itself? We may be tempted to make the following distinction: a descriptive account of

> gender includes considerations of what makes gender intelligible, an inquiry into its conditions of possibility, whereas a normative account seeks to answer the question of which expressions of gender are acceptable, and which are not, supplying persuasive reasons to distinguish between such expressions in this way. (*Gender Trouble* xxi)

Maltry and Tucker's analysis provides an example of a current mode of challenging heteronormative gender roles which can be applied in such a way that subversiveness is decided based on descriptions of appearance. As a result, potentially oppressive ideologies behind why one gender expression is acceptable (or subversive), while another is not may be left unchallenged as a new norm will already have been created. The new norm may then inadvertently serve to reinforce old hierarchies. Maltry and Tucker again illustrate this potential for the meanings behind norms to go unchallenged though their description of young femmes in riotgrrl and punk movements.

In addition to their description of Michelle Tea, Maltry and Tucker describe how many young femmes, particularly those within the riotgrrrl and punk movements, adopt "loudness" in style of clothes as well as volume of voice as a way of combating the stereotype that femme expressions, or femininity, require quiet passivity. They tell of one "grrrl" who performs dressed in "girly" clothes and "wails in her intentionally 'little girl voice,' 'suck my left one'" (100). Maltry and Tucker cite this as an example of femininity being enacted in a way that is powerful. This mix of gendered expressions may subvert expectations of what is acceptable for "girls" and may be a source of pleasure and excitement for the performer. However, positioning femininity as powerful because of the "feminine" person's reference to possessing male anatomy may not challenge the phallus as a signifier of power that is linked to male anatomy. Without further inquiry into this analysis, there is risk of the presence of "masculinity" symbolically being what gives "femininity" status. In this way femininity is still the object that requires masculinity to gain status as a subject.

While I critique ways in which individuals may have ascribed to positivist gender prescriptions that do not adequately challenge hierarchical gender norms, I do not wish to position such risks as the inevitable outcome of third wave feminist ideologies. Rather, I hope to explore such inadequacies as potential shortcomings as well as looking at how third wave feminist ideology can also be used to overcome hierarchies. For example, in the interview "I'll Be the Girl: Generations of Femme" Barbara Cruikshank discusses possibilities for femme subjectivity within a third wave feminist framework which draws from the trend within queer theory of questioning solid identities as they have been constructed within mainstream thought. Cruikshank writes about sex with her butch girlfriend during which she was "talking dirty" with her lover in a way that helped her lover construct a butch gender as a female and masculine person. Cruikshank writes about telling her girlfriend, "You put on your masculinity as a show for me like male birds show off their plumage to get the girl. Your dick is more real than any man's because yours gets made up every time we fuck; we make it real. It is never taken for granted" (107).

Cruikshank, however, saw herself as someone who had erotically constructed a femme gender expression. Yet her girlfriend was unable to conceive of such gender transgression within the context of femaleness and femininity. When Cruikshank asked her girlfriend to speak erotically about her gender expression, her girlfriend replied, "'you are the girl; you're all girl . . . you don't have to do anything different" (107–108). Cruikshank describes how she wanted her girlfriend to "give words to my fem the same way I made her butch" (108). Cruikshank concludes this section of her interview by politically framing the encounter with her girlfriend. She states:

> . . . I complained and tried to tell her that to just assume I was the girl, just because I am a girl, was sexist. This was truly no better than heterosexuality; I was "just a girl." I wanted to be a fem, and to find a way to do it that didn't depend solely on being seen with a butch. I felt dependent. If her boyness was an act, I wanted my girlness to be an act- not in the same sense of play acting, but in the sense of enacting, accomplishing something. (108)

Cruikshank's girlfriend was unable to see Cruikshank's femme expression outside dominant cultural conceptions of feminine as an inactive default for female-bodied people. Consequently, any agency Cruikshank had in constructing her femme expression was dismissed in a way that her girlfriend's masculinity was not. By challenging the inevitability of her "femininity," Cruikshank challenges the conceptualization of femininity as a "lack" of masculinity, or as the site whereupon the masculine subject acts. Instead she positions her construction of femme as part of an active, creative desire and identity. By doing this she challenges sexological and psychoanalytic misogynist ideologies regarding the female body and by extension, femininity. Femmes within the current third wave feminist era such as Cruikshank have employed queer theory in a way that challenges heteronormative prescriptions of femininity both from dominant culture and within their counter cultural communities. Though this approach is sure to prove to be a partial analysis, as were second wave feminist ideologies, grounds are beginning to be established which challenge the inevitability of conceptualizing femininity automatically playing a second and dependent status to what is seen as masculinity.

CONCLUSION

The ways in which femme gender expressions have been positioned within lesbian and queer women's subcultures illustrate how misogynist notions of female bodies can be transferred and replicated through views regarding femininity and consequently those who are associated with it. I have reviewed some of the ways in which femmes have argued that they are able to express a femme gender while being assertive and active in pursuing their desires. Within each of the examples I have discussed, femmes have asserted that they are able to construct and negotiate their identities from a powerful place. However, that femmes have had to employ such arguments attests to the fact that the social climates within their counter-cultures often replicated dominant cultural views which assumed that femininity denies a person such qualities. Femme gender expression has clearly been positioned in ways that reiterate oppressive norms. These views regarding femmes have even been perpetuated within counter-communities that are otherwise fighting against such norms.

Ideologies within sexology and psychoanalysis have become part of the cultural assumptions regarding gender that have created taken-for-granted customs. Butler refers to this as gender being simultaneously taken for granted and "violently policed" (*Gender Trouble* xix). Femmes within current queer counter cultures have challenged gender norms that were often based in misogynist ideologies regarding meanings created about female bodies often perpetuated by sexology and psychoanalysis. Often the surrounding climate of the lesbian and queer subcultures in which femme gender expressions have taken place have viewed these expressions in a way that is more consistent with such dominant cultural views of femininity than with the ways in which femmes position their own identities.

From within the third wave, queer era, many femmes stress that their femme identities are chosen subversions of gender or sexual customs, rather than concrete or obligatory roles. Despite differing frameworks, femmes across generations have argued that, "through a reshaped femininity [they] exhibit an assertive sexuality" (Harris and Crocker 1). Recently some texts have begun to bring these frameworks together and examine the ways in which femmes have contested misogynist, sexist and heteronormative conceptualizations of gender across several generations. For example, Harris and Crocker write that femme is a "contestatory lesbian identity, a radical feminist position, and a subversive queer model" (1). That such examinations are necessary is indicative of the amount of contestation concerning their gender expressions that femme-identified people have faced within their sub-cultures and communities.

That people with gender expressions linked to femininity could have the capacity to construct their expressions as part of an active engagement with feminist concerns challenges a long history of beliefs regarding what femininity can mean. The idea that femininity is a passive state, or the object of masculine desire, relates to misogynist notions based on conceptualizations of female bodies as inadequate or failed versions of male bodies. For this reason, challenging such notions regarding femininity has the potential to challenge residual misogynist constructions of femaleness. The ways in which oppressive gender norms have been extended towards femmes within lesbian and queer communities that are often feminist speaks to the depth of which such norms have become part of a taken for-granted cultural framework within dominant North American thought. It is precisely because of the insidious way that misogyny and other oppressive gender norms are embedded in Western cultural thought that exploring ways in which such norms can be replicated and contested outside of the mainstream becomes important avenue to understanding mainstream and counter-cultural communities. The ways in which the debates surrounding femme gender expressions have played out through the provide some insight into ways such insidious norms can be reproduced as well as resisted.

REFERENCES

Allison, D. *Skin: Talking About Sex, Class and Literature.* Ithaca: Firebrand Books, 1994.

Baumgardner, J., and A. Richards. *Manifesta: Young Women, Feminism, and the Future.* New York: Farrar, Straus and Giroux, 2000.

Bodies That Matter: On the Discursive Limits of "Sex." New York: Routledge, 1993.

Bright, S. *Susie Sexpert's Lesbian Sex World*. Second Edition. San Francisco: Cleis Press, 1998.

Brushwood R., C., and A. Camilleri, ed. "Introduction." *Brazen Femme: Queering Femininity.* Vancouver: Arsenal Pulp Press, 2002. 11–15.

Buhle, M. J. *Feminism and Its Discontents: A Century of Struggle with Psychoanalysis.* Cambridge, MA: Harvard University Press, 1998.

Butler, J. *Gender Trouble: Feminism and the Subversion of Identity.* Second Edition. New York: Routledge, 1999.

Califia, P. *Public Sex: The Culture of Radical Sex*. Second Edition. San Francisco: Cleis Press, 2000.

Crocker, E., and L. Harris. *Femme: Feminists, Lesbians and Bad Girls.* New York: Routledge, 1997, 1–15.

Cruikshank, B., and J. Nestle. "I'll Be the Girl: Generations of Fem." In *Femme: Feminists, Lesbians and Bad Girls*, edited by Elizabeth Crocker and Laura Harris. New York: Routledge, 1997, 105–119.

Devor, A. "How Many Sexes? How Many Genders? When Two are Not Enough." Vancouver: Simon Fraser University, February 2, 2007.

Dicker, R., and A. Piepmeier. *Catching a Wave: Reclaiming Feminism for the 21st Century.* Boston: Northeastern University Press, 2003.

Dworkin, A. *Intercourse*. New York: Free Press Paperbacks, 1987.

Freud, S. "Three Essays on the Theory of Sexuality," In *Freud On Women*, edited by Elizabeth Young Bruhel. New York: W. W. Norton & Company, 1990. 89–146.

Greenway, J. "It's What You Do with It That Counts: Interpretations of Otto Weininger," In *Sexology in Culture: Labeling Bodies and Desires*, edited by Lucy Bland and Laura Doan. Chicago: University of Chicago Press, 1998. 27–44.

Healey, E. *Lesbian Sex Wars*. London: Virago, 1996.

Heywood, L., and J. Drake, eds. "Introduction." In *Third Wave Agenda: Being Feminist, Doing Feminism*. Minneapolis: University of Minnesota Press, 1997.

Mackinnon, C. *Feminism Unmodified: Discourses on Life and Law.* Cambridge, MA: Harvard University Press, 1987.

Mitchell, J. *Psychoanalysis and Feminism: Freud, Reich, Laing and Women*. New York: Vintage Books, 1975.

Sedgwick, E. *Epistemology of the Closet*. Berkeley: University of California Press, 1990.

Storr, M. "Transformations: Subjects, Categories and Cures in Krafft-Ebing's Sexology." In *Sexology in Culture: Labeling Bodies and Desires*. edited by Lucy Bland and Laura Doan. Chicago: University of Chicago Press, 1998. 11–27.

Young B., Elizabeth, ed. "Introduction." In *Freud On Women: A Reader.* New York: W. W. Norton & Company, 1990, 3–48.

Chapter 16

Celebrating Ostara: A Ritual Performance by Gay Male Contemporary Pagans

John S. Gentile

> Spring is a resurrection of all life, and consequently of human life. In that cosmic act, all the forces of creation return to their first vigour. Life is wholly reconstituted; *everything begins afresh*; in short, the primeval act of the creation of the cosmos is repeated, for every regeneration is a creation of the cosmos repeated, for every regeneration is a new birth, a return to that mythical moment when for the first time a form appeared that was to be constantly regenerated.
>
> —liade, *Patterns* 309

On Sunday morning, March 20, 2005, I drove through Atlanta, Georgia, and enjoyed the flowering trees lining its streets that were just starting to burst into blossom. It was Palm Sunday. As I passed various churches, I saw the faithful gathering together and carrying clusters of palm branches. On a usual Sunday morning, I attend All Saints Episcopal Church where I meet my friends for mass and, afterwards, we might discuss the day's sermon while we share a meal. This Sunday was also the vernal equinox and I was forgoing mass at All Saints in order to attend a very different ritual—a contemporary pagan ritual to celebrate Ostara.

"From the 1970s onward the United States," writes Ronald Hutton in *The Triumph of the Moon*, a history of the movement, "has been the world centre of modern paganism [. . .]" (340). Even informal contact with contemporary paganism readily shows that gay, lesbian and bisexual people are welcomed within the movement and that they form a significant presence among its followers. *Voices from the Pagan Census* reports that:

> 4.8 percent [are] lesbians, 4.5 percent gay men, and 19 percent bisexual. The large number of bisexual respondents in both studies is an indication of Neo-Pagans' openness to alternatives—including sexual alternatives. (28)

My current research interest is to investigate how gay male contemporary pagans create ritual performance to express their spirituality. Contemporary paganism offers a rich field of study for its creativity: its syncretism of beliefs, its use of folklore, mythology and history (and pseudo-history) to invent a spiritual tradition, and its bricolage of old mythical images and stories. "The characteristic feature of mythical thought," Claude Levi-Strauss writes in *The Savage Mind*, "is that it expresses itself by means of a heterogeneous repertoire[. . .]" (17).

The purpose of this chapter is threefold: to establish a context by considering contemporary paganism and its relation to gay spirituality, to describe the Ostara ritual that took place in Atlanta on the morning of March 20, 2005, and, finally, to consider the ritual's efficacy.

THE CONTEXT: CONTEMPORARY PAGANISM AND GAY SPIRITUALITY

Contemporary paganism as a religious movement began in this country in the 1960s and has continued to mature in the following decades. As it gained momentum as a religious movement, contemporary paganism also developed a growing body of academic scholarship and its own field of study known as *pagan studies*.[1] My understanding of the movement is based upon my study of its scholarship as well as my reading of devotional or practical publications, my personal attendance at various pagan gatherings and rituals, and my conversations and correspondence with contemporary pagans over several years.

What is contemporary paganism? Graham Harvey cautions us in *Contemporary Paganism: Listening People, Speaking Earth*, that the religious movement "is evolving, it has no complete, codified or orthodox form" (2). However, I offer a working definition indebted to many sources, particularly Margot Adler's *Drawing Down the Moon*: it is a contemporary religious movement which identifies its origins as antedating Christianity and monotheism in the European, pre-Christian nature religions—primarily the Celtic, Greek, Roman, and Norse—as well as Eastern and Native American traditions and revives and reinvents them creatively while blending them into new forms. "Ritual," as folklorist Sabina Magliocco in her full-length study *Witching Culture* writes, "is a form of practice that unites all the Neo-Pagan traditions" (126). Contemporary pagan rituals are tied not only to rites of passage in the human life cycle but also to calendrical rites connected to the seasonal changes. "Just as rites of passage give order and definition to the biocultural life cycle," writes Catherine Bell in *Ritual: Perspectives and Dimensions*, "so calendrical rites give socially meaningful definitions to the passage of time, creating an ever-renewing cycle of days, months, and years" (102). "The Wheel of the Year," as it is commonly called in pagan circles, celebrates seasonal ceremonies of eight major sabbats. Additionally, contemporary pagans often gather for rituals performed at lunar esbats, held at the new and full moons.[2]

Contemporary paganism represents not so much a revival in any purist sense but the invention of a new religion inspired by, in highly individualistic, eclectic fashions, ancient nature-centered religions. Contemporary paganism is an invented tradition in the sense meant by Eric Hobsbawn in his book *The Invention of Tradition*:

> "Invented tradition" is taken to mean a set of practices, normally governed by overtly or tacitly accepted rules and of a ritual or symbolic nature, which seek to inculcate certain values and norms of behavior by repetition, which automatically implies continuity with the past. (1)

The central tenants of contemporary paganism include a belief in polytheism and that the sacred is immanent and inseparable from nature. "Whereas the Christian God is transcendent," writes Michael York in *Pagan Theology*, "the pagan godhead is immanent"(13).

Additionally, creativity and *Eros*, the Life force in its many manifestations, including sexuality and fertility, are considered sacred and often honored in rituals by the symbolic union of the Goddess (the feminine principle) and the God (the masculine principle). The centrality of the Goddess and the God is strongest for those contemporary pagans influenced by the writings of Gerald Gardner, whose teachings have passed into pagan folklore. Often such individuals identify themselves with Wicca, defined by Scott Cunningham as "a contemporary *Pagan* religion" that "views Deity as *Goddess* and *God*" (206). Therefore, a central tenant of contemporary pagan valorizes heterosexual union and fertility. Why does such a religion attract gay men in search of a congenial spiritual path? To answer that question, I turned to the writings in gay spirituality and spoke with gay pagans.

Called the "first book to seriously explore the spiritual complexities and gifts of being gay," Mark Thompson's book, *Gay Spirit: Myth and Meaning*, published in 1987, has also been credited by one reviewer as inspiring "a burgeoning gay male spirituality movement" (Cotton 35). Other titles include Randy P. Connor's *Blossom of Bone: Reclaiming the Connections Between Homoeroticism and the Sacred*, Brian Bouldrey's *Wrestling with the Angel: Faith and Religion in the Lives of Gay Men*, Will Roscoe's *Queer Spirits: A Gay Men's Myth Book*, and Mark Thompson's *Gay Soul: Finding the Heart of Gay Spirit and Nature* and *Gay Body: A Journey from Shadow to Self*. Writers often argue that the horrors of the AIDS epidemic coupled with the anti-gay politics and rhetoric of the Christian Right in the Culture Wars gave impetus to the gay spirituality movement. However, as early as 1978, Arthur Evans argued in *Witchcraft and the Gay Counterculture* that gay men should reclaim gay history by uncovering its links to pre-Christian spiritual traditions. Evan's book helped inspire the Radical Faerie movement and encouraged gay men to consider contemporary paganism as their own spiritual path. Christopher Pencrak, in *Gay Witchcraft: Empowering the Tribe*, chronicles his personal spiritual journey from his disillusionment with Christianity, his move into agnosticism, and eventual sense of coming home by following the pagan Wiccan path. Penczak notes that his journey may be emblematic of many gay male pagans:

> Those who felt disenfranchised from mainstream faiths, continually searching for their path, often found their way to Wicca. Quite a few of these folks were gay, lesbian, bisexual, or transgendered, coming from feelings and experiences very similar to mine, now feeling the sense of coming home again. (xiv)

What attracts gay men to contemporary paganism? "Many lesbians, gay men, and bisexuals are drawn to Neo-Paganism," writes Magliocco, "because of its accepting attitude toward all sexual orientations, especially compared with the judgmental stance of most mainstream religions" (*Witching* 62). In addition to its non-judgmental stance, I argue that gay men are attracted for the same reasons that are people of all sexual orientations: its emphasis on the individual's intellectual and personal growth, its inherent feminism and appreciation of the feminine, its response to environmental concerns, it privileging of the arts and the individual's creativity, as well as its non-authoritarian foundation which is based in its polytheism. As Magliocco explains in her essay, "Ritual is My Chosen Art Form," contemporary pagans "see themselves in contrast to the dominant hegemonic American culture: they are attempting to construct a more meaningful and satisfying moral order that includes respect for the earth, feminism, racial equality, cultural diversity, and an alternative to conspicuous consumption" (1996, 94). The Website for the Radical Faeries confirms Magliocco's study:

> [W]e tend to be Gay men who look for a spiritual dimension to our sexuality . . . Our shared values include feminism, respect for the Earth, and individual responsibility rather than hierarchy. Many of us are Pagan (nature-based religion). ("Who are the faeires?")[3]

Contemporary pagans like many gay men (pagan or otherwise) resist Christianity's tendency to demonize the human body and sexuality. As a nature religion, contemporary paganism celebrates *Eros* and the erotic, for "at its heart," writes Starhawk in her influential book *Spiral Dance*, "is precisely about the erotic dance of life playing through all of nature and culture" (9). One gay male pagan practitioner explained to me:

> We believe [our spiritual] goal is best served for ourselves in a Wiccan context for the following reasons: It is nature oriented. It sees the divine in nature rather than separate from it. It is Goddess/God oriented. It recognizes and pays attention to both the masculine and feminine aspects of divinity. It is structured enough to give us the form we want, yet it's non-authoritarian enough to provide freedom of conscience of its members. (EricM32)

Contemporary paganism's emphasis on individual growth, creativity, and eroticism along with its non-authoritarian, polytheistic understanding of the diversity and pluralities, readily invites gay men to adapt symbols and practice in ritual performance, reinterpreting the feminine-masculine polarity of the Goddess and the God to encompass a gay male sensibility.

One informant, John Skolund, explained that he felt no conflict between the traditional Gardnerian ritual with its male-female duality and his sexuality because "each of us has the other sex within us." He felt fully comfortable performing the ritual in its classic Gardnerian form. Another informant wrote:

> We've also done away with thinking in terms of male and female roles. We've taken the stand that none of us are strictly male and strictly female in a spiritual sense. We are all made of both. (Klaatu01)

This metaphoric reinterpretation recalls Jung's concept of the *anima* and the *animus* and argues that we all embody both the Goddess and the God, whatever our outward gender. Jonathan Rehm, one of my hosts for the March 20, 2005 ritual, resolves the apparent heterosexuality of the ritual Goddess-God by considering it beyond purely gender terms: "it's really all about polarity."

Gay men's spirituality groups have been influenced by their pagan members and have incorporated ritual as a central tenant of their practice. "An important part of this soul loss of our present age," states the 2005 brochure for the Gay Men's Medicine Circle, "is the absence of meaningful rituals and ceremonies in the life of the individual and the community" (4).

THE RITUAL: CELEBRATING OSTARA

My invitation to the Ostara ritual came in early March over the internet via a listserv for Gay Spirit Visions (GSV), a national community "committed to creating safe, sacred space that is open to all spiritual paths, wherein loving gay men may explore and strengthen spiritual identity" (GSV Mission 2). The importance of the internet to create and maintain community is evident in both contemporary paganism and gay spirituality (in general and GSV in particular), for both movements claim ancient roots while participating fully in contemporary postmodern, late-capitalist American culture and its reliance on electronic forms of communication/community-building. One of the hosts, Jonathan, sent subsequent messages that included driving directions and suggestions for ritual preparation, including ritual cleansing prior to the event in the form of intentional bathing.

His suggestions, like all acts of ritual preparation, were intended to heighten the experience of *separation* discussed by van Gennep in *The Rites of Passage*.

The ritual was held in the home of Jonathan and Eliot in a large apartment complex near Emory University in Atlanta. Being the first to arrive for the 11:00 A.M. gathering, I had the opportunity to talk with the hosts about their background in contemporary paganism, their preparation for the morning's company, and to observe closely the setting the hosts had created for the ritual. Jonathan and Eliot, whom I had not met prior to that morning, warmly welcomed me. Their immediate emotional openness, generosity and trust surpassed what I had already found typical of the men of GSV. From the moment of my entrance into their home to the beginning of the formal ritual, I had entered a heightened *pre*-liminal phase that further separated me from my ordinary, profane life into the sacred time and place of the ritual.

An altar table was located within the center of their small living room and served as the focus of the ritual. The images and objects upon the altar demonstrated a striking syncretism of various spiritualities, including European, Hindu, Buddhist, and Native American traditions. A large Green Man tapestry hung behind the altar draped over (and obscuring) an étagère and entertainment unit that held a television and a CD player along with books and photographs. Along with sacred objects, candles, and spring flowers, the altar held images of Eostre, an obscure Anglo-Saxon goddess of the spring. For this reason, contemporary pagan devotional and practical books identify the vernal equinox as *Ostara*, named after Eostre, whose name, the authors argue, the early Christian church appropriated in its naming of *Easter* as the celebration of the Resurrection of Jesus Christ. The books also link Eostre to Eos, the classical goddess of the dawn. Ronald Hutton in *The Stations of the Sun* traces the connection to Eostre back to the writings of Bede and follows other scholars, such as Venetia Newall in *An Egg at Easter: A Folklore Study*, in questioning whether or not the ancient Anglo-Saxons ever worshipped such a goddess.[4]

Whatever her veracity as an ancient goddess, Eostre now represents for contemporary pagans the Goddess in her maiden, or Kore, aspect, and as such is connected to beginnings and openings. The veneration of Eostre by contemporary pagans shows how a spiritual tradition is invented and how belief may be a conscious choice. Other objects upon the altar included eggs, home-baked hot cross buns, and, in a lofty place of honor atop the étagère, a store bought chocolate bunny.

This last ritual object, perhaps more than any other object, embodies the humor and pastiche typical contemporary paganism.

Along with the ritual objects and altar preparation, the hosts prepared an extensive brunch featuring a variety of egg-based entrees (including many quiches). The guests arrived, bringing with them more flowers and contributions to the brunch meal. The foodstuffs, I noted, were all homemade emphasizing a mutual giving of time and care between guests and hosts. Some of the guests changed into sarongs, which served as ritual costumes, supplied by the hosts. The tone of the morning continued to be joyful and playful. Participation in the morning ritual was highly reflexive and self-conscious. Members of company (a term I will use to include the hosts) shared comments that indicated complex levels of belief. At times, their comments expressed devotion and serious spiritual practice while at other times they expressed a comic distance or humorous perspective on the day's ritual. The emotional dialectic between gentle humor and serious devotion informed the entire morning; all participants seemed comfortable in holding the tension between faith and doubt in an emotional double-distance toward their spirituality without moving to extremes of either skepticism nor uncritical faith. They were able to participate in the ritual's meaning while recognizing it as construct by holding the ritual in symbolic consciousness. "The trick of symbolic consciousness," D. Stephenson Bond writes, "is in allowing yourself to maintain the distance—I am aware that I'm pretending, gaming, imagining—while at the same time preserving participation" (19). *Voices from the Pagan Census* confirms this understanding of contemporary pagan symbolic consciousness. Its authors note,

> Many Neo-Pagans simultaneously participate in the rituals and stand outside of them to the degree that they can reflect on the rituals as something that they created. Neo-Pagans often joke about their own rituals and seem to be taking themselves and their religious practice with a grain of salt, at the same time viewing their spiritual practices as serious. (7)

At no time did I perceive a naïve or zealous literalist belief, which is in marked contrast to my experience with members of more established religions, especially fundamentalist Christians, who demonstrate a noticeable lack of critical distance from their faith or church.

Jonathan called the company together to begin the ritual, which demonstrated both traditional and emergent qualities in its adaptation of contemporary pagan (especially Wiccan) practice. He scented each participant with burning sage and then invited four guests from among those men more experienced in pagan ritual to call the spirits of the four cardinal directions and to create the ritual circle. Based upon a scripted invocation, each spoke in turn, holding a candle, and called the spirits of the East, South, West, and North. The intent of the ritual circle was to create a sacred emotional space emphasizing protection and mutual caring. In *The Sacred and the Profane*, Mircea Eliade writes, "*the religious man sought to live as near as possible to the Center of the World*" (43). The invocation moved us into the liminal phase of the ritual and effectively created the sense of being at the *axis mundi* or sacred center throughout its duration.

"Among the most important items found upon a Pagan altar," writes Sabina Magliocco in *Neo-Pagan Sacred Art and Altars*, "are images of the deities" (26). Upon the Ostara altar were images of Eostre and Hyacinth, whom the two hosts then honored as the Goddess and the God, the female and male principles, by telling their myths. The choice of Hyacinth, a beautiful young man beloved by Apollo, as the mythic image of the masculine principle in the morning ritual, is indicative of gay spirituality's mythopoesis. Will Roscoe retells the story of Hyacinth and Apollo in his book, *Queer Spirits: A Gay Men's Myth Book*, which reclaims same-sex myths as sacred texts. Robert Drake includes Ovid's version of the myth in *The Gay Canon: Great Books Every Gay Man Should Read*. By choosing Eostre and Hyacinth, mythic figures from two different traditions, Anglo-Saxon and Greek, the hosts demonstrated the practices of syncretism and bricolage typical of contemporary paganism. Additionally, Hyacinth and Eostre, despite their different cultures of origin, represent male and female images of the archetype of the *Puer/Puella*, which Jung's identifies in "The Psychology of the Child Archetype," as concerned with futurity. Thus, they are highly appropriate deities for meditation on the season of spring and its multiplicity of meanings connected to its promise of new beginnings.

Jonathan honored the Goddess principle and offered a telling of a myth of Eostre. Immediately following, Eliot honored the God principle and told the myth of Hyacinth and indicated the hyacinths on the altar. The hosts then passed around a small bowl of hard-boiled white eggs, while Jonathan explained their symbolism as the ovaries and ova of the Goddess. Additionally, he reconfigured the symbolism of the eggs to represent for us the testes and sperm of the God. His discourse affirmed the creativity and generativity manifested in each individual, especially those present. The hosts then passed a chalice of champagne and the plate of hot cross buns among the men to drink and to eat. At this point, the hosts invited the company to the meal and to color the eggs using a variety of dyes. Along with eating, drinking, and egg dying, the remainder of our time together was spent in casual conversation and fellowship.

At the time the first guest indicated his need to leave, the hosts called us together to close the ritual, broke the chocolate bunny to share, invited the four men to thank the spirits of the cardinal directions for their presence, and gave gifts of baskets to each man present. The limen was closed; the circle was opened. The guests were invited to stay for as long as they wished. Those men remaining behind gave warm farewells to those departing as they faced reincorporation into their daily, profane lives.

THE EFFICACY OF THE OSTARA RITUAL

Ritual is a device or practice to reduce existential anxiety. "By conforming to models or paradigms that refer to the primordial past," states *The Encyclopedia of Religion*, "ritual also enables each person to transcend the individual self, and thus it can link many people together into enduring and true forms of community" (406). By linking the individual to his/her human community, the seasonal cycles of nature, the celestial bodies, the cosmic order, and divinity, ritual reduces the unbearable reality of the isolation of the human soul. The Ostara ritual certainly achieved this intention. By various means, including its feeling tone, its aesthetics, and its use to the mythology, it connected its participants interpersonally to their common humanity as well as the natural, seasonal, and celestial orders, and, ultimately, to the sacred.

Furthermore, the Ostara ritual, as an experience that affirmed, celebrated, and sanctified gayness, allowed its participants to experience *communitas*, which Victor Turner defines in *The Ritual Process* as a "generalized social bond" emphasizing "homogeneity and comradeship" (96). Mary Douglas in *Purity and Danger* discusses the concept of abomination presented in the Book of Leviticus. "Hybrids and other confusions," writes Douglas, "are abominated.[. . .]Holiness requires that individuals shall conform to the class which they belong. And holiness requires that different classes of things shall not be confused" (66–67). Gay people, by confusing heterosexual gender roles and sexuality are "hybrids and confusions" and, therefore, abominations. "If a man also lie with mankind," declares Leviticus, "as he lieth with a woman, both them have committed an abomination [. . .]" (Lev. 20:13). Deeming gay men and women "abominations" based on Biblical injunction, American society has forced them to live as second-class citizens on its social margins. The gay rights movement, particularly its recent call for same-sex marriage, has transgressed heterosexual privilege, which, in turn, has resulted in a vehement backlash by the Christian Right and the Bush administration. Against this hostile, homophobic socio-political context, the Ostara ritual offered a time and place to celebrate the Gay Man and all his creative confusions of heterosexual gender expectations. In doing so, the ritual affirmed the Gay Man in ways reminiscent of Jung's statement on homosexuality in "Concerning the Archetypes, with Special Reference to the Anima Concept":

> In view of the recognized frequency of this phenomenon [i.e. homosexuality], its interpretation as a pathological perversion is very dubious. The psychological findings show that it is rather a matter of incomplete detachment from the hermaphroditic archetype, coupled with a distinct resistance to identify with the role of a one-sided sexual being. Such a disposition should not be adjudged negative in all circumstanced, in so far as it preserves the archetype of the Original Man, which a one-sided sexual being has, up to a point, lost. (71)

Driving home, I was filled with a strong sense of wellbeing and connection to the men I had met that morning. The spring afternoon beckoned in all its beauty. I stopped at the home of my friends who had just returned from the mass for Palm Sunday at All Saints. Upon my arrival—without any prompting from me—one of them, Rob Piacentino, broke into a complaint against the service. Rob said he felt "talked down to"—"alienated," "unmoved," "bored," and "ignored." "For once," Rob continued, "I wish they would really talk to me!" Despite the beauty of the music and the church building, he experienced no sense of connection, no sense of *communitas*. The contrast between our two ritual experiences further emphasized the efficacy of the Ostara ritual. I found myself looking forward to attending Jonathan and Eliot's ritual celebrating Litha, the summer solstice:

> Spring begins in the dead of winter. This year's palms of living glory become next year's ashes of death, as the cycle repeats and the year goes around, always connected to the past, always

> moving toward the future. The movement from dead of winter to the rebirth of spring is complete, but our march toward high summer has just begun. (Santino 111)

NOTES

1. The emergence of *pagan studies* as a academic field of study may also be seen in the publication of the peer-reviewed journal devoted to the field, *The Pomegranate: The International Journal of Pagan Studies*, and the annual Conference in Contemporary Pagan Studies connected to the annual meeting of the American Academy of Religion. Additionally, the Department of Religion at the University of Florida offers doctoral program in *Religion and Nature*.

2. Many pagan books, both academic and devotional, discuss the solar sabbats and the lunar esbats. See, for example, Harvey's *Contemporary Paganism: Listening People, Speaking Earth* and Sandra Kynes' *A Year of Ritual: Sabbats and Esbats for Solitaries and Covens*. Margaret Alice Murray discusses esbats in *The Witch-Cult in Western Europe*, her highly controversial but influential book (112–23). "Most scholars believe," writes Margot Adler in *Drawing Down the Moon*, "Murray invented this term" (110). For a critique discrediting Murray's work on witchcraft, see Simpson.

3. See also Margot Adler's chapter on "Radical Faeries and the Growth of Men's Spirituality," in *Drawing Down the Moon*, 338, 48.

4. As early as 1916, Robert Haven Schauffler was questioning Bede's account of Eostre as a German goddess of the spring whose name gave the inspiration for *Easter*. See Schauffler. For a more recent consideration of the question of the authenticity of the goddess Eostre, see Cusack.

REFERENCES

Adler, M. *Drawing Down the Moon: Witches, Druids, Goddess-Worshippers, and Other Pagans in America Today*. Rev. ed. Boston: Beacon, 1986.

Bell, C. *Ritual: Perspectives and Dimensions*. New York: Oxford University Press, 1997.

Berger, H. A. *A Community of Witches: Contemporary Neo-Pagansim and Witchcraft in the United States*. Columbia: University of South Carolina Press, 1999.

Berger, H. et al. *Voices from the Pagan Census: A National Survey of Witches and Neo-Pagans in the United States*. Columbia: University of South Carolina Press, 2003.

Bond, D. S. *Living Myth: Personal Meaning as a Way of Life*. Boston: Shambala, 1993.

Campanelli, P. *Wheel of the Year: Living the Magical Life*. St. Paul: Llewellyn, 1992.

"Celebrate the Spring Equinox." *Gay Mens Medicine Circle* (brochure). 2005: 4.

Clifton, C. S., and Graham Harvey. *The Paganism Reader*. New York: Routledge, 2004.

Conner, R. P. *Blossom of Bone: Reclaiming the Connections Between Homoeroticism and the Sacred*. San Francisco: HarperSanFrancisco, 1993.

Cotton, A. "Spiritual Visionaries." Rev. of *Queer Spirits: A Gay Men's Myth Book*, by Will Rocoe, *Wrestling with the Angel: Faith and Religion in the Lives of Gay Men*, by Brian Bouldrey, and *Gay Soul: Finding the Heart of Gay Spirit and Nature*, by Mark Thompson. *Southern Voice*. July 6, 1995: 35.

Cunningham, S. *Living Wicca: A Further Guide for the Solitary Practitioner*. St. Paul: Llewellyn, 1993.

Cusack, C. "The Goddess Eostre: Bede's Text and Contemporary Pagan Tradition(s)." *The Pomegranate* 9.1 (2007): 22–40.

Douglas, M. *Purity and Danger: An Analysis of the Concepts of Pollution and Taboo*. London: Routledge, 2002.

Drake, R. *The Gay Canon: Great Books Every Gay Man Should Read*. New York: Anchor Books, 1998.

Eliade, M. *Patterns in Comparative Religion*. Cleveland: World, 1966.

———. *The Sacred and the Profane: The Nature of Religion*. Trans. Willard R. Trask. New York: Harper, 1959.

EricM32. E-mail to author. February 3, 1995.

Evans, A. *Witchcraft and the Gay Counterculture*. Boston: Fag Rag Books, 1978.

Gardner, G. B. *The Meaning of Witchcraft*. New York: Weiser, 1959.

———. *Witchcraft Today*. New York: Citadel, 1954.

"Gay Spirit Visions Mission Statement." *Visionary: The Journal of Gay Spirit Visions*. 11.1 (Winter 2005): 2.

Harvey, G. *Contemporary Paganism: Listening People, Speaking Earth*. New York: New York University Press, 1997.

Harvey, G., and Charlotte Hardman, eds. *Paganism Today: Wiccans, Druids, the Goddess and Ancient Earth Traditions for the Twenty-First Century*. San Francisco: Thorsons, 1995.

Hobsbawm, E. "Introduction: Inventing Traditions." *The Invention of Tradition*. Ed. Eric Hobsbawm and Terence Ranger. Cambridge: Cambridge University Press, 1983: 1–14.

The Holy Bible. King James Version. Nashville: Nelson, 1977.

Hopman, E. E., and L. Bond. *People of the Earth: The New Pagans Speak Out*. Rochester, Vermont: Destiny, 1996.

Hutton, R. *The Stations of the Sun: A History of the Ritual Year in Britain*. Oxford: Oxford University Press, 1997.

———. *The Triumph of the Moon: A History of Modern Pagan Witchcraft*. Oxford: Oxford University Press, 1999.

———. *Witches, Druids and King Arthur*. London: Hambledon and London, 2003.

Jung, C. G. "Concerning the Archetypes, with Special Reference to the Anima Concept." Trans. R. F. C. Hull. *The Collected Works of C. G. Jung*. Vol. 9.1. Bollingen Series 20. Princeton: Princeton University Press, 1990. 54–72.

———. "The Psychology of the Child Archetype." Trans. R. F. C. Hull. *The Collected Works of C. G. Jung*. Vol. 9.1. Bollingen Series 20. Princeton: Princeton University Press, 1990. 151–181.

Klaatu01. E-mail to author. February 11, 1995.

Kynes, S. *A Year of Ritual: Sabbats and Esbats for Solitaries and Covens*. St. Paul: Llewellyn, 2004.

Levi-Strauss, C. *The Savage Mind*. Chicago: University of Chicago Press, 1966.

Lewis, J. R., ed. *Magical Religion and Modern Witchcraft*. Albany: State University of New York Press, 1996.

Magliocco, S. *Neo-Pagan Sacred Art and Altars: Making Things Whole*. Jackson: University Press of Mississippi, 2001.

———. "Ritual is My Chosen Art Form: The Creation of Ritual as Folk Art Among Contemporary Pagans." *Magical Religion and Modern Witchcraft*. Ed. James R. Lewis. Albany: State University of New York P, 1996: 93–119.

———. *Witching Culture: Folklore and Neo-Paganism in America*. Philadelphia: University of Pennsylvania P, 2004.

McCoy, E. *Ostara: Customs, Spells and Rituals for the Rites of Spring*. St. Paul: Llewellyn, 2003.

Murray, M. A. *The Witch-Cult of Western Europe*. Oxford: Clarendon, 1921.

Newall, V. *An Egg at Easter: A Folklore Study*. London: Routledge, 1971.

O'Gaea, A. *Celebrating the Seasons of Life: Beltane to Mabon*. Franklin Lakes, NJ: New Page, 2005.

———. *Celebrating the Seasons of Life: Samhain to Ostara*. Franklin Lakes, NJ: New Page, 2004.

Orion, L. *Never Again the Burning Times: Paganism Revisited*. Prospect Heights, IL: Waveland, 1995.

Penczak, C. *Gay Witchcraft: Empowering the Tribe*. Boston: Weiser, 2003.

Piacentino, R. Personal interview. March 20, 2005.

Pike, S. M. *Earthly Bodies, Magical Selves: Contemporary Pagans and the Search for Community*. Berkeley: University of California Press, 2001.

———. *New Age and Neopagan Religions in America*. New York: Columbia University Press, 2004

Rehm, J. E-mail to author. March 2, 2005.

———. Personal interview. March 20, 2005.

Santino, J. *All Around the Year: Holidays and Celebrations in American Life*. Urbana: University of Illinois Press, 1994.

Schauffler, R. H. Introduction. *Easter: Its History, Celebrations, Spirit, and Significance in Prose and Verse*. By Susan Tracey Rice. Miami: Granger, 1976.

Simpson, J. "Margaret Murray: Who Believed Her, and Why?" *Folklore* 105 (1994): 89–96.

Skolund, J. Personal interview. April 1, 1995.
Starhawk. *Spiral Dance: A Rebirth of the Ancient Religion of the Great Goddess.* San Francisco: HarperSanFrancisco, 1989.
Turner, V. *The Ritual Process: Structure and Anti-Structure.* New York: Aldine de Gruyter, 1995.
Van Gennep, A. *The Rites of Passage.* Chicago: University of Chicago Press, 1960.
"Who are the faeries?" *About RadFae.Org.* October 18, 2001. *Radfae.org.* April 17, 2005. http://www.radfae.org/about.htm.
York, M. *Pagan Theology: Paganism as a World Religion.* New York: New York University Press, 2003.
Zuesse, E. M. "Ritual." *The Encyclopedia of Religion.* Ed. Mircea Eliade. 16 vol. New York: Macmillan, 1987.

Chapter 17

Matthew Shepard: Giving a Human Face to Anti-Gay Violence

Rodger Streitmatter

As the final decade of the twentieth century was unfolding, gay and lesbian America had reason to believe that it was approaching full acceptance into the national culture. In 1993, *Philadelphia* proved that a big-budget motion picture about a gay man with AIDS could triumph at the box office. In 1994, *Roseanne* showed that the country's television sets did not implode when their screens depicted two women locking lips. In 1996 and 1997, throngs of moviegoers wholeheartedly embraced a range of gay men—from fooh-fooh Nathan Lane in *The Birdcage* to hunka-hunka Rupert Everett in *My Best Friend's Wedding*. The *Ellen* phenomenon was a milestone as well; although Ellen DeGeneres's program didn't survive, the fact that a major TV network was willing to feature a lesbian as the leading character on a sitcom was certainly a progressive step.

And then came October 6, 1998.

It was 10:30 P.M. when University of Wyoming student Matthew Shepard walked into the Fireside Lounge not far from campus. As the five-foot-two-inch, 105-pound young man who was impeccably dressed in jeans, a sport coat, and patent-leather loafers was sitting at the bar and quietly sipping a cocktail, two local men approached him.

The pair of high school dropouts said they, too, were gay and asked their new acquaintance to come home with them, intimating that a sexual threesome would follow. By accepting their invitation, the 21-year-old student made the worst decision of his life.

As soon as the two men had Shepard inside their pickup, they began striking him with the butt of a Smith & Wesson .357-caliber handgun. But that physical brutality was only a warm-up exercise, as the thugs then drove the blond-haired, blue-eyed Shepard to a remote area, just past the local Wal-Mart, where they tied him to a rough-hewn wooden fence, burned his arms with lighted cigarettes, kicked him repeatedly in the groin, and struck his head so hard and so many times that his skull collapsed. After the men bludgeoned Shepard beyond recognition, they left him to die in near-freezing weather. When a passing bicyclist found him 18 hours later, the only spot on his entire head that was not covered in dried blood was just below his eyes—he had cried while being beaten, so his tears had rolled down his face and washed his cheeks clean. Five days later when Matthew Shepard took his last breath in a local hospital, every major print and broadcast news organization in the country reported his death.[1]

"For homosexuals, the key to winning acceptance and respect has been to make themselves familiar, visible and known," the *New York Times* stated on its editorial page. "Yet in almost 30 years of struggle, the modern gay rights movement has never achieved a recognizable public face. Now, in a victim, it has been given one."[2] The country's most prestigious newspaper had begun reporting on the incident while Shepard was still struggling to survive his injuries, prompting other major dailies and the television networks to cover the story as well. That plethora of stories helped propel mass rallies and marches in more than 50 American cities, including several thousand men and women joining Ellen DeGeneres and openly gay Representative Barney Frank for a candlelight vigil on the steps of the U.S. Capitol.[3] As Dan Rather reported on the *CBS Evening News*, "Matthew Shepard's death has set off a nationwide wave of demonstrations protesting anti-gay violence."[4]

The avalanche of news coverage that followed the attack on Shepard sent several messages. First among them was that, despite the progress that had been made by the final years of the twentieth century, a significant number of Americans continued to hate gay people. The second message was that the nation's print and broadcast news organizations were uniformly outraged at how the young man had been brutalized. A third message was more mixed, with some leading news outlets supporting and others opposing hate-crime laws that increase the penalties when a crime is based on a victim's sexual orientation. A final statement that the extensive coverage communicated was that family members are often remarkably supportive of their gay loved one.

HATRED OF GAY PEOPLE

A discussion of the degree to which the gruesome murder illuminated the hatred that many Americans of the late 1990s felt toward gay people rightly begins by looking at what motivated the vicious attack.

The *New York Times* was among the first news organizations to report on the backgrounds of Russell Henderson, 21, and Aaron McKinney, 22, who were arrested after a pistol covered in Shepard's blood was found in the back of McKinney's pickup. Henderson had dropped out of Laramie High School and worked off and on at various jobs, including as a roofer; he had been convicted twice for drunk driving. McKinney had followed a similar route and also was the father of a four-month-old son born to his girlfriend; he had recently been convicted of robbing the local Kentucky Fried Chicken.[5]

Although neither man had a steady job, every few weekends they managed to scrape together enough money to buy a hefty supply of methamphetamine—also known as crystal meth. One friend of Henderson and McKinney said they had smoked or snorted about $2,000 worth of the drug the weekend before they crossed paths with Shepard. That friend speculated, in fact, that the men may have still been feeling the effects of their recent binge on the night the attack took place.[6]

Henderson and McKinney came into the Fireside Lounge about an hour after the college student had arrived, ordering a $5.50 pitcher of beer that they paid for by pulling quarters and dimes from their pockets. The bartender told reporters that the two local men had approached Shepard, rather than the other way around, by leaving their barstools and moving to where the lone man was sitting, several feet away from them. The three men talked for awhile and then left the bar together about 1 A.M.[7]

Exactly what happened after they climbed inside the pickup is difficult to know for sure, as the only details came from Henderson and McKinney when they went on trial for first-degree murder. According to their testimony, soon after the three men were alone, Shepard placed his hand on McKinney's leg, presumably as a sign that he was ready to begin the sexual activity that he expected to take place. But that action prompted McKinney to tell Shepard, "Guess what? We're not gay, and you just got jacked. It's Gay Awareness Week!" That last sentence came in response to the fact that gay and lesbian activists had posted fliers around Laramie to promote a series of activities leading up to National Coming Out Day, which was scheduled for the next week.[8]

McKinney then began hitting Shepard, according to Henderson's testimony, with the butt of the handgun while repeatedly yelling "Queer!" and "Faggot!" Law enforcement officials speculated that hatred was the primary motivation of the two killers, as they took the $20 inside Shepard's wallet but did not steal the expensive watch he was wearing.[9]

News organizations soon reported that hatred of gay people was by no means limited to McKinney and Henderson. An *NBC Nightly News* segment included a patron of Wild Willie's Cowboy Bar in Laramie saying, "If you come to Wyoming and you're gay, you're lookin' for trouble,"[10] and the *New York Times* reported that a billboard advertising a nearby history museum had been vandalized so the original "Shoot a Day or Two" slogan would read "Shoot a Gay or Two."[11] Based on an entry in the homecoming parade at Colorado State University, according to *ABC World News Tonight*, college students were no more tolerant of gays than members of older generations; the bicyclist who found Shepard hanging from the fence had said he initially thought the body was a scarecrow, so members of Pi Kappa Alpha fraternity mocked the killing by adding a scarecrow to their float and using spray paint to scrawl the words "I'M GAY" across the figure's face.[12] (*Salon* magazine was one of the few news outlets that reported the fact that the words "UP MY ASS" were also painted on the scarecrow's backside.)[13]

Perhaps the most disturbing evidence of gay hatred was broadcast to media consumers as part of the coverage of the slain student's funeral. All of the major television networks—ABC, CBS, CNN, and NBC—covered the event, which meant that millions of viewers saw protesters standing outside St. Mark's Episcopal Church carrying pickets that read "No Tears for Queers" and "Fags Die, God Laughs."[14] The country's largest-circulation newsweekly reproduced some of the hateful signs as well. A *Time* cover story titled "The War on Gays" included a photo of an angry man shouting at members of Shepard's grieving family while he held up a sign that said "AIDS Cures FAGS."[15]

Hatred of gay people did not end with harsh words. During the previous year, according to *ABC World News Tonight*, 21 gay men and lesbians had been killed specifically because of their sexual orientation.[16]

OUTRAGE FROM THE NEWS MEDIA

Beginning with the earliest stories, it was clear that news organizations had no intention of limiting their coverage of Matthew Shepard's murder to answering who, what, when, and where. Journalistic voices immediately communicated their outrage that a college student had not only been killed but had been savagely tortured as well.

One indication of the news media's strong editorial position came through the sympathetic words they chose to use when describing the victim. The *New York Times* set the tone by characterizing him as "trusting,"[17] "clean-cut,"[18] "soft-spoken,"[19] "polite,"[20] "sweet,"[21] and "boyish."[22] The *Washington Post* followed suit, telling its readers that the slain youth had possessed a "cherubic face"[23] and had been "shy,"[24] "sensitive,"[25] and "slight of stature, gentle of demeanor,"[26] while quoting the police officer who found Shepard on the fence as saying he looked "like a child" rather than a man.[27] *Newsweek* painted a highly sympathetic portrait of the young man as well, calling him "meek,"[28] "well-groomed,"[29] "sweet-tempered and boyishly idealistic,"[30] and beginning one story with the statement: "From his first breath, life was a struggle for Matthew Shepard. He was a preemie at birth—a tiny slip of a kid who would grow up to be barely five feet tall. He was shy and gentle in a place where it wasn't common for a young man to be either. The state of Wyoming features a bronco buster on its license plate."[31]

The *Times*, *Post*, and *Newsweek* also were among the news outlets that compared Shepard to another gentle man who was savagely beaten and then left to die: Jesus Christ. "There is incredible symbolism about being tied to a fence," the *Times* said in its front-page story reporting the student's death. "Many people are comparing it to a crucifixion."[32] The *Post* made a similar observation, commenting on "the powerful Christ-like imagery of Shepard being assaulted and strapped to a fence."[33] *Newsweek*'s reference to the image came in the form of a quotation from the young victim's godfather: "The only way I can be released from the bitterness and anger I feel is when I concentrate on the Son of God being crucified, the same way as Matthew was, almost 2,000 years ago."[34]

That trio of publications also expressed outrage about the grisly nature of the crime. The *Times* said, on its editorial page, "The details of Matthew Shepard's murder are a public horror."[35] The country's most respected newspaper did not stop there, as one of its liberal columnists accused a conservative organization of being an accomplice to the crime. Specifically, Frank Rich criticized the Family Research Council for airing television ads portraying homosexuality as a disease that could be cured. "The ads ooze malice," he wrote. "In one of them, homosexuality is linked to drug addiction and certain death by AIDS." Such messages inevitably lead to physical attacks, Rich argued, like the one against Shepard. "If you wage a well-financed media air war in which people with an innate difference in sexual orientation are ceaselessly branded as diseased and sinful and un-American, ground war will follow."[36]

Washington Post columnist Richard Cohen made strong accusations as well, blaming conservative politicians for Shepard's murder. "I will figuratively place the young man's body at the doorstep of Senate Majority Leader Trent Lott," Cohen wrote. That reference was to a statement by the Mississippi senator, in June 1998, that homosexuality was a disease comparable to kleptomania. "Lott has likened a sexual preference to a wacky mental disease and also called it a sin," Cohen wrote. "In his rhetoric, he and others have, bit by bit, robbed homosexuals of their humanity." The columnist ended his piece with the statement: "Anti-gay politicians have given voice to some of the ugliest sentiments in American society—legitimizing the sort of hate that left Matthew Shepard tied to a fence, lynched on account of being gay."[37]

In *Newsweek*, angry words came from media critic Jonathan Alter. "Violence against gays is a national disgrace," he wrote. Like Cohen from the *Post*, Alter blamed Trent Lott and other Republican leaders, saying there was a direct connection between "verbal gay-bashing in Washington and gays actually getting their heads bashed in." Alter then added another element to the argument by comparing violence against gays to the physical abuse that African Americans historically had suffered. "Just as white racists created a climate for lynching blacks," he wrote, "so the constant degrading of homosexuals is exacting a toll in blood."[38]

Among the television journalists who expressed outrage at Shepard's murder was Tom Brokaw. "It's a crime that goes beyond despicable," the *NBC Nightly News* anchor said during one broadcast.[39] During another, he shook his head as he asked, with an expression of bewilderment on his face, "What causes someone to turn on another human being with such anger, such hatred?"[40] His network colleague Katie Couric provided an answer to that question when she said, on the *Today* morning show, "Conservative Christian political organizations certainly are helping to create an anti-homosexual atmosphere in many parts of the country."[41]

DEBATE OVER HATE-CRIME LAWS

Advocates of many public policy initiatives spend years trying to bring attention to their particular cause. And then, suddenly, a single event can propel that little-noticed issue into the national spotlight. Matthew Shepard's murder played that role for a proposal to expand hate-crime laws to include sexual orientation.

During the 1970s and 1980s, 40 states and the District of Columbia had passed laws that increased fines and jail time when prosecutors were able to prove that a crime had been committed specifically because of the victim's race, religion, color, or national origin, with 21 one of those states and D.C. also including sexual orientation in their laws. Shepard's attackers were not charged with a hate crime, however, because Wyoming was one of the states that did not have a hate-crime law that extended to sexual orientation. Indeed, it was one of the 10 states that had no hate-crime law whatsoever.

"Gay leaders hope that Mr. Shepard's death will galvanize state legislatures to pass hate-crime legislation or broaden existing laws," the *New York Times* reported in one front-page article. "Wyoming has been a holdout on hate-crime laws, rejecting three bills since 1994." The story also pointed out who objected to the public policy initiative, as well as why. "Conservatives, particularly Christian conservatives, generally oppose such laws, saying they extend 'special rights' to minorities."[42]

The *Times* established itself as a strong proponent of expanding the definition of a hate crime to include an attack motivated by a victim's sexuality. "Members of minority groups have often had to pay a terrible price just for being who they are," one editorial began, going on to say that African Americans and Jews were the most frequent targets of violence. "But other groups have been the victims of that murderous impulse too, and homosexuals have always been among them." After describing the attack on Shepard, the *Times* ended the editorial by stating: "His death makes clear the need for hate-crime laws to protect those who survive and punish those who attack others, just because of who they are."[43]

In the months following the incident and as the trials of Russell Henderson and Aaron McKinney approached, the *New York Times* continued to campaign—in news stories as well as in editorials—for hate-crime laws that included sexual orientation. Indeed, some articles on the issue sounded like they had come directly from press releases crafted by advocacy groups. "The National Gay and Lesbian Task Force says the laws are valuable because they shape the way society thinks about itself and they draw boundaries of what society will tolerate," one story read. "Advocates argue that society speaking out, clearly and specifically, against crimes directed at members of a minority group can make the members of that group feel less isolated and threatened. And, they say, police officers might become more vigilant about such crimes if the laws require training on the issue, as the laws in eight states do."[44]

One of several occasions on which the *Times* promoted the issue on its editorial page came in the wake of Henderson's decision to plead guilty to murder charges in exchange for avoiding a possible death sentence. The paper applauded the judge who sentenced the killer to two consecutive life terms, but it criticized the Wyoming legislature for failing to enact any type of hate-crime law. "In the days and weeks after Matthew Shepard's murder, it seemed that the nation would be awakened to the virulence of anti-gay beliefs that propelled the murder," the *Times* stated. "Yet in a very short time, the old prejudice that homosexuals are not discriminated against and do not warrant 'special' protection has resurfaced."[45]

Various other major news organizations echoed the *Times*'s position. "While laws can't stop hate, they do send the message that society will not tolerate such bigotry," an editorial in the *Boston Globe* argued. "They also reinforce the constitutional guarantees that should extend to all individuals in a civilized society."[46] *USA Today* also supported hate-crime laws that include provisions regarding sexual orientation, saying that opponents of such legislation were wrong when they insisted that it would give special rights to gay people. "Such statutes help punish crimes that are committed because of who or what the victim is: black or brown; Muslim or Mormon; male or female; gay or straight," the nation's largest-circulation newspaper stated. "If that's part of some mysterious 'homosexual agenda,' then so is the preamble to the Declaration of Independence and the equal-protection clause of the Constitution."[47]

Not all liberal-leaning news organizations, however, endorsed hate-crime laws—whether related to sexual orientation or other factors.

A *Washington Post* editorial dubbed the effort to enact such laws "misguided,"[48] with a commentary piece in the same issue illuminating the *Post*'s reasoning: "What Henderson and McKinney allegedly did was a terrible, evil thing. But would it have been less terrible if Shepard had not been gay? If Henderson and McKinney beat Shepard to death because they hated him personally, not as a member of a group, should the law treat them more lightly?"[49]

Regardless of the arguments for and against hate-crime laws, Shepard's murder prompted considerable debate on the issue, in Wyoming and several other states. Ultimately, however, neither the media attention nor the widespread discussion led to any additional laws being enacted. As NBC anchorman Tom Brokaw put it in 1999, "It appears the death of Matthew Shepard has done little to change any minds."[50]

LOVE FOR A GAY SON

In 1993, the film *Philadelphia* had depicted a young gay man whose family supported him during a difficult time in his life. Five years later, the news coverage that revolved around Matthew Shepard spotlighted real-life parents whose love was every bit as powerful and as unconditional as those that had been portrayed in the landmark motion picture.

Television viewers met Dennis and Judy Shepard on the day the grieving parents buried their son. Cameras showed the father and mother, tightly gripping each other's hand, standing somberly outside the church as snow fell around them, determined to tell the world about their son. "Matt was the type of person who, if this had happened to another person," Dennis Shepard said, "he would have been the first one on the scene to offer his help, his hope, and his heart." Before the father finished his brief statement, his wife broke down and cried openly, the cameras capturing the image and broadcasting it nationwide. Across the street, protesters could be seen carrying signs that read "God Hates Fags" and "Matt in Hell." The correspondent for *ABC World News Tonight* finished her report by saying that the Shepards "chose to ignore" the protesters. "Instead, they gave thanks to the thousands of well wishers from around the world who have comforted them in their time of sorrow."[51]

Katie Couric of NBC gave television viewers a much more intimate look at the couple when she interviewed them on the *Dateline* news magazine show four months after the funeral. "He wanted to go into diplomacy," Dennis Shepard said of his son, "and work overseas for human rights." Judy Shepard spoke during the program as well, but her voice was so soft that listeners had to strain to hear her words. "He wasn't just my son," the mother said. "He was my friend, my confidant, my constant reminder of how good life can be."[52]

Dennis and Judy Shepard had been living in Saudi Arabia when their son was attacked, the father working as an engineer for an oil company. They flew to Wyoming to be with Matthew as he lay comatose in the hospital and then to bury him. But when Dennis Shepard returned to his job halfway around the world, Judy Shepard stayed in the United States. She wanted desperately to retreat into the privacy of her personal grief while returning to her role as a stay-at-home wife, but gay rights activists convinced her that she could be a uniquely effective public spokeswoman against anti-gay violence.

When reporters—whether they worked for the *Atlanta Journal,*[53] *Los Angeles Times,*[54] or *Minneapolis Star Tribune*[55]—asked her why an affluent woman who wanted nothing to do with the public limelight had agreed to give up her comfortable life with her husband to crisscross the country, usually traveling by herself, to speak before dozens of groups in such far-flung towns as Murfreesboro, Tennessee, and Willimantic, Connecticut, Judy Shepard's answer was always the same: "I'm doing this for Matthew."[56]

Journalists also repeatedly asked Shepard about when and how she and her husband had learned of their son's sexual orientation. They had suspected Matthew was gay long before he came out to them, she said in a *Boston Globe* story, so she read everything she could find about how parents could make it easier for gay children during the often-traumatic process of acknowledging their sexuality. "I tried to educate myself," she said, so she and her husband could react as supportively as possible. After absorbing what experts and other parents of gay children had to say, Judy Shepard concluded that the ideal response would be to accept the news matter-of-factly. She and her husband even rehearsed the conversation that they knew was coming, she said, so when Matthew—at age 18—finally told them, they didn't so much as blink an eye. "We acted like it was no big deal, even though our hearts were pounding a mile a minute," she recalled. "That seemed to us like the ideal reaction, so that was how we reacted. Matthew's well-being always came first."[57]

Judy Shepard shared other details about her son's life as well. He had become fluent in three foreign languages—French, German, and Arabic—while attending boarding school in Switzerland, she said, and had worked to raise money for AIDS research. Not all aspects of Matthew's life had been pleasant, however, as his mother also told of how, during a trip to Morocco during his senior year in high school, he had been gang raped by six men. "After that, he had the posture of a victim," she said. "He was the kind of person whom you just look at and know that if you hurt him that he's going to take it—that there's nothing he can do about it, verbally or physically. When he walked down the street, he had that victim walk."[58]

Even though the stories painted Dennis and Judy Shepard to be remarkably caring and compassionate people, the public was still unprepared for the extraordinary act of human generosity the couple performed in November 1999. After Aaron McKinney was found guilty of first-degree murder, the Shepards asked the judge to show leniency to the man who had tortured their son. Because of that request, McKinney was sentenced not to death but to life in prison. Dennis Shepard delivered the news to a stunned courtroom. "I would like nothing better than to see you die, Mr. McKinney," the father told the killer. "However, this is the time to begin the healing process—to show mercy to someone who refused to show mercy to my son."[59]

"THE CRUCIFIXION OF MATTHEW SHEPARD"

When looked at from an analytical perspective, some of the messages sent by the heinous killing of Matthew Shepard and the extensive news coverage of that crime were conflicting. On the one hand, the incident served as a sobering wake-up call, communicating that a critical mass of Americans continued to hate gay men as much as people from earlier eras had. On the other hand, the myriad statements of outrage voiced by the nation's leading news organizations indicated that many of these powerful institutions were appalled that such a despicable crime had been committed. Efforts to broaden hate-crime laws to include sexual orientation offered mixed messages as well; the prestigious *New York Times* fervently supported the proposal, but other liberal journalistic voices such as the *Washington Post* opposed it. One of the few topics related to Matthew Shepard's murder on which there was no ambiguity was that his parents loved him—completely and unconditionally.

In the context of the evolution of the media's treatment of gay people, the most intriguing question about this case study is: Why did this particular incident of anti-gay violence attract so much attention and thereby propel the issue of anti-gay violence into the national spotlight like no event before or since?

Clearly part of the answer involves the gruesome nature of the crime. Two homophobic thugs lured a gay college student out of a bar, took him to a remote area, tied him to a fence, tortured him, and brutally beat him—the kind of details that create a riveting story. But Matthew Shepard was by no means the only gay man who had been the victim of inhuman treatment. Five months after the highly publicized murder, an Alabama man was bludgeoned to death with an ax handle and his lifeless body was then burned on a stack of rubber tires,[60] and, a few months after that, an Army private stationed in Kentucky was dragged from his bed and killed by fellow soldiers who beat him with a baseball bat.[61] And yet the name of neither man—Billy Jack Gaither nor Barry Winchell—became part of the public consciousness or the collective American memory to the degree that the name Matthew Shepard did.

Vanity Fair magazine attempted to identify the specific factors that set the Wyoming incident apart from others that had occurred during the same general time frame. A 15-page story titled "The Crucifixion of Matthew Shepard" concluded that the major factor was how the media portrayed the victim. "Parents throughout the country felt that Matthew could have been their son, an idea many had never contemplated before about a gay person," the magazine argued. "In part, this may have been a result of the fact that while he was described as gay, the press did not portray Matthew as a sexual adult. He was depicted as having parents, rather than partners, and those parents were loving and affluent." Shepard's physical characteristics added to his media appeal, *Vanity Fair* continued. "Photographs in the press showed him as having a fragile, childlike appearance—a look of pale purity, the translucent beauty favored in religious art."[62]

The various words and phrases that journalistic organizations used to describe the murder victim clearly contributed to this impression that the college student, despite being 21 and therefore legally an adult, was really more of a boy than a man. The *New York Times* called him "trusting," "sweet," "boyish"; the *Washington Post* spoke of his "cherubic face," his "shy" and "sensitive" nature, his "slight" stature, his looking "like a child"; and *Newsweek* added that he was "meek" as well as "sweet-tempered and boyishly idealistic." The comparisons to Jesus Christ nailed to a cross reinforced the image of a victim who was both guileless and blameless; the gay and lesbian news magazine *The Advocate* observed that the mainstream media "painted him as a veritable gay saint."[63]

In short, Matthew Shepard was portrayed as a waif-like child who had been taken advantage of because he was weak and vulnerable. Billy Jack Gaither and Barry Winchell had clearly been men, not boys. The first was a middle-aged, working-class man with only average looks; the other was a muscular, battle-ready soldier who had fought his attackers, losing only because they outnumbered him. Neither Gaither nor Winchell was a pampered member of the upper-middle class and neither was incapable of defending himself. Matthew Shepard was the only one of the three, therefore, whose appearance was consistent with the traditional stereotype of homosexuals as weak and effeminate beings. And so the nation's news outlets eagerly ushered him into the media spotlight.

NOTES

1. See, for example, James Brooke, "Gay Man Dies from Attack," *New York Times*, October 13, 1998, A1; Tom Kenworthy, "Gay Wyoming Student Succumbs to Injuries," *Washington Post*, October 13, 1998, A7; *CBS Evening News*, October 12, 1998 (the newscast was anchored by Dan Rather; the segment was reported by Cynthia Bowers); CNN, October 12, 1998 (the newscast was anchored by Judy Woodruff; the segment was reported by Brian Cabell); *NBC Nightly News*, October 12, 1998 (the newscast was anchored by Tom Brokaw; the segment was reported by George Lewis in Laramie, Wyoming, and Pete Williams in Washington).

2. "The Lesson of Matthew Shepard," *New York Times*, October 17, 1998, A14.

3. Allan Lengel, "Thousands Mourn Student's Death," *Washington Post*, October 15, 1998, A7.

4. *CBS Evening News*, November 24, 1998 (the newscast was anchored by Dan Rather; the segment was reported by Richard Schlesinger).

5. James Brooke, "Men Held in Beating Lived on the Fringes," *New York Times*, October 16, 1998, A16.

6. JoAnn Wypijewski, "A Boy's Life," *Harper's Magazine*, September 1999, 62. In November 2004, the ABC news magazine program *20/20* aired a widely discussed segment in which Aaron McKinney stated that his primary motivation for beating Matthew Shepard was not to hurt a gay man but to rob the well-dressed student so he could fuel his methamphetamine binge.

7. James Brooke, "Men Held in Beating Lived on the Fringes," *New York Times*, October 16, 1998, A16.

8. James Brooke, "Witnesses Trace Brutal Killing of Gay Student," *New York Times*, November 21, 1998, A9.

9. James Brooke, "Witnesses Trace Brutal Killing of Gay Student," *New York Times*, November 21, 1998, A9.

10. *NBC Nightly News*, October 9, 1998 (the newscast was anchored by Tom Brokaw; the segment was reported by Roger O'Neil).

11. James Brooke, "After Beating of Gay Man, Town Looks at Its Attitudes," *New York Times*, October 12, 1998, A9.

12. *ABC World News Tonight*, October 14, 1998 (the newscast was anchored by Peter Jennings; the segment was reported by Lisa Salters in Fort Collins, Colorado).

13. Lily Burana, "Letter from Laramie," *Salon*, October 16, 1998 (http://archive.salon.com/news/1998/10/16newsb.html).

14. *ABC World News Tonight*, October 16, 1998 (the newscast was anchored by Peter Jennings; the segment was reported by Lisa Salters in Casper, Wyoming, and Rebecca Chase in Atlanta); *CBS Evening News*, October 16, 1998 (the newscast was anchored by Dan Rather; the segment was reported by Cynthia Bowers); CNN, October 16, 1998 (the segment was reported by Joie Chen); *NBC Nightly News*, October 16, 1998 (the newscast was anchored by Tom Brokaw; the segment was reported by Roger O'Neill in Casper, Wyoming, and Pete Williams in Washington). Many of the signs were carried by followers of the Rev. Fred Phelps, an anti-gay minister who led a group of protesters to the funeral from his Westboro Baptist Church in Topeka, Kansas.

15. Steve Lopez, "The War on Gays: To Be Young and Gay in Wyoming," *Time*, October 26, 1998, 39.

16. *ABC World News Tonight*, October 16, 1998 (the newscast was anchored by Peter Jennings; the segment was reported by Lisa Salters in Casper, Wyoming, and Rebecca Chase in Atlanta). The death figure was attributed to the National Coalition of Anti-Violence Programs.

17. "Murdered for Who He Was," *New York Times*, October 13, 1998, A18.

18. Michael Cooper, "Killing Shakes Complacency of the Gay Rights Movement," *New York Times*, October 21, 1998, A1.

19. Frank Rich, "Journal: Loving Him to Death," *New York Times*, October 24, 1998, A17.

20. Frank Rich, "Journal: Loving Him to Death," *New York Times*, October 24, 1998, A17.

21. Frank Rich, "Journal: Loving Him to Death," *New York Times*, October 24, 1998, A17.

22. James Brooke, "Wyoming City Braces for Gay Murder Trial," *New York Times*, April 4, 1999, A14.

23. Justin Gillis and Patrice Gaines, "Pattern of Hate Emerges on a Fence in Laramie," *Washington Post*, October 18, 1998, A1.

24. Tom Kenworthy, "Hundreds Gather to Remember Slain Man as 'Light to the World,' " *Washington Post*, October 17, 1998, A3.

25. Allan Lengel, "Thousands Mourn Student's Death," *Washington Post*, October 15, 1998, A7.

26. Tom Kenworthy, "Gay Man Near Death after Beating, Burning," *Washington Post*, October 10, 1998, A1.

27. Wil Haygood, "Honor Thy Son," *Washington Post*, July 13, 2003, D1.

28. Howard Fineman, "Echoes of a Murder in Wyoming," *Newsweek*, October 26, 1998, 43.

29. Howard Fineman, "Echoes of a Murder in Wyoming," *Newsweek*, October 26, 1998, 43.

30. Mark Miller, "The Final Days and Nights of a Gay Martyr," *Newsweek*, December 21, 1998, 30.

31. Howard Fineman, "Echoes of a Murder in Wyoming," *Newsweek*, October 26, 1998, 42.

32. James Brooke, "Gay Man Dies from Attack," *New York Times*, October 13, 1998, A1.

33. Tom Kenworthy, "Hundreds Gather to Remember Slain Man as 'Light to the World,' " *Washington Post*, October 17, 1998, A3.

34. Howard Fineman, "Echoes of a Murder in Wyoming," *Newsweek*, October 26, 1998, 42. The godfather's name was Steve Ghering.

35. "The Lesson of Matthew Shepard," *New York Times*, October 17, 1998, A14.

36. Frank Rich, "Journal: The Road to Laramie," *New York Times*, October 14, 1998, A23.

37. Richard Cohen, "Legitimizing Hate," *Washington Post*, October 15, 1998, A23.

38. Jonathan Alter, "Trickle-Down Hate," *Newsweek*, October 26, 1998, 44.

39. *NBC Nightly News*, October 9, 1998 (the newscast was anchored by Tom Brokaw; the segment was reported by Roger O'Neil).

40. *NBC Nightly News*, October 12, 1998 (the newscast was anchored by Tom Brokaw; the segment was reported by George Lewis in Laramie, Wyoming, and Pete Williams in Washington).

41. John Corry, "Murder in Wyoming," *American Spectator*, December 1998, 72.

42. James Brooke, "Gay Man Dies from Attack," *New York Times*, October 13, 1998, A1.

43. "Murdered for Who He Was," *New York Times*, October 13, 1998, A18.

44. Rick Lyman, "Hate Laws Don't Matter, Except when They Do," *New York Times*, October 18, 1998, D6.

45. "A Stiff and Proper Sentence," *New York Times*, Apri1 6, 1999, A26.

46. "Wyoming's Lesson About Hate," *Boston Globe*, October 14, 1998, A18.

47. "A Brutal Assault Boosts Case for Expanding Hate Crime Laws," *USA Today*, October 15, 1998, A12.

48. "A Murder in Wyoming," *Washington Post*, October 14, 1998, A14.

49. Michael Kelly, "Punishing 'Hate Crimes,'" *Washington Post*, October 14, 1998, A15.

50. *NBC Nightly News*, February 5, 1999 (the newscast was anchored by Tom Brokaw; the segment was reported by Roger O'Neil in Ft. Collins, Colorado).

51. *ABC World News Tonight*, October 16, 1998 (the newscast was anchored by Peter Jennings; the segment was reported by Lisa Salters in Casper, Wyoming, and Rebecca Chase in Atlanta).

52. Dennis and Judy Shepard interview by Katie Couric, *Dateline*, February 5, 1999.

53. Kirk Kicklighter, "Mother's Tale of Murdered Son Briings Quiet, Then Tears," *Atlanta Journal*, January 2001, 19, E1.

54. Julie Cart, "Matthew Shepard's Mother Aims to Speak with His Voice," *Los Angeles Times*, September 14, 1999, A5.

55. Terry Collins, "Matthew Shepard's Mom Fights the Hatred that Killed Her Son," *Minneapolis Star Tribune*, March 29, 2001.

56. Julie Cart, "Matthew Shepard's Mother Aims to Speak with His Voice," *Los Angeles Times*, September 14, 1999, A5.

57. Adrian Walker, "Mission Found After Son Is Lost," *Boston Globe*, March 25, 2000, B1.

58. Melanie Thernstrom, "The Crucifixion of Matthew Shepard," *Vanity Fair*, March 1999, 267.

59. Angie Cannon, "In the Name of the Son," *U.S. News & World Report*, November 15, 1999, 36.

60. Kevin Sack, "2 Confess to Killing Man, Saying He Made a Sexual Advance," *New York Times*, March 5, 1999, A10.

61. Francis X. Clines, "Killer's Trial Shows Gay Soldier's Anguish," *New York Times*, December 9, 1999, A18.

62. Melanie Thernstrom, "The Crucifixion of Matthew Shepard," *Vanity Fair*, March 1999, 272.

63. Chris Bull, "All Eyes Were Watching," *The Advocate*, November 24, 1998, 33.

Index

About the Editor and Contributors

EDITOR

Jim Elledge's most recent book, *A History of My Tattoo* (Stonewall, 2006), won the Lambda Award for poetry and was a finalist for the Thom Gunn Award. His collection of prose poems, *H*, an impressionistic biography of Henry Darger, is due from Busman's Holiday Press in 2011. His poems have appeared in *Barrow Street, Denver Quarterly, Five Fingers Review, Hayden's Ferry Review, Indiana Review, North American Review, Paris Review*, and others. His essay on Tina Turner, "Tina and I," appears in *My Diva: 65 Gay Men on the Women Who Inspire Them* (ed. Michael Montlack, 2009), and his "Dunstan Thompson's 'beautiful and butcher beast' Unleashed and on the Prowl" is forthcoming in *Dunstan Thompson: On the Life and Work of a Lost American Master* (eds. D. A. Powell and Kevin Prufer, 2010). He directs the MA in Professional Writing Program at Kennesaw State University, just outside of Atlanta, and the Writers Workshop of Puerto Rico, a summer study program in San Juan, Puerto Rico.

CONTRIBUTORS

Marlon M. Bailey is an Assistant Professor of Gender Studies and African American & African Diaspora Studies at Indiana University, Bloomington. He is also a former Chancellor's Postdoctoral Fellow in Gender and Women's Studies at the University of California-Berkeley. Marlon's most recent essays have appeared in *Souls: A Critical*

Journal of Black Politics, Culture and Society and the *Journal of Gay and Lesbian Social Services*. He is currently completing a book manuscript titled, *Butch/Queens Up in Pumps: Gender, Performance and Ballroom Culture in Detroit*, a performance ethnographic study of Ballroom Culture in Detroit that will be published by the University of Michigan Press.

Alison Bancroft is a specialist in interdisciplinary approaches to modern culture and media and is committed to thinking across media forms, theoretical domains, and cultural contexts. Her research interests include visual culture and theory, psychoanalytic thought and cultural life, and sexualities. She teaches at Queen Mary, University of London, and has published several papers on her current interest, psychoanalysis and fashion. She has recently been awarded a PhD from the University of London, and her thesis "Jacques Lacan and an Encounter with Fashion" is the basis of a forthcoming book and exhibition.

Barclay Barrios is an Assistant Professor of English and Director of Writing Programs at Florida Atlantic University. His research focuses on writing program administration, composition/rhetoric and technology, and the intersections of queer identities and composition/pedagogy.

David R. Coon is an Assistant Professor of Media Studies at the University of Washington Tacoma, where he teaches courses in film and television studies and video production. His research interests include gender and sexuality in the media, visual representations of cities and suburbs, and the work practices of media professionals. He has published articles in the *Journal of Popular Film and Television* and *Feminist Media Studies*.

Lyn J. Freymiller is on the faculty of the Communication Arts & Sciences department at Penn State University. He received his MA from the University of Wisconsin - Milwaukee and his PhD from Penn State University. His research focuses on issues of gay identity and media portrayals of gay characters. He has analyzed such television programs as *Six Feet Under*, *Queer as Folk*, and *Will & Grace*.

John S. Gentile is Professor and Chair of the Department of Theatre and Performance Studies at Kennesaw State University. He received an MA and PhD in Performance Studies from Northwestern University and an MA in Mythological Studies from Pacifica Graduate Institute. He is the author of *Cast of One: One-Person Shows from the Chautauqua Platform to the Broadway Stage* (University of Illinois Press) and the founding co-editor of *Storytelling, Self, Society: An Interdisciplinary Journal of Storytelling Studies*. His stage production inspired by Joseph Campbell's work, *The Hero's Journey: Mythic Stories of the Heroic Quest*, was featured as a plenary session at the international Mythic Journeys conference, and his adaptation of Herman Melville's *Moby Dick* received the award for Best Performance at the Casablanca Theatre Festival in Morocco in 2009. His essay, "The Pilgrim Soul: Herman Melville's Moby Dick as Pilgrimage," is forthcoming in *Text & Performance Quarterly*.

Mark John Isola, who earned his PhD in literature from Tufts University, is an Assistant Professor of English at the Wentworth Institute of Technology in Boston. Mark John's interests include American literature, gay studies, AIDS literature, and critical theory. Isola has published journal articles in the *Nordic Journal of English Studies* and *eSharp* and has contributed to several GLBTQ reference collections, including critical essays on the Violet Quill and the impact of AIDS on literature. He has been selected to chair panels and present papers at several national-level conferences, including MLA, ALA, and PCA/ACA, and he serves as the LGBT Studies Area Chair for the Mid-Atlantic Popular/American Culture Association.

Richard Kenney is a media ethicist, former journalist and the Scripps Howard Endowed Professor of Journalism at Hampton University in Virginia, where he teaches media writing, ethics, and law. Dr. Kenney's research has been published several times in the *Journal of Mass Media Ethics*, and he contributed several chapters to the textbook *Doing Ethics in Journalism*. Kenney has also presented and published work on the ethics of language choice in media coverage of LGBT issues. He is an Ethics Fellow with the Poynter Institute for Media Studies. He earned his PhD from the University of Georgia.

Bryan Luis Pacheco is a Community Initiatives Associate for The Gay Lesbian Straight Education Network (GLSEN). He is the recipient of a highly competitive 2009/2010 Public Allies apprenticeship. He attended Middlebury College on a prestigious POSSE full-tuition scholarship, majoring in Spanish Literature, with a minor in Teaching

Education. Pacheco has been an avid pro-wrestling fan for 12 years, watching it as a young boy with his brother Brandon. As a gay man, he often questioned the way Queers were represented in pro-wrestling and in general on television. Bilingual, he has taught in Costa Rica and has devoted much of his young career to working with marginalized groups in educational settings. He is currently researching the injustices that occur on the Mexico/U.S. border and how they affect queer people. He hopes to use writing as a tool to bring attention to urgent Latino and queer issues.

Christal Seahorn currently teaches at the University of Louisiana at Lafayette where she is working on her PhD in Rhetoric and Folklore. She travels each summer experiencing Pride festivals around the world. To date, her Pride roster includes Houston, New York City, London, Amsterdam, and, of course, San Francisco.

Malgorzata Skorek is currently a PhD Candidate in Social & Cognitive Sciences at the University of California, Merced. Her major research interest is in the ways mass media portray men and women and in the effects these often-stereotypical portrayals have on the viewer's perception and behavior. She is conducting content analyses of diverse mass media and experiments of short-term exposure to selected imagery. She received her MA in International Communication and BA in Integrated Social Sciences from Jacobs University Bremen in Germany.

Anika Stafford is a PhD student in Women's and Gender Studies, where she determinedly writes about education, critical disability studies, and sordid queer theory. Her previous publications include "Beyond Normalization: Challenging Heteronormativity in Children's Picture Books," in *Who's Your Daddy? And Other Writings on Queer Parenting* (Sumach Press). For the past 15 years she has been hosting workshops and organizing events on myriad anti-oppression topics. She currently resides in Vancouver, British Columbia.

Rodger Streitmatter is a Professor in the School of Communication at American University in Washington, D.C. He is the author of eight books, including *Unspeakable: The Rise of the Gay and Lesbian Press in America*, *Empty Without You: The Intimate Letters of Eleanor Roosevelt and Lorena Hickok*, and *From "Perverts" to "Fab Five" ~ The Media's Changing Depiction of Gay Men and Lesbians.* Streitmatter is a former reporter for the *Roanoke Times & World News* in Roanoke, Virginia, and he holds a PhD in U.S. History from American University.

Katharina Vester is the Acting Director of American Studies at American University in Washington, D.C. She specializes in transnational cultural studies and the dynamics of power in everyday practices. She was assistant professor of American Studies at the University of Bochum (Germany) from 2002 to 2007, where she earned her PhD summa cum laude. She holds an MA in American Culture from the University of Potsdam and the Free University of Berlin. She is completing a book manuscript on the construction of identity narratives and resistance to hegemonic norms of gender, race, and sexuality in culinary discourses. She is the editor, with Kornelia Freitag, of *Another Language: Poetic Experiments in Britain and North America*, in the series: Transnational and Transatlantic American Studies (2008).

C. Todd White earned his PhD in anthropology from the University of California, where he studied the Los Angeles-based origins of the homosexual rights movement. He is an editor for *BeforeStonewall: Activists for Gay and Lesbian Rights in Historical Context* and author of *Pre-Gay L.A.: A Social History of the Movement for Homosexual Rights.* White is a frequent participant in American University's Lavender Languages and Linguistics Conference and a contributor to LGBT periodicals, including *Gay and Lesbian Review Worldwide.* With Jonathan Ned Katz, he helped to launch the OutHistory.org Web site, hosted by the Center for Lesbian and Gay Studies, and has also created Web sites for the Homosexual Information Center, the Society of Lesbian and Gay Anthropologists, and the Committee on Lesbian, Gay, Bisexual, and Transgender History. He lives with his partner in Rochester, New York, and teaches anthropology at the Rochester Institute of Technology and at the University at Buffalo.